A Gunner in Lee's Army

CIVIL WAR AMERICA

Gary W. Gallagher, Peter S. Carmichael,
Caroline E. Janney, and Aaron Sheehan-Dean, editors

*This landmark series interprets broadly the history and culture
of the Civil War era through the long nineteenth century and
beyond. Drawing on diverse approaches and methods, the series
publishes historical works that explore all aspects of the war, biographies of leading commanders, and tactical and campaign
studies, along with select editions of primary sources. Together,
these books shed new light on an era that remains central to our
understanding of American and world history.*

A Gunner in Lee's Army

THE CIVIL WAR LETTERS OF

Thomas Henry Carter

EDITED BY Graham T. Dozier

The University of North Carolina Press CHAPEL HILL

This book was published with the assistance of the Fred W. Morrison
Fund for Southern Studies of the University of North Carolina Press.

Designed and set in Merlo types by Rebecca Evans
Manufactured in the United States of America

The paper in this book meets the guidelines for permanence
and durability of the Committee on Production Guidelines for
Book Longevity of the Council on Library Resources.

The University of North Carolina Press has been a member
of the Green Press Initiative since 2003.

Cover illustration: Postwar watercolor portrait of
Thomas Henry Carter in Confederate uniform.
Courtesy of James F. Turrell.

Library of Congress Cataloging-in-Publication Data
Carter, Thomas Henry, 1831–1908.
A gunner in Lee's army : the Civil War letters of
Thomas Henry Carter / edited by Graham T. Dozier.
pages cm.— (Civil War America)
Includes bibliographical references and index.
ISBN 978-1-4696-1874-6 (pbk : alk. paper)
ISBN 978-1-4696-1875-3 (ebook)
1. Carter, Thomas Henry, 1831–1908—Correspondence. 2. United
States—History—Civil War, 1861–1865—Personal narratives, Confederate.
3. Confederate States of America. Army—Officers—Correspondence.
4. Soldiers—Confederate States of America—Correspondence.
5. United States—History—Civil War, 1861–1865—Artillery operations,
Confederate. 6. Carter, Susan Roy, 1834–1902—Correspondence.
I. Dozier, Graham T., editor. II. Title.
E605.C29 2014
973.7′82092—dc23
2014007433

18 17 16 15 14   5 4 3 2 1

FOR MY FATHER

CONTENTS

ILLUSTRATIONS

FOREWORD

Artillery officer Colonel Thomas Henry Carter witnessed the rise and fall of Robert E. Lee's Army of Northern Virginia, but he did not describe his escapades as a crusade of heroism or as an epic adventure. Carter simply refused to write theatrical war stories, the kind of sensational copy that played well with general audiences at home. He had seen too much blood to be seduced by the drama of battle. In his lengthy and richly detailed letters to his wife, Susan Roy Carter, he wrote with a fearless realism, an approach that brings the reader into the many dimensions of organized warfare that include the battlefield, military leadership, discipline in the ranks, religion, Confederate nationalism, privations on the home front, and the collapse of slavery. All of these subjects Carter scrutinized with a critical detachment that eluded most of his peers, who typically chronicled the hard facts of their existence as if their letters were hard truths carved in stone tablets. Although Carter's perspective flowed from a deep political and ideological commitment to the Confederacy and its slave-holding class, he was not afraid to fire a critical shot back at his nation for its military failures or internal shortcomings. His ability to break with the "official" voice of his country—a message that always proclaimed the superiority of southerners in all things and rarely admitted any deficiency—is truly exceptional. Carter, for instance, thought that Northern armies were more successful in disciplining their troops than the Confederates, whose independent dispositions encouraged acts of self-preservation under fire that bordered on cowardice. Carter, who favored any measure that advanced Confederate military authority over the rights of the individual, blasted his government for lacking an effective bureaucratic apparatus to punish or banish questionable officers who allowed their men to run amuck on the battlefield. "We are anxious to remodel the army organization," Carter opined in 1864, "to abolish the elective system for officers &

to inaugurate a discipline which will make the men obey on the battlefield & elsewhere. Unless we do we are lost. The Yankee discipline is immeasurably superior to ours."

Carter's penetrating criticisms were not those of a bitter outsider. In rising up the ranks to eventually command the artillery of the famed 2nd Corps, Carter rubbed shoulders with some of the most prominent officers of the army, including Lee, Thomas "Stonewall" Jackson, Jubal Early, John B. Gordon, and Richard Ewell. His opinions, on the whole, offer a balanced commentary on the merits and weaknesses of these famous men, though at times he could be vicious in his characterizations of his fellow officers. No other set of letters from a veteran of Lee's army evaluates Lee's lieutenants with such brutal honesty. Yet his frank opinions are not distorted by personal ambition or darkened by jealousy. In the fall of 1864, after a string of Confederate defeats in the Shenandoah Valley, he wrote that his commander Early "is smarting under the newspaper articles at this time. His civil & political life renders him particularly sensitive to these strictures. I have known no man in the army so morbidly sensitive on this subject as himself. His jealousy & hatred of Gordon is openly displayed, a most unfortunate circumstance, for could they work in harmony a great victory might be won. I believe Early to be a patriot but a selfish man who is desirous of monopolizing all the glory." Though Early had lost favor with Carter, the latter had the capacity to empathize with those in command, knowing that the helter-skelter nature of warfare often exceeded the powers of any man, regardless of their natural military abilities or leadership style.

Although Carter breathed the "rarified" air of the Confederate high command, he never lost his feel for the ground level of war. His deep concern for his wife's welfare, who remained on the family's extensive plantation in King William County, Virginia, and his need to manage his farm and slaves from afar made him extremely sensitive to how the war had ripped apart the lives of his fellow southerners and how all men, regardless of rank, were caught in a crossfire of demands that weakened their military reliability. Rarely did he reduce the outcome of a battle to simple questions of duty or courage. He understood that the men in the ranks were not only soldiers but also husbands and fathers whose worries extended beyond showing up for roll call or doing guard duty. Men were pulled in conflicting and contradictory directions, and the preservation of self and family often trumped the high ideals of a national cause. Food shortages, runaway inflation, and labor demands were the cries for help that all men heard from home. Carter encountered similar problems, especially with his slaves, who were not as compliant as he would have preferred when the Yankees were in his neighborhood. These troublesome issues weighed upon Carter, whose letters demonstrate that no soldier was insulated from the disruptions of the home front. He lashed out at free blacks for their entrepreneurial spirit, since they "took advantage" of the simple laws of supply and demand in charging more for their goods. Carter was also frustrated with his own slaves, especially those who accompanied him in the army. He never saw them as loyal and trusted Confederates ready at any moment to shoulder a gun for the cause, but as unruly and unreliable "rascals" who lost their sense of loyalty when Union armies were in close proximity. These dislocations at home did not discourage Carter. He thought the war was a fight to the death for a political and social world where he and his family stood at its very pinnacle of power.

Thanks to the superior editing of Graham Dozier, we are fortunate to have one of the most significant collections of letters to come from a member of Lee's high command. Although the text of Carter's letters contain the predictable grumblings of a soldier who longed for home and who was frustrated by the restrictions of the ranks, his words transcend the daily grind of army life and reveal the inner world of an extraordinarily intelligent and insightful man whose pen brought a degree of coherence, deep reflection, and purpose to a world rattled by the unending and unpredictable tremors of war.

PETER S. CARMICHAEL

ACKNOWLEDGMENTS

After the Civil War, Thomas Henry Carter's letters passed to his youngest daughter, Anne Willing Carter Dulany. They then went to her son, Henry Rozier Dulany Jr., and then to his widow, Kate Weems Dulany, known to the family as "Tolly." At some point, Tolly gave the box of letters to her late husband's cousin, Eda Atkinson Carter Williams, the oldest daughter of Tom Carter's youngest son, Spencer Leslie Carter. When Eda Williams moved into a retirement community in Richmond, the undisturbed letters came into the possession of Eda's younger sister, Susan Roy Carter Williams. In 1995 the wartime letters of Thomas Henry Carter were donated in the name of the two sisters to the Virginia Historical Society (VHS) by Eda's daughter, Eda Carter Williams Martin, and Susan's son, Fielding Lewis Williams Jr.

I must acknowledge several of the living descendants of Colonel Carter. Eda Martin and Fielding Williams, his great grandchildren, deserve my sincerest gratitude, not only for preserving the letters for future generations by giving them to the VHS but also for helping me many times during the project by answering a steady stream of questions. I owe Fielding, in particular, a tremendous debt for allowing me to take on the task of publishing his great-grandfather's letters. Fielding's nephew, the Reverend Dr. James F. Turrell of Sewanee, did an early version of the transcription of Carter's letters, which he generously shared with me and for which I am very grateful. Jim saved me a lot of time in the initial phase of the project. Finally, I wish to thank Robert E. L. deButts Jr., whose great-grandfather, Robert Edward Lee Jr., married Tom Carter's oldest daughter, Juliet. Rob graciously shared information and copies of materials relating to his Carter ancestors. Colonel Carter would be very proud of his descendants.

Tracking down all the bits and pieces of information about Tom Carter was often challenging but always a rewarding experience. What made it much easier than it could have been was the help I received from the following individuals and their institutions: George K. Combs, manager of Special Collections at the Barrett Branch Library in Alexandria, Virginia; John Coski, historian, and Teresa Roane, archivist, at the Museum of the Confederacy; Diane B. Jacob, head archivist at the Virginia Military Institute; C. Jared Loewenstein, reference librarian at the Alderman Library of the University of Virginia; and Mary Thomason-Morris, archivist at the Clarke County Historical Association. All of these folks were generous not only with their valuable time but also with the materials they shared with me.

Several of my colleagues at the VHS helped me throughout the process of transcribing the letters, researching the annotations, and writing Carter's biography. First and foremost, Nelson Lankford, my boss and mentor, helped make this a much stronger work through his constant support and editorial advice. I owe him my warmest thanks. Frances Pollard runs one of the best research libraries in the country. She and her staff—Katherine Wilkins, John McClure, Brenna McHenry Godsey, and Amber Jones—assisted me over the past several years. Lee Shepard let me catalog the Carter papers soon after they arrived at the VHS, which first brought them to my attention. And Jamison Davis granted me the permission necessary to include in this book Carter family images from the society's collections.

The field of Civil War history, particularly the part of it that deals with the Army of Northern Virginia, is rich in scholars, many of whom are willing to offer advice and lend a hand. I was fortunate to have several of them help me with my project. Gary W. Gallagher and Robert K. Krick, both having seen Jim Turrell's transcription, encouraged me to edit Carter's letters for publication. Throughout the process, they shared advice and information and read the manuscript. Robert E. L. Krick, a good friend and Civil War scholar, offered plenty of help. With his keen eyes and vast knowledge of General Lee's army, Bobby caught various mistakes and identified several individuals in the annotations. Keith S. Bohannon and Joseph Pierro both answered numerous questions and sent along bits of information that proved very helpful. To all of these scholars, I say thank you.

At UNC Press, I wish to thank the editors of the Civil War America series—Peter Carmichael, Carrie Janney, and Aaron Sheehan-Dean—and the anonymous readers of my manuscript for their willingness to support the publication of Carter's letters. In particular, I thank former series editor Gary Gallagher for all he did to smooth the way. Editorial director Mark Simpson-Vos, assistant editor Caitlin Bell-Butterfield, and project editor Jay Mazzocchi were a delight to work with throughout the process and were always happy to answer the many questions I had along the way. The press contracted Michael Taber to compile the index, and I thank him for his excellent work.

Finally, I need to thank a few people who have been a source of inspiration to me for a far longer period than the time I have spent working on this book. F. Powell Johann Jr., Amos Lee Laine, and James I. Robertson Jr. all taught me history at different times in my life. They each in their own way excited and nurtured my interest in the subject and deserve my deepest gratitude and respect. Kemp and Mimi Dozier, my father and stepmother, have been a great source of encouragement and support to me. Their gentle nudges, mostly consisting of questions about the project, kept me on track. But it is to my father, who has put up with me for far longer than anyone else mentioned here and who has always stood behind me in my life, that I affectionately dedicate this book.

EDITORIAL METHODS AND NOTES

This book brings together 103 letters written by Thomas Henry Carter between 22 June 1861 and 7 March 1865. He wrote 101 of them to his wife, Susan. He sent the remaining two to his stepmother, Ann Willing Page Carter, and to his wife's brother-in-law, John Coles Rutherfood. All but three of the letters reside in the collections of the Virginia Historical Society (VHS). Photocopies of the three that are not at the society but which are included here were generously provided from a private collection. The majority of the letters come from one collection at the VHS, the Thomas Henry Carter Papers, 1861–96 (Mss1C2466a). The three from the private collection and one from another collection of Carter's papers at the VHS have been identified in the lead note for those specific letters.

Readers will note that there are three significant gaps within the time span of the letters. The first occurs between 1 May and 15 August 1862, during which period Carter's battery fought in the Seven Days Battles. The second takes place in 1863 between 25 June and 18 September, depriving the reader of Carter's description of the Battle of Gettysburg and its aftermath. The final gap is in the summer of 1864 during the hectic Overland Campaign. Why those gaps exist is largely a matter of conjecture. During that first period, for example, it could be explained by Carter's location near his family's King William County home. When not fighting against the Union army east of Richmond in late June, he could have been spending some of his peaceful moments with his wife. Throughout his letters, Carter describes his attempts to find Susan nearby accommodations. That may account for the missing letters in the summer of 1863. As far as the final period in 1864 is concerned, the opposing armies were in almost daily contact between 5 May and 3 June. It is likely that Carter simply did not have the time to compose thoughtful letters home. There is one final theory that may account for the gaps. In a letter written in 1915 by Tom

Carter's son Thomas, he mentions that some of his father's wartime letters were in the hands of an Episcopal priest in Hanover County and that he does not know what became of them. It is impossible to know if those are the same letters mentioned above that eventually made their way to the VHS or if they are the missing letters that would have filled many of those gaps.

Thomas Henry Carter's prewar background as a cadet at the Virginia Military Institute and as a medical student at the University of Virginia and the University of Pennsylvania is evident in his clear, well-written wartime letters. They are quite legible, even when he succumbed to the practice of cross-writing to save paper. To ensure ease of reading as well as to maintain the accuracy of the original letters, a number of editorial decisions have been made. Like many of his contemporaries, Carter was an inconsistent speller. Those misspellings, however, have not been corrected, nor has the [*sic*] notation been inserted to indicate a mistake. The same goes for his use of capital letters for words within a sentence or for proper nouns. They remain as written. Carter was also somewhat inconsistent in his use of punctuation marks; he tended to use dashes instead of periods at the end of many sentences, and he did not like to use many commas. He also did not bother to make the effort to indent new paragraphs. One gets the sense that he was an impatient writer. In the case of dashes at the end of sentences, they have all been silently replaced with periods. Missing commas and other missing punctuation marks that might lead to unclear sentences for modern readers have been added in brackets []. Where it is clear that a new paragraph begins, the modern rule of indention has been applied. Abbreviated words that would be confusing if left as written have been completed with the missing letters placed within brackets—yr or yrs have been rendered as y[ou]r and y[ou]rs, evr as ev[e]r, and recd as rec[eive]d. Also, words represented by one or only a few letters have been expanded with the missing letters included in brackets—R as R[ichmond] or Fdg as F[re]d[ericksbur]g. Carter almost always used wd, cd, shd, altho, tho, whi, and thro instead of would, could, should, although, though, which, and through. All such cases have been silently corrected without the use of brackets, which would have been an unnecessary distraction for readers. Commonly understood abbreviations for personal names, military ranks, unit designations, and place names—such as Wm and Jno for William and John, Col and Genl for Colonel and General, Arty and Bttn for Artillery and Battalion, and Richd for Richmond—have been left as written. Words that are missing some of their letters because of damaged

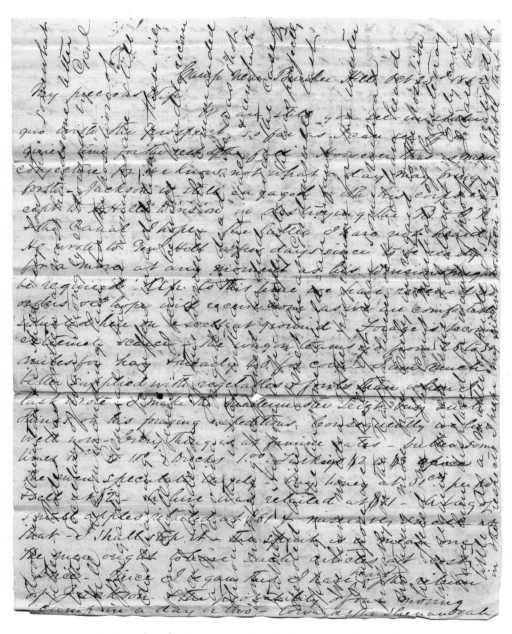

Letter written by Tom Carter to his wife, Susan, on 23 October 1862
(Virginia Historical Society)

paper have been reconstructed within braces {}, and lost words have been replaced with braces and ellipsis points { . . . }. Missing pages have also been indicated with ellipsis marks.

Abbreviations Used in the Footnotes

CSR	Compiled Service Records
CSR-Officers	Compiled Service Records of Confederate General and Staff Officers and Nonregimental Enlisted Men
IBC	Isabelle Burwell Carter
NARA	National Archives and Records Administration
OR	U.S. War Department, *The War of the Rebellion: A Compilation of the Official Records of the Union and Confederate Armies*, 128 vols. (Washington, D.C.: Government Printing Office, 1880–1901). Unless otherwise noted, citations are to Series 1. Citations consist of volume number, part (if applicable), and page number(s).
RDD	*Richmond Daily Dispatch*
SRC	Susan Roy Carter
THC	Thomas Henry Carter
THCP	Thomas Henry Carter Papers
TNC	Thomas Nelson Carter
UVA	Albert and Shirley Small Special Collections Library, University of Virginia
VHS	Virginia Historical Society, Richmond
VMI	Archives, Preston Library, Virginia Military Institute, Lexington

A Gunner in Lee's Army

Introduction

Major Thomas Henry Carter sat in his tent on the night of 15 March 1863 and pondered his situation in the Army of Northern Virginia as he scratched out a letter in the dim light to his wife, Susan. He had been in Confederate service since the late spring of 1861 and had risen from command of an artillery battery to that of a battalion in the South's most successful army. Now he faced an important decision. His former division commander, Major General Daniel Harvey Hill, had left the army. Hill's questionable health and stormy relationship with General Robert E. Lee were the main factors that prompted his resignation. The prickly general now commanded Confederate forces in North Carolina. A month after he left, Hill wrote to Carter with a tempting proposition. "I have just received a flattering invitation from Genl Hill to join him in N. Carolina," Thomas informed Susan. Would the Virginian join Hill as his chief of artillery—a position that would undoubtedly bring "more prospect of distinction on less fighting"? It was a lot to consider, and the major took pen in hand to share the weight of the decision with his wife. "I shall not accept," he promised, "certainly not before consulting your wishes."

This scene offers a revealing look not only at the close relationship between Thomas Henry Carter and his wife but also at the candid and thoughtful nature of his correspondence. Such frank views on the numerous events and people that shaped his wartime service, written with clarity and style, are what make Carter's letters stand out in the subgenre of published materials relating to the Army of Northern Virginia's artillery. Though their content does not match the depth of analysis found in E. Porter Alexander's personal recollections, *Fighting for the Confederacy*, Carter's letters offer the kind of thoughtful observations and insight into the army and its leaders that are found in the writings of other Confederate artillerists, including William M. Owen's *In Camp and Battle with the*

Washington Artillery and William T. Poague's *Gunner with Stonewall*. But unlike these postwar publications, including Alexander's, Carter's honest and engaging correspondence is all the more remarkable because it was written from a wartime perspective—one not colored by knowledge of the outcome, by the passage of time, or, in some cases, by decades of postwar reflection. Consequently, his unvarnished evaluations of such topics as conscription, morale, military strategy, and the debate in late 1864 concerning the enlistment of African Americans in the Confederate army, as well as his descriptions of fellow officers, will be prized by those interested in Lee's army for years to come.

—⚌—

The story of Thomas Henry Carter's life comes down to us in bits and pieces. His service as one of Lee's finest artillerists can be traced through mention of his name in various tables of organization, correspondence, and reports in published official records and by occasional appearances in later recollections. His career can be summarized briefly. Carter enlisted as a captain in the spring of 1861 and led the King William Artillery at Seven Pines, the Seven Days Battles, and Antietam before earning a promotion to major after Fredericksburg and to lieutenant colonel in February 1863. At Chancellorsville and Gettysburg, he commanded a battalion of artillery. In 1864, as a newly promoted colonel, he fought against General Ulysses S. Grant's army in the Overland Campaign and served as the chief of artillery in General Jubal Early's Army of the Valley. The following spring, he commanded artillery in Lee's thin lines east of Richmond and joined the retreat to Appomattox.

Some details about Carter's life and personality are sadly lacking. In fact, the only comprehensive study of the artillery of the Army of Northern Virginia—Jennings Cropper Wise's *The Long Arm of Lee*—contains multiple references to Carter at various stages of his military career, but it misidentifies him as Thomas "Hill" Carter. How Wise came up with that incorrect middle name is unknown. Unfortunately, his mistake took hold and appeared in other works on Lee's army. Up until today, Tom Carter has merely taken his place among the midlevel officers of that army who occasionally emerge in the narrative of a battle, then just as quickly disappear into the background when the story continues.

In Carter's case, however, it is possible to discover a great deal more about not only his role as a Confederate artillerist but also his personality. During the war, he wrote more than 100 letters to his wife, Susan Roy

Carter. Taken as a whole, these letters show Carter to be a literate man who held nothing back in his observations of people and events. They also reveal his character, one ideally suited for service in the Southern army. And finally, the letters bring to light Carter's exceptional relationship with his wife.

Tom Carter took careful notice of the people around him in the army and freely shared his frank opinions with Susan. His descriptions of Confederate officers, though not lengthy, are apt and revealing. Earl Van Dorn and Pierre G. T. Beauregard, Carter's superiors in the fall of 1861, appeared outwardly fastidious and concerned with public opinion, but according to the inexperienced captain, both possessed strong leadership qualities. Likewise, Generals Richard S. Ewell and Jubal A. Early initially drew high praise. In both cases, however, the passage of time and their conduct on the battlefield tempered Carter's attitude toward them. The general with whom he would be associated most during the war, Robert Emmett Rodes, always impressed Carter. On the negative side of the scale in Carter's estimation stood men like General Samuel Cooper and President Jefferson Davis. Both represented to him the detached and self-serving leadership style that he felt characterized the Confederate government. While he described Cooper as "an imbecile," Carter also had little good to say about Thomas Jordan, Beauregard's assistant adjutant general, whom he dubbed "that arrant humbug." His opinion of Robert E. Lee, unlike that of Ewell and Early, rose steadily over the course of the war. At the end of 1861, Carter shared the common perception that Lee was too cautious, but by September 1862, he declared that Lee "has the entire confidence of the Army."

Carter's judgments of these and other officers in the Army of Northern Virginia reflect not only his view of them at a given moment in time but also his ideas toward leadership and what the army needed in that regard. Several months after the Battle of First Bull Run, in which he did not fight, Carter joined the chorus of those who believed the Confederate army should have immediately advanced on Washington. On 13 October he told Susan that "the blame is put on Davis' shoulders here," the lesson being that "Politicians will ruin us forever." Two years later, while in a similarly reflective mood, Carter bemoaned the fact that the army lacked decisive and aggressive generals. "It is time to get rid of men when they fail," he proclaimed on 10 November 1863. Carter unleashed perhaps his most damning criticism of his own army in the fall of 1864 after his best and worst day as an artillery commander. At the Battle of Cedar Creek, his guns pounded fleeing Union soldiers in what had at first looked like an overwhelming Confederate victory. But a halt in the action of several hours allowed Union general Philip Sheridan to gain control over his disorganized army and launch a counterattack that turned the tide of battle. Two days after the humiliating Southern defeat, Carter explained how "[o]ur Company officers & many field officers are utterly worthless exercising no authority whatever at any time. . . . Had we a system which could at once reduce these men to ranks something might be done. We are too democratic to have a good army." In all of these cases, Tom Carter's strong sense of discipline, developed and encouraged during his years as a cadet at the Virginia Military Institute, and the premium he placed on aggressive leadership inform his letters and exemplify a personality well suited to that of an officer in the Civil War.

It was no accident that Carter formed an artillery battery when he decided to cast his lot with the Confederacy. As he explained to his wife in the spring of 1862, a captain of artillery exercised a degree of independence not enjoyed by the same rank in the infantry or cavalry. That quality of independence likely appealed to Carter because of his background as a plantation manager. Beginning in 1854, he ran his father's large plantation in King William County, which included more than 100 slaves. That autonomous existence no doubt shaped his personality. It definitely affected his attitude toward the larger government that he now found himself serving. In describing the chaos surrounding the implementation of the Conscription Act in the spring of 1862, Carter lashed out in frustration at the situation. "After the Old State is lost the Confederacy may go hang," he informed Susan. "We shall be ruined & I have no faith in the permanency of the Southern Confederacy." Carter, being a member of one of the most prominent families in Virginia, definitely knew where his ultimate allegiance lay.

Finally, the content of the letters themselves reveals much about the strong bond between Tom Carter and his wife. From the first letter to the last, he held nothing back from Susan. His long descriptions of army news—incidents of camp life, battles, promotions, artillery reorganizations, the state of morale—indicate that he was writing to someone who understood his life and wanted to know everything that he was experiencing. Theirs was as much a partnership as a marriage. As described above, when General D. H. Hill asked Carter in March 1863 to serve in North Carolina as his artillery chief, Carter wrote to Susan about the offer. The new position promised higher rank and "less fighting." But he assured his wife that he would not accept the post without hearing from her first. His letters also shed light on the culture of family and community that existed within the Army of Northern Virginia. During the quiet periods of the war, officers' wives and children often stayed in nearby towns or homes, granting the men a chance to reclaim some of the comforts of their prewar lives. Judging by the number of times that Carter discusses Susan's travel prospects, he and his wife took full advantage of the hospitality of friends and relatives throughout Virginia. Clearly, as indicated by the tone and content of the letters, the Carters shared a close partnership that survived the war and lasted until her death in 1902.

Whether in Richmond training his men in 1861, in winter camp in March 1863 pondering his future, or in the Shenandoah Valley in the late fall of 1864 trying to make sense of recent defeats, Carter reveals himself to be a thoughtful observer of the people around him and of the events in which he is a witness or participant. His letters offer a unique glimpse of a profound experience from a well-educated and insightful perspective.

CHAPTER ONE

———— ⁓ ————

Life before the War

Thomas Henry Carter was born in 1831 at Pampatike, the King William County, Virginia, plantation of his parents, Thomas Nelson Carter and Juliet Muse Gaines Carter. Tom, as the family knew him, was named after his father and his maternal grandfather and was the second son and the third of four children. The Carters occupied a prominent position among the leading families in Virginia. John Carter, the first of that name to arrive in Virginia, came from England sometime before his election to the colony's House of Burgesses in 1642, in which he represented Upper Norfolk (later Nansemond) County. That same year, he received a grant of land in Lancaster County, where he established the family seat of Corotoman. By the 1660s, John Carter had amassed more than 4,000 acres through grants, purchases, and patents. With large land ownership came an increase in social prominence and political power, culminating in his election to the governor's council in 1658.[1]

As high as John Carter and his wife, Sarah Ludlow Carter, rose, however, no member of the family would match the accomplishments of their son Robert. Born around 1664, Robert Carter followed in his father's footsteps, serving as a commander in the local militia and representing Lancaster County in the House of Burgesses. From 1699 to 1705, Robert was treasurer of the colony, and from 1700 until his death in 1732, he served on the governor's council. Where Robert differed from his father—and what established his place in Virginia history—was in his passion for acquiring

---

1. TNC to IBC, 14 Jan. 1915, THCP, 1850–1915, VHS; Quitt, "John Carter," 72–73; Heinemann and others, *Old Dominion, New Commonwealth*, 48. This letter, written by Tom Carter's son, Thomas Nelson Carter, to his daughter Isabelle is essentially a forty-page memoir about his early life at Pampatike. In it, he describes his grandparents and his father's early life, Confederate service, and postwar years. Tom Carter's middle name is occasionally mistakenly identified as "Hill." For reasons unknown, Jennings Cropper Wise, author of the only comprehensive history of the artillery of the Army of Northern Virginia, identified him as "Thomas Hill Carter."

land. Like his father, he accumulated acreage through grants, purchases, and patents, but the amounts varied tremendously. In Robert's time, vast stretches of land between the Rappahannock and Potomac Rivers became available in what was known as the Northern Neck Proprietary. Robert acquired at least 295,000 acres of land in the Northern Neck by the time of his death. The political power he wielded and the vast wealth he accumulated through land ownership, tobacco farming, and other ventures earned him the apt nickname of "King" Carter.[2]

The Carter family remained politically prominent throughout the eighteenth century. "King" Carter's son John and grandson Charles both served on the governor's council and managed the vast estates inherited from their illustrious predecessor, including the James River plantation known as Shirley that John II and his wife, Elizabeth Hill, built by 1738. Charles Carter owned more than 13,000 acres in thirteen counties and at least 710 slaves. Like his grandfather, he represented Lancaster County in the House of Burgesses. Charles remained in that body until the outbreak of the American Revolution. Marriage to his second wife, Ann Butler Moore, resulted in the birth of several children, including son Robert Carter in 1774.[3]

Robert chose a different path than his ancestors. His father gave to him one of the many Carter family properties, a plantation in King William County called Pampatike. The 1,200-acre farm on the north bank of the Pamunkey River promised a prosperous life for Robert. As much as he may have wanted to follow in the tradition of his family, however, Robert was never comfortable with the institution of African slavery. In a letter to his children, written in 1803, he stated: "I conceive a *strong disgust* to the *slave trade* and all its barbarous consequences. This aversion was not likely to be *diminished* by becoming a slaveholder and witnessing many cruelties." Instead of managing Pampatike, Robert Carter pursued a medical career. He studied under Dr. Benjamin Rush and received his medical degree from the University of Pennsylvania in 1803. Nine years earlier, in 1794, he had married Mary Nelson, a union that enhanced the well-established Carter dynasty. Her father, Thomas Nelson of Yorktown, Virginia, was a planter, signer of the Declaration of Independence, and governor of Virginia fol-

2. Berkeley, "Robert Carter," 84–86.
3. Tillson, "Charles Carter," 57–59; Evans, "John Carter," 73–75. Robert's older sister, Ann Hill Carter (1773–1829), later became the second wife of Henry "Light Horse Harry" Lee (1756–1818), a union that produced several children, including Robert Edward Lee (1807–70). When she named her son, Ann Lee chose to honor her two favorite brothers, Robert and Edward Carter (Freeman, *Lee*, 1:12; Pryor, *Reading the Man*, 14).

lowing Thomas Jefferson. At Shirley on 8 October 1800, Mary gave birth to her second son and fourth child, Thomas Nelson Carter.[4]

The future father of Thomas Henry Carter grew up among his Carter relatives at Shirley and in northern Virginia. Tragedy, however, intruded early in Thomas's life. In 1803 his mother died shortly after she and Robert returned to Virginia from Philadelphia. Two years later, Thomas's father, who had largely been absent studying medicine in Europe, died shortly after returning home on 14 November 1805 at the age of thirty-one. A few bits of parental guidance that Thomas received from his father survive in a letter Robert wrote to his children, in which he advised that they "be *humane* to [their] slaves and dependants" and that they "consider ardent spirits as one of the greatest moral and physical evils with which it has ever pleased God to inflict man." Following his father's death, Thomas became the ward of a relative, William Carter. He attended schools at Kinloch, the Turner family home in Fauquier County, Virginia, and at Moffett's near Richmond. Family tradition maintains that he went to Princeton College but remained there only one night before returning home, and that he entered the U.S. Navy only to resign shortly thereafter. After traveling through the Deep South because he was "uneasy about his lungs," Thomas returned home, where he met Juliet Muse Gaines, a young woman who taught at a school at Aylett's, not too far from Pampatike. The couple married in 1824. Her grandfather, Henry Gaines, from whom Thomas Henry Carter derived his middle name, represented King and Queen County in the Virginia General Assembly during the first decade of the nineteenth century. Juliet's sister Cornelia, who lived with the Carters, believed that "whatever sense or intellect [the Carter children] had was inherited from the Gaines family."[5]

A reserved man, Thomas Carter spent most of his life dedicated to the practice of farming. Pampatike thrived in the 1830s under his management. It nearly doubled in size to 2,250 acres after he bought Goodwin's Island on the Pamunkey and had a dam built along the river to reclaim swampy land. Like fellow farmer Edmund Ruffin, Carter experimented with a variety of fertilizing methods to produce a healthy crop of corn and

4. Robert Carter to His Children, 12 Oct. 1803, VHS; Norfleet, *Saint-Mémin in Virginia*, 151–52; Carter Family Bible Records, 179[?]–1811, VHS.

5. TNC to IBC, 14 Jan. 1915; Robert Carter to His Children, 12 Oct. 1803; Mary Carter Buckner to Tom [?], 16 April 1924, Carter Family Genealogical Files, Clarke County Historical Association, Berryville, Va.; Leonard, *General Assembly of Virginia*, 240, 244, 257. While attending Moffett's, Thomas Carter lived at the St. Charles Hotel in Richmond, located on the north side of Main Street between 12th and 13th Streets.

wheat. In this atmosphere of prosperity, Thomas and Juliet had four children. Thomas Henry Carter, the couple's third child, was born at Pampatike on 13 June 1831. Events beyond King William County that year would
help shape the world that Tom Carter would inhabit and crystallize the
issues that would divide the nation thirty years later: William Lloyd Gar-
rison published the first issue of the *Liberator*, which became the "most
prominent voice" of the abolition movement; Virginian Cyrus McCormick invented the reaper, which almost overnight made wheat farming
more profitable and further fueled the demand for more slave labor; and
Nat Turner's rebellion in Southampton County shocked white Virginians
and resulted in tighter controls over the enslaved population.[6]

Though Tom Carter would spend the majority of his life at Pampatike, his earliest residence there ended abruptly when he was four years
old. Like his father, Tom lost a parent when he was very young. In 1834
Juliet Carter died, leaving her four small children without their mother.
Realizing that he could not manage his large plantation and raise his children, Thomas Nelson Carter found someone to fill the role left by his
wife's death. A year after losing Juliet, he married Anne Willing Page, the
daughter of William Byrd Page and Evelyn Byrd Nelson Page of Clarke
County, Virginia. Known as "Sweet Anne," she was described as "attractive
in every way, in mind, character, and appearance." The family lived briefly
at Pampatike, but by 1840 they had moved to Clarke County after Thomas
Carter purchased Annfield, a late Georgian-style stone house situated on
a 216-acre farm near Berryville, Virginia.[7]

At Annfield, where he later claimed he "learned to ride, to shoot, and to
speak the truth," young Tom Carter grew up around his extended family,
which, by virtue of many years of Carter family marriages, included the Ar-
misteads, Burwells, Randolphs, Byrds, Pages, Grymeses, Tayloes, and Lees.
He attended schools with friends and family members in Clarke County
at Mt. Airy, the Burwell family home, and at Clay Hill, the nearby plantation of Francis Beverley Whiting. Whiting had established his school for

6. TNC to IBC, 14 Jan. 1915; 1830 Census, King William County; "Experiments with Bone
Manure," 28; Howe, *What Hath God Wrought*, 323–27, 425–26, 535. According to an 1836 gazetteer of Virginia, in 1830 King William County had a population of 9,319, consisting of 3,389
white and 5,930 black residents (Martin, *Gazetteer of Virginia*, 204).

7. TNC to IBC, 14 Jan. 1915; Magill, *Beverley Family of Virginia*, 471; Annfield Title Abstract,
1900, Clarke County Historical Association, Berryville, Va.. Tom Carter's two older siblings
were Robert and Mary Nelson (d. 1914), who later married Dr. Robert Buckner of Baltimore.
Tom's younger brother, Julian, also served in the Confederate army and was killed in July 1862
(Magill, *Beverley Family of Virginia*, 471).

his own children but had welcomed Tom Carter and other children from the neighborhood.[8]

In the fall of 1846, Carter matriculated to the Virginia Military Institute (VMI), a military college located in Lexington that had been founded seven years earlier on the site of a state arsenal. Though regulations stated that no entering cadet could be under the age of sixteen, Tom Carter had just celebrated his fifteenth birthday in June. In addition, rather than graduate in 1850 with the rest of the first-year (or Fourth Class) cadets who entered in 1846, Carter was placed with the second-year (or Third Class) cadets, who would graduate in 1849. The principal professor of the institute did have the authority to exempt qualified students from attending first-year classes. Precisely why Tom Carter was permitted to enter VMI a year early and as a second-year student is not known. Most likely it is attributable to a combination of family connections and the quality of his Clarke County education.[9]

Cadet Carter and his classmates underwent a strict combination of academic and military training. In his first year, he studied mathematics (algebra and geometry), French, and landscape drawing. French turned out to be Carter's strongest subject and math his weakest. At the end of his first year, he stood fourteenth out of a class of thirty-five. The school day at VMI consisted of classes from 8:00 A.M. to 1:00 P.M. and again from 2:00 to 3:30 P.M. After 4:00 P.M., the cadets assembled on the drill field for their military education, which mostly consisted of drill, inspection, and marching. The strict regimen left cadets with little time of their own. That is not to say that they could not find ways to engage in social activities. Carter later remembered how he and his fellow cadets "delighted" to attend the Reverend William White's Presbyterian church in Lexington "rather more, I fancy, to see the pretty girls that there did most frequent, than to hear his godly admonitions."[10]

When Cadet Carter returned for his second year, he did so starting

8. Tyler, *Men of Mark*, 4:61; TNC to IBC, 14 Jan. 1915; Meade, "Col. Thomas H. Carter, C.S.A.," 41. In 1807 Mary Lee Fitzhugh Custis (1788–1853) was visiting her cousin Ann Randolph Meade Page (1781–1838) at Annfield when she gave birth to her daughter, Mary Anna Randolph Custis (1807–73), the future wife of Robert E. Lee (Pratt, *Guide to Early American Homes*, 21).

9. McMurry, *Virginia Military Institute*, 5, 9; Class Standings, VMI. Carter's class, which had matriculated in the fall of 1845, was VMI's first four-year class. Before then, cadets attended the institute for three years (McMurry, *Virginia Military Institute*, 20).

10. Class Standings; McMurry, *Virginia Military Institute*, 20; THC to Joseph R. Anderson, 1 July 1889, Thomas Henry Carter Alumni File, VMI. At the end of his first year, Carter finished twenty-seventh in mathematics, sixteenth in drawing, sixth in French, and eighteenth in conduct (Class Standings).

in July 1847 with the annual summer encampment, during which cadets experienced what amounted to basic training. They lived in tents on the drill field and spent their days learning to handle arms, engage in small-unit drills, and practice the care and firing of artillery pieces. Academic classes began again in September. Carter's courses in his second year included more math (analytical geometry and calculus), Latin, drawing (topographical), and mechanics. This time, his strongest subject proved to be drawing and his weakest mechanics. Carter's records also indicate that he received no demerits for poor conduct. Either he was an exceptionally well-behaved cadet or he knew how to avoid getting caught. In any case, at the end of the term, Tom Carter had improved his class rank by three, finishing eleventh out of twenty-eight cadets.[11]

During his time at VMI, Carter shared the classroom and barracks with cadets who were either engaged in current U.S. military service or would later see Confederate service. While he and his fellow cadets marched and drilled in Lexington, the United States was at war with Mexico. On 14 April 1847, the corps gathered to witness "a national salute of thirteen guns" that were fired in honor of recent American victories in Mexico. The occasion was all the more poignant because twenty-six former and a few current cadets were then serving in Mexico. Three members of Carter's class took part in the war, including Benjamin Franklin Ficklin, future Confederate soldier and a founder of the Pony Express. Of the fifty-one cadets who matriculated into the class of 1849, thirty-five would later serve in the Confederate army or navy. Samuel Garland Jr., the third-ranking member of the class, would achieve the rank of brigadier general in the Confederate army and die at the Battle of South Mountain. Several of Carter's professors would also fight for the Confederacy, including Francis Henney Smith, John Quincy Marr, Raleigh E. Colston, and Robert Emmet Rodes. Carter's own Confederate service would be closely linked throughout the war with Rodes.[12]

Tom Carter's final year at VMI began shortly after he turned seventeen. The courses he took reflected a much heavier emphasis on military-

11. McMurry, *Virginia Military Institute*, 23–34; Class Standings. Of the twenty-eight cadets in Carter's class, only eight, including Carter, managed to avoid earning a single demerit. At the end of his second year, Carter ranked fifteenth in mathematics, nineteenth in mechanics, ninth in drawing, and fourteenth in Latin (Class Standings).

12. Couper, *One Hundred Years at V.M.I.*, 1:164; *Register of Former Cadets*, 13–14; 1848 Regulations, VMI. Men like Rodes and Marr taught as assistant professors at the institute before they graduated. That privilege was extended to high-ranking upperclassmen (McMurry, *Virginia Military Institute*, 24).

related subjects. They included military and civil engineering, tactics (infantry and artillery), and math (optics and astronomy). Other First Class subjects included French, Latin, drawing, natural philosophy (physics), chemistry, and rhetoric. Carter finished with his highest marks in French and struggled most in tactics, which is ironic considering his later abilities as a Confederate artillerist. On 4 July 1849, Tom Carter graduated eighth out of a class of twenty-four cadets.[13]

Carter returned to Clarke County after his graduation, apparently not finished with his education. At some point during his days at VMI, or perhaps after he got home, he decided to pursue a medical career. Having chosen that profession, he enrolled in the medical school at the University of Virginia for the 1850–51 session. Over the course of the next year, Carter studied chemistry, medicine, physiology and surgery, and anatomy. In June 1851 he and fifteen others received the degree of doctor of medicine.[14]

At that time, the curriculum at the University of Virginia was designed around the theoretical study of medicine. The college offered little clinical instruction. Carter therefore decided to follow in the footsteps of many other graduates, including his grandfather Robert Carter, and continue his medical education at the University of Pennsylvania, a school known for offering "hands-on instruction in clinics and hospitals." Whether he knew it or not, Tom Carter was also participating in a noticeable movement of young men from the South to the city of Philadelphia. In the antebellum period, there was a sizeable migration of southern medical students to the city. It had a prosouthern reputation, and its medical schools were known for turning "southern men into American gentlemen, not merely physicians." From 1800 to 1860, 51.5 percent of those who matriculated into the medical school of the University of Pennsylvania were from southern states. Of that number, 12.5 percent—the highest from any state south of the Mason-Dixon Line—came from Virginia, including forty-six in Tom Carter's class of 410 students.[15]

13. 1848 Regulations; Class Standings; *Register of Former Cadets*, 13–14. Of the fifty-one cadets who matriculated into Carter's class, twenty-four graduated in 1849. Cadet Carter's final year proved to be more eventful, as indicated by the fact that he accumulated twenty-seven demerits for unrecorded infractions. At the end of his final year, he finished fifteenth in mathematics, sixth in French, fourteenth in Latin, ninth in drawing, thirteenth in natural philosophy (physics), thirteenth in chemistry, seventh in rhetoric, eighteenth in tactics, and tenth in engineering (Class Standings).

14. *Catalogue of the University of Virginia, Session of 1850–'51*, 9; *A Sketch of the University of Virginia*, 28.

15. Tyler, *Men of Mark*, 4:61; Kilbride, "Southern Medical Students in Philadelphia," 698, 704, 709; *Catalogue of the University of Pennsylvania, Session 1851–52*, 27.

Once again, Carter seemingly accomplished the impossible. He had just turned twenty in June 1851 and had been accepted into a school whose students had to be at least twenty-one. Nor had Carter met several of the other strict entrance requirements. The one that mattered most, however, stated that "medical students who have attended one complete course in a respectable Medical School, where the attendance on two complete courses is necessary to a degree, where the same branches are taught as in this [school] . . . are permitted to become candidates by an attendance here for one full course." Carter's medical degree from a reputable school and the fact that his grandfather attended the University of Pennsylvania most likely earned him a spot in the class.[16]

Over the next year, Tom Carter studied at the university and had clinical instruction at the Pennsylvania Hospital. The medical school, which had been operating since 1765, was located at Ninth and Chestnut Streets. It had moved its facilities to that site in 1802 and originally shared with the university the building that had been the presidential mansion when Philadelphia served as the first national capital. The mansion was torn down in 1829, and the medical school moved into a newly constructed building on the site. There, Carter took courses in anatomy, surgery, chemistry, and the "diseases of women and children." Though students underwent a more rigorous clinical curriculum at the medical school, they still had to study the theory and practice of medicine as well. Carter's training at the University of Virginia no doubt prepared him well for that. At the end of the 1851–52 session, the young medical student graduated with his second degree in medicine.[17]

Instead of returning home to Clarke County after graduating, the newly christened Dr. Carter remained in Philadelphia to gain practical experience in a local hospital. One such institution that offered opportunities for a young physician to practice his skills was the Blockley Almshouse, which had as part of its facility a small hospital that specialized in the treatment of, among other diseases, smallpox. Sometime in the fall of 1852, Carter began a two-year tenure at Blockley, where he hoped to put into practice what he had learned over the previous two years. By the following February, however, he had begun to reevaluate his plans to remain at the hospital for the full two years. As with many young men, Carter was in a hurry to progress in his field. Remaining in one place seemed to be

16. *Catalogue of the University of Pennsylvania, Session 1851–52*, 35.
17. Ibid.; Nitzsche, *University of Pennsylvania*, 119; *General Alumni Catalogue of the University of Pennsylvania*, 524.

standing still. "I have been through all the wards & have seen every kind of disease," he reported to Lucy Randolph in Clarke County, and "[a]nother year would be but a repetition of the same duties & a loss of time, which of course is invaluable to a young man." Time at the hospital also took a personal toll on Carter. In that same letter to Mrs. Randolph, he described a poor female patient who was so afraid to die that she refused the visit of a priest. Carter became "deeply interested" in her case and "stayed with her almost the whole time." Though she showed signs of improvement, after five days she "was attacked with congestion of the Brain & died." The young doctor wrote: "This is one of the pains of the profession."[18]

While living in the City of Brotherly Love, Carter did not entirely devote himself to his medical career. As a young man of twenty-two who lived with a cousin, Charles Carter, he engaged in a fairly active social life. The city provided many diversions for the sons of the Virginia elite. Close ties between the city's "bluebloods and their southern peers" offered an entrée into Philadelphia high society. "The F.F.V.s are at a premium in Phila[delphia] & therefore are shown much kindness & attention," according to Carter. To Lucy Randolph he reported that he had "been to a number of large balls & parties . . . & was quite pleased with many of the young ladies. But in truth I will say that I think there are no young ladies like those of Old Virginia." When not on duty at the hospital, Dr. Carter managed to travel as well. Baltimore, Maryland, was a favorite destination. When his older brother Robert came to Philadelphia in the winter of 1853, the two traveled to Baltimore to visit family and friends and "indulged to such an extent in its gaieties, such as balls, parties, theaters, concerts, dancing schools & soirees." His parents, with his younger half siblings Charles Shirley (called "Shirley") and Evelyn, spent time in Philadelphia as well. On one occasion, the whole family attended a children's party at which six-year-old Evelyn "enlivened the time . . . by a fight with Susy Burwell . . . in which contest the courage of the Burwells & Carters was exhibited to much advantage before the admiring Philadelphians."[19]

In the winter of 1853, Tom Carter considered his plans for the future. He knew that he did not want to remain in Philadelphia. As much as he

18. TNC to IBC, 14 Jan. 1915; THC to Mrs. Randolph, 7 Jan. 1853, THCP, 1850–1915, VHS. Though Carter never identifies the recipient of the letter, internal evidence indicates that it was Lucy Nelson Wellford Randolph (1810–82) of Clarke County, Va., the wife of a relative, Dr. Robert Carter Randolph (1807–87) (Magill, *Beverley Family of Virginia*, 173).

19. TNC to IBC, 14 Jan. 1915; Kilbride, "Southern Medical Students in Philadelphia," 710; THC to Mrs. Randolph, 7 Jan. 1853.

enjoyed his social life and the work at the almshouse hospital, he was determined to return to Virginia. "I am extremely unwilling," he wrote, "to leave the old state." With that thought in mind, he briefly considered setting up a medical practice in Alexandria, Virginia. Opportunities there were limited, however. Carter noted that "[u]nless [the city] is growing it would be useless to go there for the old physicians have the practice among the old inhabitants & of course are secure of it." In any case, he figured that he had time to choose his future course. He informed a friend that he expected "to go first to the lower country [and] visit my friends & relations there." After that, Carter hoped "to go to Europe for eight months or a year." Sometime in the early spring, he followed through on his plans to visit friends and family in the "lower country"—meaning King William and Hanover Counties. The Braxton family, cousins who lived at Ingleside in Hanover County, hosted the young doctor on one such occasion. Elizabeth Braxton wrote to her sister on 26 April and reported that "Tommy Carter dined here today." She announced that "he looks just as he always did with the exception of a moustache & is . . . a 'very sweet fellow.'" As far as traveling abroad, before Carter could even begin to make plans, family circumstances conspired to change the course of his future.[20]

The unexpected death of his father's overseer at Pampatike left the family in a bind. Wheat farming in Virginia in the early 1850s was a profitable business that required lots of land to cultivate the crop. Large plantations like the Carter farm in King William County not only had enough land— more than 2,000 acres—but also the labor force to harvest and ship the wheat. In 1850 more than 100 enslaved African Americans lived at Pampatike. From his home in Clarke County, Thomas Nelson Carter depended on an overseer to manage the daily operations in King William County. Sometime in the fall of 1852 or early in the winter of 1853, the overseer at Pampatike died. Rather than risk losing a season of harvesting and selling his wheat crop, Thomas Carter asked his son Tom to manage the farm. They came up with a plan whereby Tom would rent Pampatike from his father for $5,000 a year, a sum easily raised from the large wheat crop. Having made all of the arrangements, the young doctor moved back to his birthplace to begin life as a farmer. He took to it quite well. Carter proved himself more than capable of managing the slaves who worked the land and kept the house. He maintained a regular schedule at Pampatike for

20. THC to Mrs. Randolph, 7 Jan. 1853; Elizabeth Braxton to Lucy Lindley Braxton, 26 Apr. 1853, J. Ambler Johnston Papers, 1784–1902, VHS.

Susan Roy Carter, ca. 1858 (Courtesy of Fielding L. Williams Jr.)

those whose labor he managed and for himself as well. He would "[get] up and out at day break all the year round except Sunday."[21]

It was not all work for Carter. Once he reestablished himself in King William County as a "gentleman farmer," he began to take part in its social world. Visits with friends, neighbors, and extended family offered welcome distractions for the young farmer. "House parties," where men and women throughout the county would gather at neighboring estates and come together in one grand occasion, always attracted Carter. At one such party in 1854 or early in 1855, Pampatike played host to a number of male friends and family members who intended to travel the seven miles to Chericoke, the home of the Braxton family. There, Tom Carter met and became infatuated with a young woman named Susan Elizabeth Roy, known as Sue to her family. A brief courtship followed, culminating in their marriage on 7 November 1855 at her family's estate, Green Plains, in Mathews County.[22]

21. Heinemann and others, *Old Dominion, New Commonwealth*, 203; TNC to IBC, 14 Jan. 1915; 1850 Census, King William County, Slave Schedules.

22. Dulaney, *Some Recollections*, 1–2; TNC to IBC, 14 Jan. 1915; Mathews County Marriage Records, 1854–1935, Library of Virginia, Richmond.

Carter's new bride was the daughter of William H. Roy, a prosperous Mathews County resident who, at the time of Susan's birth in 1833, represented the county in the House of Delegates. The Roy family had roots in Virginia that stretched almost as far back as the Carters. Dr. Mungo Roy, a Scottish physician, arrived in the colony sometime in the first decade of the eighteenth century and settled in Essex County, where from 1720 to 1740 he served as justice of the peace. Like the early Carters, the doctor purchased land and enhanced his social status, acquiring acreage in Essex and Orange Counties. His descendents inherited his lands and married into many of the families living in the eastern part of the state. Susan's mother, Anne Seddon Roy, who died when Susan was only eighteen months old, came from Fredericksburg. Though her father later remarried, Susan spent considerable time in Fredericksburg with her Seddon relatives, including her uncle James Alexander Seddon. "Uncle Alex," as she and Tom knew him, later became the longest-serving Confederate secretary of war.[23]

After less than two years together, Tom and Susan Carter welcomed their first child on 2 May 1857. According to Tom, William Roy, despite being named for Susan's father, had the appearance of a Carter. To help nurse the child, known by family as Roy, Tom chose an enslaved women named Celia Grymes. She had been born at Pampatike and after Roy's birth seemed the best choice as a nursemaid. Celia would spend the rest of her long life at the farm taking care of the Carter family. In the white southern tradition of the faithful house servant, Celia became a beloved member of the family. During the Civil War, Tom Carter often asked his wife about Celia and passed on to her his kindest regards.[24]

Sometime later that fall, Susan became pregnant with their second child, and everything at Pampatike appeared to be prospering. Any feelings of joy and anticipation that Tom and Susan may have felt, however, received a heavy blow in the spring of 1858, when young Roy died. Susan, in particular, was devastated at the loss of her little boy. In May she wrote a letter to her aunt in which she expressed her overwhelming grief: "I cannot help being very sad. I wonder if I shall ever get accustomed to my baby's absence. It seems to me now that I miss him more than ever." At the same time, she and Tom looked forward to the birth of their second

23. Williams and Johnson, *Roy Genealogy*, 4, 11; Lancaster, *Historic Virginia Homes*, 231; Martin, *Remarkable Women of Pampatike*, 4; TNC to IBC, 14 Jan. 1915.

24. Martin, *Remarkable Women of Pampatike*, 6; THC to Sarah Seddon Bruce, 15 June 1858, Bruce Family Papers, 1665–1926, VHS; TNC to IBC, 14 Jan. 1915.

child. To handle his grief, Tom focused on the impending arrival. As Susan explained to her aunt, "My dear husband looks for so much happiness and comfort from his new baby. I trust that it may come soon and be healthy." It did—and on a date of special significance to Tom Carter as well. On 13 June 1858, the day her husband turned twenty-seven, Susan gave birth to another boy, whom the couple named Thomas Nelson after Tom's famous great-grandfather. Two days after his son's birth, Tom proudly wrote to Susan's aunt, Sarah Bruce, announcing the blessed event. In the letter, he noted that "he was a fine large boy . . . born by a singular coincidence on my own birthday." In a moment of bittersweet emotion, Tom also described the child as "a Roy in appearance as our precious little boy was a Carter."[25]

To further distract himself from his grief, Tom Carter could always turn to his business affairs. Not only was he busily engaged in managing Pampatike, but he also was a one-third partner in a new venture. On 30 March 1858, Carter, his father, and his half brother, William Pleasants Page Carter, purchased 1,027 acres in Madison Parish, Louisiana, for $39,737.50. Like many southerners of the Upper South, the three men wanted to expand their holdings to include a cotton plantation in the Deep South. Land in Louisiana along the Mississippi River offered a high financial return for landowners. Payment for the property was spread over a four-year period. The three Carters made the first payment of $10,000 in March and agreed to send similar payments on the first of January for the next three years. Tom and his father raised their shares of the initial payment by selling state stocks through the Richmond-based firm of Edwin Wortham and Company. To populate the Louisiana property with enough labor to farm the cotton, Tom Carter and his father agreed to send forty slaves; Tom sent twenty-three from Pampatike, and his father sent seventeen from Clarke County. The new venture did indeed prove lucrative. In January 1859, Tom wrote a letter to a Mr. Richardson advising him to invest in land in Louisiana near the Carter holdings. He explained that "[t]he profits are fully double those of this state & with the same strict personal attention that we give here would probably be triple."[26]

25. SRC to Sarah Seddon Bruce, 1858, and THC to Sarah Seddon Bruce, 15 June 1858; both in Bruce Family Papers, 1665–1926, VHS.

26. Thomas Henry Carter Account Book, 1859–88, VHS; A. R. Hynes to THC, 14 Jan. 1864, Private Collection; THC to Mr. Richardson, 25 Jan. 1859, THCP, 1850–1915, VHS. As part of the arrangement, Tom and his brother William paid $1,694.19 to ship their family's slaves to Louisiana.

Susan Carter also commented on the success of the Louisiana farm in a letter she wrote to her uncle William Patterson Smith in July 1860. "Dr. C[arter]'s brother William is with us, he is just from Louisiana & reports most favorably of our prospects there." She went on to note that there were "fine crops of corn & cotton with no serious sickness among the servants" and that her husband planned to travel to Louisiana later that fall to "see how everything is getting on." In that same letter, Susan mentioned her young family, which had grown by one. On 6 April 1860, she gave birth to a girl, whom she and Tom named Juliet in honor of his mother. In describing her children, Susan reported that "[m]y little ones are quite well just now. Thomas has been a little puny with occasional attacks of indisposition but seems to be improving & Juliet is as fat & good as she can be. I really never saw a better or more sprightly baby & it is well she has something to redeem her homely exterior. I hope she will verify the old saying that an ugly baby makes a pretty woman."[27]

With his wife and two healthy children and his established position as a prosperous gentleman farmer in King William County, Tom Carter was poised to live a life worthy of his family name. Events beyond Pampatike, however, soon interrupted his plans. A decade of growing sectional tensions that threatened to tear the nation in two culminated in 1860. The election of Abraham Lincoln as president proved to be the last straw for South Carolina. On 20 December the Palmetto State officially seceded from the Union, followed by the six other states from the Deep South by 1 February 1861. Virginia, however, had remained in the Union during that initial period of the secession crisis. Its leaders continued to debate throughout the winter months. Only with the fall of Fort Sumter on 13 April and Lincoln's call two days later for 75,000 troops from those states still in the Union did Virginians decide. On 17 April, by a vote of 88 to 55, the Virginia Convention passed an ordinance of secession. The commonwealth had cast its lot with the recently established Confederate States of America.

War fever swept through King William County in the spring of 1861, and Tom Carter succumbed to its power. On 23 May, when Virginians in the central and eastern parts of the state voted overwhelmingly for secession, King William County residents traveled to their polling places and supported secession by a vote of 496 to 0. Tom Carter stood among those who could no longer justify their allegiance to the United States.

27. SRC to William Patterson Smith, 13 July 1860, THCP, 1850–1915, VHS.

Though he never explicitly stated his reasons for supporting secession, Carter gave a hint in a letter he wrote to Susan in January 1862. In sharing his concern over the issue of what to do about the approaching expiration of the initial enlistment period in the Confederate army, Carter remarked that "[u]nless this 12 mo[nth]s volunteer business can be altered by a re-enlistment nothing can prevent the ruin of Virginia. After the Old State is lost the Confederacy may go hang." Clearly, he viewed his ties to the commonwealth as the primary motivation for his military service. Thus Carter most likely accepted the reality of disunion only after Virginia's leaders passed the ordinance of secession following Lincoln's call for troops to put down the rebellion.[28]

Sometime in the spring, Tom Carter joined the rush to form a military company and offer its services to the state. In his case, he decided to form an artillery battery. The precise moment when Carter began to gather recruits is unknown, but by 24 May the *Richmond Daily Dispatch* announced that a battery was being formed in King William County. Why he chose artillery is also not clear. A comment in a wartime letter to his wife suggests a possible reason. "My command [of a battery]," he explained to Susan, "unlike that of a Captain of Infantry is separate & independent." Having established himself as a successful manager of a large plantation—a mostly autonomous and isolated world within a world—Carter may have been drawn to the independent nature of battery command versus the notion of leading one company among nine others in an infantry or cavalry regiment. Because the population of available recruits in King William County was limited to begin with, and with other units mobilizing there as well, he could only form a company-sized unit. A captain in command of an artillery battery ultimately had more responsibility and a greater chance of distinction than did a captain in command of an infantry or cavalry company. Whatever his personal reasons were, Tom Carter became captain of the King William Artillery on 1 June. The battery officially enlisted for twelve months with seventy-one men at Bond's Store near Rumford Academy, on the road that ran from Ayletts to King William Court House.[29]

28. Long, *Day by Day*, 77; *Richmond Enquirer*, 31 May 1861; THC to SRC, 8 Jan. 1862.

29. *RDD*, 24 May 1861; THC to SRC, 8 Jan. 1862; Thomas Henry Carter's CSR; Atkinson, *King William County in the Civil War*, 23. The location of Bond's Store was derived from a map of Caroline County drawn by the Confederate Engineers Office under the direction of Lieutenant Colonel Jeremy F. Gilmer (Map of Caroline County, 1864, Jeremy Francis Gilmer Collection, VHS). According to the monument that stands in front of the original King William County courthouse, the county contributed 450 men to Confederate military service. Most of the sol-

Carter spent the next several weeks organizing and equipping the unit, while Susan and the children were largely absent from Pampatike. In mid-June, they visited the Braxtons at Ingleside. The new captain, just short of his thirty-first birthday, stood a little over five feet, nine inches tall and weighed about 165 pounds. With a mustache and a goatee, he looked the part of a dashing hero. Part of Captain Carter's duty involved traveling to Richmond to purchase supplies and coordinate his activities with the state's military forces. After one of his visits to the capital city, Carter took time out to write the first of his many wartime letters to Susan.[30]

—∿—

Pampatike[31]
June 22nd [1861]

My dearest Wife,

I am unable to see you this evening in consequence of an attack of Dysentery which came on me in Richmond yesterday. I am doing better today in some respects though still suffering with considerable pain at times. If I have a good night I shall be over in the cool of the morning. Shirley started for Clarke this morning, via Staunton as the authorities do not allow persons to pass the Manassas Junction.[32] I saw your Uncle Seddon.[33] He was all kindness & affection as usual. You will see by the papers that he is [a] delegate to the Southern Congress from the State at large. I send the paper of today. We had a little brush with the enemy near Cumberland in which we captured two cannon & killed several yankees.[34] The Valley is considered safe—400 or 500 Maryland-

---

diers served in the following units raised in the county: the King William Artillery, companies D and H of the 53rd Virginia Infantry, and Company H of the 9th Virginia Cavalry (Atkinson, *King William County in the Civil War*, 27).

30. TNC to IBC, 14 Jan. 1915.

31. THC to SRC, 22 June 1861, Private Collection.

32. Shirley is Charles Shirley Carter (1840–1922), Tom Carter's younger half brother.

33. James Alexander Seddon (1815–80) was the younger brother of Carter's mother-in-law, Anne Seddon Roy. In June 1861 Seddon was elected to represent Virginia in the Confederate Provisional Congress, which had moved to Richmond from Montgomery, Ala., at the end of May. Seddon served in the Congress for eight months, after which, on 20 November 1862, he became Confederate secretary of war. He held that post until 5 February 1865 (Schlup, "James Alexander Seddon," 576).

34. Carter is referring to a brief fight that took place near Romney, Va. (now W.Va.). Federal troops, commanded by Colonel Lew Wallace, moved south from Cumberland, Md., to aid pro-Union citizens of the town who were reportedly being mistreated. A small skirmish resulted in Wallace's force withdrawing back to Cumberland (Long, *Day by Day*, 85).

ers hold Harpers Ferry. The remainder are at Winchester. We also hold Romney. The enemy have retreated. I feel easy for the present in relation to Clarke. I trust & pray our little darling is better. Tell me about her. I sent the port wine by Harrison. I send your things by Charles.[35]

You must not be uneasy about me. I am better today but find it best to keep the recumbent posture. This disease is very prevalent in Richmond. Gresham of King & Queen went up with me & was ill last night[,] so much so as to require Dr Cornday [or Counday] all night.[36] We were at the American (a perfect hog hole) the other hotels being full.[37] William returned with me & will enter my company taking the chances of office.[38] I saw the Washington Artillery drill & pass in review before the President & Genl Lee.[39] I was somewhat disappointed in the manouvres[,] the horses being new & untrained. Met Martha Clarke[40] & Mrs Claiborne there.[41] The latter was perfectly enamoured of Genl Lee who really was superb[,] mounted on Sir Equal in uniform. The horse stood fire so badly that the Gen had to ride off for fear of running into the ladies. He is a magnificent rider.

35. Harrison and Charles were enslaved African Americans who accompanied Tom Carter while he served in the Confederate army.

36. Gresham and Dr. Cornday (or Counday) have not been identified.

37. The American Hotel was located in Richmond at the corner of Main and 11th Streets (*Richmond City Directory 1860*).

38. William Pleasants Page Carter (1843–1927) was Tom Carter's younger half brother. He enlisted in the King William Artillery on 1 June as a sergeant and was promoted to first lieutenant later in 1861. In 1862 he was wounded at the Battle of Seven Pines and at the end of the year earned promotion to captain. From then until his capture at Spotsylvania Court House on 12 May 1864, he commanded the King William Artillery. William P. P. Carter spent the remainder of the war as a prisoner in South Carolina, Georgia, and finally at Fort Delaware (CSR).

39. The Washington Artillery mustered into Confederate service in New Orleans, Louisiana, on 26 May 1861 as a battalion of five companies. Shortly thereafter, Companies 1 through 4, under the command of Major James Burdge Walton (1813–85), left for Virginia. The 5th Company served in the western theater. The Washington Artillery was a pre–Civil War organization that dated back to 1838. It fought in the Mexican War as the Native American Battery and later reorganized in 1852 as the Washington Artillery (Crute, *Units of the Confederate States Army*, 159–60).

Jefferson Davis (1808–89) of Mississippi, former secretary of war and U.S. senator, had been elected by the Confederate Congress to serve as provisional president of the Confederate States of America on 9 February 1861. In November he became president of the "permanent" government in its first and only presidential election.

At this point in the war, Robert E. Lee, who had been promoted to the rank of full general on 14 June 1861, was serving in an unofficial capacity as military adviser to President Davis. Earlier in the spring, after he had resigned from the U.S. Army, Lee had commanded all military and naval forces in the state of Virginia (Freeman, *Lee* 1:529–30; *OR* 2:775).

40. Martha Clarke has not been identified.

41. Carter may be referring to Mary Anna McGuire Claiborne (1819–64) of Fredericksburg and Richmond, Va.

The news relatin[g] to the capture of Gen Lyons in Missouri is not confirmed & probably untrue.[42] My company will be mustered into service Friday. I hope I may recover from this complaint at once.

God bless you my darling Wife
I wish I could see you.
Thos. H. Carter

Much love to all at Ingleside.[43] Gen Patterson crossed the Potomac at Williamsport with fifteen hundred but returned to the Maryland side.[44] I saw Baldwin, an old college mate & brother of our Inspector Gen.[45] He was in the ordnance department, United States service, & stationed in Maine. He escaped & ran the blockade near Mr Newton's— Westmoreland.[46] He says enormous preparations are being made at the north. Men from manufacturing & commercial interests are thrown out of employment & enter the ranks for employment & a livelihood. They are better equipped & armed than our men[,] having all the latest improvements. He seems to fear the Northwestern men more than the New Englanders. Braver & better shots. The cities of the North are getting up petitions for peace but they do not represent the masses. You remember they were conservative in their vote.

42. Brigadier General Nathaniel Lyon (1818–61) of Connecticut commanded Union forces in Missouri. He was later killed on 10 August 1861 at the Battle of Wilson's Creek (Warner, *Generals in Blue*, 286–87).

43. Ingleside, which was built between 1838 and 1840 by Carter Braxton (1789–1855) and his wife, Mary Grymes Sayre Braxton (1805–88), was located in Hanover County, Va., south of the village of Old Church. During the war, Carter Braxton's daughter, Nora Crena Braxton Macon (1824–92), and her husband, Dr. William Macon (1819–90), owned the two-and-a-half-story brick home. In June 1864 Lieutenant General Ulysses S. Grant used the house as his headquarters during the Battle of Cold Harbor. Tom Carter's great aunt, Mary Carter, was Carter Braxton's mother (*Old Homes of Hanover County*, 27–28; Colvin, *On Deep Water*, 26; 1850 Census, Hanover County).

44. Major General Robert Patterson (1792–1881) commanded the U.S. Department of Pennsylvania in June 1861 (Eicher and Eicher, *High Commands*, 418–19).

45. James William Baldwin (1828–75) was an 1849 graduate of the Virginia Military Institute (McMurry, *Virginia Military Institute Alumni*, 89). His twin brother, Lieutenant Briscoe Gerard Baldwin (1828–98), was on duty at the Ordnance Bureau in Richmond in 1861. He later served as assistant adjutant general on the staff of Robert E. Rodes and as an ordnance officer under Robert E. Lee (Krick, *Staff Officers*, 66).

46. Carter is most likely referring to "Linden," the Westmoreland County, Va., home of Willoughby Newton (1802–74), member of the Virginia House of Delegates, U.S. congressman, and cofounder with Edmund Ruffin of the Virginia Agricultural Society. Newton built the two-story Classical Revival house around 1830. Union army foragers raided the property in February 1863 and came away with Newton's carriage horses and many of his sugar-cured hams. Newton's son, William Brockenbrough Newton (1832–63), served in the 4th Virginia Cavalry (*Biographical Directory of the United States Congress*, 1567–68; Norris, *Westmoreland County*, 283–84, 375).

CHAPTER TWO

———— ∿ ————

1861

15 September–29 December 1861

On 25 June 1861, Captain Tom Carter wrote the commandant of the Virginia Military Institute that he had "a company of untrained men, about seventy in number. . . . My men are uniformed & thoroughly equipped." One week later, the King William Artillery arrived in Richmond, where a correspondent for the *Richmond Daily Dispatch* described the men as "stout, able-bodied fellows." On 2 July the unit, led by Carter, mustered into Confederate service on Capitol Square. For the next two months, the battery encamped on the grounds of Richmond College on the outskirts of the city. There, Carter trained a battalion of artillery that consisted of his own and two other batteries. On 1 September, when its initial period of training came to an end, the King William Artillery received its first guns and encamped at nearby Allen's Grove. In early October, Carter and his battery left the Richmond area for northern Virginia, where, after a two-day journey by train, they joined the main Confederate army near Manassas Junction.[1]

Following the Battle of Bull Run on 21 July, which Carter and his battery had missed, the opposing armies settled into a relatively peaceful period. With the exception of the small fight at Ball's Bluff on 21 October and some skirmishing between cavalry units, both sides spent most of their time fortifying and watching each other's movements. Carter and his men initially encamped near Fairfax Station on the Orange and Alexandria Railroad and later occupied positions at Union Mill near Bull Run Creek and at Davis's Ford near the Occoquan River. On 2 November the King William Artillery was formally attached to Robert Rodes's brigade in Earl Van Dorn's division in the Confederate Army of the Potomac. For

1. THC to Francis H. Smith, 25 June 1861, Thomas Henry Carter Alumni File, VMI; *RDD*, 3 July 1861; Thomas Catesby Jones, "War Reminiscences," VHS; Macaluso, *Morris, Orange, and King William Artillery*, 20.

Carter, the remainder of 1861 was a period of adjustment as he got to know his men.[2]

—〰—

Fairfax Ct House
Sunday
Sept. 15th [1861]

My darling Wife,

I have only a moment to write to say that I have arrived safely & am well. I reached Manassas Thursday evening 4 P.M. having passed nearly two days & a night on the road. The rolling stock is in bad order from incessant use & the freight train laid over from time to time to avoid collision with the passenger. I reported the same evening to Johnston & encamped at Manassas until yesterday morning.[3] Expecting to remain some days there I was in no hurry unfortunately to visit the Battle field & was suddenly ordered here to report to Beauregard.[4] I passed Mitchell's Ford on Bull Run a few hundred yards above Blackburn's Ford where the fight of [the] 18th occurred. The country [is] open rolling & beautiful in scenery. Fortifications abound at Manassas & Bull run. Troops are posted all through this country & the number must be large. In the last few days an advance of the whole army has been made. Johnston's Headquarters are still at Manassas. Beauregard is here. I am about to report to him now & am as dirty as a pig, the baggage having been sent by rail to Fairfax Station 3 1/2 miles distant. Wagon transportation is most difficult. The men encamped in the open air without tents last night. I am in Dorsey's room. He moves today with his 4th Brigade (of which he is Medical Director now) to Falls Church.[5] Hall's Hill was taken night before last which is

2. Macaluso, *Morris, Orange, and King William Artillery*, 20–21; *OR* 5:936, 960–61.

3. General Joseph Eggleston Johnston (1807–91) of Virginia was the fourth-ranking general in the Confederate army (Warner, *Generals in Gray*, 161–62).

4. General Pierre Gustave Toutant Beauregard (1818–93) of Louisiana commanded the Confederate forces in Charleston, South Carolina, that forced the surrender of Fort Sumter and, with Joseph E. Johnston, led the army that won the Battle of First Bull Run. In September he commanded the Confederate Army of the Potomac (Eicher and Eicher, *High Commands*, 123–24).

5. John Syng Dorsey Cullen (1832–93) was a prewar physician who practiced in Richmond, Va.. Dorsey Cullen served briefly in the 1st Virginia Infantry before taking up his duties as a surgeon in the Confederate army on 3 May 1861. In October he became the medical director of James Longstreet's division and, in 1862, his corps. In 1863 Cullen served as the medical director of the Confederate Department of Virginia and North Carolina (*Richmond City Directory 1860*; *OR* 51[2]:357; Davis, "John Syng Dorsey Cullen," 595–96).

said to protect Munson's Hill. Genl. George M. Smith reached here yesterday, one of the first military men in the country.[6] He, Beauregard[,] Longstreet &c. met in military conclave yesterday.[7] Something is in the wind. Kiss the precious children for me & give my love to your uncle, aunt[8] & family & remember me to Celia.[9] I must be off to report & get my tents[,] luggage &c. The 1st Regiment is just starting to Falls Church with four days provisions[—]no tents.[10]

> In great haste
> your devoted husband,
> Thos. H. Carter

Direct your letters here. Will write again in a day or two at greater length.

—⁂—

> Camp "Masked Battery"
> Near Fairfax Station
> September 27th 1861

Since my last letter my darling wife two letters from Rock Castle[11] have reached me & it is needless to tell you the pleasure I derive from them & the gratitude to God I experience in knowing that my precious family is in the enjoyment of health & other blessings. Nothing of interest has occurred since my last letter. I am kept closely at the encampment

6. Carter is referring to Major General Gustavus Woodson Smith (1821–96) of Kentucky, whom Carter misidentified as "George M. Smith" (Warner, *Generals in Gray*, 280–81).

7. Brigadier General James Longstreet (1821–1904) of South Carolina commanded an infantry brigade in the Confederate Army of the Potomac (Warner, *Generals in Gray*, 192–93).

8. Carter is most likely referring to Charles Bruce (1826–96) and his wife, Sarah Alexander Seddon Bruce (1829–1907). Sarah was the sister of Carter's mother-in-law, Anne Seddon Roy. The Bruces lived at Staunton Hill in Charlotte County, Va. ("Genealogical Notes of Seddon Family," Bruce Family Paper, 1715–1906, VHS; Bruce, *Bruce Family*, 113).

9. Carter is referring to Celia Grymes (1806?–1907), a Carter family slave. Her obituary appeared on the front page of the 7 June 1907 issue of the *Richmond Times-Dispatch*.

10. The 1st Virginia Infantry was organized in Richmond in April 1861 and was commanded by Colonel Patrick Theodore Moore (b. 1823?) (CSR).

11. Rock Castle, named for its location on a rocky cliff overlooking the James River, was the Goochland County, Va., home of John Coles Rutherford and his wife, Ann Seddon Roy Rutherfoord, the sister of Carter's wife, Susan Roy Carter. The original colonial home, known as the "Queen Anne Cottage," was built by 1732 by Tarleton Fleming. In 1843 John Rutherfoord, following his one-year term as governor of Virginia, purchased the property as a summer home. His son John C. Rutherfoord inherited the house and added an Italianate front to the structure. In 1932 the original colonial "Queen Anne Cottage" was rediscovered and moved to the garden (Bullard, *Goochland County Yesterday and Today*, 114).

by the drill & occasionally by an order from Beauregard to Ewell[12] to hold ourselves in light marching order to move at an instants warning with three days provisions & forty rounds of ammunition. We never have three days provisions ahead nor forty rounds of ammunition (for infantry), a fact which Ewell says he has not failed to communicate [to] Beauregard but which has not been regarded. The only effect of this order is to keep us all closely at home for not the least preparation is made & no one expects any movement. I wish we had an efficient Sec. of War & that Lee instead of being in the West with an army triply outnumbered & on half rations without the possibility of accomplishing any object save that of keeping back the enemy, was at his former post in Richmond.[13] Old Cooper is an imbecile I am inclined to think.[14] There is a screw loose all around in our army since the victory. The opinion of the army is that a tremendous mistake was made in not advancing on to Alexandria immediately after the Bull Run fight. The blame I am told lies at Davis' door. I really do not think we are in a state now to invade Maryland with success. The fortifications at Evansport (about twenty miles distant) progress slowly, & everything goes on slowly. A part of the Railroad between this place & Springfield (twelve miles towards Alex[andria]) where several Regiments are stationed needs slight repair & yet I suppose wagons will haul for weeks where the R[ailroad] would do the work in half the time. And every thing in this way. Johnston is a man of splendid abilities & every inch a soldier but I take it he is lazy if I may judge from the want of system evinced on every side. Some think G. W. Smith the "coming man" for the times. He is regarded as a great man by the Army officers. I have not seen him. We expect to move in a few days to the neighborhood of Fairfax Ct. H. again. Our Brigade is attached to the 1st Corps under Beauregard & he will post his brigades near his Headquarters. I should prefer to be in Smith's Corps. The opinion here of Beauregard is that he would make a good Brigadier but no higher. I think we shall go into winter quarters here. Possibly a column may cross at Evansport into

12. Brigadier General Richard Stoddert Ewell (1817–72) of Virginia commanded the 2nd brigade of the Confederate Army of the Potomac (Eicher and Eicher, *High Commands*, 229).

13. Judah P. Benjamin (1811–84) was secretary of war from 17 September to 21 November 1861 (ibid., 8). Carter is referring to Robert E. Lee's brief, lackluster service in western Virginia (now West Virginia) as coordinator of Confederate operations against Union forces in the region. Lee remained there until the end of October (Gallagher, "Robert E. Lee," 1154).

14. General Samuel Cooper (1798–1876) of New Jersey was the highest-ranking officer in the Confederate States Army. He served in Richmond as adjutant and inspector general from 16 May 1861 until 19 April 1865 (Eicher and Eicher, *High Commands*, 184–85).

Maryland. Twelve guns have been placed there—forty or fifty ought to be in position & something might be done.

Genl. Ewell entertained several ladies at a dinner a few days since[—] Mrs Genl David Jones &c.[15] The same day Wm Payne[16] & Bob Randolph son of Charles Randolph of Fauquier gave the officers a dinner made up of the contents of a box from home.[17] We enjoyed ourselves quite much. While at dinner two fugitives came up & dined with us. One was Lieut. Dunott of a company in the Wm Gordon's Reg. He was captured at Bull Run.[18] Mrs Clements daughter of John C. Calhoun gave him a suit of clothes & aided him in his escape.[19] The other[,] Adjutant or Lieut Alexander of Portsmouth[,] who was in the St Nicholas with Col Thomas (Zavoner), escaped by jumping from the walls of Fort McHenry. He swam some hour or two in the water around the fort & finally escaped in the bottom of a carriage beneath the hoops of two young ladies. The same night he acted [as] bolster for them. Lu Carroll[,] daughter of Judge Thompson[,] gave some assistance.[20] I see a good deal [of] Wm Newton.[21] He is a noble fellow. So unpretending & yet so talented. This evening he received a box from home & sent me a portion of his sweet &

15. Sarah Rebecca Taylor Jones, wife of Confederate general David Rumph Jones, was a niece of President Zachary Taylor (Bearss, "David Rumph Jones," 201).

16. William Payne has not been identified.

17. Robert Randolph (1835–64) enlisted as first lieutenant in Company H of the 4th Virginia Cavalry on 25 April 1861 at Warrenton, Va. On 19 September 1861, he was elected captain of the company, known as the Black Horse Troop. Randolph served with the unit—earning promotions to major, lieutenant colonel, and colonel—until his death on 12 May 1864 during the fighting near Yellow Tavern, Va. (CSR). His father, Charles Carter Randolph (1788–1863), was a veteran of the War of 1812 and a large landowner in Fauquier and Stafford Counties, Va. (McGill, *Beverley Family of Virginia*, 201–2; 1860 Census, Fauquier County; Krick, *Lee's Colonels*, 316).

18. Third Lieutenant Henry H. Dunot (b. 1833?) of the 27th Virginia Infantry. A prewar civil engineer, Dunot enlisted in the 27th Virginia on 22 April 1861. He was captured at First Bull Run and imprisoned in Washington, D.C. Dunot escaped from prison and returned to the unit on 23 September 1861 (CSR).

19. Anna Maria Calhoun Clemson (1817–75) was the daughter of John C. Calhoun and the wife of Thomas Green Clemson, the founder of Clemson University. The couple lived in Bladensburg, Md., before the war (Clemson University, http://www.clemson.edu/about/history/figures/annaclemson.html [accessed 20 August 2010]).

20. Lu Carroll has not been identified.

21. William Brockenbrough Newton (1832–63) enlisted as a first lieutenant in Company G of the 4th Virginia Cavalry at Ashland, Va., on 9 May 1861. On 27 September 1861, he was elected captain of the company to replace the newly promoted Lieutenant Colonel Williams Carter Wickham (1820–88), Tom Carter's first cousin. Newton was the son of Willoughby Newton (1802–74), who represented Westmoreland County in the Virginia House of Delegates from 1826 to 1832 and served one term in the U. S. Congress from 1843 to 1845. Young Newton graduated from the University of Virginia in 1852 and settled in Hanover County, where he practiced law and farmed. In 1859 he was elected to the House of Delegates (CSR; Leonard, *General Assembly of Virginia*, 470; *Biographical Directory of the United States Congress*, 1567–68).

irish potatoes & butter. By the way[,] these three articles & ham & fish & molasses are the great standbys of soldiers. The whiskey goes rapidly but I do not care to replenish it. The little I need can be kept in my trunk. When a bottle is taken from the box the men dispatch it quickly. Wm & Julian rejoice in each other's society[,] sleep together & he usually takes meals with us.[22] He is as boyish as ever. I don't think really he is fit for any commission. Their peals of laughter & jokes can be heard anytime. At night a large fire is made near our tent & all gather around including a large portion of the company & have music which is really quite good. Wm is a great favorite with his set & Newman[,][23] Cocke[,][24] Dabney[,][25] Ryland[26] & Walker Hawes.[27] My mess is an excellent one. The lieuts are all gentlemen[,] amiable[,] kind & obliging & all of us on the most cordial terms. I have not yet seen the Clark boys. You would be astonished to see how much separated we are by a few miles up here. Last night there was some skirmishing at Springfield. Three Yankees killed & one of Rhodes' men wounded.[28] We have two ~~much~~ Regiments down there from this

22. Julian M. Carter (1834?–62) was Tom Carter's younger brother. On 8 May 1861, Julian enlisted in Richmond as a private in Company I of the 4th Virginia Cavalry. Though his exact birth date is not known, Julian is listed in the 1850 census as being sixteen years old, thus he was most likely born in 1834 (CSR; 1850 Census, Clarke County).

23. William B. Newman (1831–62) enlisted as a first sergeant in the King William Artillery at Bond's Store on 1 June 1861. When the battery reorganized in April 1862, the men elected Newman to serve as first lieutenant. A month later, he was killed in action on 31 May during the Battle of Seven Pines (CSR).

24. Edward J. Cocke enlisted as a corporal in the King William Artillery on 1 June at Bond's Store. He was promoted to sergeant sometime before his mortal wounding at the Battle of Seven Pines on 31 May 1862 (CSR).

25. Alexander F. Dabney (1836–62) enlisted as a sergeant in the King William Artillery at Bond's Store on 1 June 1861 (CSR). Carter also mentions Dabney in his letters of 29 April, 18 August, and 4 October 1862.

26. Robert Semple Ryland (1838?–1925) enlisted as a second lieutenant in the King William Artillery at Bond's Store on 1 June 1861. When the unit reorganized in the spring of 1862, he was not reelected and was discharged on 14 May. On 18 August 1862, Ryland enlisted as a private in Company H of the 9th Virginia Cavalry. He was captured by the enemy in King William County, Va., on 16 March 1865 and confined at Point Lookout, Md., until his release on 17 June. Ryland was described as being six feet tall with brown hair and hazel eyes. After the war, he represented King William County in the Virginia House of Delegates from 1877 to 1879 (CSR; 1860 Census, King William County; Leonard, *General Assembly of Virginia*, 526).

27. Walker Aylett Hawes (1840–1914) enlisted as a second lieutenant in the King William Artillery at Bond's Store on 1 June 1861. When the battery reorganized in the spring of 1862, Hawes lost his position, and in August he enlisted as a private in Company H of the 9th Virginia Cavalry. He was wounded at the Battle of Brandy Station (9 June 1863) and later was shot in the groin near Reams' Station (27 August 1864) and in the hip in January 1865 (CSR).

28. Carter is referring to Colonel Robert Emmett Rodes (1829–64) of Lynchburg, Va., who he misidentified as "Rhodes." At this time, Rodes commanded the 5th Alabama Infantry (Warner, *Generals in Gray*, 263). Carter spent the rest of the war in close association with Rodes—initially

Brigade—under Longstreet who has command of the advance. Write to me as often as you can my darling. Kiss my precious little children for me. Talk to Thomas about me.[29] Tell him I will bring him a gun. & that dear little cherub Juliet. How I long to hear her say Papa. I want to see you terribly—& dream of you. God almighty bless you my own dear wife.

Ever y[ou]rs,
Thos. H. Carter

—〰—

Camp "Masked Battery"
Near Fairfax Station
October 13th 1861

Your last letter from Richmond my darling wife, was received on Friday just on the eve of a march with two of my guns to gather forage in the neighborhood of Pohick Church.[30]

Thursday evening three Regiments of Ewell's Brigade[,] two of Early's Brigade & my Battery were ordered to be ready to march Friday morning at 3 o'clock with three days provisions & without tents or baggage.[31] We were of course ignorant of our destination. At 1 o'clock I aroused the company & just as we were ready to mount & be off a courier rode up through the pitchy darkness & the order was rescinded by the Earl Van Dorn.[32] He ordered[,] however[,] one Reg. & two of my pieces to be ready to march at 7 A.M. & Rodes (the Col), & myself to report to him at that hour. This was simply a foraging expedition. He then explained to us his plan in the 3 o'clock expedition. It was to march to Springfield[,] cut off a comp'y of troops, attack the battery on Bush Hill[,] which he

---

as a battery commander attached to his brigade and later as a battalion commander attached to Rodes's division.

29. Carter is referring to his oldest son, Thomas Nelson Carter (1858–1917), who he named for his father, Thomas Nelson Carter.

30. Pohick Church, located in southeastern Fairfax County, Va., was a colonial Episcopal church built between 1769 and 1774. Both George Washington and George Mason had served as vestrymen. Later in the war, Federal troops used the building as a stable, which resulted in the destruction of much of the church's original interior woodwork (Loth, *Virginia Landmarks Register*, 160).

31. As of the end of August, Brigadier General Richard Stoddert Ewell's brigade consisted of the 5th, 6th, and 12th Alabama and the 12th Mississippi Infantry regiments, while Brigadier General Jubal Anderson Early's brigade included the 5th and 11th North Carolina and the 24th Virginia Infantry regiments (*OR* 5:825).

32. Major General Earl Van Dorn (1820–63) of Mississippi commanded a division in the Confederate Army of the Potomac (Warner, *Generals in Gray*, 314–15; *OR* 5:889).

had heard was a trifling earthwork, destroy all the property in reach & form a junction across on the turnpike between Fairfax Ct. H. & Alexandria with Longstreet. This attack would have been a diversion while the wagons hauled off the forage on the Potomac.

Well it was very brilliant & might have been very bloody but would have accomplished no object worthy of the risk & loss of life.

He had been granted permission by Beauregard but it was afterwards withdrawn[,] he knew not why. He is an inch or two lower than myself[,] slender, hazel eye, dressy & fancy fellow—fights for effect & evidently loves it. Very successful & altogether a dashing Genl. His aids are liked accordingly, & looked sappy-headed accordingly. Would not give Ewell for him. He will risk largely for a great object—not otherwise. The Earl looked quite distingué in his shirt & drawers of the latest cut. In the foraging expedition we had to guard two roads outside of our pickets several miles beyond Pohick. I sent one gun under Pat [Fontaine][33] with Rodes & took the other with the wing under Major Morgan to guard the telegraph road.[34] The pickets thrown out on the road beyond Rodes by him fired into a Cavalry comp'y of 60 which came unsuspectingly down the road [and] only killed one horse. The firing was heard by us & we immediately prepared for action. Not hearing the cannon I knew it was nothing serious & we soon calmed down. At night I stretched out my India rubber blanket by the fire & slept comfortably until midnight when the rain began to fall. I then put on my India rubber greatcoat which is a great invention. At 3 1/2 A.M. we were ordered back. I took no cold & am perfectly well. Until I had my bed tick stuffed with hay I slept in great discomfort from cold. Since [then] I sleep delightfully. Walker Hawes has suffered for some time with a perineal abscess.[35] I shall endeavor to get him a furlough for ten days. He is getting well. Ryland has been jaundiced but is well again. Pat is also restored to his usual health & appetite.

33. Patrick Henry Fontaine (1841–1915), a Baptist minister from King William County, enlisted as a first lieutenant in the King William Artillery at Bond's Store on 1 June 1861. He was not reelected when the battery reorganized in May 1862 and decided to return home to his ministry. In August 1863 Fontaine entered the service once again as a chaplain in the 53rd Virginia Infantry, which was commanded by his cousin, Colonel William Roane Aylett (1832–1900). After the war, Fontaine preached in numerous churches in North Carolina and southern Virginia (CSR; Taylor, *Virginia Baptist Ministers*, 6th series, 14–17).

34. Carter is most likely referring to Major John Tyler Morgan (1824–1907) of the 5th Alabama Infantry. Morgan was a prewar lawyer and member of the Alabama secession convention who eventually rose to the rank of brigadier general and served in the western theater (CSR; Warner, *Generals in Gray*, 221–22).

35. A perineal abscess is an abscess located between the anus and the scrotum.

You might inquire as to the grinding of the wheat at a country mill but they are too far to haul there & back & the cost would be nearly as great as hauling to Richmond which I think entirely impracticable. If the mill at the foot of { . . . }tain's Hill were fit for anything it might be done. I see nothing to do as it is but to await the opening of the blockade. Possibly some mill down the Pamunkey River might grind forward the flour[,] but every thing in the country is in a small scale & the flour[,] if at all inferior[,] might be rejected by the government. In new enterprises it is necessary to move with great circumspection as shoals & concealed dangers lie ahead. Still inquiries will do no harm. The shoes ought to be made quickly & as economically as possible. Nat is wasteful with the leather unless watched.[36] I understand a third of the negroes have been impressed from King William to work on the fortifications at Yorktown.[37] This must have put back the operations at Pampatike. I hope every thing will go on well there. Make them keep things up about the yard—the fencing[,] gates[,] latches & whitewashing & keep down the weeds as far as possible. I hate to see a dilapidated establishment. I fear you will need James. If so look out for a free servant for me & I will return him. It is dangerous here to have him & I would prefer to send him home. Many have escaped from this Brigade already & [I] should not feel at all surprised to hear any morning that he & Anthony were off. Anthony is Walker Hawes' negro & a lazy trifling scamp. There is not the least difficulty in getting James back.[38] He would reach Hanover Ct. House by 1 P.M. & home the same day. He is fat & dirty as possible. A good servant ought to be hired at 12 dollars a month. Holman has a first rate at 10$.[39] Send a free one if possible.

Wm Edwards soon backed out—only stayed long enough to see the country & then vamosed.[40] Too much bluster to be fit for anything. I will send you most of my pay when I get it so you need not call on Wortham

36. Nat was one of the Carter family slaves at Pampatike.

37. Throughout the fall of 1861, Major General John B. Magruder used slave labor to build fortifications on the Virginia Peninsula. On 7 September he was authorized to impress one-half of the male slaves from farms in various eastern Virginia counties (including King William) to work for fifty cents per day. In December, Magruder hired slaves at the rate of $100 a man to work at Gloucester Point and on the Peninsula (OR 4:654, 715).

38. James was a Carter family slave who traveled with Carter and served as his camp servant.

39. William H. Holman (b. 1841) enlisted as a first lieutenant in the 1st Company of the Fluvanna (Va.) Light Artillery on 20 June 1861. Eight days later, he was promoted to captain. Holman served with the battery until relieved of his duty on 16 May 1862 (CSR).

40. William Edwards (b. 1829 or 1831) enlisted as a sergeant in the King William Artillery (CSR).

oftener than necessary.[41] Forty dollars per month is an abundance
up here. I will send you the 100 but the difficulty is to get it. The men
up here have not in many instances received a cent. Largely over half &
those too who joined early in the difficulty. Some companies have been
paid up to the 1st July by Virginia but have not received a dime from
the Confederacy. There is a tendency among the men to regard the war
as over since the Bull run fight & to get off home[,] being homesick &
having an idea that there is no danger of another draft if they can only
escape now. An advance will remove this delusion. Such a movement
is attended with gigantic difficulties now. The golden opportunity was
allowed to pass on the 21st July & a great sacrifice of life will be the
consequence. They have rallied & we have lost by sickness more than
[the] heaviest battle could have destroyed after the 21st at Washington.
Still, I think we are about to move somewhere—not upon the fortifications I think but around into Maryland I presume—but everything is
conjecture save what I have told you about the transportation[,] sick &
superfluous baggage.

You had best send my box by someone. It is altogether uncertain that
I will ever receive it if sent by the freight train or express. Capt Wood of
the Transportation department on Bank Street will forward it free of expense but send it under the care of someone.[42] Wait until Walker Hawes
returns. He is one of the nicest little fellows I ever knew. So gentlemanly
always & one of the best-informed officers I have on military matters.
I am glad to hear you will reach home so soon. You will aid greatly in getting the servants comfortable for the winter. Their winter clothes, socks
& shoes ought to be attended to at once. I heard from Robt. lately.[43]
Stephen is dead. After this war is over & the taxes paid to remove the
debt thereby incurred we shall have but little to live on. So my darling
bestir yourself in the morning—be energetic & economical. I will send
my order for pay by Walker Hawes. You can have a hundred of it. Noth-

41. Edwin Wortham (b. 1812?) was a commission merchant in Richmond, Va. His business,
E. Wortham & Co., was located at the corner of Cary and 5th Streets. Carter had been a client
of Wortham's since before the war, and his letters to Susan constantly refer to dealings with the
commission merchant (Thomas Henry Carter Account Book, 1859–1888; *Richmond City Directory 1860*).

42. Carter is probably referring to Captain David Henry Wood of Winchester, Va., an assistant quartermaster in Richmond who was responsible for arranging transportation for soldiers.
Wood, later promoted to major, served in this capacity until he received a parole in the city on
16 May 1865 (*City Intelligencer*, 17; *Stranger's Guide*, 8; Krick, *Staff Officers*, 308).

43. This is most likely Carter's older brother, Robert Carter (1827–1911).

ing new up here except that the Blockade at Evansport is now effectual. They allowed one of our boats to be burnt there with capacity to carry 1000 men by a tug. Not a shot was fired. An order to this effect was given. Don't know why. The expectation here is that so far from going into Maryland we will be attacked here. They certainly outnumber us as admitted on all sides two to one & some suppose three to one. Our fighting force here is put down at 50,000 men—not over. An order has been sent to Brig. Genls[,] Cols & Capts. of Artillery that certain signals by Rockets mean an attack on the right[,] center or left. These signals not to be told to any other officer. Capts. of Artillery are big characters. I think a fight is pending from all the signs & orders but it may be some days or weeks hence. Under Providence I think we shall whip them notwithstanding their advantages. Nothing can exceed the stupidity of not advancing after the Bull Run. All admit it now & the blame is put on Davis' shoulders here. Politicians will ruin us forever.

We gained nothing strategically by the 21st fight. In fact lost it in this respect[,] for we are now encamped where Ewell's Brigade was the 1st [of] July & the enemy are behind an impregnable base line—fortified at every point. Morally we did gain greatly but the Manassas fight must be fought over again on account of the fatal blunder of somebody. You might send on the servant by Walker Hawes if no opportunity occurs sooner, & I will send James down to Hanover Ct. H. with some friend. I will write here after Saturdays & Wednesdays so that my letters will reach you Tuesdays & Fridays but remember that an order to march will often prevent me from writing.

May God Almighty bless you & my precious little children always[,] prays your devoted husband. Remember me to Celia.

—⁊⁊⁊—

Union Mills near Manassas Junction
October 17th 1861

You see by the above caption my dearest wife that we have changed our quarters & for this reason I did not write yesterday which was my regular day for sending off a letter to reach you tomorrow morning. This will not reach you until Tuesday which I regret as I know you are anxious about me. My precious wife you must not think me forgetful of you & the darling little children. Always you are in my most tender remembrance, but often it is inconvenient to write in Camp. Still unless very actively engaged I intend to write twice a week. Day before yesterday we were planning a grand review of our Brigade & Genl. Ewell & I were measuring off distances, clearing away brush &c &c. This review of our Brigade was preparatory (by Genl. Earl Van Dorn) to a Division review on Sunday by Genls Beauregard & Johnston. A Division is two or more Brigades commanded by a Major Genl.

In the evening I had marched my Battery to a fine creek & washed off the mud & ordered a general cleaning up. On my return Genl. Ewell suggested that I should accompany Bob Mason to Manassas at Daybreak to escort Mary Lee to Ravensworth[44] or rather as far as his Headquarters & from that point he would take her on.[45] I was to return by 10 1/2 A.M. in time for the review. Mary Lee would reach Manassas at 7 3/4 A.M. I went to my tent to shave off my siders, to touch up my moustache & goatee & to improve the outer man generally[,] when alas for our well-laid project[,] almost as I dismounted orders arrived from Genl. Van Dorn to prepare for a march at a moments' warning & a short time after another, to be ready in an hour. We eat supper, packed up, & soon struck tents, hitched horses & waited all night. This is the way these fools do who think they are wondrous wise because they have commanded a parcel of low Irish & Dutch mercenaries against Indians & who think that volunteers, accustomed to every luxury in life, can stand the rough usage of regulars. Ewell is the most considerate man in regard to his troops I know at all but Van Dorn has had us up half the night several times already. For my own part I did not mind it a great deal. I took my cot from the wagon & slept soundly by a fire for a short time. The men however had their blankets packed in their knapsacks & walked to this point (eight miles off) the next day. A little before daybreak we commenced moving with the wagons which were sent ahead. The whole Division then fell back[,] halting from time to time. The road is hilly & in places bad. The soil of a red clay, sticky & fine for caulking wagons. I can form

44. Ravensworth, located in Fairfax County, Va., was built between 1796 and 1800 by William Fitzhugh (1741–1809). The house passed to Fitzhugh's son, William Henry Fitzhugh (1792–1830), and then upon his death to his niece Mary Anna Randolph Custis Lee (1808–73), the wife of Robert E. Lee. Early in the war, Mrs. Lee lived at Ravensworth until the advances of the Union army made that impossible. At different times after the war, two of General Lee's sons, George Washington Custis Lee (1832–1913) and William Henry Fitzhugh Lee (1837–91), lived there, and both died there. Ravensworth was completely destroyed by fire in 1926 (Green, Loth, and Rasmussen, *Lost Virginia*, 39; McGill, *Beverley Family of Virginia*, 216).

45. Major Robert French Mason (1834?–1902) was assistant quartermaster on the staff of Brigadier General Richard S. Ewell. Later in the war, Mason served as quartermaster and assistant adjutant and inspector general on the staff of his cousin Major General Fitzhugh Lee. Mary

some idea now of the Bull run retreat of the Yankees. For our Division[,] about 8000 strong I suppose[,] there were a hundred wagons. Such baulking & cursing among teamsters you cannot conceive. The whole army has fallen back to a line from this point resting on the Bull run (the bank next to Alexandria) to Centreville & beyond (on the turnpike leading to Fairfax Ct. H. & Alex.). A ridge broken here & there extends to that place; in our rear is Bull Run Valley & we occupy the extreme right flank of the army. We are encamped on an immense hill overlooking the Bull run creek, the ford & the Railroad bridge. The ridge ends in a point formed by the junction of Pope's Head creek with Bull R. Across this deep ravine of Pope's Head creek runs the road by which we came called Sangsters road. The ravine is very deep & steep. The cliffs on each side are 4[00] or 500 yds apart, & a hundred or more feet high. Across this my artillery is to play to guard the Sangsters road leading to the ford on Bull run which lies just at the junction of the two creeks. Right across Bull Run at the ford, on the Manassas side, is another ~~ford~~ cliff up the side of which slopes the road. The cliff across Pope's Head is rather higher than mine & the Yankees will have the advantage in that respect. They talk of throwing up a breastwork on my point which will protect against shot but not against shell which you know burst over the head. I do not know the reason why the army advanced to Fairfax Ct. H. only to fall back in a few weeks. It is rumored that the enemy have advanced in a column of 50,000 towards Leesburg perhaps with the intention of cutting off that wing which is distant from the center.[46] Now I suppose this wing will be withdrawn towards Centreville. I thought it possible that the advance to Fairfax Ct H might have been made to mask the Evansport work while in process of construction. Now it is complete. It is about as far from this point as from Sangster's Crossroads (our old Headquarters). My Post Office is Manassas & add on the directions ~~care of~~ Ewell's Brigade at Union Mills.

The messenger is about to leave & I must hasten to close. I write again tomorrow for the Tuesday mail, but as you will get this Tuesday

Custis Lee (1835–1918), also a cousin of Bob Mason, was the second child and oldest daughter of Robert E. Lee.

46. Union troops were moving west from Washington on the opposite side of the Potomac River, intending to launch an attack on Nathan Evans's brigade, which was then guarding the fords near Leesburg, Va. Carter overestimated the size of the Federal force. The actual number was closer to 12,000, most of whom returned to Washington before the much-smaller Union force crossed the river on 21 October and engaged Evans's Confederates in the Battle of Ball's Bluff (Salmon, *Civil War Battlefield Guide*, 21).

I don't know that I will write so soon again as tomorrow unless I have something of interest to tell. I received a letter from Mama yesterday.[47] She had heard nothing from Wm & myself, although we wrote long letters ten days since. Nothing is more annoying than to write a letter ten pages long that is never received. She had made a plan to visit us in the carriage but Papa objected on account of his horses.[48] Don't know where she would have stayed. This country is desolation itself as to inhabited houses, although the soil is good. She is anxious to hear about Pampatike. You owe her a letter. I wish you would always answer her letters promptly. Tell her everything about Pampatike & tell me also in your next.

I have not yet written to Dr Turner but will do so soon.[49] Remember me to him most kindly. Beauregard has made his Headquarters here also Van Dorn & Ewell. Don't know where Johnston is. I must look up Genl. Ewell. I like him extremely. He is so honest & high-toned & intelligent. I wish Mary Lee would marry him. He is a great favorite of Genl Lee. Much love to all. Julian received a letter yesterday from Pauline. She is boarding at a Hotel in Natchez, a poor place, too poor to rent or buy a house.[50] Wm Page [is] at Alfred's house in great comfort & luxury.[51] Talk of buying Oakly in Clarke for next summer.[52] Very low spirited.

47. Carter is referring to Anne Willing Page Carter (1815–91), his father's second wife. Known by the family as "Sweet Anne" Page, she grew up at Annfield, the Page family home in Clarke County, Va.

48. "Papa" is Thomas Nelson Carter (1800–1883), the father of Thomas Henry Carter. During the war, he and his wife, Anne Willing Page Carter, lived at Annfield in Clarke County, Va.

49. Carter is likely referring to Dr. Robert R. Turner (b. 1810?) of King William County, Va., who is listed in the 1860 census along with his wife, Eleanor (b. 1813?), and his daughters, Eliza (b. 1844?) and Mary (b. 1853?) (1860 Census, King William County). Doctor Turner is mentioned in several of Carter's letters as helping Susan Carter sell her crops and transact some financial investments.

50. Probably Pauline Davis Carter (b. 1839), Tom Carter's sister-in-law and the wife of his older brother, Robert. The couple were living in Mississippi, looking after Carter family property (Magill, *Beverley Family of Virginia*, 471).

51. Carter may be referring to William Byrd Page (1848–64). He was the youngest son of Judge John E. Page, an uncle of Carter's stepmother, Anne Willing Page Carter (Page, *Page Family in Virginia*, 148).

52. Oakley, which Carter misspelled, was the prewar home of Francis Otway Byrd (1790–1860), a veteran of the War of 1812 and a relative of Carter through Byrd's grandmother, Elizabeth Hill Carter of Shirley. Oakley was located in Clarke County, Va., about two miles west of Annefield, where Tom Carter grew up and where his father and stepmother still lived. Francis Byrd and his wife had moved to Baltimore, Md., in the 1850s, and he died there in 1860. Presumably, that was the reason that the house was for sale in the fall of 1861 (MacDonald, *Clarke County: A Daughter of Frederick*, 14–15).

Saw Dr Randolph at Manassas yesterday.[53] All the sick well or better in Clarke. Belle Burwell to be married next Wednesday to Peter Mayo.[54] Mr Geo Burwell was operated on for cataracts [and] could not see yet.[55] Renshaw is going to Richmond in a day or two I suppose to get his pay though Mama did not say so. He is lieut in [the] militia.[56]

God bless you my darling wife & take care of you & my dearest little children every moment of your lives. I pray for you all many, many times daily. Put your trust in God always. I do not know that we shall fight immediately but it must come this fall I suppose.

Write regularly.

Always your own devoted husband
T.H.C.

—⚬—

Union Mills
Oct 22nd [18]61

Your dear letter, my darling wife, from Ingleside on Friday last was received yesterday & I write in answer today instead of tomorrow (Wednesday) because it is raining & something might occur to prevent. Nothing new has happened since my last written on Friday, except a variety of rumours, one of which states that there was a small fight at Leesburg yesterday in which 600 of the enemy were repulsed with a small loss

53. Carter is probably referring to Dr. Robert Carter Randolph (1807–87) of New Market, Clarke County, Va. According to the 1860 census, he and his wife, Lucy, lived with their six children on an estate valued at $30,000 and held property worth $17,500 (McGill, *Beverley Family of Virginia*, 173; 1860 Census, Clarke County).

54. Isabella Dixon Burwell (1841–1912) married Peter Helms Mayo (1836–1920) on Wednesday the twenty-third of October. At the time of the wedding, Mayo was a corporal in Company I of the 4th Virginia Cavalry. He left the unit at the end of October 1861. In March 1864, Mayo served in Richmond as a captain and assistant quartermaster in the transportation department (Brown, *Burwell Kith and Kin*, 40; CSR).

55. George Burwell has not been identified.

56. Robert Henry Aloysius Renshaw (1834–1910) of Bristol, Pa., was married to Tom Carter's half sister Lucy. He was the son of an English diplomat and a Spanish mother and a graduate of Harvard College. Early in the war, Renshaw served as a hospital steward. In March 1864 he was appointed captain and assistant quartermaster, though his commission was not confirmed. In November 1864 Renshaw was reappointed as captain and on duty with the Army of Northern Virginia's reserve ambulance train. In 1881, long after Lucy's death in September 1865, he married Anne Carter Wickham (1851–1939), a cousin of Tom Carter (Brown, Myers, and Chappel, *Persons Buried at Old Chapel*, 82; McGill, *Beverley Family of Virginia*, 466; Krick, *Staff Officers*, 252).

by 100 Mississippians.[57] Wm Walles commissary of Col Bev Robertson's
Reg. of Cavalry told me this & regarded it as undoubtedly true.[58] He saw
a man who left Leesburg after the fight. 16 of the enemy reported killed
& an equal number taken prisoners. Several wounded on our side, none
killed. Our scouts report a large force has left Alexandria & advanced
up the Potomac with a view it is thought of cutting off Evans' Brigade
some 3000 strong at Leesburg.[59] Jackson (Stone-wall as he is here called)
who has lately been promoted to Major Genl. has gone to that point
with his Division.[60] He went yesterday & I judge some movement up
there is anticipated. It is supposed the column from Alexandria has gone
up to guard the crossing of Banks near Leesburg.[61] Robertson reports
that 10,000 crossed the Chain Bridge night before last. The line selected
by our army from this point to Centreville & beyond is very strong &
being rendered impregnable. Since I wrote Friday I have rode over the
larger portion of it, & found the fortifications going on rapidly & on a
complete & elaborate scale. Some of them are enclosed works. They are
chiefly near Centreville, which is five miles from this point. We are the
extreme right flank. An earthwork is in progress 4 miles beyond Centreville on the Middleburg turnpike. It seems that our extreme right & left
wings are quite distant. Evansport near Dumfries is about 25 miles to our
right & only 12 miles above Acquia Creek. Leesburg is about 22 miles to
the left of Centreville. The gaps are considerable & I have an idea that
we are fortifying so strongly from here to Centreville in order that a

57. The "small fight" referred to by Carter was the Battle of Ball's Bluff, fought on 21 October. Federal forces under Colonel Edward Dickinson Baker, a former congressman and current sitting senator and a close friend of Abraham Lincoln, crossed the Potomac River near
Leesburg, Va. Confederates under Brigadier General Nathan Evans ambushed the Federals and
drove them back across the river. In the engagement, the Union lost 921 (48 killed, including
Baker; 158 wounded; and 714 captured or missing) and the Confederates suffered 149 casualties
(33 killed, 115 wounded, and 1 missing) (Boatner, *Dictionary*, 41).

58. Private William Walls (not Walles) enlisted in the 4th Virginia Cavalry on 8 May 1861
(CSR). Beverly Holcombe Robertson (1827–1910) was elected colonel of the 4th Virginia Cavalry in September 1861 (Davis, *Confederate General*, 5:97).

59. Brigadier General Nathan George Evans (1824–68) of South Carolina commanded a brigade that consisted of the following units: the 13th, 17th, and 18th Mississippi Infantry and the
8th Virginia Infantry (*OR* 5:825).

60. Brigadier General Thomas Jonathan Jackson (1824–63) of Virginia was promoted to
major general on 7 October 1861 and assigned to command a division in the Confederate Army
of the Potomac. Two weeks later, on 21 October, he became the commander of the newly designated Valley District of the Department of Northern Virginia. His nickname of "Stonewall"
came as a result of his brigade's performance at the Battle of First Bull Run (Warner, *Generals in
Gray*, 151–52; *OR* 5:892, 896, 909).

61. Major General Nathaniel Prentiss Banks (1816–94) of Massachusetts commanded a division in the Army of the Potomac (Eicher and Eicher, *High Commands*, 115).

small force may hold this line while the major portion of the army can be spared to either wing should it become necessary. In this way small numbers can prevent a flank movement by large bodies of troops. The present line is I think much stronger than the Bull Run valley. This stream is being bridged at a number of points so that if compelled to fall back the stream will be no impediment. At Blackburn's ford where the fight of the 18th occurred[62] & where poor Carter Harrison,[63] Jim Lee,[64] & c. fell[,] the enemy had greatly the advantage in position—the cliff being on their side & the meadow on our own side & so too at many other points that I observed. My own impression is that the rascals will never come here. They may try the flank movement at the same time making a demonstration on our front to conceal their real point of attack. But I should not be at all surprised if there is no fight this fall. The winter is fast approaching & if the battle does not come on soon Jack frost will put in his veto, & it would be impossible for the enemy to advance even if they gained a victory. They would leave behind their cities with comfortable houses for soldiers to invade a country desolated by our armies & where winter quarters would be necessary to build. Thus far they have fortified as far as they have come & seem to intend taking the South by parallel lines, a slow mode of getting over distance from Washington to New Orleans. When one recollects their loud boasts & the start of their grand army to overwhelm us & cast our flesh to the birds of the air[,] he is reminded of the story of Goliath & David. There was heavy firing at Evansport yesterday probably batteries opening on some passing vessels. I am told that the firing of our guns there is execrable[,] doing but little damage. Beauregard speaks of sending some of the batteries from this

---

62. Carter is referring to the Battle of Blackburn's Ford, which took place on 18 July 1861, three days before the Battle of First Bull Run. At Blackburn's Ford, a Confederate brigade under James Longstreet successfully defended the Bull Run crossing against a strong Union reconnaissance, led by Colonel Israel B. Richardson's brigade. The small engagement cost the Federals nineteen killed, thirty-eight wounded, and twenty-six missing; the Confederates suffered fifteen killed and fifty-three wounded (Long, *Day by Day*, 96).

63. Carter Henry Harrison (b. 1831?) enlisted in the 11th Virginia Infantry at Walton's Mill, Cumberland County, Va., on 22 April 1861. He was promoted to major on 28 May and was killed in action at Blackburn's Ford on 18 July 1861 (CSR). Harrison graduated from the Virginia Military Institute in 1850, a year after Tom Carter.

64. James Kendall Lee (1829–61), a thirty-one-year-old lawyer from Richmond, enlisted as captain in Company B of the 1st Virginia Infantry on 24 April 1861. He died on 4 August from wounds sustained in the 18 July action at Blackburn's Ford. In 1860 Lee prepared *The Volunteer's Handbook*, which was an abridgement of William Joseph Hardee's *Rifle and Light Infantry Tactics* (1853–55), the standard textbook for infantrymen (CSR; 1860 Census, Henrico County; Warner, *Generals in Gray*, 124; Wallace, *1st Virginia Infantry*, 103).

army to do better. It is said we took a vessel of hay & one of army over-coats. I hope this is true. I ride a good deal with Wms Wickham & Wm Newton.[65] The latter desired to be remembered to you. He is a noble fellow. Sunday I went with him to Jackson's Brigade then at Centreville (he now commands a Division). We spent the day with Dr Smith his brother-in-law.[66] There I saw Mr Lee (Mama's brother-in-law) who is Lieut. in a Jefferson company in Jackson's Brigade.[67] Nothing new in Clarke. In returning I met Nat Burwell of Glenview & Frank Whiting.[68] The latter is a private, [the] former a sort of independent fighter & goes to & fro at pleasure. Saw Archie Page yesterday.[69] Hugh Nelson is his Capt.[70] They had a skirmish ~~yesterday~~ a few days ago—lost one man[,] killed two & took two prisoners.[71] Hugh was absent. In reference to the

65. Williams Carter Wickham (1820–88) was a lieutenant colonel in the 4th Virginia Cavalry. In August 1862 he was promoted to colonel of the regiment and on 1 September 1863 received a commission as brigadier general. Wickham was Carter's first cousin (Warner, *Generals in Gray*, 335–36).

66. Dr. Smith presumably was William Newton's brother-in-law, surgeon John Philip Smith (1822–84) of the 2nd Virginia Infantry. Smith was a graduate of the University of Virginia and the husband of William Newton's sister Sarah (b. 1830) (CSR; Brockenbrough Family Bible Records, 1778–1887, VHS; Blanton, *Medicine in Virginia*, 415; Smith's obituary in *Winchester Evening Star*, 7 Jan. 1885).

67. Richard Henry Lee (1821–1902) enlisted as a first lieutenant in the 2nd Virginia Infantry on 18 April 1861. He served with that unit until the fall of 1862, when he was assigned as judge advocate for the 2nd Corps of the Army of Northern Virginia. Lee's first wife was Evelyn Byrd Page Lee (1823–89), the half sister of Tom Carter's stepmother, Anne Willing Page Carter (CSR; Lee, *Lee of Virginia*, 480–81).

68. Nathaniel Burwell (1819–96) of Glenvin, Clarke County, Va., was a member of Company E of the 122nd Militia, a local unit that had been called out on 13 July 1861 (Hughes, *Old Chapel*, 65–66; Wallace, *Military Organizations in Virginia*, 252). Francis B. Whiting (b. 1826?) of Millwood, Clarke County, was a private in the 2nd Virginia Infantry (CSR). Whiting characterized his occupation as "gentleman" upon his enlistment on 18 April 1861.

69. Most likely Archie C. Page (b. 1830?) of Millwood, Clarke County, Va. Page enlisted as a private in the 6th Virginia Cavalry on 3 September 1861. In October 1862 he left his unit, apparently without proper permission, and was subsequently listed as a deserter. Two months later, Page returned bearing a surgeon's certificate and managed to avoid any disciplinary action. Beginning on 27 September 1863, he served in the quartermaster's department in Harrisonburg, Va., where he distributed grain to the army. His war ended in Winchester, Va., where he was paroled on 19 April 1865. The 1860 census lists Archie Page as living in Clarke County with Benjamin and Matilda Harrison and their son, Benjamin (CSR; 1860 Census, Clarke County; see Carter's letter of 8 October 1862 for Ben Harrison reference).

70. Hugh Mortimer Nelson (1811–62), a prewar teacher in Charles City County, Va., and lawyer in Baltimore, Md., enlisted as captain of Company D of the 1st Virginia Cavalry on 21 July 1861. Two months later, he was transferred to Company D of the 6th Virginia Cavalry, from which he was dropped when the unit reorganized in April 1862. On 4 May 1862 Nelson, with the new rank of lieutenant, joined Major General Richard S. Ewell's staff as an aide-de-camp. Nelson suffered a slight wound at the Battle of Gaines's Mill, and on 6 August 1862 he died of typhoid fever (CSR; Krick, *Staff Officers*, 230).

71. Carter is referring to Third Sergeant William A. Gibson (1839–61) of Company D of the

corn, you can tell Dr Turner I think he had better sell decidedly, at $3 per barrel at the landing, to be delivered after the 10th [of] November as seeding will continue until that time I presume. Receipts should be taken & carefully preserved. Pat Fontaine talks of going down tomorrow on sick furlough. He is a little jaundiced & full of notions about himself when sick. I advised Dr Hancock to recommend a short leave of absence.[72] Walker Hawes will probably return this week. When you send boxes it would be much better to send them by some friend—indeed it is useless to send them unless you do as they will probably never reach me. Moreover put them up yourself instead of Wortham except groceries as it is cheaper this way. I shall send this letter by Pat. We are encamped now on a red clay corn field which holds water for days—it is always damp notwithstanding its height & rocky formation. The consequence is that a number of the men are sick. There is no reason why the battery should be placed exactly where it is to defend & I will apply this evening to Genl. Van Dorn to allow me to encamp on a hill opposite which is drier. Col Robertson is about to vacate it to encamp at Sangsters Station. They are now to leave our Division & to be put under Gen Stuart.[73]

Van Dorn is much annoyed at having no cavalry. I begin to like him better. He comes with a great reputation for success & is full of dash & fight. He talks I hear of asking for a transfer to the West. I suppose he thinks the times too slow here for him. Julian & Wm are both well. The former much dissatisfied as usual & mad because he can't get a transfer to this company or be orderly to some Genl. I hope there is a good deal of corn. Though the negroes did not use the improved corn, only the stock. There is probably a plenty of that but no great deal of good corn. I wish to write to Dr Turner tonight. He has been very kind & of great service to my interests. I don't know what Papa will do for his five thousand dollars. He will have to take small portions of it from Wortham until the

---

6th Virginia Cavalry. Gibson was killed on 15 October in a skirmish near Annandale, Va. (CSR). Captain Hugh Nelson was able to return from the fight with Gibson's body and two Federal prisoners (Hewitt, Trudeau, and Suderow, eds., *Supplement to the Official Records of the Union and Confederate Armies* 69:780).

72. Probably Francis W. Hancock, a surgeon who served in the Confederate Army of the Potomac in 1861. Later in the war, Hancock was the surgeon in command of Jackson Hospital in Richmond, Va. (CSR).

73. Brigadier General James Ewell Brown "Jeb" Stuart (1833–64) commanded a brigade of cavalry that included Colonel Robertson's 4th Virginia. On the day that Carter wrote his letter, Jeb Stuart was assigned to command the cavalry in the Potomac District of the newly established Department of Northern Virginia. Later in the war, he commanded all of the cavalry of Lee's Army of Northern Virginia (Warner, *Generals in Gray*, 296–97; OR 5:913).

wheat is sold. In a letter from Bott he says on the 14th of October he had out 50 or 60 bales of cotton & 125 bales probably open in the field. I told you of the death of Stephen, the servants suffering with chills &c. The crop [is] better than he expected. I must also write to Palham about having the deed recorded.[74] Mama seems to think that when the war is over, it will be best to divide that place. Probably it will if there is anything to divide. Wm would be thrown out of occupation. However that is far enough ahead to take care of itself. I will send down my account by Pat for two month's 280. What will you do with it[?] I shall want another uniform out of it, & one or two more pants. Send my nice black cloth pants up & I will wear my chocolate pants everyday. My blue uniform pants are worn out. The cloth is wretched. But that Wendlinger is such a scamp[,] I would order a suit by my measure there.[75] I hope to get rid of James if another servant can be obtained. He is truly indifferent[,] lazy, & dirty & requires constant watching & scolding & pushing to get anything out of him. I think if you can possibly do without him it would be best to send him to the field. In my absence from Pampatike he would be intolerable about the house. I would sometime if there is a good servant in the world[,] one that will attend to his business without eternal trouble. They are the filthiest creatures. The truth is every officer requires a servant & in our mess there are but two. Hawes took his servant home & expects to hire a free one. Ryland & Pat Fontaine have none. There is a rumor today that we took 200 prisoners at Leesburg—hardly true. How do you manage for carriage horses[?] Nelson has been fat & lazy but much admired.[76] He is now sick with distemper & looks badly. I wish you had a good pair of carriage horses. You must stay at home as much as possible—war is an awful time & your presence is needed there to take care of my interests & to take [care] of the negroes. Their shoes ought to be made now & winter clothes. If stamps are convenient send me some. It is the hardest work getting Silver to mail letters.[77] My heart yearns to see you & those precious little darlings. God grant that we may all meet again in peace & health. Much love to all. Have not seen Jack for a long time. Best love to all.

Ever your devoted husband
T. H. Carter

74. Mr. Palham has not been identified.
75. C. Wendlinger, a merchant tailor, had a shop at 146 Main Street in Richmond (*Richmond City Directory 1860*).
76. Nelson was one of Carter's horses.
77. Silver was one of Carter's camp servants.

I send my will & the power of attorney to Wortham who can draw it & pass it over to you. You had better deposit it in some Bank or with him, subject to your draft. You had better send another blanket. The bed tick is of untold comfort to me—filled with hay it is a delightful bed. Until I did this I found it impossible to keep even tolerably warm. Now however I am very comfortable. Send candles[,] butter[,] vegetables, such as will keep, pickles[,] preserves, hams. I doubt if poultry will keep unless you are certain the box will come straight through. Send two pairs of yarn socks. I am wearing those Cousin Mary gave me & my heavy boots. My feet are warm. Pack the box tight & put nothing in it of value in the way of glass or crockery as we throw them away every move. I should like a stout pair of pants of gray or dark cloth. Pat thinks he could get them for me. Don't forget the nice black pair. The officers that I associate with dress very nicely & fare well. If you have any whiskey at home you may put me up some bottles. God bless you my own dear one. Remember me to Celia & the other servants.

—〰—

Union Mills
Oct 25th [18]61

Although it is Friday night my darling wife, I write to send by the mail messenger in the morning that my letter may be certain to reach you Tuesday. I have nothing new to tell you that you have not seen in the newspapers. The glorious victory of Evans at Leesburg is in the mouth of everyone. It is perhaps the most brilliant affair of the war when the disparity of numbers is considered & other advantages of the enemy, such as position[,] artillery &c. We are fortifying rapidly & very completely & elaborately, infinitely more so in the short time already here than in all the time at Manassas. Indeed the earthworks at Manassas are very trifling. Immediately at the point they are sufficient but along Bull Run except at Mitchell's Ford they are nothing—were put there between the 18th & the 21st fights.[78] Our line, I mean of our Brigade, is thrown forward several hundred yards to another line of hills, a much stronger position than the other. The change I think was brought about chiefly by the strenuous efforts of Rodes who has great influence with the Genls & deservedly so. He has now superintendance of the fortifications & is

78. Mitchell's Ford is one of the major crossing points on Bull Run Creek.

conducting them rapidly & skillfully. It is rumoured this evening that he has received a commission of Brig. Genl.[79] He was spoken of in that capacity for the Brigade now commanded by L. P. Walker[,] late secretary of War[,] & no doubt was far better qualified than he for the post.[80] I hope he will not be removed from our Brigade. My Battery is to be divided in the event of fight, two pieces on the right to guard the Sangster road & two pieces in front to guard the Fairfax Ct. H. road.

Earthworks with embrasures for my guns are being erected as well as long lines of the same across the hills for the Infantry. A great deal of work has been done & in a short time. Last night the Infantry worked until 10 o'clock. Today we cut down a large of surface of wood which obstructed the fire on one of the roads. The impression among the Genls is that we shall have a fight soon. I think not. Certainly they will have a warm time should they try this route or the Centreville road. Great energy has been shown in the work since we fell back & I think we can[,] with God's help, whip them whenever they come, but I don't believe one word of their ever coming this route except as a feint, & since the failure of the Banks column to pass the Potomac it is probable McClellan has new strategic arrangements to make.[81] My own impression is that the real point of attack will be Evansport if anywhere on this army. The blockade is annoying & a source of privation & disgrace to them. It is reported here by the scouts that many troops have been removed from Alexandria probably to the West.

There is much sickness among my men since the change of position owing to the dampness of the soil. Now I hope it will improve as I have moved my camp three quarters of a mile front on an excellent ground. I want three men sent to the rear (either to Manassas or home) with the Camp Fever. Tom Bosher & Pat Fontaine I am sorry I even allowed to go home.[82] The former was simply a childish homesickness & an

79. Robert Emmett Rodes received his commission as brigadier general on 21 October 1861 (CSR-Officers).

80. Leroy Pope Walker (1817–84) of Alabama had served as the first Confederate secretary of war from 21 February to 16 September 1861. The day after his resignation from that office, he was appointed a brigadier general in the Confederate Provisional Army and given command of garrisons at Mobile and Montgomery, Ala. Walker never secured a field command and subsequently resigned his commission on 31 March 1862 (Warner, *Generals in Gray*, 320–21).

81. Major General George Brinton McClellan (1826–85) of Pennsylvania commanded the U.S. Army of the Potomac (Warner, *Generals in Blue*, 290–92).

82. Thomas J. Bosher (b. 1837?) enlisted in the King William Artillery on 1 June 1861 at Bond's Store. He later earned a promotion to sergeant before being discharged on a surgeon's certificate of disability on 18 August 1862 (CSR).

attempt to back out entirely & the latter a case of notions, with slight indisposition. The result is that every man with sore finger or knee wants to go home. Sick men I desire to be sent home, it is the place for them. It is hard to know who to trust. Tom Bosher is a man of means—worth 50[,000] or 60,000 dollars & was regarded as one of the truest men in the company. Lately he has been trying to get a substitute & whining with homesickness until everyone of any spirit has been disgusted. Tell me everything about home in your letter. I see corn is 85 cents in Richmond. Can't we get some more for that at Pampatike than 60 per bushel? I hope Wortham will sell that he has in store at this price. Shall write to him to do so.

Last night was a stinger—a heavy frost.[83] It is hard matter to keep warm. If we have blankets enough to keep warm in a tent they may be lost for want of transportation. The teams to two of the wagons are wretchedly weak. My battery horses are very fat still & much desired— a little balky unless constantly used, & no place to drill here [because] the country is so steep. To keep warm at night we dig a hole in the bottom of the tent, line it with rocks & fill it with live coals which do not smoke.

We are still in a country of pine holes & can go into winter quarters whenever ready. Then I hope to see you my precious one & the sweet little chicks. I suppose you received my letter by Pat Fontaine. I expect one from you tomorrow morning. Your last was from Ingleside. The mails from King William are very irregular. God bless you my own one. I would give worlds to see you tonight.

Your devoted husband
Thos. H. Carter

—⁓—

Union Mills
Nov 2nd 1861

Your dear letter of the 26th Ult. my darling wife, was received the 31st.[84] It gives me heartfelt pleasure & gratitude to our Heavenly Master to learn you are all well & that things progress favorably at Pampatike.

---

83. The temperature recorded in Washington, D.C., at 9:00 P.M. on 24 October was 45 degrees. At 7:00 A.M. the next morning, it was 39 degrees with a report of "heavy white frost" (Krick, *Civil War Weather*, 37–38).

84. "Ult." is the Latin abbreviation for *ultimo mense*, which means "last month."

May they thus continue is my earnest prayer. Nothing of much interest has occurred since my last letter of the 29th. Gov[ernor] Letcher has been on a visit to Centreville & has had a handsome review of the Va. troops, some 7[000] or 8000 men.[85] Not knowing it was to come off[,] I was not present. President Davis is expected in a day or two & will stay with Genl Van Dorn. My company was paid off for two months ending 31st Aug; on Tuesday last. If you have any difficulty in getting my pay (the acc't for which I sent by Pat) I shall regret that I did not wait & send it by two gentlemen here from King Wm, Hill King & Mr Ambrose White.[86] They came up Tuesday to see their sons who are in my Comp'y.[87] They report everything after the old fashion in King Wm except an excellent speech delivered at Ct on Monday by Garnett.[88] I do not know whether an election will be held or not in the Camps for President on Wednesday next. Politics are at a low ebb in Camp as you may suppose. Should you have trouble in collecting my pay let me know & I will get it here. In relating to James you need not bother yourself further about a substitute. If you have procured one send him & Pat & Ryland will take him. When the trains of wagons fall back or any movement is made I like to have someone to whom my things may be entrusted. Free negroes from Richd are generally great rogues & I am disposed to think it best to bear the ills we have rather than fly to others we know not of. He washes quite well & irons my shirts & collars (which I now wear) as nicely almost as is done at home. The iron I bought him he managed to lose[,] but Ryland sent for an excellent one. It is a large shell of iron in the shape (except much higher & larger) of a flat iron. The top is removed & the shell filled with live coals. In the broad end is a hole with a slide to graduate the draught. At the top of the point in front is a small chimney. When coals can not

85. John Letcher (1813–84), former U.S. congressman from 1851 to 1859, was the governor of Virginia from 1860 to 1864.

86. James Hill King (b. 1802?) and Ambrose White (b. 1805?) were farmers from King William County, Va. (1860 Census, King William County).

87. Festus King (b. 1833?) and James White (b. 1840?) enlisted as privates in the King William Artillery on 1 June 1861 at Bond's Store. Private King stood five feet, ten inches tall and was described as having light hair, a light complexion, and blue eyes. White served with the battery until October 1862, when he was discharged on a surgeon's certificate of disability. In May 1864 White returned to active service when he enlisted in Company H of the 9th Virginia Cavalry (CSR for both men). For more on Festus King, see Carter's letter of 23 September 1863.

88. Carter is referring to Muscoe Russell Hunter Garnett (1821–64) of Essex County, a former member of the U.S. House of Representatives who withdrew from Congress when Virginia seceded. In May 1861 he was chosen to serve in the Virginia Convention, and in November he was elected to the Confederate States Congress. Garnett died of typhoid fever in February 1864 (*DAB*, 158).

be found a small fire of light wood can be used. This irons admirably & retains the heat an hour. The heat being graduated by the draught hole & slide.

In reference to the corn I think the sale a good one. It is much higher in Richd at this time but you know how fluctuating the market there is & the expenses p[e]r bus[hel] would have been 11 or 12 cents with great risk of injury on the Railroad even if it is possible to send it by that route. Mr Hill King thinks there is no difficulty on that score[,] that return trains are empty. It is not so on the [Virginia] Central for Wm says his father has been unable to send his wheat to market by the cars.[89] A fair price at the landing is always a great desideratum but particularly now that there is a peak of bulk at the White House.[90] In regard to the wheat I wrote you that I did not see how it is possible to haul to Dabney's Mill. My wagons & teams would not begin to do it & the road is a hilly one & will soon be too deep. Moreover they are needed about the corn crop. I see no alternative but to send to Richd if that be possible by the river & cars. I dislike this plan on acc[oun]t of the risk to the grain & should prefer to sell at the landing but this is I presume impracticable. The price is too low to warrant the risk I think & I feel disposed to wait longer to see the result of the storm now brewing in England & France. The recent circular of Seward's looks squally to the North & if we gain another victory here (should there be a fight) the blockade may be raised.[91] When things are at their worst they must better & I suppose wheat cannot be lower.

We are in the midst of one of the most violent North-east storms I have ever witnessed.[92] I trust it is another wonderful interposition of

89. The Virginia Central Railroad ran north from Richmond to Hanover Junction before heading west to Gordonsville. From there, it continued southwest into the Shenandoah Valley (via Charlottesville), where it passed through Staunton on its way to its termination at Covington in the Allegheny Mountains. The distance of the railroad that linked Richmond with the Shenandoah Valley was slightly more than 195 miles (Freeman, *Lee's Lieutenants*, 1:681).

90. White House was a small community in New Kent County, Va., on the south shore of the Pamunkey River. Its location on the newly constructed Richmond and York River Railroad made it a good place to transport crops from King William County to Richmond. The community was named after the nearby eighteenth-century plantation that had been the home of Martha Dandridge Custis (1731–1802), the future wife of George Washington. At the beginning of the Civil War, Robert E. Lee's son William Henry Fitzhugh "Rooney" Lee owned the White House. His mother, Mary Anna Randolph Custis Lee, and sisters lived there after they left Arlington. They remained on the plantation until the Army of the Potomac confiscated it during the Peninsula Campaign and used it as a supply base (Green, Loth, and Rasmussen, *Lost Virginia*, 46).

91. William Henry Seward (1801–72) was the U.S. secretary of state.

92. A violent rainstorm swept through northern Virginia on 2 November (Krick, *Civil War Weather*, 40).

Providence in our favor to thwart the designs of our enemies by sea. If that expedition is off Cape Hatteras[,] Yankeedoodle will wish himself elsewhere & in vain.[93] The rain pours in torrents occasionally & fitful gusts of a heavy gale flap our tents until they crack like pistols. With deep trenches around & good pegs they stand the storm but woe to those that are not so pitched. Two have fallen but they are easily put up without further damage than a ducking to the inmates. The trenches around some were not properly made. Last night a few of the men awoke with a stream of water under them. You know how I enjoy a storm at night when the rain patters on the roof. Far more so now when the drops sound close to me. The sense of security & comfort is delightful, except my darling that I wake up far away from you. My tent is perfectly dry. You need not send me more shirts. I have an abundance. I have not yet heard from Mama. It is strange she does not receive my letters nor those of William. I wrote again to her yesterday. You receive my letters regularly do you not? I usually mention when the last was written. In this way you can tell.

I hope Lee has done more in Western Va than is generally supposed for there is some disappointment in his career out there in which I myself participated. But I see now that Rosencranz by making his rapid movements, so much lauded at the time, killed his men more effectually than Lee could have done.[94] The Yankee papers are now pouring on him their vials of wrath & from his abandonment of the country it would seem a virtual defeat unless indeed the rumor here is true that he has turned up between Romney & Martinsburg. No one here believes it.

The great difficulty in this rain is the impossibility of cooking. We happen now to have some boxes brought by the King Wm gentlemen. How is your garden & "henery" (Mrs Tooley)[?] I wish you had some of the nice beef we enjoy. It is fat[,] young & tender. As Captain I receive from the men presents on every occasion from their boxes. The butter & bread from King William is beautiful. Mrs Hill King sent up a few loaves almost equal to the Brandon bread.[95]

93. Carter is referring to the U.S. naval expedition against Port Royal, S.C. The force, under the command of Flag Officer Samuel F. Du Pont (1803–65), left Hampton Roads, Va., on 29 October with seventeen wooden cruisers carrying nearly 12,000 soldiers under Brigadier General Thomas West Sherman (1813–79). Port Royal fell on 7 November (Long, *Day by Day*, 132, 136).

94. Brigadier General William Starke Rosecrans (1819–98) of Ohio commanded the Federal army facing Robert E. Lee in western Virginia in the fall of 1861 (Warner, *Generals in Blue*, 410–11).

95. Rosena King (b. 1811?) was the wife of James Hill King (1860 Census, King William County).

Yesterday these gentlemen went to the battle field of the 18th & 21st. They went on my battery horses, were perfectly charmed with their day. I have never yet been but hope to do so soon. Today in the storm they rather wish themselves home. Mrs Ryland sent me an excellent pair of yarn socks. Two p[ai]r more will be sufficient for me & perhaps Wm wants some.

How are my sweet little children, dear dear little things? I long so much to fold all of you in my arms in peace & happiness once more. I begin to hope the war will end next spring. Should not be surprised if a portion of this army should be sent to the Cities to winter. If so I hope to get to Richmond & be with you. Still fortifying here & at Centreville. Jack has gone home for a while. He is sick Dorsey Cullen says[,] whom I saw yesterday.

God bless you my best of wives & take care of you & your dear little family. Remember me to Celia.

I received a long & affectionate letter from Lucy Lindley.[96] She is a dear girl. Don't be jealous my precious. You have no earthly cause to be you know.

Ever y[ou]r devoted husband
Thos. H. Carter

Health of the men almost restored by the change of encampment & late fine weather.

—⟪⟫—

Union Mills
Nov. 9th 1861

Your letter, my own precious wife, of last Friday the 1st inst. was received on Thursday.[97] I was not aware that my letters were at all despondent. My health is perfect & that of the Comp'y excellent since the change of encampment with the exception of one case of camp fever. That in so large a number is a very favorable state of health. You are also mistaken in supposing that I have not received your letters. They are some time on the way but I think all have been received. The long one written immediately after your arrival at Pampatike was received &

96. Lucy Lindley Braxton Temple (1835–62) was a cousin of Tom Carter. She grew up at Ingleside, the Hanover County, Va., home of the Braxton family. In 1854 she married Dr. Thomas Price Temple (McGill, *Beverley Family of Virginia*, 494).

97. "Inst." is a Latin abbreviation for *instante mense*, which means "this month."

answered. The letters I supposed lost (to Mama) were received after a while. William got one from her a day or two since. Wm Nelson [is] well again & will return to his company in a month or so. Yesterday Willie Randolph & Archie spent the day with us.[98] The former has recovered entirely from his attack of Typhoid & is remarkably fat & robust. He says Papa & Mr Renshaw left Clarke about a week since for Evansport. Mr R. had heard from some friend there that he could probably get an appointment in the Quartermaster department, & Papa for the drive possibly started but if he set off when Willie thinks he did[,] viz on Friday the 1st[,] he probably was turned back by the storm. The letter from Mama was mailed at Warrenton & I then thought it was done by Papa. Yesterday, Jackson's old Brigade to which William R. belongs left for Winchester. I suppose to confront the enemy at Romney[,] Grafton &c. McClellan's flank movements seem more successful than those at the centre. I really do not like the success of the fleet on the Georgia coast. Today Van Dorn reports that three forts off Port Royal have been taken—Pulaski[,] Tybee & a third name unknown. I hope the report relative to the Pulaski is untrue.[99] An intelligent young man from Savannah told me today that he did not credit it. Pulaski was a strong fort. But the telegraphic despatch may be right. The expedition was certainly a most formidable one—the largest by far that has been raised on this continent. We hoped here that the fleet would be too much crippled by the tremendous gale of Saturday [the] 2nd to be dangerous but it seems not. The great harm done by these affairs is that a foothold on our soil is gained, which is at once fortified & supplied by water—the easiest

98. Carter is referring to William Wellford Randolph (1837–64) and his brother Archibald Cary Randolph (1833–87), the sons of Dr. Robert Carter Randolph (1807–87) of New Market, Clarke County, Va. William enlisted as a private in the 2nd Virginia Infantry at Millwood, Va., on 18 April 1861. He was elected captain of Company C when the unit reorganized in April 1862. Promotion to lieutenant colonel came two years later on 26 April 1864. William Randolph was killed on 5 May at the Battle of the Wilderness (CSR; 1860 Census, Clarke County; McGill, *Beverley Family of Virginia*, 173, 175). Archie Randolph, a graduate of the University of Virginia (1852) and the Jefferson School of Medicine (1857), enlisted as an assistant surgeon in the 1st Virginia Cavalry on 25 May 1861. He also served with the 1st Virginia Infantry and, following his promotion to surgeon on 26 September 1862, as chief surgeon of Fitzhugh Lee's cavalry division. Randolph remained with the army until its surrender at Appomattox Court House on 9 April 1865 (CSR; 1860 Census, Clarke County; Blanton, *Medicine in Virginia*, 413).

99. Fort Pulaski, a coastal fortification constructed near Savannah, Ga., between 1829 and 1847, was occupied by local militia on 3 January 1861 and later transferred to Confederate authorities. The Port Royal expedition that Carter is referring to did not result in the capture of Fort Pulaski. Nearby Tybee Island was evacuated on 10 November, and its Confederate defenders entered Pulaski. The fort did not fall until 11 April 1862 (Lattimore, *Fort Pulaski National Monument*).

transportation of all—& the alarm thus created keeps back thousands of troops. Ten thousand men at Old Point & New Port News keep idle 20,000 under Magruder & 10,000 under Huger.[100] Our numbers are inferior to theirs & we can't afford to swap three for one. I hope[,] however[,] these troops at the South are composed of those who would not enlist to go to a distance. When a state is invaded the militia can be called out. I don't believe McClellan will attack us here unless the Evansport blockade compels him to do so. I saw today Major Thomas Williamson my old Prof. at the Institute.[101] He has been the Engineer on the works here & on the Potomac. He thinks the blockade not yet effectual—that vessels pass at night. Matthias Point he regards as the best place to fortify on the river & so reported it. I presume it was not fortified because the support of troops was insufficient. At Evansport, if necessary, we could sustain them. If this Southern expedition succeeds many persons suppose McClellan will advance. I doubt it. Such a success would perhaps satisfy the public sentiment at the North for the time & allow him to postpone his attack which he evidently desires to do because as Johnston remarked the other day he is afraid he has too much at stake—position[,] reputation & the ruin to their cause consequent upon another disastrous defeat here. He hopes the flank movements South & West will divert our troops from this point until so weak here that he can easily master us. It is good strategy & without a navy it is what we can't thwart. They have infinitely the advantage of us in all, save courage[,] cause & officers, & I begin to believe that McClellan is equal if not superior to any we have. His youth & energy are a great advantage. I believe Johnston fully his equal in ability & probably his superior but he is lazy & almost past the age for great deeds. At his age habits are formed of thought & action[,] running in old ruts. No originality I imagine in these old Army officers who have gone

100. Major Generals John Bankhead Magruder (1807–71) of Virginia and Benjamin Huger (1805–77) of South Carolina commanded, respectively, the Confederate Army of the Peninsula and the Department of Norfolk in the fall of 1861. Official returns for Magruder's army for the month of December stated an aggregate present for duty of 16,825; Huger reported 13,451 present in his department on 30 November (Warner, *Generals in Gray*, 143–44, 207–8; *OR* 4:706, 716).

101. Thomas Hoomes Williamson (1813–88), a graduate of West Point, joined the faculty at the Virginia Military Institute in 1841 as a professor of engineering, tactics, and drawing. Following Virginia's secession, Williamson entered the Confederate Provisional Army as an engineer with the rank of major. In July 1861 he served as chief engineer to General P. G. T. Beauregard. In early May 1862, Williamson, now a lieutenant colonel, briefly served as engineer on the staff of his former VMI colleague Major General Thomas J. Jackson. The following year, he commanded a company of Home Guard troops in Rockbridge County, Va. Williamson continued to teach at the institute until 1887 (Krick, *Staff Officers*, 305; Wise, *Military History of the Virginia Military Institute*, 49).

in a certain routine through life & have been taught never to question the propriety of anything. Taken as a class they are inferior to great men in other profession. They lead an idle life, are paid a stated salary, are promoted in regular order & therefore have no incentive to exertion in time of peace. Still they pass down to future ages as great.

Today I went with Willie Randolph[,] Archie[,] Dr Ellerson & William to the Battlefield.[102] It commenced raining hard & our ride was rather more hurried than I wished it to be. I do not believe since examining the ground that we were so nearly whipped as has been stated. A small force (4000) met the enemy in advance & were driven back a mile or less across a wide sloping ravine of open land but when the enemy came up the ascent & met at the crest a force about half their own then they were stopped. On this crest within a hundred & fifty yards of each other were killed Bartow[,] Bee & Fisher.[103] Where Bartow fell is a round stone column four feet high with this inscription "They have killed me boys but never give up the field." Willie R. showed us where he stood when three men around him were wounded (one killed afterwards). Where Wm Nelson was wounded. Where Mr Harrison's brother & the two Conrads were killed & laid out together all under one cloak.[104] Where Beauregard complimented them. Where Sherman's Battery was taken.[105] The 4th Alabama Reg. nearly cut to pieces.[106] Where Pendleton's Battery was placed &c &c.[107] Graves & horses are thick of course.

102. Doctor John Hanckel Ellerson (b. 1802?) was Tom Carter's uncle by marriage to his wife's aunt, Laura Roy Ellerson (b. 1820?). The couple lived in Hanover County, Va., and had five children (Tyler, *Encyclopedia of Virginia Biography*, 5:662; Williams and Johnson, *Roy Genealogy*, 17; 1860 Census, Hanover County).

103. Colonel Francis Stebbins Bartow (1816–61) of Georgia commanded a brigade in the Army of the Shenandoah (*OR* 2:470; Krick, *Lee's Colonels*, 45). Brigadier General Barnard Elliott Bee (1824–61) of South Carolina commanded a brigade in the Army of the Shenandoah. Before receiving a mortal wound during the Battle of First Bull Run, Bee reportedly bestowed the nickname "Stonewall" on Thomas J. Jackson (Eicher and Eicher, *High Commands*, 125). Colonel Charles Frederick Fisher (1816–61) commanded the 6th North Carolina Infantry at Bull Run (Krick, *Lee's Colonels*, 138).

104. Sergeant Holmes Addison Conrad (1837–61) and his younger brother, Private Henry Tucker Conrad (1839–61), both in Company D of the 2nd Virginia Infantry, were killed at the Battle of First Bull Run (CSR).

105. "Sherman's Battery" was most likely Company E of the 3rd U.S. Artillery, which was attached to Colonel William Tecumseh Sherman's brigade at First Bull Run (*OR* 2:314).

106. The 4th Alabama Infantry served in Brigadier General Barnard Bee's brigade at First Bull Run. In the fight, the regiment suffered 197 total casualties (40 killed and 157 wounded). The unit, which began the day with 750 soldiers, sustained losses of more than 26 percent (*OR* 2:569–70; Crute, *Confederate States Army*, 5).

107. Carter is referring to the Rockbridge Artillery, which Colonel William Nelson Pendleton commanded at the Battle of First Bull Run (*OR* 2:470).

It is late my love & I can't write much more. I have enough stamps now, don't send any more. I have some idea of closing for my new crop of corn at 65 cents at the landing. Can it be done. I have written to Dr Turner[,] not on this subject however. I should like to know from Wortham what prospect there is for a high price for corn. It would not be dry enough to shell until after Christmas. I do not know where we shall go into winter quarters. I see by the papers of today that McClellan does not intend to go into winter quarters. He holds that threat over us[,] he having houses for his troops. An attack would be the best thing he could do for us. Probably enable us to follow into Alexandria. He won't do it I am sure. I long to see you my precious. I shall get off when I can but the difficulty is great as Captain of a battery. I want to go to Evansport for a night but can't go just now. Mary Frances Page—engaged to Dr Powell brother of Lee Powell—a fair man I am told.[108] She is a fine girl. I am sorry to hear of Armistead. The sooner whiskey kills him now the better.

Love to all my friends.

Embrace & kiss my sweetest little children & may God bless you & them. Amen.

Y[ou]r own,
Thos. H. Carter

———✦———

Union Mills
Nov. 16th, [18]61

I have reproached myself frequently my own sweetest wife since Wednesday last for allowing that day to pass without my customary letter fearing you may have been uneasy (you know you are always uneasy) about me. On that day, I went to see a handsome review of Stuart's Brigade of Cavalry with which I was much pleased.[109] That night I went to see Rodes to ascertain if he had letters to be mailed in the morning before the cars started, hoping to send a letter in that way in time for the Friday's mail, but he has no official mail sent in that morning, as mail [is]

108. Carter is most likely referring to Mary Francis Page (1840–78) of The Briars, Clarke County, Va., who was a cousin of his stepmother, Anne Willing Page Carter. In 1867 Mary Page married John Esten Cooke (1830–86), the postwar author and former member of Jeb Stuart's staff (McGill, *Beverley Family of Virginia*, 526; Krick, *Staff Officers*, 102).

109. Brigadier General Jeb Stuart's brigade consisted of the 1st, 2nd, 4th, and 6th Virginia Cavalry; the 1st North Carolina Cavalry; and the Jeff Davis Legion (*OR* 5:1030).

allowed only I believe to Genls. Johnston & Beauregard. I intend to write to you twice weekly (as I have done) but you must not be alarmed when they do not arrive. Often little circumstances like the aforementioned prevent. Let me know if my letters reach you at the proper time. For instance, this is Saturday night & this letter will be mailed tomorrow morning after the cars leave for Rich'd. It then goes down Monday & ought to reach you Tuesday morning—does it do so? The same rule ought to hold good of my ~~Wednesday~~ Tuesday night letters. They should reach you the Friday morning after. While I think of it I wish to tell you to write at once to the Whig & Examiner to send those papers to you.[110] They come to me with great irregularity & would be a pleasure to you. I can get papers here. Rodes takes them all I believe & I go to his office nearly every morning. At all events take the Whig[—]that is a good commercial paper & will keep you posted on the state of the markets. I shall write to the editor myself but it usually requires two or three joggings of the memory to force him to act. I have today written to Mr Wortham to ask his advice relative to the 65 cts. per bushel for new corn at the landing. I feel disposed to take it & they may ship as soon as they choose after it is gathered. They of course taking the risk of heating in the corn shelled in too damp condition. As they would probably use it immediately this might be no risk at all in cold weather. I am so little informed now on the probability of the prices for produce in the future that I am unable to decide, & therefore asked Wortham his advice. I think it very possible that corn in Virginia may be scarce as it is close to the large bodies of men & animals to be fed & therefore *easy* of *transportation*, a point now of *immense* importance, as transportation now on the railroads from other states (supposing a large surplus crop in them which I do not know to be the case) is almost impossible. In that case corn in Virginia will be high. I will let you know when I hear Wortham's opinion. I am pleased to hear of the sale of straw. Unless it was all ricked, which is not usually done, the sooner it is pressed (baled) the better. The wet summer may have already damaged it. Long forage is however such a consideration with us here that any kind is craved. My horses for a long time have had but little & now have none at all, eating corn alone three times daily. It is

110. Carter is referring to two of the major newspapers in Richmond. The *Richmond Whig*, a longtime organ of the Whig Party, began the war as a lukewarm supporter of the Confederacy and remained critical of the Davis administration throughout the conflict, while the *Daily Richmond Examiner* supported the Democratic Party and thus advocated secession from the beginning of the war (Andrews, *South Reports the Civil War*, 28–29).

annoying to see them gradually depreciate. They have been the admiration of all. When my men get their new uniform now in contemplation, which is to be a handsome & expensive one for dress occasions only[,] costing perhaps the $21 allowed semiannually, & I get the brass pieces which I design[,] taking from Yankeedoodle (!!!), then Washington Artillery look to your laurels. All admit the fine drilling of my men. The fighting (the point at last) is yet to be proved.

By the way Willie Randolph & Dr Ellerson say there is no doubt whatever that one battery of the Washington Artillery was deliberately skulking away at Manassas when met by Genl Jackson (Stonewall). He asked where they were going & the Capt stammered out something about ammunition exhausted. Jackson turned him back. This Wm Randolph saw with his own eyes.

You did right to sell only the spare straw. If the chaff has been preserved it is possible that some of the shucks may be sold but there is time enough for this. You have gotten on swimmingly with the shoes as well as other matters. As soon as possible after Xmas the carpenters should go on new quarters, patching the old ones to make them comfortable. I wish now to continue that job until a new set is made. They should be off the ground. I can't tell what to do about salting pork. Salt is $20 per sack I understand. { . . . } folks suggest some partial (at least { . . . }) substitute.

After this month I suppose we shall go into winter quarters—indeed tools are already coming we hear on the cars. One car became detached a few days since at Manassas & ran down the grade to Bull Run by us— pitching over the abutment of the bridge lately was washed away into the creek. It was filled with axes, hatchets[,] froes &c. &c. which looks like work on winter quarters. I think I told you that one Reg. here had commenced without orders. The houses are log-huts [with] daubed-roofs of chestnut boards four feet long—weighted down with logs— so that no nails are used. The floors of chestnut slabs. It is intensely cold tonight but my tent is comfortable from a roaring fire in the flue. This becomes so heated that the hand can not be held on it. The doors I sewed buttons on last evening & Willie & I are snug as bugs in a rug. The sentinel tonight will put in the wood from time to time for his own benefit as well as mine. Ryland & Hawes have one also. You ask about Wm & myself—we of course get on as well as possible. What put the notion in your head[?] I do not show him your letters because I don't like anyone to see them somehow. My mess is as pleasant as it could be—all gentlemen on the most familiar & cordial terms. My standing with the company is just the same so far as I know. All satisfied. I should not be surprised when the army goes into winter quarters if the rules relative to furloughs are still rigid. Otherwise there would be no army here until spring. If there is any difficulty on this point I will endeavor to find some place here where you can stay at least a short time now & then with me. I doubt if more than one furlough will be allowed me this winter & that a short one. The Battery Captain is a sort of right hand man with the Genls. of brigades & Divisions.

I was shocked to hear y[ou]r account of Jack's illness. Is it Typhoid Fever[?] Dorsey told me he had gone home a little sick & you mentioned he was sick at Fanny's but I was entirely unprepared for your announcement of his hopeless illness, & still hope it is an exaggeration.[111] I at once wrote to Fanny to express my sympathy & to ask his condition at this time. I do trust God may spare him. I can not but hope that his powerful constitution[,] youth & previous good health will enable him to weather the storm. In such a case in the absence of severe symptoms of the head or chest if proper nursing is afforded, the diarrhea checked & beef *essence*[,] brandy &c. &c. regularly administered[,] I think the chances most decidedly in his favor. You know the family are easily alarmed by sickness. His poor wife too in her situation I do sincerely sympathize with. She is a fine woman.

The generals here still talk of a fight. I don't believe a word of it. The season is too far gone. We have only some 33,000 troops here exclusive of one Brigade at Leesburg 3,000 strong & for 8,000 at Evansport. Jackson you know has gone to the Valley to meet Genl Kelly who is trying to replace the Baltimore & Ohio R.[112] Kelly has 6,000 at Romney, 1800 at Wmsport, 200 [at] Harper's Ferry[,] 800 across at Shepherdstown. Jackson ~~Pendleton~~ has his Brigade [of] 3,000 & 1,400 Militia & 16 pieces of artillery. Our position here is strong & a part of it strongly fortified & should McClellan come we will with God's help drive him back & I hope winter in Alexandria & Washington.

---

111. Fanny Churchill Braxton Young (1822–94) and her husband, John Brooke Young (1813–86), lived at Westbrook in Henrico County, Va. She and her brother Jack Braxton grew up at Chericoke in King William County. Their grandmother, Mary Walker Carter Braxton (1763–1845), was a half sister of Tom Carter's grandfather, Robert Carter (1774–1805) (Horner, *History of the Blair, Banister, and Braxton Families*, 157–58).

112. Brigadier General Benjamin Franklin Kelley (1807–91) of New Hampshire commanded U.S. troops in West Virginia, where, in August 1861, he was assigned to protect the Baltimore & Ohio and the Northwestern Virginia Railroads from Confederate attacks (Warner, *Generals in Blue*, 260–61; OR 5:552).

Direct your letters to Rodes' Brigade same place. Give my love to the Callaways.[113] I hope you will see a great deal of them this winter. Embrace my precious children for me. Tell Thomas he must be a good boy & mind what you tell him & ask him what his dear Papa must bring him[—]a whip or cap or toy or p[ai]r [of] shoes or what. Do you think that other little cherub would appreciate a doll baby—dear dear innocent little things. May God ever bless every moment of your days[,] guide & protect you under all circumstances[,] prays your devoted husband. Your last letter was dated the 12th inst. Always mention my last letter to you. I feel so sorry for you alone at Pampatike dearest, but remember this is a season of trial to us all. Bear up bravely & trust in God who will make everything work together for good to those who trust in him. Even my little looking glass is broke[n]. Send me another when you can.

Ever your devoted husband.

Remember me to Celia & the servants. James, Anthony & sundry others stay in a tent heated like mine.[114] James does better—washes quite well.

—⚹—

Union Mills
Nov. 23rd 1861

Your last sweet letter, my precious wife, of Tuesday night & Wednesday morning, was received today (Saturday) & I am grateful to God to hear of the continued health of my dear family. My leg of which I told you in my last of Tuesday night is much better. Indeed I have never been confined with it. By limping I have been going about all the time. Wednesday & since I rode & except a little stiffness which is wearing off it is nearly well. It was a mercy the fall did not seriously injure me, as I fell with great force. The vile beast got out that night with one of the finest animals in the Battery & neither has ~~not~~ been heard from since. Stealing horses seems one of the amusements here. The sentinels were greatly to blame & as a punishment I have kept them on guard alternate nights since the escape of the horses. I hope to pick them up somewhere yet. We are still quiet here, with no immediate prospect of a battle that

113. Unable to identify.
114. Carter took James and Anthony, two of his slaves, with him into Confederate service. Their duties typically consisted of cooking meals, maintaining Carter's tent, and delivering messages to and from his wife.

I can see. It is thought that Evansport may occasion a fight soon or late. The suffering in Washington with the blockade there will be excessive. It is now said that 2000 men are employed in Washington fitting out gunboats & vessels[,] probably for an attack on Evansport.

Van Dorn's Division will be ordered there in such an event. He thinks it possible that it may be sent there soon, without regard to the anticipated attack. I hope not, as the place is 17 miles from Manassas where its supplies are furnished. Seventeen miles on these roads with poor horses will be a slender chance for provisions. With a railroad here it is impossible to get supplies for horses & sometimes for men. Could we have the river open, which is impossible of course, the place would be pleasant enough. A chance with the rifled guns at the passing vessels now & then would relieve the monotony of our lives. Today, I took the Company out & practiced firing. It is the second time this week we have fired. Yesterday Holman who is in Early's Brigade, our Division, practiced.[115] It was on an open field at a graveyard 800 yards off[,] about half the distance at which we first practised. I ranged his guns[,] cut the fuse & aided in everything that I could & then the scamps went off & boasted that they had beat me badly. Today I determined to show them that the pupils was not yet equal to the preceptor (for I have taught them nearly all they know as one of my men told them) & I invited them to the same spot to see our shooting. The firing was firstrate[,] although the wind blew high. The men were wild with delight. In five shots with the rifled gun at a poplar tree a foot & a half in diameter seven hundred yards off[,] two struck the trunk in the center & passed entirely through & on, showing the immense force with which the gun shoots. The shell & spherical case burst beautifully in & around the objects.

Van Dorn is now 1st Maj. Genl. & has command of the 1st Division of the Army [of the] Potomac.[116] Johnston & Beauregard are simply Generals commanding[,] one a corps & the other the whole Army of the Potomac (Johnston). Van Dorn has a large command[,] twenty three Regiments & five Batteries, by the new organization Brigading according to States. He has Mississippi[,] Alabama[, and] Louisiana troops.[117]

115. Holman's unit was the 1st Company of the Fluvanna (Va.) Light Artillery. The battery mustered in on 20 June 1861 and served in the reserve artillery of the Confederate Army of the Potomac in November 1861.

116. Earl Van Dorn was promoted to major general on 19 September 1861 (Warner, *Generals In Gray*, 315).

117. In the fall of 1861, the Confederate army in northern Virginia was reorganized into three districts: the Valley District, commanded by Major General Thomas J. Jackson; the Potomac

Robert E. Rodes
(Library of Congress)

The batteries will not be so arranged. I shall therefore remain with
Rodes. He is very kind & a capital officer[,] as good I believe as any of his
rank—& better than nine-tenths. Van Dorn I like too, he is a gentleman,
not profound or striking in any way. You have seen thousands equal to
him in every respect except perhaps Tactics & for ought I know some
hidden military talents which explain his success hitherto. He is very
dressy & fond of reviews. Rides a superb horse presented by the Texans,
& just received. His manners are pleasant.

I have today heard from him the latest news from Fort Pickens. Last
night at 7 P.M. the firing ceased & Bragg was satisfied with the day's
work. The Niagara injured badly, & a breach made in the bastion of Fort
Pickens. The Navy Yard set on fire several times but extinguished. I do
trust in God that we shall defeat them there. If so, the expedition will be

District, placed under General P. G. T. Beauregard; and the Aquia District, led by Major General Theophilus H. Holmes. Each of these districts operated under the newly formed Department of Northern Virginia, which was commanded by General Joseph E. Johnston. Earl Van
Dorn, a major general, led the first division in Beauregard's Army of the Potomac (*OR* 5:913–14,
960–61). Carter's mention of "Brigading according to State" is a reference to an important
aspect of the army's reorganization. The idea was the brainchild of President Davis, who believed that units from the same state should be kept together to foster pride and cohesion. He
remarked in a letter to Beauregard that the men "will be stimulated by extraordinary efforts,
when so organized that the fame of their State will be in their keeping" (*OR* 5:903).

a failure.[118] The Beaufort capture[,] while a disgrace to South Carolina on account of the wretched arrangements & the poor defence[,] has given the enemy no material advantage at all equal to the expenditure & expectations of the expedition.[119] The advance of the enemy in Kentucky & Southwest Va. must be soon stopped by winter & the impossibilities of getting supplies. The Mississippi expedition may give trouble—but I doubt it.[120] The success of the enemy at Beaufort has stimulated to the highest degree our water batteries & we have desperate energy in emergencies.

The Capture of Mason & Slidell is bad on some accounts but while England will hardly take any decided steps in the matter, it will tend to bind her to our cause & widen the gap between herself & the North.[121] Her large commerce makes her cautious in regard to war but her interests are too plainly with the South & against the North to make her course doubtful. Cotton[,] free trade (or nearly so) & the manufacturing wants of the South on one scale—the Morrill tariff[,] blockade & bullying on the other.[122] No one can doubt her course ultimately. In relation to the wheat I do not see what you can do except to send it by vessels & cars to Richmond. The 600 bushels p[e]r week to Fiskhall would be slow & no one to see after them on the route or there[,] so be objectionable.[123] Besides the teams are needed to gather the corn & to plow the low grounds or any stiff land for corn next spring, whenever it can be

118. On 22 and 23 November 1861, Union-held Fort Pickens and the USS *Niagara* and *Richmond* bombarded Confederates at Fort McRee, Fort Barrancas, and Pensacola Navy Yard. The strength of the attack almost convinced Braxton Bragg, the Confederate commander, to abandon his positions (Long, *Day by Day*, 142).

119. Beaufort, S.C., fell to Federal forces on 9 November (Long, *Day by Day*, 138).

120. Carter is most likely referring to Brigadier General Ulysses S. Grant's expedition on the Mississippi River, which culminated in the Battle of Belmont on 7 November (Long, *Day by Day*, 136).

121. Carter is referring to the capture at sea of Confederate diplomats James Murray Mason (1798–1871) and John Slidell (1793–1871) by Captain Charles Wilkes (1798–1877) of the U.S. Navy on 8 November 1861 in what became known as the *Trent* Affair. Mason and Slidell were on their way to England on board the British mail steamer *Trent* when Wilkes, commander of the Union warship *San Jacinto*, stopped the British vessel and had the two Confederate commissioners removed and brought to Boston. The incident stirred anti-Union feelings in Britain and increased sympathy there for the Confederate cause. United States secretary of state William Seward ended the crisis on 10 January 1862 when he ordered the release of Mason and Slidell, thus avoiding a possible armed conflict with Great Britain (Boatner, *Dictionary*, 516, 765, 847, 925).

122. The Morrill Tariff was a protective tariff law adopted on 2 March 1861. The act, named for Representative Justin Morrill of Vermont, received the support of almost all the northern representatives, while most southern representatives opposed it.

123. Fiskhall has not been identified.

done. I am willing to sell at the present prices, but should like to do so at the landing. However I would not stand on that as a purchase at the landing is now rarely effected, but ship it whenever you can. The tan vats I should certainly make at home. It will teach the other servants the mode of tanning & make a larger portion of our leather. I was glad to hear the corn turned out 300 barrels. Did not expect so much was left of the good corn. None of the injured corn was sold. I suppose I wish Davis could ride over the farm with Chenault & learn all its peculiarities.[124] I hope to be there by ~~Spring~~ Xmas to explain but can't say. When we enter winter quarters I shall stand a better chance. As Christmas is the time I should be at home to instal him I shall probably wait till then before I apply for furlough—a month off. It seems long long long to be absent from you my darling wife. I fear you will have an unwelcome visitor in Papa. Mama writes that he is getting tired of Annfield & thinks he ought to see after & help me in my business.[125] She opposes it because she says he will interfere[,] she fears[,] in my business. She spoke of your affectionate invitation to her to spend the winter but thought she could not. The family is large & I don't see how they can go unless she & Papa should do so & leave Lucy & Renshaw at Annfield.[126] It will end I think in two or three visits from Papa during the winter & spring of a week or so at a time with Renshaw. They went to Evansport to get some place in the Quartermaster department for Renshaw under Gen Trimble.[127] He promised to do what he could, if the place was vacated. Or perhaps it was the Commissary department. I don't recollect which. They passed close to us but Papa was so disgusted with one night at Dumfries that he turned

124. Davis was most likely John Davis, a former overseer for the farm. Carter mentions him in his letter of 24 September 1863 as having been "engaged as an overseer at Pampatike." B. Chenault (or Chinault) was listed as a twenty-nine-year-old overseer in the 1860 census for King William County. His name, and those of his wife and two sons, appear immediately below Carter's in the census schedule, suggesting that he worked for the Carters (1860 Census, King William County).

125. Annfield, located in Clarke County, Va., was the home of Carter's parents, Thomas Nelson Carter and Anne Willing Page Carter. It was built around 1790 by Matthew Page, who named it for his wife, Ann Randolph Meade Page (1781–1838). Following his marriage to Anne Willing Page, Thomas Nelson Carter purchased the property. Tom Carter spent his youth there, and his sister Lucy lived at Annfield during the war with her husband, Robert Henry Renshaw. Annfield was also the birthplace of Mary Anna Randolph Custis, who later married Robert E. Lee (Brown, Myers, and Chappel, *Biographical and Genealogical Record*, 82–83).

126. Carter is referring to his half sister Lucy Carter Renshaw (1838–65), who married Robert Henry Renshaw in April 1859 (McGill, *Beverley Family of Virginia*, 472).

127. Brigadier General Isaac Ridgeway Trimble (1802–88) of Virginia commanded a brigade in Major General Gustavus W. Smith's division in the winter of 1861 (Warner, *Generals in Gray*, 310–11; *OR* 5:961).

back immediately. I don't object to one more house near Henry's for Celia's children.[128] It will not do to have many there—wood is scarce & the present location of the quarters, a good one. Lucy's family is becoming large.[129] I hardly know how to lessen the number in that room.

I told you in my last that I wanted the carpenters after Xmas or as soon as they could to work steadily on the new quarters. The old ones must be repaired to make them habitable & comfortable. Give them plank floors & make them daub their chimneys. If this were done they would last longer. Some houses will last a while longer with new sills. Building at Pampatike is slow, slow. Some of the quarters need boarding badly. I hear Jack is better.[130] They are right fussy about sickness. Another review tomorrow (Sunday), so I must stop. I miss church badly, but say my prayers & read. Lately it has been too cold to have prayers for the men in the open air at night. Kiss those dear children for me—how I yearn to hear their prattle, sweet little innocents.

God bless you my own dear wife now & forever in every way. Pray fervently.

Y[ou]r own
Thos. H. Carter

—m—

Union Mills
Nov. 26th 1861

I received your letter of Saturday the 23rd on yesterday, my precious wife, & was surprised to learn that my letter of today week (the 19th) had not reached you on Friday 22nd. It was written & sent to the office. Why it miscarried, I cannot tell. I also wrote last Saturday as usual & this should have reached you today. I am not at all wearied of writing twice weekly my darling & only omitted one mail two weeks since when I went to Centreville to a review. I have recovered almost entirely from my fall & walk now without limping. The clay & vinegar is a most excellent application to sprains & bruises. My knee was a combination of both. Nothing yet of the two horses. They are stolen on every side now. What with the distemper & want of long forage they will die in larger numbers this winter. I understand dead horses line the road already from Centre-

128. Henry was a Carter family slave.
129. Lucy was a Carter family slave.
130. Jack was a Carter family slave.

ville to Manassas. The former is the bleakest place I know. The wind sweeps with force & with a peculiar chill from the Bull Run mountain parallel to the ridge on which it is situated. Sunday we had a grand Division Review[—]some six thousand troops. It passed off well & much to the satisfaction of the little Earl. Beauregard reviewed us. I took my Battery through in the most approved style. Holman's Battery was present under the command of the 1st Lieut., H[olman] being sick. The 1st Lieut. [,] Gay[,] was in a peck of trouble but finally informed me he would do exactly as I did[,] which he did most literally.[131] Kemper's Battery in Bonham's Brigade in our Division was also present, in most dilapidated condition.[132] You recollect he acquired considerable distinction at Manassas, coming up at a critical time & place & he now scorns all "playing soldier" as he terms it[,] but says "when any killing of Yankees is to be done no one can do more." At the University Wm Newton says he was ordinary enough. Wm's theory & doubtless a correct one is that there is a deal of luck in this thing of military distinction & mentions him as an instance. Certainly he seems a most indifferent officer. My men in their heavy overcoats with capes looked remarkably well & the horses too are fine. Beauregard looked all over the French man as he is. He wore an immense overcoat coming down to his ankles & similar to that of Bonaparte. He was beautifully mounted on a Chestnut. By his side dashed little "Van" on his splendid Texas charger—his cap & sleeves covered with gold braid. Behind them Longstreet[,] Ewell[,] aides & escort swept along all dressed in gorgeous style on splendid horses with gay trappings, jingling spurs & clanging sabres. It really is an inspiriting sight. The brass bands discoursing music all the while. The Earl told me Beauregard was greatly pleased & even surprised at the fine display. These reviews while they do seem as if "playing soldier" do good. They excite pride in the men, oc-

131. First Lieutenant William Gay (1823–93) joined the 1st Company of the Fluvanna (Va.) Light Artillery on 1 July 1861. He later resigned his commission when the unit reorganized on 15 May 1862 (CSR).

132. The Alexandria Light Artillery (also known as Kemper's Battery) formed in Alexandria, Va., on 15 March 1861. The battery mustered into state service on 17 April and into Confederate service on 30 June. It saw action at First Bull Run (attached to Brigadier General Milledge Bonham's brigade) and in the Peninsula Campaign (attached to Brigadier General Joseph Kershaw's brigade). In 1864, after conversion to heavy artillery, it became Company E of the 18th Virginia Heavy Artillery Battalion and served in the defenses of Richmond. The unit's first commander, Captain Delaware Kemper (1833–99), was a prewar teacher in Alexandria. He earned promotion to major on 25 June 1862 and to lieutenant colonel on 2 March 1863. After the war, President Grover Cleveland appointed Kemper to serve as U.S. consul to China. He returned to Alexandria in 1897, where he died two years later (OR 2:440, 11[2]:485, 11[3]:532; CSR).

casion a general rubbing & cleaning up, & break in upon the monotony of camp life. Monday (yesterday) all the troops were ordered into line near their respective encampments. Genls. Johnston, Beauregard & staff passed by taking a view at a little distance, somewhat after the fashion of an inspection. Genl. McClellan did the same the 20th at Bailey's Crossroads. He had[,] Tom Jordan says (Beauregard's Adj. Genl.)[,] 80 Regts. of infantry[,] 7 Regts. Cavalry & 20 Batteries estimated in the aggregate at 75,000 troops.[133] They again talk of a fight. On Johnston's staff is young Washington[,] Ella's stepson.[134] He is good looking[,] well dressed & rides the famous iron grey horse of Barton Key that figured in the Sickles case.[135]

How does Lewis Washington pass his time at Clover Lea, or is he there?[136] His home is hardly safe. I received an affectionate letter from Fanny stating that Jack is better. I am glad of it. She mentioned opening

133. The review of the Union army took place on 20 November in front of a large crowd, including President Lincoln and his cabinet. George McClellan wrote that night to his wife that the "Grand Review went off splendidly . . . not a mistake made, not a hitch"; while Private Robert Sneden of the 40th New York Infantry claimed that despite being "hungry, thirsty, and cold" by the end of the review, the men returned to their camps "much elated" (Sears, *Papers of George B. McClellan*, 137; Sneden, *Eye of the Storm*, 6). Carter's estimate of 75,000 Union soldiers present at the review falls slightly above that of the 65,000 mentioned in McClellan's message to his wife and that of 70,000 stated in an article about the event that appeared in an issue of *Harper's Weekly* (Sears, *Papers of George B. McClellan*, 137; *Harper's Weekly*, 7 Dec. 1861).

Thomas Jordan (1819–95) was an 1840 graduate of West Point—where he had been a roommate of William Tecumseh Sherman—and a veteran of the Seminole and Mexican Wars. He spent his entire Confederate career as a staff officer, beginning in 1861, when he served as General Beauregard's assistant adjutant general. Later, Jordan served in the western theater under Albert Sidney Johnston and Braxton Bragg (Warner, *Generals in Gray*, 167–68).

134. James Barroll Washington (1839–1900) of Baltimore, Md., was a lieutenant and aide-de-camp to General Joseph E. Johnston. He served on Johnston's staff until he was captured during a reconnaissance mission at the Battle of Seven Pines on 31 May 1862. After his exchange in September 1862, Washington was transferred to ordnance duty in Montgomery, Ala. (Krick, *Staff Officers*, 297). His stepmother was Ella More Bassett Washington (1834–98) of Jefferson County, Va. (now W.Va.). She and her husband, Lewis William Washington (1812–71), were living at Clover Lea, the Hanover County, Va., home of her parents (Ella More Bassett Washington to Winfield Scott Hancock, 25 July 1865, VHS).

135. Philip Barton Key (1818–59), the son of Francis Scott Key (1779–1843), author of "The Star-Spangled Banner," was the U.S. attorney for the District of Columbia when he was shot and killed at Lafayette Square in Washington, D.C., by Congressman Daniel Edgar Sickles (1819–1914) for having an affair with Sickles's wife. Sickles was subsequently tried and, for the first time in American jurisprudence, found not guilty by reason of temporary insanity. After the war broke out, Sickles became a brigadier general in the Union army on 3 September 1861 (Warner, *Generals in Blue*, 446–47).

136. In January 1863 Lewis Washington applied for a position as a paymaster in the Confederate army. His service records include many letters written by prominent members of the Confederate and Virginia governments supporting his application. Before the war, Washington lived at Beall Air in Jefferson County, Va. During John Brown's raid on Harpers Ferry in October

a letter from you to Bunny.[137] Clay Dallam has an office in the Treasury Department with a salary of $1000 per annum.[138] In relation to the wheat I think you had better get a vessel as soon as you can conveniently & ship it. I will write to Mr Wortham tonight & tell him to aid you in securing it. I don't think wheat will be lower & probably will be much higher[,] but in view of the uncertainty on that point & a hundred others such as risk of fire, loss, &c. &c. I am well satisfied with the present prices. Wortham may be able to sell it at the landing. If not he must give strict attention to it from the White House up to Richmond which part of the route is most exposed. I like to settle up everything at Xmas—another inducement to a sale now. There is not the least occasion to dispose of the money to Papa that is in the Savings Bank. Ever since it has been there you seem to have had an itching to spend it in this way or some other. Far better to save it & add to it for a rainy day. Wortham will advance to Papa any amount he needs at Xmas on the expectation of the wheat crop then on the way. He is always willing to advance when the sale of the crop is promised, & perhaps by that time the wheat may be there—if not no matter. My sale of corn was so large that it will I trust cover all expenses though I know they are enormous. Mules, taxes— war taxes[,] slaves, salt[,] groceries &c. &c. I owe John Haw a large sum for the repair of my wheat drum & the new horse power.[139] Price's[,] Chenault's & Dr Turner's bills will be very heavy say nothing of Watt's. Still I trust most earnestly that the wheat & corn will cover everything & bring us out square. Money matters always trouble me when I think of them so I will write no more about them tonight. I really think one cause of my good health here has been the absence of all care on this point. Nothing in all my past life has harassed me half so much as the fear of debt. I do not ~~desire~~ aim to accumulate. Next to disgrace & death it is the great end of life. In a temperament like mine too practical to be sanguine it would be an endless source of mortification & misery.

1859, Lewis Washington was held captive by the raiders and later served as a witness during their trial (George Washington Bassett to James Alexander Seddon, 17 Jan. 1863, in Lewis Washington's CSR; Rasmussen, *Portent*, 25).

137. Bunny is most likely Carter's cousin Lucy Tomlin Braxton (b. 1845), the youngest daughter of Corbin and Mary Braxton of Chericoke.

138. Henry Clay Dallam (b. 1827) of Baltimore, Md., was married to Elizabeth "Bettie" Pope Braxton (b. 1835?). Bettie, one of the daughters of Corbin and Mary Braxton of Chericoke in King William County, Va., was Tom Carter's cousin (Horner, *History of the Blair, Banister, and Braxton Families*, 160).

139. Possibly John O. Haw (b. 1830?) of Henrico County, Va., who was listed as a carpenter in the 1860 census (1860 Census, Henrico County).

But to turn to more pleasant topics. Mother you must not call our little darling baby "ugly." She has the dearest sweetest eyes & brow in the world. Can she walk well? I long to see her dumpy little figure toddling about the room. & my precious big man with his loud voice & boyish ways—tell him Papa says he must be a good boy & mind his Mama & Papa will bring him his whip. William & Ben Nelson, who is the best natured fellow in the world, have one of Thomas' sayings, "Give me some goodies." Ben is constantly with us[—]I mean, in our tent[—]for he is a member of the Company.[140] He is a perfect gentleman in all his instincts & in his raising, first cousin of Mary Newton. Has two children. I am glad you are gradually getting the servants back from Yorktown.[141] I think you have done wonderfully to finish the shoes so soon. I hope they get on as well in proportion to the amount of work to be done with the clothing. In my last letter I told you about the quarters & the leather. The latter I think decidedly best to be made at home. The other servants will thus learn the process of tanning. Pat I expect tomorrow from your letter. I shall be delighted to see the box which has been packed by yourself. The silk gown will be a great comfort. We are still in tents but perfectly comfortable. Some talk of going to Evansport this week. I hope not this winter for my own part. All supplies to be hauled from Manassas, semiweekly mail.

Holman I found so sick yesterday (or day before) that I advised him seriously to go home. He has been puny for weeks & now has Camp or Typhoid Fever. I got him a furlough & he started this morning, & goes up the Canal tomorrow evening. Tom Bosher I have ordered back. If he is physically disabled the Brigade Surgeon will decide & discharge. He is a poor concern. The example is what I want in bringing him back.

Wortham wrote me ~~yesterday~~ Saturday that he had sent the box with whiskey[,] candles & a looking glass ordered by you to the transportation office. It has not yet arrived & I am getting uneasy about it. The

140. Benjamin Cary Nelson (b. 1831) enlisted as a private in the King William Artillery at Bond's Store on 1 June 1861. He served with the unit until he was wounded in the right knee by a shell fragment at Gettysburg on 3 July 1863. Unable to remain on active duty, Nelson was reassigned to the War Department in Richmond, where he served as a clerk until his retirement in November 1864 (CSR).

141. Carter is referring to the use of some of his slaves as laborers on Confederate fortifications then being constructed along the west bank of the Warwick River near Yorktown, Va. Throughout the fall of 1861, Major General John B. Magruder had been hiring free and enslaved African Americans to build his defensive line. According to a form letter sent to various counties in the region, slaves and free blacks would receive fifty cents a day for their labor. The slaves' wages would go to their owners (OR 4:654).

pilfering on that Railroad is a crying shame & outrage. He ought to have seen it put on the cars at the depot. I shall mention it in my letter to-night. The bombardment has ceased at Pensacola. I hope the whole naval expedition will prove an utter failure & so far it is. Now if the Mississippi raid fails, the skies will be bright. The East Tennessee movement seems at an end. The Mason & Slidell affair will do us good indirectly—make John Bull wrathy & add to the current now setting in our favor.[142] I see the Convention still hangs on to the dear Democracy Government. For fear of offending the dear people. Universal suffrage in every respect is the order of the day. Conventions never go back. This Confederacy will not last ten years with Democracy & Demagoguerism in full growth in its infancy.[143] States already jealous & the army organized according to States will increase this feeling. Could we come out of this revolution as our forefathers out of the Old Revolution[,] purified by the fiery ordeal[,] we might look for lofty patriotism.

Embrace my own sweet little children, my darling wife. I think so tenderly & lovingly of you all. May God be with you & bless you now & forever.

Y[ou]r fond husband.

—⁓—

Union Mills
November 30th, [18]61
Saturday night

It is late, my precious wife, but I cannot allow the mail to pass without sending you a letter. I did not receive today as I expected your letter of Tuesday but it may come in the morning. However as you wrote on that day by Pat you may not do so by the mail. Your box arrived this evening after a passage through many vicissitudes. I need not tell you my darling how much pleasure it gave me to open it & to think of your affection & thoughtfulness. Many of the inner boxes are not yet unclosed. A number of the Company as usual gathered around & greatly enjoyed the cakes &c. & for fear of consuming everything at once I closed it for the pres-

142. John Bull is a nickname for an Englishman.
143. Carter is likely referring to the convention then in progress in Wheeling, Va., to decide the fate of the far western counties of the state. West of the Allegheny Mountains, fifty counties sent representatives who voted to secede from Virginia and to remain in the Union as the new state of West Virginia. It was formally admitted to the Union on 20 June 1863 (Lause, "West Virginia," 2090–91).

ent. The gown is a great comfort & I am now writing in it, as warm as a bug in a rug. Wm too is much pleased with his articles which were unexpected. He had made a bed tick of bags ripped & sewed up properly but this gives him a change, for these ticks have to be changed & washed. The socks are beautifully made. I had no idea you were a proficient in knitting. Was the yarn spun at home? The sausages—not yet opened—are kept in remembrance. You recollect my penchant on this dish.

Pat reached here Wednesday night, looking remarkably well, weighing 175 lbs. & if he will only think himself hearty no doubt he will be so. I very flatly put down his whims about himself on every occasion. If allowed to be humoured they will ruin his health. He is eternally feeling his pulse & pinching Muriate of Ammonia to swallow, when he is the fattest[,] heartiest[,] strongest man we have. Considering he came as "food for powder" he takes wonderful care of himself. Papa himself is not so bad on this point. However[,] Pat is so obedient & gentlemanly that I can't help liking him. He left the boxes at Hanover Ct. H. On account of their weight they were retained for the freight train. I never expected to see them again but they were forthcoming yesterday much to our joy. My box from Wortham has never reached me although it was sent to the transportation office last Saturday. The stealing at Manassas & all along the route is intolerable. White[,] one of my men (Quartermaster Sergeant)[,] arrived last night from Rich'd with some things & was compelled to guard them at the depot.[144] He saw a man break open the head of a barrel & the sentinel joined in. Another wiped out the name on a box & walked off with it. I sent White down for a variety of things for the Battery & to contract for a uniform for the Comp'y. It was impossible to get any cloth in Richd. The Crenshaws have contracts on hand to fill until the 1st Feb.; after that they will not contract with anyone, but will auction off their cloth to the highest bidder once a week or month.[145] Wendlinger asked $70 for a uniform for me. A cap for me cost $8 & so on in everything. He (White) is selling or expects to ~~selling~~ sell flour ground by Dabney for $9 per barrel. The difficulty of transportation will render

144. James G. White (b. 1820) enlisted as a private in the King William Artillery at Richmond on 17 July 1861. He served as Carter's quartermaster sergeant until he was discharged on 30 June 1862 upon completion of his one-year term of service and for being too old. White, a native of King William County, Va., stood five feet, seven inches tall and had a fair complexion, blue eyes, and dark hair (CSR).

145. Most likely Crenshaw & Co., a commission merchant located on Basin Street between 10th and 11th Streets in Richmond (*Richmond City Directory 1860*).

wheat high in Virginia this winter. Have you heard from Wortham relative to my wheat[?] I asked him to send a vessel to you as soon as possible if the York R. R. is practicable & told him I should be glad to sell at the landing—if he could do so. Have you heard anything more of the straw sale[?] I hope it is a bona fide sale—$1 per hundred baled. They to furnish the baling machine & to bale it or show how. Mr Edwards tells me Hill King sold his straw at 50 cts per hundred. You are a great manager Pat tells me. He thinks you are better than I am. I am much of the same opinion. In regard to those extra pigs you mentioned some little time since you intended to sell[,] I advise against it. The hogs are small at Pampatike & a large number required to supply enough meat. Is the salt you have fine or coarse salt? The meat should be well salted & the salt mixed.

Jno Edwards has a little fever, if it continues I shall send him home before he is worse.[146] Two or three men have been kept here too long & suffered the consequence. One, I understand, John Tuck is expected to die.[147] I hope not. Although the measles have passed through the Comp'y none have yet died. They are unusually healthy now. I attribute the good health under Providence to good police & thorough airing of everything each day & once a week I inspect the comp'y drawn up in ranks. When they have Typhoid Fever I get them off quickly. There has been quite a stir this week. The Genls have rode over our ground twice in two or three days—heavy baggage was sent to the rear & a fight predicted on Thursday. My heavy baggage (for the whole comp'y) was sent to the rear with three men & a large tent. All this I did not tell you in my last letter because it would have alarmed you unnecessarily. All has passed off quietly now & I have no idea that the Yankees will fight till spring. Fitz Lee with 50 Cavalry dashed into 100 Infantry a short time since, took ten prisoners[,] killed three or four, had his horse killed under him.[148] He is a dashing & fine little fellow.

146. John Duval Edwards (b. 1831) enlisted in the King William Artillery on 1 June 1861 at Bond's Store (CSR).

147. John C. (or H.) Tuck enlisted as a private in the King William Artillery at Bond's Store on 1 June 1861. Records indicate that he served with the unit until he was captured on 5 July 1863 during the retreat from Gettysburg. From then until his exchange on 18 February 1865, Tuck remained in Union prisoner-of-war camps, including Fort McHenry, Fort Delaware, and Point Lookout. He returned to the unit and was paroled at Appomattox on 12 April 1865 (CSR).

148. Carter is referring to a skirmish that took place near Fairfax Court House, Va., on 27 November 1861 between elements of the 1st Virginia Cavalry, commanded by Lieutenant Colonel Fitzhugh Lee (1835–1905), Robert E. Lee's nephew, and a small Union force (Driver, *1st Virginia Cavalry*, 26; Eicher and Eicher, *High Commands*, 343).

I am so overpowered with sleep tonight my darling that I must stop. If Jno Edwards goes down I will send messages. Did you learn whether Wortham drew my pay[?] I forgot to ask him in my letter. I am glad you are to have an overseer. Davis is spoken of in the highest terms by all who know him in this Company. He is above all suspicion as to honesty. You think I am overscrupulous about leaving as Virginius Croxton &c. are at home, but you must remember that I command the only Battery in the Brigade & as long as there is the remotest prospect of a fight I could not think of leaving.[149] Even if I wished to go, a furlough would be flatly denied. A few weeks ago I was not allowed to spend a night at Evansport where I wished to go. The men too must have an example. They are crazy to go home. If I were to leave it would do harm. Pat & Bosher have ruined themselves by their furloughs when but little was the matter with them. Many cases have been far worse but have stuck to their posts here & recovered. As soon as we are regularly fixed in winter quarters I hope to go. I think we will be quartered here[,] I hope so, it is convenient to supplies, mail, wood[,] water &c.

With the planks of the boxes I intend to make a floor to my tent which adds greatly to its comfort & cleanliness. I am much pleased with Pat's bed but my own is good enough. Bosher has returned looking very well—but with a long face. I promise myself much pleasure in opening quietly my box. James was in high delight at the opening this evening. Do you receive my letters regularly[?] Did you receive the missing letter of last week[?] Dr Randolph & Archie were here a few days since. All well at home. They are building a railroad from Manassas Junction to Centreville about eight miles long.

Nothing new up here.

Has Dr Macon recovered from his injury[?] Where is Rooney[,] Charlotte & child[?][150] There is a rumor that Matthews has been invaded. It is exposed.

I have looked at the handkerchiefs from my precious big man. Kiss him for his Papa also that other little sweetness. God be with you & bless

149. Lieutenant Colonel William Virginius Croxton of the 9th Virginia Cavalry was on leave in November because of illness (CSR).

150. William Henry Fitzhugh Lee (1837–91), known as "Rooney," was Robert E. Lee's third child and second son. In 1861 Colonel W. H. F. Lee commanded the 9th Virginia Cavalry. His wife, Charlotte Georgianna Wickham Lee (1840–63), lived at Hickory Hill, her family's home in Hanover County, Va. The couple had two children, a boy and a girl, both of whom died as infants (Warner, *Generals in Gray*, 184–85; McGill, *Beverley Family of Virginia*, 218).

you & my darlings. I will come to you at the earliest moment that I possibly can with propriety.

Good night.

Your own dear Husband.

The gown is delightful—the warmest I ever felt. Do you hear from Sister Ann[?][151] Where is your Uncle Jack[?][152]

—ᴡ—

Manassas Junction Post Office
Davis Ford
Dec. 11th 1861

Your two letters of the 3rd & 7th inst. my darling wife were received yesterday, the first having taken an excursion elsewhere I presume from the length of time on the way. I have written once since my arrival here[,] on the 8th it was mailed. I hope it reached you yesterday the 10th. There is nothing new. The excitement of the expected battle has worn away in consequence of its improbability. Even little Van has abandoned all hope. Johnston still thinks it possible but it is his duty so to think. To be prepared should it come. My opinion all along has been that no battle would be fought until next May. Once or twice I have been swerved from this belief by the confident assertion to the contrary of our leading Gens. Their information is unreliable necessarily. Their corps of spies & correspondents are doubtless faithful but what can they learn? What would McClellan's spies discover by passing through our lines? Something probably of our force but nothing of the plans of our Generals. Before the 21st July Battle the Yankees confident of success were less rigid in their interruption of travel through their lines & less cautious [in] every way. Now McClellan is secret enough. Every day there is firing at

151. Ann Seddon Roy Rutherfoord (1831–1908) was Carter's wife's sister. She was married to John Coles Rutherfoord (1825–66), and the couple lived at Rock Castle in Goochland County, Va.

152. Most likely John Seddon (1826–63), who was the brother of Susan Carter's mother, Ann Seddon Roy (d. 1834). From 1855 to 1861, he represented Stafford County in the Virginia House of Delegates before enlisting as captain of Company D of the 1st Virginia Infantry Battalion on 14 May 1861. Until 7 June 1861, Seddon acted as assistant adjutant general on the staff of Colonel Daniel Ruggles (1810–97). Promotion to major came on 20 May 1862. For much of his service, however, Seddon was in poor health, which eventually forced him to resign from the battalion on 11 October 1862. John Seddon died at Snowden, his home near Fredericksburg, Va., on 5 December 1863 (CSR; Krick, *Staff Officers*, 262; Warner, *Generals in Gray*, 265–66). John's older brother, James Alexander Seddon, was the Confederate secretary of war.

Evansport & I do not understand why their fleet does not bombard the place. Genls. Whiting & others consider it weak & unable to stand an attack by water & it is a source of unceasing annoyance & inconvenience to the Washington Army & people.[153] Their fleet seems to be idle on the Southern coast unless it is designed to blockade simply. Perhaps they are awaiting the formation of the second fleet. We are hard at work erecting a shed stable for the Battery horses & clearing a spot in an oak wood for cabins. The place I have selected is a good one, an oak ridge half mile long ending on the Occoquan River, a deep ravine on each side from which we get water & some four hundred yards from Rodes' Headquarters. Quite a variety of plans are proposed for the cabins. Rodes suggests stakes eight feet long driven into the ground two feet & the tent placed on top[,] a door made in one side & chimney on the other. This gives a room only the size of a tent. Where few are in a tent it suits well enough. When crowded a larger room would be needed. Rodes proposes to tack oznaburg on the outside of the row of stakes & newspaper on the inside.[154] The latter plan with men would be impracticable. Difficult to get the paper & it would tear when rubbed against. The principle is good, however. Dr Hancock gave me a large hospital tent twice the usual size. I shall fix this in [the] manner suggested by Rodes, using mud daub instead of newspapers. The country abounds in game. Two pheasants killed by one of my men have just been shown me & wild turkeys are seen every day. It is as thinly settled as any country I have seen & yet close to the Railroad. Hardly a house can be found for miles for the Headquarters of the Generals. Rodes has a small affair with two rooms. The upper was filled until a day or two since with wheat. He telegraphed his wife at Charlottesville to come on. She was expected yesterday but was too sick with fever of some sort to come. He has had a bad cold but is not confined to his room. Finney (Lieut Col in Harry Heth's Regt under Floyd) came on a visit to Rodes.[155] He was convalescent from a severe attack of Typhoid Fever. While here he had a relapse & has returned

153. Brigadier General William Henry Chase Whiting (1824–65) of Mississippi commanded a brigade in Major General Earl Van Dorn's division (*OR* 5:960; Warner, *Generals in Gray*, 334–35).

154. Osnaburg is a coarse textile fabric made from flax.

155. "Finney" is most likely Nehemiah Finney, who served as a lieutenant in the 45th Virginia Infantry. Around 15 December 1861, he was promoted to the rank of captain. Finney later served in the 23rd Virginia Infantry Battalion (CSR). The 45th Virginia was commanded by Colonel Henry Heth (1825–99), who earned eventual promotion to major general. Brigadier General John Buchanan Floyd commanded the Confederate Army of the Kanawha in December 1861 (Eicher and Eicher, *High Commands*, 237).

to R[ichmond] very sick. Were you not surprised at the nomination by the President of H. Hethe for Maj. Genl comdg Arkansas & Missouri & ranking Price & McCullough?[156] It was not confirmed by Congress. He is a gentlemanly[,] nice man but I should not suppose fitted for such a post. However he is equal to many of the Maj. Genls here. I do not know how it may be in a military point of view, but in other respects some of the Brigadier Genls are greatly superior to the Maj Genls here.

I hope Genl. Lee may accomplish something in the South.[157] He has lost ground in the army. He is personally popular with the Generals & officers but regarded as too cautious by the army & lacking in confidence in volunteers. Many of our Volunteer Regts. have fought with more courage than regulars. It is reported here that Rooney Lee's Companies have disbanded—I suppose for the winter only. Mary Lee came to Genl. E. Kirby Smith's review at Centreville a few days ago.[158] John Lee[,] her Cousin[,] has some office in this Division.[159] She went to Genl. Ewell's house & dined or lunched. This looks like yielding to the tender passion. The old fellow has also entertained all night Mrs Brown of Tennessee, mother of his aid Campbell Brown & some relation of his.[160] If Mary

156. Colonel Henry Heth (1825–99) of Virginia commanded the 45th Virginia Infantry in 1861. When President Davis sought to appoint an overall commander of Confederate forces in Arkansas and Missouri to alleviate the tension between Benjamin McCulloch (1811–62) and Sterling Price (1809–67), the two officers who commanded those troops, he put forward Heth's name. On 10 January 1862, the Trans-Mississippi Department was established with Earl Van Dorn, rather than Henry Heth, as its commanding officer. On 18 January Heth, who became a brigadier general on 6 January, took command of Confederate troops at Lewisburg, Va. (now W.Va.). Heth served in western Virginia and Tennessee in 1862 before returning to the Virginia theater in March 1863. He eventually rose to the rank of major general (OR 8:701, 745, 5:1038; CSR; CSR-Officers).

157. Carter is referring to Robert E. Lee's service, since early November, as commander of a department covering the coast of South Carolina, Georgia, and east Florida. From his headquarters in Savannah, Ga., Lee mainly oversaw construction of coastal defenses in South Carolina. The general remained there until President Davis abruptly ordered him to return to Virginia on 2 March 1862. Lee's replacement in South Carolina was Major General John C. Pemberton (OR 6:312, 400, 402).

158. Major General Edmund Kirby Smith (1824–93) of Florida commanded the Fourth Division of the Confederate Army of the Potomac. In 1862 he was assigned to the western theater, where he eventually rose to the rank of lieutenant general in command of the Trans-Mississippi Department (Warner, Generals in Gray, 279–80; OR 5:939, 1078).

159. Lieutenant John Mason Lee (1839–1924) was the younger brother of Fitzhugh Lee and a cousin of Mary Custis Lee. He enlisted in the Confederate army on 18 May 1861 and on 7 October became an aide-de-camp to Brigadier General Isaac Trimble, whose brigade was in Major General E. Kirby Smith's division. Lee later served on the staffs of his cousin William Henry Fitzhugh Lee and Williams Carter Wickham (Krick, Staff Officers, 199; OR 5:967).

160. Elizabeth McKay Campbell Brown (b. 1820) of Spring Hill, Tenn., was a first cousin of Richard Ewell. He courted Mrs. Brown, known as Lizinka, and later in the war, the two mar-

don't take him & the widow wants him she can succeed I think. His admiration of her is extravagant.

Two of the Louisiana Tigers were shot day before yesterday at Centreville for attempting to kill their Captain & to rescue from the Guard tent some prisoners under trial.[161] They died with the utmost sangfroid. Their own company were made to shoot them.

I received a letter from Sister Ann a day or two since. She was at home alone. Mr R[enshaw] had gone to the Legislature. She expects to go down after hog killing. Richmond is much crowded. John Patton's house [is] for rent[162] & she wrote at once to inform your Aunt Sally.[163] Nothing new. We are still in the enjoyment of your box. It unfolds daily some new delicacy & the deeper we dive the more we find. The sausage is unexceptionable, is eaten at every meal & so is nearly gone. Some of the things I have sent to Rodes as I am much at his house. Poor Finny was much refreshed by the tea & white sugar while sick. Last night while at Rodes' I sent down for four bottles of whiskey & some eggs with the intention of having eggnog. We decided however to take apple toddy. He asked me for some potatoes which by the way I have entirely forgotten to send. Xmas will soon be here now & I hope to be with you then.

You must not talk about yourself as a "poor plain, 'old' wife." On the contrary you are a *fat*, stylish young wife. I want a daguerreotype of your picture without the frame, or rather with the frame rubbed off after taking the daguerreotype to Mrs Rodes when she comes.[164] You do not take well yourself & the picture can be exactly imitated if the likeness of the

ried. George Campbell Brown (1840–93), Lizinka's son, enlisted in April as a lieutenant in the 3rd Tennessee Infantry and on 1 July became aide-de-camp to General Ewell (Jones, *Campbell Brown's Civil War*, 2, 12; CSR).

161. Privates Michael O'Brien and Dennis Corcoran of Company B of the 1st Louisiana Infantry Battalion were executed for their crimes on 9 December 1861. They were the first soldiers in the Virginia army to suffer that ultimate punishment. The Louisiana Tigers included the 1st Louisiana Infantry Battalion and the 6th, 7th, 8th, and 9th Louisiana Infantry regiments (CSR; Jones, *Lee's Tigers*, 40).

162. Carter is probably referring to John Mercer Patton (1826–98), an 1846 graduate of the Virginia Military Institute and a Richmond lawyer who was then serving as a lieutenant colonel in the 21st Virginia Infantry. The Patton house in Richmond was located on 10th Street between Marshall and Clay Streets (Krick, *Lee's Colonels*, 300–301; 1860 Census, Henrico County).

163. "Aunt Sally" is Sarah Alexander Seddon Bruce, the sister of Carter's mother-in-law.

164. Carter is referring to a portrait of his wife that was painted in Richmond in the late 1850s by the French artist Louis Mathieu Didier Guillaume (1816–92) (Wright, *Artists in Virginia before 1900*, 65). The Guillaume portrait of Susan Carter is in the possession of her great-grandson, Fielding Lewis Williams Jr. Robert E. Rodes married Virginia Hortense Woodruff Rodes (1833–1907) of Tuscaloosa, Ala., in 1857 (Collins, *Robert Rodes*, 38, 45).

frame could be erased. Can it be done[?] We are having a beautiful spell of weather now—for building.

I love to hear about our sweet little children[,] precious little darlings. Keep them from the Diphtheria cases. I pray they may not have it. Dear Mama always believed in the camphor bags. Keep the Quarter Children from Mr Chenault. I am pleased to hear Mr Chenault is trying to do well. You are right as to his motive. Don't talk against him to Celia. He will continue to do well with the hope of getting back. He has no chance of getting such another birth in this life & he is now awaking to the fact. Where does he go next year[?] Do you know[?]

Much love to all my friends. Jack is in luck to be posted in Richmond. When will his wife be confined[?]

God bless you my own. Kiss the little chicks for me & believe me always.

Y[ou]r devoted & loving husband,
Thos. H. Carter

Did you ever learn if Wortham drew my pay[?]

—⁕—

Davis Ford
Dec. 17th 1861

Your letter of the 13th inst. my darling wife, came to hand this morning. I do not know why my letter of the 10th did not reach you on Friday. It went to Manassas the 11th ought to have gone to Richmond the 12th & to Old Church the 13th.[165] The office in R[ichmond] is probably in fault, or it may be Manassas. I wrote again a short letter on Sunday evening which should have been received this morning. We are hard at work with the winter quarters. Nearly all the men are putting up houses—quite good ones they are. Some to be covered tents[,] some with boards & some with poles[,] leaves[,] brush & dirt like a hen house & of the same form. Plank is scarce & nails also. The most economical methods have to be adopted. Pat & myself are well quartered in the large hospital tent.

165. Old Church, named for a colonial-era church, was a small village in Hanover County, Va., centered around a tavern and a post office. Roads intersected there that ran east and west across the county and north to the Pamunkey River. Most of Carter's letters to Susan came through the Old Church post office. From Pampatike, Carter's wife could cross the Pamunkey at nearby Piping Tree Ferry and take the road southwest to Old Church to collect her mail (*Old Homes of Hanover County*, 39).

On one side two widths of the tent cloth are ripped up & a fireplace larger than that in the dining room is placed. It is made of logs & lined with rocks & daub. A delightful fire now burns in it. Wood abounds all around[,] from two feet of the door to a half mile, oak[,] hickory &c. Indeed, it is too near, for last night the wind rose high & I feared a dry limb might find its way through my cloth house & through your humble servant. I shall cut them down tomorrow. The tent is fifteen feet square giving ample room for locomotion. Plank is all I want now for the floor, & the difficulty of getting it is remarkable. Still I hope to succeed soon. When that is jointed & laid I shall be fixed for the winter. I am building a large stable too for the Battery horses, sixty-four stalls & shall need more, as ten more horses are to be sent in a day or two to make up six to each piece. I fear the glanders has broken out among them. A horse doctor was sent yesterday to decide a case[,] whether distemper or glanders.[166] With great solemnity he pronounced it glanders, & I shot the horse without being in the least concerned of the necessity of the act. The glanders is contagious to man & beast & fatal to both—requiring in man inoculation of the virus through an abraded surface. Another horse similarly affected but varying in the stage of the disease he decided had distemper. Today I have practiced firing shells. Capt Alexander Chief of Ordnance having discovered the defect in the shells & the remedy[,] he wrote me to try & report result to him.[167] I did so & the remedy is perfect. Some failed to explode but this is due to the composition used in the fuse. After testing these I shot at the dead horse, between ~~three~~ 3 & ~~four~~ 4 hundred yards off. Four shells out of five struck him, to the great delight of the men & spectators among whom were Rodes & his wife. Tomorrow we fire again. I see a great deal of Mrs Rodes. She seems a fine woman[,] fond & proud of her husband & he quite as adoring of his dulcinea.

They live in a small house about a quarter of a mile from me. Van Dorn & staff are quartered seven miles from here between Manassas & Union

166. Glanders is a contagious disease of horses and mules, but it can infect humans as well. It is characterized by swelling beneath the jaw and a profuse mucus discharge from the nostrils (Centers for Disease Control and Prevention, "Glanders General Information," http://www.cdc .gov/glanders/ [accessed 20 December 2013]).

167. Major Edward Porter Alexander (1835–1910) of Georgia was chief of ordnance and chief signal officer for the Confederate Army of the Potomac. Carter mistakenly referred to Alexander as a captain in this letter. He had enlisted as an engineer on 16 March 1861 and had been promoted to major on 1 July. On the last day of the year, he became a lieutenant colonel. Later, Alexander would rise to command an artillery battalion and, as a brigadier general, eventually command the artillery of the 1st Corps of the Army of Northern Virginia (CSR; Eicher and Eicher, *High Commands*, 101).

Mills. Nothing new here. All prospect of a fight seems to have faded away. Possibly the navy may take a turn at Magruder by way of feeding the Northern greed for excitement. By water they are more successful than by land. They can play from "long taw," & at a safe distance.[168] Their nerves are steadier & with their fine ordnance, good powder &c. they can beat us. In close quarters the case is different. The furlough question seems to occupy all minds. I hope some arrangement will be made soon, though it is certain all cannot be gratified. The new act offering a bonus to those who reenlist for two years or the war is thus far a failure.[169] Men fear there is some catch in it. The volunteer system will not conduct this war to its close should it continue a year or two longer although Southerners say thousands of volunteers can still be had from the cotton states if arms can be furnished. Drafting is the only mode to raise an army for next summer, & the worst feature of the case is that the 12 mo[nth]s volunteers go out in the midst of the next campaign—May[,] June[,] July &c. If the Militia is to furnish the next army, it should now be drilled & put into camp as soon as possible. In my judgment some plan should be devised to keep the old troops in the field although personally I am indifferent. The old troops are well drilled, in many instances have been under fire & are in the field without difficulty of transportation. As far as I am concerned I suppose I shall have to continue in the service as long as the war lasts. When my Company disbands however I can have a breathing spell & get some other good post on somebody's staff or in the Surgical Department or in Artillery, my favorite arm. I can't help hoping however that this war must be coming to end next summer. It is strange no news is received of the Mason & Slidell Affair. It will amount to nothing except a little diplomatic lying on Seward's part. I am glad to hear Lee's Rangers are at Evansport.[170] I may see something of them.

Present me most kindly to your Aunt Laura & her little girl.[171] I am

168. "Long taw" refers to a game of marbles in which players attempt to strike each other's marbles by tossing from a distance one of their own and taking any that they hit.

169. Enacted on 11 December 1861, the Bounty and Furlough Act stated that all "privates, musicians, and non-commissioned officers" were entitled to a $50 bounty and a furlough of up to sixty days if they reenlisted in the Confederate army for three years or for the war (*Statutes at Large*, 223).

170. Lee's Rangers, named for its first commander, Captain W. H. F. Lee, was a cavalry company that formed in King William County, Va., on 10 June 1861. The unit became Company H of the 9th Virginia Cavalry on 18 January 1862 (Wallace, *Military Organizations in Virginia*, 50–51).

171. Carter is referring to Laura Roy Ellerson (b. 1820?) and her daughter Mary (b. 1850?) (1860 Census, Hanover County). Laura's brother William was Susan Carter's father. The 1860 census taker mistakenly recorded the last name as "Ellyson."

glad she is with you & that you drive out more than usual. Remember me also to Elija Turner.[172] I shall try to get down about the first of the year but nothing is more uncertain. When everything is blocked with snow & mud as it must be soon there can be no reason for keeping me here.

The weather lately has been most beautiful & the nights as bright as day.

Has Magruder sent home the other two men[?] Has Bodye improved[?] Joan & Nelly's child are gone from the original lot & none have come. I hope no more will die. Has Davis been over the farm with Chenault[?] I am glad everything progressed favorably. When the hands are sick it is better if they look badly to rest them awhile & give them light work. Don't forget to have the Daguerreotype of your picture taken for me when you have an opportunity.

Mother my heart swells with tenderness when I think of those dear little children—sweet little things. You don't tell me half enough about them. Tell me everything they say & do. Put Thomas in pants. He must not grow too fast[,] he will pass the doating age. Dear dear wife & children[,] I long to see you more than I can describe.

God bless you my own good wife.

Y[ou]r fond husband,
Thos. H. Carter

Your home manufactured envelope is ingenious & as good as any that can be made. My box from Wortham's with the looking glass[,] whiskey & candles has never arrived.

—⁓⁓—

Davis' Ford
Dec 25th 1861

Your last letter my dearest wife was received yesterday. I am truly concerned to hear of the Militia draft. I had hoped overseers would be exempt.[173] It is hard to know what course is now best to pursue. Should

172. Elija Turner has not been identified. Carter may have written "Eliza" Turner, in which case he is referring to the seventeen-year-old daughter of Dr. Robert R. Turner (1860 Census, King William County).

173. Carter is most likely referring to the act passed on 29 November 1861 by the Virginia General Assembly entitled "An Ordinance to Reorganize the Militia," which designated all white male citizens between the ages of twenty-one and thirty-one as active members of the state militia. The act did not exempt overseers from potential service, much to Carter's disap-

the militia be soon returned I greatly prefer employing some manager temporarily in Davis' place as he is said to be an excellent overseer. Mr Pae would probably be the most suitable person for that case.[174] He is highly spoken of by all, lives close to you, by Mr Warner Edwards,[175] has sons grown so that he would most likely agree to stay until the return of Davis. On the other hand[,] if Davis is permanently fixed in the army perhaps Dudley would be the best man.[176] He is well spoken of by all here. Mr Pae is probably too old for so large a business for the whole year, although very suitable for a short period in the winter. Dr Turner under all the circumstances can give you better advice than myself. Some steps must be taken soon. I wish sincerely I could be with you now & had fully promised myself that joy this week, but I have thought best to wait a fortnight & give way to Robt. Ryland who had set his heart on going. My furlough was written & Rodes advised that only one commissioned officer should be allowed leave of absence at one time. It is as well probably as it is now doubtful whether any will be signed for a fortnight, another fight being "talked of." A system of furloughs has been instituted by which ten men from each company of average size are allowed to be absent at one time. Under this head ten men have sent in furloughs from my Company, also R. Ryland. I trust some way will be opened to you by receipt. Some one here said that overseers on estates of over thirty hands were exempt. This must be a mistake. If you could only learn how long the militia would be detained on the peninsula you could act well enough. Possibly you will have heard by the arrival of this letter. I am pleased to see your interest in everything. It will benefit you in every way. But I regret you should not enjoy yourself in Richd as you expected. I suppose you drive about from time to time. This will direct your mind from trouble & keep you posted in news. I wish you had some

---

pointment (Virginia State Convention of 1861, "An Odinance to Reorganize the Militia," VHS). The Confederate government was debating at the time over how to address the issue of maintaining the strength of its various armies after the end of the original ninety-day enlistment period. Those debates resulted in the passage of the First Conscription Act on 16 April 1862. That act did include an overseer exemption clause. For a more detailed discussion of the conscription act, see Carter's letter dated 21 April 1862.

174. Mr. Pae has not been identified.

175. Warner Edwards was a fifty-nine-year-old neighbor of the Carters in King William County. According to the 1860 census, he was head of a seven-member household, had real estate valued at $15,000, and owned $20,000 worth of personal property (1860 Census, King William County).

176. Susan Carter hired Mr. Dudley to work as the overseer at Pampatike (see misdated letter of 27 December 1861 in chapter 3).

one to stay with you. Pampatike is out of the way & you must be lonely. But you must recollect my own precious wife that you are doing your duty. War is hard time on all especially on women & children. Don't send the daguerreotype. I will get it when I go down. Everything is lost that is sent to me except your box. Sutton sent me 5 gallons of whiskey & some candles by the Express last Friday. Lost as the other box was of the same kind.

I am so anxious to see my dear little man in his pants & my little[,] dumpy[,] sweet daughter with those dear eyes. Mother I hope soon to see you all.

God grant it & bless you prays your own fond husband,
Thos. H. Carter

I dine tonight with Rodes. Miss Rodes sent down before breakfast to invite me to an eggnog drinking, as I was invited to dinner & was not ready to go then. Rodes has taken on his staff a Mr Spencer France son of the Lottery man in Baltimore.[177] Married a Miss Williams of the Eastern Shore—a very pretty woman Wm says. He & Wm are old friends. He is a nice[,] gentlemanly[,] intelligent man who came down as a substitute for a few days for his cousin Mr Leach in the Blackhorse troop.[178] Rodes was pleased with him & took him on his staff.

—⁂—

Headqrs, Rodes' Brig.
Davis' Ford
Dec 29th [1861]

I have received no letter this week my {dear} wife since your last Saturday's letter. I suppose however there is some good reason for your omission to write. I trust everything goes well & that you have been able to learn something about a new overseer. Should it appear probable that

---

177. Spencer Leslie France of Baltimore, Md. France's service record indicates that he served as a private in the King William Artillery and later as a captain and assistant adjutant general of the 2nd Corps artillery. From 1 October to 31 December 1863, he was a clerk on Carter's battalion staff (CSR).

178. Charles Hunton Leach (1837–1910) of Fauquier County, Va., enlisted as a private in Company H of the 4th Virginia Cavalry (the "Black Horse Troop") on 25 April 1861. In December 1861, he served as a courier for Brigadier General Robert E. Rodes. Leach was captured during the cavalry fight at Gettysburg and was not exchanged until 18 February 1865. According to his parole of honor, which he received at Fairfax Court House on 9 May 1865, the twenty-eight-year-old Leach was six feet tall with black hair, dark eyes, and a dark complexion (CSR).

Davis will soon return & possibly you may learn this from Magruder indirectly[,] you might make some temporary arrangement. But I believe the next summers campaign will be the crisis & will be fraught with many difficulties calling for every exertion that this government can make. God grant that the people may awake to the fact in time to save the Old Dominion. If I am right in the above opinion the militia will be subject to draft at all times in [the] future & even should Davis return now he might be summoned at any time next summer in the midst of the most important farming operations. Therefore I fear some one else will have to be employed. I am truly sorry for he is regarded as a good man & competent manager & { . . . } hoped that your trouble on that would be at an end.

{ . . . } Militia now must be resorted to { . . . } the next army. The twelve months volunteers will go out of service in the very midst of the fighting season. The late act of Congress authorizing a bounty of 60 days leave[,] $50 extra pay & transportation free to & fro to all reenlisting for 2 years or the war will not at all answer to reenlist this army. The men are actually diseased on the furlough question. The mania is such that it unfits many for duty, but for all that they are not disposed to reenlist[,] fondly hoping & foolishly too that when they go home next summer there they will remain. In vain they are told that their services are necessary to carry on the war & that they will be drafted on their arrival. That is a far-off evil & not believed. They are told that eight or nine tenths of the Army of the Potomac are 12 months vol. that will march home next summer as McClellan marches to Richd. Man is selfish—patriotism a thing you read of. They hope in a new organization to get some office. Some few offer here & there to reenlist & they are so many gained, but the new army must be organized from the militia which ought to be placed in Camps of instruction & drilled now. This is the only plan I know of, & even this is not entirely satisfactory[,] for the new army will not equal the present force. The army now in the field are composed of the flower of the Southern people[,] are well drilled, accustomed to fire in many instances & on the spot. Still it is the only feasible plan I know of. Why Congress does not move I know not. It is full time. My Company to a considerable extent will reenlist they say if I will promise to command them, but the act is not yet gone into effect & when the time comes I do not count on many. Popular favor is altogether uncertain & I have two or three unpopular officers to sustain & bear along as I best can, which often exposes me to injustice & to misapprehension.

I hope Dr Turner has been able to give you some advice on the over-seer subject. I was greatly shocked to hear of Genl. Cocke's suicide.[179] It is said here that he has been suspected at times of slight insanity. Tell me the circumstances when you write. I still hope to get a furlough soon, though it is uncertain. They are constantly denied. Wms Wickham was refused. Wm Newton got off in some way. I hardly know how. McClellan keeps the authorities in constant expectation—doubtless to prevent the furlough reenlistment. By the way[,] that bounty could not be carried out to its full extent for too many men would leave at one time & be absent too long were it adopted generally. Robert[,] my brother[,] wrote to me from the Exchange [Hotel in] Richmond. I hope he has been to Pampatike. Wm Page spoke of going to Clarke. They came on about the Sequestration Act.[180]

Do write to me about yourself & the children. I long so much to see them & yourself. I hear their childish { . . . } constantly. Dear little ones. {God} forever bless you my darling wife.

McClellan had another sham battle yesterday evening. Such firing I never heard. The smoke could be seen here. All this does good—accustoms his men to the confusion of fire &c. &c. He will come out in the spring with a fine army. I doubt not our ultimate success but fear Old Virginia will be sacrificed for the Southern Confederacy, unless speedy measures are taken for another army.

God bless you my own wife.

Ever y[ou]rs most devotedly,
Y[ou]r husband

179. Philip St. George Cocke (1809–61) of Virginia commanded the 5th brigade of General P. G. T. Beauregard's army at Bull Run. Later in the year, while suffering from poor health, he returned to his Fluvanna County home, where he committed suicide on 26 December 1861 (Warner, *Generals in Gray*, 56–57).

180. The Confederate States Congress passed the Sequestration Act on 30 August 1861. The act declared that all real and personal property of "alien enemies" (i.e., U.S. citizens) could be confiscated by Confederate authorities. For example, in October Monticello, the Albemarle County, Va., home of Thomas Jefferson, was confiscated because it was owned by U.S. Navy captain Uriah P. Levy. The legislation demanded that southern citizens report any alien property and turn it over to the proper authorities. The act was in retaliation for the Confiscation Act passed by the U.S. Congress on 6 August. (For the act itself, see Moore, *Rebellion Record*, supplement, vol. 1, 19–23; for the confiscation of Monticello, see Hamilton, "Confederate Sequestration Act," 380.)

CHAPTER THREE

———————— ⚊ᴠᴠᴠ⚊ ————————

From Northern Virginia to the Peninsula

8 January–1 May 1862

The new year found Captain Carter and the men of the King William Artillery encamped in winter quarters at Davis's Ford in Prince William County. Dull daily routines filled their days and nights, and false reports of enemy movements were all too frequent. Carter informed Susan in mid-January that "[w]e have had . . . alarms so often that they are but little regarded." The new year also brought with it distressing news for the Confederacy. Union victories in Tennessee and on the coast of North Carolina in February dampened Southern morale. At the same time, many units in the Confederate armies were fast approaching the end of their initial twelve-month period of enlistment. The Conscription Act, which had passed the Confederate Congress in December 1861, would shortly go into effect. Its goal was to solve the manpower needs of the various Southern armies, but it also had the potential to cause chaos and confusion in the ranks. Carter, like many others in Joe Johnston's army, spent a great deal of his time trying to obtain a furlough to visit his family.[1]

On 7 March the Confederate army, anticipating the long-awaited Federal advance, began to pull out of its positions in northern Virginia. Carter's battery evacuated its camp on the eighth and marched southwest alongside the tracks of the Orange and Alexandria Railroad. After resting several days near the Rappahannock River, the battery made its way to Rapidan Station, where it arrived on 20 March. The army did not remain in central Virginia for long. To counter the movement of Union general George B. McClellan's Army of the Potomac down the Chesapeake Bay to the tip of the peninsula between the York and James Rivers, Johnston's

---

1. Macaluso, *Morris, Orange, and King William Artillery*, 22; THC to SRC, 27 Dec. 1861. Carter misdated the 27 December letter. His references to events that took place in the first weeks of the new year suggest a more likely date of 12 January 1862. The letter appears in the correct chronological location but retains its original date.

army reinforced the smaller Confederate force at Yorktown. Tom Carter and his battery arrived at the old colonial port on 11 April and immediately occupied a defensive position on the Warwick River line. On 28 April the King William Artillery officially reorganized under the provisions of the Conscription Act and unanimously reelected Carter as its captain.[2]

—⁊⁊⁊—

Davis' Ford
Jan 8th 1862

My precious Wife,

Last night, which was the usual time for my letter to be written, I was so much fatigued by my ride to Centreville that I postponed my letter 'till today. All the morning I have been engaged in having the Battery horses rough shod for the slippery state of the roads in accordance with the emphatic orders lately received to that effect. A battle is still talked of here—none of us believe it but I always obey orders so that no blame can attach to me if possible to avoid it. The orders lately since the sailing of the Burnside fleet have all been most warlike but that armada is probably intended for the Southern Coast.[3] I wish the alarms would end or the battle come off—in either case I could get away. As it is now the furloughs of several Infantry Captains have been returned to Rodes [and] refused in consequence of an impending battle. Battery Captains being on the footing of Cols of Infantry are of course required to remain. My command unlike that of a Captain of Infantry is separate & independent. In the event of a battle no one could command it but a Lieut. In Infantry the Comp[an]y would be in a regiment & if under the Col it would matter but little whether the Captain is present or not. With a battery which acts alone[,] you see[,] everything is different. No regimental organization except in the case of Col Pendleton who is assigned to the defense of the breastworks at Centreville & therefore he commands a Regt. of Artillery.[4] On the field a regiment would be entirely unmanageable.

2. Long, *Day by Day*, 180; Macaluso, *Morris, Orange, and King William Artillery*, 23; THC to SRC, 22 Mar. and 29 Apr. 1862.

3. Carter is referring to the combined Union naval and army force under the command of Brigadier General Ambrose Everett Burnside (1824–81) of Indiana, which sailed from Hampton Roads, Va., to the North Carolina coast. There, it landed troops on Roanoke Island and defeated the small occupying Confederate force on 8 February (Boatner, *Dictionary*, 108).

4. Colonel William Nelson Pendleton (1809–83) of Virginia was General Joseph E. Johnston's chief of artillery in January 1862. On 26 March 1862 he became a brigadier general, and from

Otherwise "they say" your husband would have gone up a button or two sometime since.

Rodes is desirous that I should open books & reorganize the Company for the war. Those not reenlisting would go home at the end of the twelve months & submit to the risk of militia draft. I expect in some way to be compelled to remain in the service. Artillery I prefer[,] though there is no chance of promotion for the reasons above stated, but it is decidedly the most pleasant. Military distinction is a matter which is of little moment. All of us must remain in the field until this abominable war is over or the state will be overrun. I have more fear of next summer's campaign than anytime yet experienced. Unless this 12 mo[nth]s volunteer business can be altered by a reenlistment nothing can prevent the ruin of Virginia. After the Old State is lost the Confederacy may go hang. We shall be ruined & I have no faith in the permanency of the Southern Confederacy. The officers must set the example. I want to know what you think of it. I can not tell you my darling how the prospect of an indefinite continuance of this war depresses me. One can endure anything for a limited time but a future without a ray of light—without a hope of that sweet domestic happiness we once enjoyed seems at times almost intolerable. Of course the risk of death is greatly increased also but the times seem to require sacrifice of everything save honor.

I wish you to write to me on this subject. I still have hopes of getting on this furlough list about the middle of this month when I will talk more fully on the subject.

If we could only be together I think I could endure anything.

Rec'd a letter from Robert—don't think he'll come. Pauline threatened to come after him with the children & Dave as an escort. He seems much exercised on the subject & fears to start home lest he should be passed on the route, & fears his route may be cut off as the enemy are said to be at Huntersville & arming for some point on the East Tennessee road.

Tell me how my precious little daughter is Mother. God grant she may be better. I feel their little arms around my neck, see you in the chamber upstairs as when I formerly saw you when I came from riding everyday & long for the quiet days of peace once more. May God grant that we may

---

then until the end of the war, he served as chief of artillery for the Army of Northern Virginia (CSR-Officers; Warner, *Generals in Gray*, 234–35).

once more be united never to part in this life & that peace may yet come sooner than supposed.

So many persons are supported by the war I fear it will be prolonged as long as possible. The people however are in favour of peace. England may yet find some pretext to break the blockade & enter the ring.

God bless you my own sweet wife.

Ever y[ou]rs
Thos. H. Carter

—m—

Head Quarters 2nd Brig. 1st Divis. 1st Corps A.P.
Davis' Ford
Decr. 27 1861[5]

My dearest Wife,

Your last letter of the 31st was duly received yesterday. I wrote one the 1st day of the year & sent it by Dr McKinney to the office & he was reminded of it three times. He may have forgotten until he reached home at Charlottesville. If so you will get it Tuesday with this one. Last night at 12 1/2 A.M. a courier came with a long letter from Genl. Beauregard to Van Dorn & one from the latter to Rodes. The first stated that a telegram just from Richmond gave information that the fleet under Burnside from Annapolis & lately lying in Hampton Roads had started somewhere & no one could know where this blow would fall. Therefore this Division should be ready to be thrown across the Occoquan at Woodyards Ford on the Bull Run Branch & Wolf Run Shoals Ford on the Occoquan. Van Dorn ordered three days' rations to be issued & the troops to be ready to march in light marching order at a moment's warning. We have had these alarms so often that they are but little regarded. So I turned over & went to sleep again. I am always ready except as to provisions & they can be issued in a few moments. On former occasions, I have had the provisions issued & cooked & the result has been a great waste & old[,] hard[,] tough biscuits for the men to eat for time specified, when I was very certain that the alarm was false. The Genls of course are right to be always on the guard whether they believe the reports or not. When orders of the kind come next spring they will be obeyed literally for then the time will be at hand for heavy fighting. The information to Genl.

5. See note 1 above for an explanation of the incorrect date.

Johnston from four *unknown* sources has all been of the same tenor—
that conjointly with the fleet attack on Evansport a demonstration will
be made here at Leesburg & Romney—that the demonstration may be
converted at any moment into a real attack by the success on the flanks.
I don't believe a word of any part of it except the possibility of an attack
on Evansport & perhaps a demonstration through here to prevent our
giving aid at Evansport, & this I think improbable. The fleet is probably
destined for some other point.

These summons unfortunately for me serve to prevent my getting a
furlough at present. I still hope to be with you by the middle inst. I am
glad you will make a visit to Richmond. It will buoy up your spirits. I
telegraphed Robert yesterday [at the] Exchange Hotel that I would meet
him at Manassas Monday evening.[6] I don't know whether he will stick
up to the arrangement or not. I lost the first man in my comp'y [on] new
year's day. He died at Culpeper Ct House of Typhoid Fever. Had they
obeyed my earnest solicitation that he might be sent home he might have
been saved. His name was James Donald Moore—[from the] lower part
of King Wm County.[7] Considering the number of cases of measles & the
number of men (101) & the length of service { . . . } this does well. I hope
Edwards will recover.[8] The Genls had all concluded to send their wives
home on this alarm—but they have changed their minds. On the 2nd[,]
four ladies & Major Genls met at an eggnog party at Genl. Van Dorn's.
We had a delightful day—Mrs G W Smith[,][9] Mrs E Kirby Smith[,][10]
Mrs Col Duncan Smith[11] & Mrs Rodes. Mrs Duncan Smith is a charming

6. The Exchange Hotel and Ballard House stood at the corner of Franklin and 14th Streets in
Richmond, Va. (*Richmond City Directory 1860*).

7. James Donald Moore (1836?–62) enlisted as a private in the King William Artillery at Richmond on 10 July 1861. On 12 January the members of the battery assembled to pass a resolution
concerning Moore's death. Five days later, a Richmond newspaper published the resolution
(CSR; *RDD*, 17 Jan. 1862).

8. John Duval Edwards of the King William Artillery was on sick leave until 22 March 1862.

9. Lucretia Bassett (1822–81) of New London, Conn., met Gustavus Woodson Smith while
he was serving in the U.S. Army Corps of Engineers. The couple married on 3 October 1844 (*The
Confederate War Department*, "Gustavus Woodson Smith," http://www.csawardept.com/history/
Cabinet/GWSmith/index.html [accessed 30 Sept. 2013]).

10. Cassie Selden (b. 1836) of Lynchburg, Va., met Edmund Kirby Smith while he was stationed there in April 1861. The couple married on 24 September 1861 (Moore, *Rebellion Record*,
3:27; Parks, *Edmund Kirby Smith*, 125).

11. Georgia P. King (b. 1833?) married William Duncan Smith (1825–62) of Augusta, Ga., in
the summer of 1861. Georgia's father was Thomas Butler King (1800–1864), a prominent coastal
farmer who served five terms each as a state senator and a U.S. representative. During the Civil
War, King traveled to Europe as a commissioner for both Georgia and the Confederacy (*Bio-*

little woman. Longstreet was there but not his wife.[12] Every thing since has been dull enough. We had a little snow which is very slippery & the weather is cold. James sleeps in my tent & keeps up the fire.

We still have a little hope about the Mason & Slidell affair as England is evidently desirous to break the blockade. Davis & Genls Johnston & Beauregard are at loggerheads. These politicians will ruin any government on earth. Davis is anxious to organize the army by states [so] that Mississippi & his favorites may have the lion's share.[13] The Genls very wisely oppose it as jealousy[,] dissatisfaction & a desire to return home on the part of the Southern troops will necessarily follow. No steps yet taken to establish another army for next summer. I am told Davis speaks openly of the Blunder of Johnston when the whole army knows he made the grand blunder of all—preventing the pursuit of the 21st. He is afraid Johnston & Beauregard will get a little more popular favour than himself. He is no Washington unfortunately for us.[14]

You must tell me more of my dear little ones Mother. I love to hear of their sweet little ways. I dare say you have done wisely in employing Dudley. I wish I could get off & install him. If these alarms will ever cease I will leave at once. Best love to all friends.

Ever y[ou]r own,
Thos. H. Carter

—⁂—

graphical Dictionary of the U.S. Congress, "Thomas Butler King," http://bioguide.congress.gov/scripts/biodisplay.pl?index=K000215 [accessed 30 Sept. 2013]). In 1861 Duncan Smith commanded the 20th Georgia Infantry. His regiment, like Carter's battery, served in Earl Van Dorn's division. Smith later became a brigadier general and died of yellow fever at Charleston, S.C., on 4 October 1862 (Warner, *Generals in Gray*, 285–86).

12. In early January, James Longstreet's wife, Maria Louisa Garland Longstreet of Lynchburg, Va., and their four children were boarding in Richmond. When the children became ill in the middle of the month, Longstreet traveled to Richmond to be with his family. The situation worsened, and during the last week of January three of the general's four children died from scarlet fever (Wert, *James Longstreet*, 46, 96–97).

13. As described in note 115 of chapter 2, President Davis believed that the morale of troops in units from the same state, if brigaded together, would grow stronger and that these units would become a more cohesive and effective fighting force (Freeman, *Lee's Lieutenants*, 1:118).

14. George Washington (1732–99) was considered by most Americans at the time to be the greatest soldier in the country's history. It was inevitable that Union and Confederate commanders would be compared to the hero of the American Revolution.

My dearest wife,

Your last letter was duly received & I am most thankful that our little daughter has recovered from her attack of sore throat, which I feared from a former letter might prove to be Diptheria, & that everything progressed satisfactorily at Pampatike.

I am sorry to hear of Davis' shortcomings, which I shall not mention. However I don't know that he is to blame for the partiality of the Coalters to himself. Our Major General Van Dorn has just left us for the West—Missouri & Arkansas.[16] We are sorry to lose him. He is a nice gentlemanly man, & except for the very absurd staff he had around him there is no fault to find with him. He will be heard from in his new field when the Spring opens. He has great energy & activity, & though not at all remarkable in intellect is quick of observation & has experience in the realities of the battlefield. We do not know who will take his place— Harry Heth[,] Genl Longstreet or Kirby Smith. Of the three we prefer Longstreet. Davis found it impracticable to organize by states[,] the Genls commanding very properly opposing it strongly, [and] sent Van Dorn to a new field. In this light it is fortunate he has gone. It is rumored that Brig Genl. Whiting has been deposed & placed in his command in the regular service[,] Major in the Cavalry service & sent to Western Virginia.[17] I doubt it. He is a man of firstrate parts but dissipated. The

15. This letter may have been written and sent on 13 January instead of the twelfth because of a reference in the beginning of Carter's letter of 14 January to his application for a twenty-day leave, which he mentioned at the end of the letter dated 12 January 1862.

16. On 10 January, Major General Earl Van Dorn was relieved of divisional command in the Confederate Army of the Potomac and ordered to report to Richmond. From there, he traveled west to take command of the newly established Trans-Mississippi Department (*OR* 5:1027, 8:734).

17. The rumor did indeed prove false. In late October 1861, President Davis devised a plan whereby brigades in Johnston's army would be reorganized to consist of regiments from the same state, the idea being that such a measure would strengthen unit morale and foster healthy state rivalries between brigades (see note 13 above). Brigadier General Whiting strongly disagreed with the plan, describing it to Gustavus W. Smith as "a policy as suicidal as foolish" and "inconceivable folly." Whiting went so far as to make his thoughts known to the president, who in turn threatened to remove him from brigade command. In the end, General Johnston managed to hold on to Whiting. He remained with the army and commanded a division in the Peninsula Campaign and the Seven Days Battles. When Robert E. Lee reorganized his army in October 1862, Whiting was reassigned to Wilmington, N.C., where he oversaw construction of Fort Fisher at the mouth of the Cape Fear River. Except for brief service back in Virginia during the Bermuda Hundred Campaign in May 1864, he remained at Wilmington until he

rumour goes that the difficulty originated in an unpleasant correspondence between him & the President. It is said that Davis has determined to take the field in the Spring in command of the army. God forbid! My opinion of him is going down like mercury in a thermometer [on] a cold day. He has reinstated a Capt Montgomery of an Alabama Battery who was cashiered by a Court Martial, & sentence approved by Genl Johnston for drunkenness[,] theft, incompetency &c.[18] I can testify to the last deficiency. Davis did this to vent his spleen against Johnston showing a vindictiveness I was not prepared to see. Johnston has better abilities & more force than Davis.

Nothing new. We have sent up our furloughs again. None have returned ~~but~~ & it is doubtful if they will be allowed. Some of the men have re-enlisted & tried the furlough system. I have sent up my application for twenty days leave of absence but have not much hope it will be granted. I trust & pray it will. Julian is here & well. He is in a hurry to start so I must end this letter as I wish to show him a new road. Kiss my precious children for me, & take many my darling for yourself. If I fail to get this furlough I will make some arrangement by which we can be united— but Mother I must see those dear little ones.

God forever bless you
Y[ou]r own
Thos. H. Carter

—᠁—

---

was wounded and captured when Fort Fisher fell on 15 January 1865. Despite being severely wounded, Whiting was transferred to Fort Columbus on Governor's Island in New York Harbor. He died there of his wounds on 10 March 1865 (*OR* 5:913, 1011–12, 18:770, 19[2]:684; Denson, "William Henry Chase Whiting," 150–51; Hewitt, "William Henry Chase Whiting," 132–33).

18. Joseph T. Montgomery (b. 1839?) formed the Jeff Davis Artillery in Selma, Ala., at the end of June 1861, and on 1 July he became its first captain. By October his poor conduct had made him unpopular with his men, and General Johnston sought to replace him with a competent officer. The only way to do this was through a court-martial. One was convened on 13 December 1861 and ruled that Captain Montgomery be dismissed, to take effect on 3 January 1862. As Carter mentioned in his letter, President Davis reinstated Montgomery. After Davis did so, the men of the battery reacted immediately. Several of the officers handed in letters of resignation. In his letter to the secretary of war, Second Lieutenant Robert S. Walker wrote that Montgomery was "a man in whom I have no confidence as a commander to whom it is most grinding to pay the respect due a superior officer, and under whom I cannot with honor to myself serve" (Walker's CSR). By early February, it was clear to Captain Montgomery that he had lost control of the battery; therefore, on the seventh he officially resigned and left the unit. President Davis later promoted Montgomery to lieutenant colonel and sent him back to Alabama to form an artillery battalion (Laboda, *From Selma to Appomattox*, 14–15).

Your letter of the 10th my dearest wife has just reached me & in accordance with your request I write immediately to Richmond. In my letter of Sunday I told you of my application for a furlough of twenty day's. It has not been returned yet & there is much doubt whether it will be granted. A number of my men have reenlisted & applied for furloughs. Nothing has been heard of them. Tom Jordan, that arrant humbug, will have his way & is the power behind the throne. His lordship rises from his couch about midday & signs as few papers as possible. He has issued an order that no one shall present his application in person but it must go through the couriers. His august presence can not be contaminated by association with anyone lower than a General.[19] If the furlough is granted I will at once start for Richmond. If not I will endeavor to make some arrangement for you up here—but not just yet. The ground is covered with snow & the roads terrible & really I don't know how to manage the matter. There are no houses near here except miserable huts & they not under guard, & the country filled with soldiers, among whom are those notorious scoundrels the New Orleans Tigers. Mrs Rodes has returned to Lynchburg for a short time. Nothing new. We are sorry to lose little Van. He is a fine, gentlemanly, dashing fellow whom you will hear of when the Spring opens in weal or woe. I had no idea I was so much attached to him until now. He left Sunday.

Love to Robt. I should have written to him, but hoped everyday to hear from the furlough, & to see him in person. He expected to leave tomorrow. Also my love to Wm Page, & all my friends[,] your Aunt Sally[,] Mr B. Tompkins[20] &c. I am thankful to hear of the recovery of the dear little daughter. May God bless you all. No chance of a battle now. It is of the last importance that our public men should act promptly in organizing at once another army. Thomas' resolutions I prefer.[21] The furlough might be shortened [by] half.

19. Carter was not alone in his criticism of Jordan. In his postwar memoirs, James Longstreet's aide, G. Moxley Sorrel, noted that "Jordan was considered a brilliant staff officer, and justly so; but there appeared something lacking in his make-up as a whole that disappointed his friends" (Sorrel, *Recollections*, 22).

20. Mr. B. Tompkins has not been identified.

21. Henry Wirtz Thomas (1812–90) represented Fairfax County in the Virginia state senate from 1850 to 1863 and from 1871 to 1875. During the latter period, he served as the president pro tempore of the senate and was lieutenant governor from 1875 to 1878 (Morris, *Virginia's*

But the dear people I fear will be humoured & fondled with some absurd plan of raising men which will not work in practice & Spring will find us without any definite plan. The problem is of easy solution but the dear creatures mustn't be forced to do anything they don't like else Mr Delegate is forever defunct. They will have to face the music & draft for the war in the present organization of Companies & Regiments[,] giving them the privilege of electing new officers if desired & men from the same localities of said Companies & Regiments can be drafted to fill them to the maximum. They can either draft or give up Virginia.

I hope the choice will soon be made. There is not a single war Regiment from Virginia. Fortunately many Southern troops are for the war. It is roughly estimated that two thirds of the Army [of the] Potomac are twelve months volunteers.

God bless you.

Ever y[ou]r devoted husband
Thos. H. Carter

—⁓—

Wednesday [January] 15th 1862

This letter my darling was written yesterday to be mailed in the evening. The messenger reached the office too late. I open it to say that the furloughs have not returned, but furloughs of the Regiments, some thirty five in number, were granted, to take effect from the 20th & 25th inst provided the movements of the enemy at that time will permit.

I imagine the same answer will be returned on those from this Company. In reference to mine it is more doubtful. I see by the papers that the Military Committee in the Legi[slature] requested to be relieved from the attempt to devise a plan to reorganize the Va. forces—frightened by the howl from the camps, in letters of remonstrance to the papers. I am sorry to see it. God knows what is to become of Virginia. She has already half her territory under foot of the enemy & the men in the field so crazy to be relieved from the hardships & dangers of war that they have lost all reason & insist on being disbanded in the midst of next

Lieutenant Governors, 72). On 7 January, Senator Thomas proposed a seven-point plan for the reorganization of the Virginia army. The major points included the designation of all current volunteers as being drafted for the war, the granting of thirty-day furloughs to men then in active service, and the methods by which company and regimental officers would be chosen (*Daily Richmond Examiner*, 8 Jan. 1862).

summer[']s campaign. The Dispatch says compulsion would be ruinous. What then? Volunteering is long since at an end. I suppose when the time arises the militia will be called out untrained[,] undrilled[,] with shotguns &c. to be shot down like sheep. Well I hope something may turn up to show the volunteers that to save the state they must continue in the service. If they are to reorganize it ought to be done now while the enemy are kept back by the season.

God bless you.

—ᨈᨈ—

Davis Ford
January 19th 1862

My darling Wife,

Your last letter from Chericoke was duly received.[22] I regret that you were disappointed in your trip to Richmond. In the lonely life you now lead I rejoice to hear of any arrangement which will divert your thoughts from the troubles which from the nature of things, must surround you. I trust you will yet take the trip. There is nothing to relate. As yet the furloughs have not returned. Those of the 12th Mississippi remained there four weeks & by the same rule we have three weeks nearly of suspense to endure.[23] I am about making arrangements for enlisting for the war a battery of six brass guns. Rodes would aid me in a battalion of ten guns but the men I find are opposed to such an arrangement as they say they would not be satisfied with my promotion to the Majority. I really care nothing for it, for it would give me the place of a supernumerary, the Captain actually being the commander of the Battery.

Some of the men have re-enlisted for two years & many more would do likewise if the provisions of the recent act of Congress could be carried out, viz the furlough of thirty days at home. I always knew that arrangement would not work in practice. It is absurd to talk of allowing half the army to go on furlough for 30 or 60 days. Such portion in

22. Chericoke was the King William County home of the Braxton family. The original structure, built in 1770 by Carter Braxton, was destroyed by fire in 1775. The house that Tom Carter knew was constructed in 1833 by Corbin Braxton (1792–1852). Carter and his family regularly made the seven-mile journey to visit the Braxtons of Chericoke before the war ("Notes on Chericoke," Alice Cabell Horsley Siegel Papers, 1898–1963?, VHS).

23. The 12th Mississippi Infantry formed in Corinth, Miss., on 23 May 1861. In January 1862, the regiment served in Brigadier General Robert Rodes's brigade (*OR* 5:1029).

each Company as can be spared have as a general rule already enlisted & no more can go until their return. Tomlin's Bill which appeared in yesterday's paper is a good one in strict justice—but it will give an army for next summer's campaign vastly inferior to the present in quality. It proposes to fill the vacancies in each comp'y from non-re-enlistment, by draft according to lot of the militia now at home. This is fair & gives the number required, but unfortunately the militia now at home is a very inferior class of men compared with the present army of volunteers, & while we should have the same number the army would not compare in efficiency. He offers no bounty to those re-enlisting in the way of furloughs & no fear of militia draft to those that disband & go home. The consequence will be that re-enlistment from want of inducement of fear or favor, will amount to few.[24] It seems hard, it is true, that Volunteers who have already encountered the brunt of the war should be forcibly kept in service while militiamen are staying quietly at home, but this could be obviated either by bringing all into the field (& they will be needed) save exceptional cases of useful men such as physicians[,] Magistrates[,] overseers &c. &c.[,] or by discharging the most inferior men in each Comp'y & supplying their places from the Militia. The whole question is a knotty one. I think I prefer Thomas' of Fairfax to any. You saw them probably, but they will not be passed. Wms Wickham's resolutions are liked by many. It proposes to discharge one fourth & fill vacancies from Militia. The present organization as far as possible should be aimed at augmenting the army from Militia as much as needed. I hope to have this suspense in reference to the furloughs soon relieved. It is worse than positive disappointment. I can tell you how I long to see you & my pre-

24. Harrison Ball Tomlin (1815–96), though born in Hanover County, Va., was a planter for most of his life in King William County. A graduate of the University of Virginia, he represented King William for seventeen years in the Virginia House of Delegates, including during the war. Tomlin also served in the Confederate army as colonel of Tomlin's battalion in 1861 and of the 53rd Virginia Infantry from January 1862 until his resignation on 7 January 1863 (Krick, *Lee's Colonels*, 378).
Delegate Tomlin's bill to organize the state troops and volunteers of Virginia offered commanding officers of regiments or battalions the choice either to recruit men directly to fill vacancies or to draw them from the state militia by means of a lottery. Tomlin offered no incentive, as Carter noted, for soldiers to reenlist whose original term of enlistment would end in the spring of 1862. Those men would simply be allowed to return to their homes and "not be subject to any compulsory military duty for the present" (*RDD*, 18 Jan. 1862). Carter favored Senator Henry W. Thomas's plan regarding the reorganization of the Virginia army because it called for all volunteers then in service to be considered drafted for the war. Vacancies would be filled by a statewide draft (*Daily Richmond Examiner*, 8 Jan. 1862).

cious little children. I think of you daily & nightly. My last letter was sent to Richmond care of Wortham as directed. I fear he will keep it some time with the expectation that you will arrive in Richd.

The rain pours & McClellan can not advance, so that I could leave now with impunity. As you see from my letters I feel uneasy in regard to our next campaign. It will be the crisis. The new Congress may devise some plan. McClellan will from selfish & ambitious motives exert his utmost ability but at heart I believe he desires this war to end. It would leave him high in power & reputation—its continuance must bring failure in the end. I hope much from the money pressure at the North & from the possible demand of England & France that the blockade shall be raised.

Nothing new from Clarke. Kiss my own dear little children for me & take any number for yourself from your own fond husband.

—ↀↀↀ—

Davis Ford
January 28th 1862

Your last letter from Pampatike, my dearest wife, was received yesterday, & I am thankful you found the dear little ones well on your return. I have nothing new to relate. I have abandoned all hope of a furlough for the present. The applications sent up it is understood are not to be returned. I cannot obtain leave of absence to recruit a war company as there are no men in King Wm to enlist. I am disappointed more than I can express—indeed I am so irritable that I have to exercise constant control over myself to prevent getting into some difficulty. The men of my company will not re-enlist unless they receive a quid pro quo in the shape of a furlough, nor will any of the 12 mo[nth]s volunteers[,] except a few cases. You misunderstood me in regard to a remark in reference to my men not desiring my promotion. It was simply intended by them to express a preference for me as their Captain & it was rather egotistical in me to have mentioned it as it really meant nothing, popular favor being as fickle as the winds, & he who trusts to it, if determined to be governed by duty, leans on a broken reed. But there is no chance of promotion in Artillery as I have mentioned before & I should care nothing for it if there were, as a Capt of a Battery occupies a sufficiently high place. I do not know whether the present organization of the Vol Companies will be retained & the three Divisions of Militia gradually incorporated, or new Companies be formed in toto & the 12 mo[nth]s Vol. allowed to go home. If this last arrangement obtains, we are lost. The present organization is worth three times its number of militia even if they were drilled from this date. Drill is out of the question until April on account of the inclemency of the weather & recruits introduced into Camp at this season will be decimated by measles & its sequels[,] Typhoid Fever & Pneumonia, & moreover the militia now at home is a craven[,] spirit-less[,] pitiable material at best. I shall wait quietly & see what steps the Legi[slature] will take & be governed by them. I am I know disposed to gloomy views but I find the most sanguine among my friends agree with me that this period is the most critical that has yet arisen.

A committee from Congress has waited on Beauregard with the request that he will take command in Kentucky under A. S. Johnson.[25] His name on acc[oun]t of his immense popularity in the country will be a tower of strength in that section. He consented to go temporarily on the express condition that he should return here in the Spring when the next campaign opens. I imagine when he once undertakes a campaign in that state he will be unable to return as long as operations continue active at that point. He leaves in a day or two. I trust he may repair the terrible disaster we have sustained under that besotted creature Crittenden.[26] He goes it is said to Columbus. The enemy have a most wholesome fear of his prowess.

Wm rec[eive]d a long letter today from Mama. Papa unwell & weather bad, speaks of two pretty pieces of poetry by Wm in the Winchester Republican, 2000 sick in Jackson's Army, Mrs Hopkins taking boarders, [and] Robt Renshaw still absent in the Army.

I have sent up an application for a sick leave for Lieut Ryland. He is suffering with Dysentery & threatened with Typhoid Fever[,] having a bad tongue fever &c. He will probably remain home three weeks from

25. On 26 January, General Beauregard was ordered to report to General Albert Sidney John-ston (1803–62) at Bowling Green, Ky., before continuing on to Columbus to take command of Confederate forces there. On 30 January, Beauregard was officially relieved of his duties in Virginia (OR 5:1048, 1053). General A. S. Johnston (not "Johnson," as Carter wrote) of Kentucky was appointed full general in the Confederate army on 31 August 1861 and given command of all Confederate troops west of the Allegheny Mountains. He was later killed at the Battle of Shiloh (CSR; OR 4:405; Warner, Generals in Gray, 159–60).

26. Carter is referring to the defeat of Confederate forces under Major General George Bibb Crittenden (1812–80) at the Battle of Logan's Crossroads on 19–20 January. Crittenden was later censured for his poor performance, and in October 1862 he resigned his commission (War-ner, Generals in Gray, 65–66; Long, Day by Day, 162).

the last of this week. I want more shirts (white). The bosoms of these I have are in shreds, & the cotton weak & rotten. Would it not be as cheap to buy them ready made[?] I have quite a sum of money with me & another months wages due in a day or two. I must send it down I think. I hardly know what to do with it. Had it been in y[ou]r possession while in Richd you might have paid the debts at Prices &c.

I have also at the request of Pat applied for one week's furlough for Phil Fontaine to bring him a horse, the old one having been rendered useless by disease. It is doubtful if this will be granted, if so you might send anything by him on his return as he expects to come on the cars. The authorities will allow a man to be detailed on a special service when they will refuse a furlough per se. I must write to Wortham in relation to my affairs. I had so confidently expected to go down sooner or later that I have not written regularly. He ought to place $5000 to my father's credit. Had he any idea when the vessel could go for the wheat? I shall see the Comdg Genl. & explain to him the necessity for me to visit home. I am sure I can't tell how Dudley is to conduct matters until my system is explained[,] as well as a hundred peculiarities of the farm. However, military men do not allow usually such excuses. I shall know that I have done my best. A Brig. Ct Martial will detain me some ten days longer. I have no objection to y[ou]r taking Winny in the kitchen, but I never expect to have good servants around me, as the price of such is eternal vigilance & [a] system & I never had the patience to carry out these requirements.[27] Mama spoke of a long & pleasant letter from you. I wish you would write regularly & tell her everything about the farm. She enjoys letters more than anyone I know. I will write soon. Wm Newton & Julian dined with us yesterday. Neither Julian nor Willie have re-enlisted—indeed no one has as the furlough system is a dead letter.

Robert spoke of you as a firstrate manager to Mama in a letter. She had seen Wm Page. The South suffers greatly for want of meat. What became of Chenault[?] Did he get business & with whom? My sick men are gradually coming in looking well. Has Mr Bruce gone south?[28] Mama you

27. Winny was a Carter family slave at Pampatike.
28. Charles Bruce (1826–96), a prewar legislator from Charlotte County, Va., was Carter's wife's uncle by marriage to her aunt Sarah Alexander Seddon Bruce. On 23 September 1861, Bruce formed the Staunton Hill Artillery in Charlotte County and served as its first captain. In January 1862, the unit was stationed on the coast of South Carolina. When the battery reorganized in April, Charles Bruce was dropped from the unit by his own request (CSR).

must dote on those precious little babes for me. I feel their arms around my neck & their soft cheeks against mine but it is only in imagination.

May God bless you all.

Ever y[ou]r devoted husband.

Let Dr Turner examine Henry. I hope it is not an abscess or Syphilis. Don't mention the last word to ears polite.

—⁓—

Davis Ford
Jan 31st 1862

Your letter of the 29th has just reached me my darling wife & if any place could possibly be found it would rejoice my heart to have you but it is utterly impossible to find accommodations here & as deeply as I regret it you must abandon your trip. The country is one sea of mud. The roads impassable except to wagons & in a few days if the rains continue pack horses will be used in their stead.

I can only advise you to try to endure our separation as one of those trials we all have to encounter sometime in life. As to your anxiety about my spiritual welfare I don't know that you have more cause of uneasiness than usual. Camp life is not particularly religious but I have prayers every night in my tent & all attend who desire to do so—no compulsion being used.

I know that I am very sinful but I never pretended to a high state of holiness & trust if I am killed I shall reach heaven through the mercies of Christ. None of us can do more in my opinion. If works are to save me I read my Bible & pray as I did at home. I believe I do pray for you & the children more than myself but I hope that fault if it be one may be overlooked.

I am still on the Genl. Ct Martial, & now that the novelty begins to wear off I am somewhat tired of it. It is useful in acquainting me with the regulations which I never could bring myself to read before. I see Douglas' resolutions in reference to reorganizing the Va. forces have passed the Senate[,] not the house as yet.[29] It will give us a better army for the Spring campaign than Tomlin's but the breaking up of the present orga-

---

29. Beverley Browne Douglas (1822–78) represented King William, King and Queen, and Essex Counties in the Virginia senate (Leonard, *General Assembly of Virginia*, 482).

nization in the Spring—at a time when McClellan will advance his war Reg'ts—trained & seasoned—will I fear be fatal to poor old Va. The militia now at home is poor material to work on & will die with Camp maladies at this season as with some fearful epidemic. Not one man should be allowed to leave his post on these lines but more men should be brought here. As far as my individual command is concerned it matters little for I can get some good position always, but that the sacrifice & blood thus far & the old state itself perhaps should be lost for want of nerve enough to order these men to remain when their times expire is criminal in the highest degree. No fear of rebellion in the ranks if the order is issued for they will see the necessity of such a measure down deep in their hearts. My darling I know the pain this letter will give you. I hate to send it, but you can't find a place here to stay at. I shall see Genl. Johnston next week after the adjournment of the Ct Martial. Perhaps he will give me a week's furlough.

Ryland went home this morning with on a surgeon's certificate of sickness. He was threatened with Typhoid Fever & looks badly. He will let you know the time of his return[,] probably the 18th February if well enough. I asked him to get me six ready made shirts fourteen & a half inches round the neck, collars fifteen inches. Should you get them let him know. He has the money. He is a noble fellow, & true as steel. He may recruit while at home if he escapes the Typhoid attack. Send a box by him, my flute, your daguerreotype as I asked you to have it taken. I told Ryland to look at my coat ordered at Wendlingers & if a really good one to take it. Suppose you look at it Monday. I want to send my horse down & buy another. You need him & his health is bad—at home he will soon recover. Don't give up all hope. I trust to manage the furlough yet.

Kiss my darling children for me & keep me in their remembrance. Love to Sister Ann & Aunt Sarah & my kindest regards to the Rutherfords. I am glad to hear Mr Rutherford's health is better. What part of the coast will Mr Bruce be ordered to[?] Will Aunt Sarah accompany him[?]

God bless you always my precious wife.

In haste
Y[ou]r devoted husband.

—w—

No letter has reached me, my darling wife, since your last from
Richmond. I presume you were prevented by your trip home this week
or possibly one is now in the office for me as the mail has not yet come
today. It is with grief that I have to tell you that since the passage of the
Va Bill Johnston will not allow officers to go home recruiting. A few got
off for that purpose just before the bill was known in the papers, but
as we never hear anything down here until it is old or countermanded
I knew nothing of it until the evening that the leaves of absence for
recruiting were revoked. Johnston sent a letter to Rodes sometime since
stating that furloughs would not be granted to Commissioned officers
but they would be allowed to go home to recruit as soon as a bill then
before Congress should become a law which was expected daily. Each
day I inquired if the recruiting bill had become a law & if Johnston had
communicated anything in regard to the matter. The invariable answer
was no. Thursday, I thought I would ride to the 4th Cavalry & there to
my astonishment heard that a number of officers had just gone home
recruiting. I returned home thinking that at last there was a certain
prospect for my trip home. That night Rodes returned from Centreville
where he had seen Johnston who ordered that no more Virginians should
be allowed to leave as the State had arranged to supply her army. The 4th
Cavalry are near Manassas & as Robinson the Col. is a relative of Johnston's wife & he often at Centreville & therefore posted on all matters[,]
he got his men off before we even heard of it here.[30] Wm Newton got
his furlough & knowing the liability of a countermand at once mounted
his horse & went some six miles down the railroad to Bristoe. That day
he left[,] the order was revoked. In the same way he got off at Xmas &
the furloughs were then revoked the day he left. The only chance is to
seize the first opportunity & leave at once, but our misfortune is never to
know anything here in time for speedy action. Centreville is ten miles off
& the roads in such condition that the ride there & back is a days journey. The Southern officers are still allowed to go home recruiting the late
order applying only to Virginians. Rodes assures me that there is not the
least possible chance of a furlough & from what I have seen I believe it to

30. Carter is referring to Colonel Beverly Holcomb Robertson (1827–1910), commander of
the 4th Virginia Cavalry who was promoted to brigadier general on 9 June 1862 (CSR; Warner,
Generals in Gray, 259–60).

be true. Many men get off on sick leaves of absence & it is possible that if their wives are dying they would be allowed to go, although some have been refused in this event. I should not trouble them with my importunity in such a case but go home as deliberately as I ever did anything in my life. There is reason in all things. Not one of them have the success of our cause more deeply at heart than I have & I hope to fight for it while I have life, but I have not bound myself body & soul to any man or set of men.

I shall ride around this country for some miles & see if I can get two rooms for you & the children. If I can get a tight house & something decent for the children to eat I should prefer that they should be with you for I will not be allowed to visit you more than once or twice a week I fear & you would be lonely without some company. Permission has to be obtained to spend a single night, & I am told that a Lieut Col. Hairston of Early's Brigade whose wife is with him is only allowed to spend a single night in the week.[31] If you could be boarded anywhere near here I might be allowed to go oftener. The rules here are very much more stringent than elsewhere because of the fact that we face the enemy. At Fredericksburg & the Peninsula furloughs are obtained more easily. It is of serious importance that my business should be arranged for next year but such claims are not recognized as military & are disregarded. Truly war is a terrible state of things. Wm Newton met his wife & children on the cars & next morning all returned. The fact that I have a separate command would go against the possibility of my getting a furlough. Do not put too much trust in my getting rooms. I shall do my best. Any place on the railroad would be too distant & at any place this side you would be mud bound. Would you be afraid to bring the children should I succeed? What on earth would you do all day by yourself? Had I known all this, I should have built a log house. Then however the children might have taken cold. The men are re-enlisting considerably in consequence of the recent reverses. I doubt if there will be any battle here if the old army can be kept together.

My darling you must try & bear up as I do under our separation. My spirits are so depressed at times that I am very miserable. My sweet little infants too I yearn to see. Sometimes I can hardly bear up but I strive against this as there are thousands exactly in my situation & not

31. Carter is referring to Lieutenant Colonel Peter R. Hairston (1835–1915) of the 24th Virginia Infantry. Hairston was later wounded at the Battles of Williamsburg and Second Bull Run. He resigned on 9 April 1863 (Krick, *Lee's Colonels*, 171).

allowed to go home—who are farther off & have been longer away. Tell me how every thing goes on at Pampatike. I must write to Richmd & tell Wortham to settle up my accounts for last year & to hurry up the vessel. Have any of the river farmers got off their grain[?] I am seriously afraid we shall have another crop on hand before this is sold which would be ruinous. When the Spring opens I suppose the Railroad will be more used than now. What seems to be the difficulty about the vessel[?] Wheat loses so much by keeping. The corn crop will have to be sent off too. I wonder if we shall ever be quietly & happily at home again enjoying the blessings of peace. God grant it.

Farewell darling
Y[ou]r own devoted husband.

Did you succeed in getting the cloth for my coat[?] If Shafer could get my measure I should like him to make it.[32] He is a great rascal but a beautiful tailor. I should like no gilt except on the Shoulder Straps, & the red cuffs & red collar without the red edging around the coat.
Wm & Julian both at Annfield.

—⁓—

Davis Ford
Feb 19th 1862

My darling wife
No letter has come from you since you left Richd. Doubtless some good cause has prevented your writing. In my last I told you of the impossibility of getting a furlough & told you I should endeavor to get rooms somewhere in the neighborhood. After reflecting upon the condition of the roads, the danger to the children & y[ou]r loneliness without them & my absence from you while here a considerable portion of the time, I am forced to the conclusion that the whole plan had better be abandoned. While this war lasts our separation except for brief periods, is necessary. These meetings bring but temporary relief & deepen the subsequent loneliness. We can only bear it as we may, trusting in God that the days of peace may once more reign in our midst. Most of the men in the army are denied the privilege of seeing their loved ones & I

---

32. John C. Shafer was a merchant tailor whose shop was located in Richmond, Va., on 14th Street between Main and Franklin Streets (*Richmond City Directory 1860*).

am only on the same footing—with the advantage of hearing constantly from you. This war is now assuming gigantic proportions. The days of trial have come. Our victories of last summer have demoralized the army & the whole South. While the Yankees, with characteristic industry & perseverance[,] doubly augmented by the humiliating defeat of Manassas, have quietly but on an enormous scale prepared for the next campaign. The crisis. Money has not been spared as proved by the unparalleled debt incurred thus far. They found an old government in operation with army & navy & manufacturing capabilities & uninter-rupted commerce so far as their wants are concerned. We started with nothing but enthusiasm which took us through last summer with success & so elated us as to induce the belief that the victory was easy & at hand. We must arouse ourselves now or be ruined. Had the public sentiment of the North allowed McClellan to wait until Spring & then to launch his hosts upon us[,] our ruin would have been certain for the time, but the want of money now & their fanaticism has hastened matters & forced an onward movement at such a time as to make their success doubtful & we may prepare before the worst of the storm bursts upon us.

It is rumored here that we were defeated at Fort Donelson & that A. S. Johnson has capitulated. I don't believe the latter. The rumor may be true of the former.[33] If so the loss is heavy every way. I wrote to Wortham yesterday urging him to exert himself in getting a vessel to take off the wheat. Dudley ought to burn the shells & haul out the lime on such places as it is needed & spread it on the ploughed surface so as not to turn it down deep, but harrow or work it with a crop of corn. I have al-most forgotten which fields come in cultivation. The sand field comes in peas & the lime on the ploughed surface will be splendid for them. The river field comes in corn, I think. The lime from the Island landing would therefore have to be hauled to one or the other of these fields. The cut in Pampatike field next to the Piping tree needs lime badly. When the mares drop their colts they should be kept separate from all other horses. The yard is the best place if they give birth at different times. I hope no accident will happen to them. I saw a Mr Shultice yesterday from

33. Fort Donelson, located on the Cumberland River in Tennessee, was captured on 16 Feb-ruary 1862 by a combined army and naval force commanded by Union general Ulysses S. Grant. Between 7,000 and 8,000 Confederates surrendered as a result. Joseph Johnston was not pres-ent at the battle. Brigadier General Simon Bolivar Buckner (1823–1914) of Kentucky surren-dered the Confederate army to Grant at Fort Donelson (Boatner, *Dictionary*, 395–97).

Goochland[,] son of Dr Shultice of Matthews.[34] He says his Father got his servants ready to move them to Goochland & most of the men ran off. He hopes all have not escaped. The troopers were in search—a large reward was offered. He says Mrs Roy has lost all but one man. This is an exaggeration I suppose. He says four of his men are out from ~~at~~ his home in Goochland & that Billy Brown was allowed to go home Xmas. Has he returned[?] I have no faith in the promises of Cuffry. I received a letter from Lucy Lindley & one from Cousin Mary rating me soundly for a doleful letter I [had] written to the former on the state of the country & begging that you would come to them. They are dear people. How are they at Chericoke[?] Cousin Polly[35] is said to have left 3,000 each to Armistead[36] & Jack,[37] 2000 each to the daughters,[38] 95000 to Smith Lee[39] in State Stock (left in money of course) & Charles Carter & Skipwith[40] residuary legatees[,] afterwards altering Charles because of condition of country & increasing thereby Skipwith's. Also 20,000 to John Hill Carter. How is y[ou]r garden[?] & Henry[,] is he better?

34. Carter is most likely referring to Oscar Shultice (b. 1835?). Shultice was a private in Company F of the 4th Virginia Cavalry (CSR). His father, William, was a wealthy physician and farmer in Mathews County, Va. Oscar appears in the 1850 census as a fifteen-year-old student living in Caroline County, Va. Ten years later, he is listed as an employer of sixteen of his father's slaves in Goochland County, Va. (1850 Census, Caroline County; 1860 Slave Schedules, Goochland County). William Shultice (b. 1806?) was listed as a physician and farmer in the 1860 census. He lived in Mathews County, Va., with his wife, Mary, and their five daughters and owned $80,000 in real estate and $120,000 in personal property, including forty-eight slaves (1860 Census, Mathews County).

35. "Cousin Polly" is Mary Walker "Polly" Carter Cabell (1788–1862), the granddaughter of Charles Carter (1733–1802) and his first wife, Mary Walker Carter (1736–70). Tom Carter was the great-grandson of Charles Carter and his second wife, Anne Butler Moore Carter (1756?–1810?).

36. William Armistead Braxton (c. 1825–64) lived in King William County, Va., where, in 1860, he owned $30,000 worth of real estate and personal property valued at $25,000. He was the oldest child of Corbin and Mary Williamson Tomlin Braxton and a cousin of Tom Carter. Armistead, as he was called, enlisted on 21 October 1864 as a private in the 43rd Battalion of Virginia Cavalry (Mosby's Partisan Rangers). He was killed in action on 15 November 1864 near Berryville, Va. (1860 Census, King William County; Colvin, *On Deep Water*, 26; CSR).

37. Tomlin "Jack" Braxton (1832–92) was the second son of Corbin and Mary Williamson Tomlin Braxton and the younger brother of William Armistead Braxton. He was a cousin of Tom Carter (Horner, *History of the Blair, Banister, and Braxton Families*, 157–58).

38. The "daughters" probably refers to Fanny Churchill Braxton Young, Elizabeth "Bettie" Pope Braxton Dallam, and Lucy Tomlin Braxton. They were the sisters of William Armistead and Jack Braxton (ibid.).

39. Smith Lee is either Sydney Smith Lee (1802–69), Robert E. Lee's older brother, or Smith's son Sydney Smith Lee (1837–88).

40. Skipwith has not been identified.

Are you putting [in] vegetables for next summer[?] What [do] you do for salt[?] I will send you money by the first opportunity. My precious wife & children I would give worlds to see you.

God bless you all
Thos. H. Carter

Julian has enlisted in Wm Newton's Company.[41] I advised him to stay in Cavalry as he is perfected in the drill. Wm Newton is a noble man, one of the finest characters I know.

—⚹—

Davis Ford
Feb 27th 1862

My dearest Wife

Your letter of the 24th was received last night. I wrote to you a few days ago & directed the letter to the Spotswoods, advising you to go home with Aunt Sally. Now you will be compelled to do so as we are under marching orders. All sick [men] & extra baggage have been sent to the rear. We know nothing of the movement on foot. It is one of three projects, a change of position with [the] whole army to some point further back, an expected attack here, or a transfer of a position of this army to the valley. By tomorrow I will know.

I have sent back my trunk, reserving such things as I need in Fontaine's trunk. When I hear where you are, will send you the key to my trunk. In it is the coat from Wendlinger's. It fits me very well, but the objection is that the material is very poor. I wish the cloth to be of the best quality similar to my old coat, no shoulder straps, *genuine* lace, the waist longer in *front* (*only*). The trunk will be sent to Wortham's by Express in a few days. The shirts fit well except the new ones which are too small. Walker Hawes took them. I enclose Mama's letter.

I am glad Davis openly denounced in his message the cowardly conduct of our troops at Roanoke & Donelson.[42] Shaw is said to be a New Jerseyan. Will write again tomorrow or as soon as I know anything of our movements.

41. William Newton commanded Company G of the 4th Virginia Cavalry (CSR).

42. Davis, in describing Confederate defeats in North Carolina and Tennessee in his "State of the Confederacy Address" of 25 February 1862, called the surrender of Roanoke Island "deeply humiliating" and admitted that he was "not only unwilling but unable to believe that a large army of our people have surrendered without a desperate effort to cut their way through investing forces" at Fort Donelson, Tenn. (*OR*, Series 4, 1:950–51).

Some think it a general fall back to the Rappahannock line. Should not be surprised myself if it is a valley movement.

Love to Aunt Sally & Nanny & Sister &c. Kiss my dear little ones for me & tell me about them.

God bless you darling.

In haste, y[ou]rs devotedly,
Thos. H. Carter

Tell me where to direct my letter in Richd.

——⁓——

Davis Ford
March 1st 1862

My darling Wife,

I have written twice to Richmond, once to the Spotswood House & once to the care of Wortham & Co.[43] The last enclosed a letter from Mama & told you of our anticipated movement on this line. We are still as much in the dark as when I last wrote. The orders to reduce baggage are so stringent as to allow officers only twenty pounds of baggage including bedding & blankets. This brings us nearly to the Georgia costume—a state of nudity not to be desired in this weather[,] the coldest we have had to the feelings whatever it may be by the thermometer. I have sent back my trunk & the key in an envelope care of Wortham. I wish you to take out the coat & return it with the order that another must be made like it, with a few exceptions mentioned before, but of the best materials.

Rodes seems to think this order to reduce baggage is simply to prepare for any movement that may become necessary in future developments. From the minute details in reference to transportation I should think otherwise. At Manassas the Railroad agents are at work all day & n{ight} taking back flour[,] a large {quan}tity of which had collected there. Several hundred men are at work there on the fortifications. This however may be a strategic blind as this country & army abound in spies, or it may be intended to cover a retreat. Johnston as usual has

43. The Spotswood House Hotel was located at the southeast corner of 8th and Main Streets in Richmond, Va. The five-story hotel, a little more than a year old in March 1862, survived the war only to be destroyed by fire on Christmas Day in 1870 (*Staunton Spectator*, 27 Dec. 1870; Sale, "Disaster at the Spotswood," 18).

exercised the strictest secrecy & he is right. I doubt if many of the Maj. Genls understand this movement. Of course the atmosphere is loaded with rumours. Among them is a statemen[t] { . . . } Jackson has evacuated Winchester & fallen back to Strausburg & that one Brig. has reached Manassas.[44] I was deeply grieved yesterday to see by the papers that Dabney Harrison was killed at Donelson. He has made a good exchange but his poor wife & children.[45] How singularly unfortunate that fam{ily} has been thus far. The figh{ting} at Donelson seems to have been desperate but the surrender was unpardonable. It is clear by the recent accounts that the fleet was disabled & defeated & had A. S. Johnston sent forward 5000 or 10000 troops we should have won the day. Our army was overcome by the heavy odds against them of Infantry. We have discovered that their gunboats will not stand the heavy rifled guns. I begin to think Floyd with all his rascality is equal to any of these Genls. A. S. Johnston is overrated. His first initials are bad. Beauregard should have the Western Command. Some of his letters show a lack of common sense but he has the wonderful talent of the French for military matters & is thoroughly versed in every department. Moreover he is the idol of the Army—full of enthusiasm & energy & of dauntless courage personally & as a leader. I sometimes think that notwithstanding J. E. Johnston's superiority to him intellectually & as a General[,] yet in view of the above qualities Beauregard may be the "Coming Man." Tell me in y[ou]r letters where to direct mine.

   Much love to Aunt Sally & Sister. Mother dote on those dear dear little ones for me. Tell Aunt Sally not to be uneasy as to Mr Bruce.[46]

44. Rumors of General T. J. Jackson's evacuation of Winchester proved false. His Valley Army did not leave the town until 12 March, which was after General J. E. Johnston pulled the main army out of northern Virginia beginning on 7 March, and Union general Nathaniel Banks moved his command toward Winchester (Long, *Day by Day*, 180, 183–84).

45. Dabney Carr Harrison (1830–62) entered Princeton at the age fifteen and later studied law at the University of Virginia, after which he practiced in Martinsburg, Va. (now W.Va.). He soon abandoned the legal profession, however, and enrolled in the Union Seminary in Prince Edward County, Va., where he also taught for two years. He was the minister of First Presbyterian Church in Lynchburg, Va., and in 1857 became chaplain of the University of Virginia (Hoge, *Sketch of Dabney Carr Harrison*). When the war broke out, Harrison enlisted at Mechanicsville, Va., as a captain and formed Company K of the 56th Virginia Infantry on 6 August 1861. He was wounded at Fort Donelson, Tenn., on 16 February 1862 and died of his wounds while being transferred to Nashville. In his will, dated 3 January 1862, he left books, furniture, and $500 in Confederate bonds to his wife, Sally Pendleton Buchanan Harrison (b. 1833), who also filed a claim for Confederate back pay in the amount of $329.00. In 1896 Dabney's widow published in the *Confederate Veteran* magazine a request for information on the location of her husband's grave ("Widow's Moan," 40).

46. Charles Bruce and his Staunton Hill Artillery had been ordered to report to General

Robert E. Lee
(Library of Congress)

Lee will certainly put him behind breastworks. Lee is very cautious—too much so it is said by some. This remains to be seen. He had no army in Western Va.

God bless you my precious wife.

E[ve]r y[ou]r devoted
Thos. H. Carter

—∞—

Camp near the Rapidan Station
March 22nd 1862

My darling wife,

I know you have felt uneasiness about me & our movements on this line, but I have been unable to relieve you as I wished to do. The mail has been kept so far in our rear that it has been {im}possible to communicate with {you.} By Sutton I sent you a message & on his return to

---

R. E. Lee at Coosawhatchie, S.C., in mid-January (see Bruce's CSR). Lee remained in command of Southern coastal defenses there until his return to Virginia on 4 March to serve as President Davis's military adviser (*OR* 6:400).

us a few days since he has stated it had been forwarded to you.[47] This I trust explained my silence & relieved your anxiety. Sutton has gone to R[ichmond] again with a dispatch from Rodes. Had I known this plan I could have written. We commenced our march backwards on Saturday the 8th inst & reached here Thursday the 20th a distance of fifty five miles. At the Rappahannock River we remained several days to allow the troops to come up & to rest, also to give time to the citizens to pull back with their effects. The loss in negroes was heavy, hundreds leaving every night, some were caught. The people were much alarmed & distressed & complained that {they} should have been forewarned. {This} however might have endangered the success of the movement. The country we have crossed & abandoned is the best portion of Virginia, but it was a necessary movement since the reverses in the West. At Manassas we were at a deadlock & had to keep a fine army idle awaiting the pleasure of the enemy[,] he being impregnably fortified at Washington. Here we prevent the flank movements of the Valley or the navigable Rappahannock. Jackson has no army in the former to check the enemy (5,000 being his number) & the Rappahannock is defenseless.[48] Harry Heth has no troops to oppose the movement on foot in Western Va. which is aimed probably at our Western Railroad & in view of this state of things Gordonsville is the main point to hold. Jackson {will} hold the other end of the Central at Staunton as long as possible I presume & Heth will join him when forced back. Things look to a concentration, as in the west & then will come the tug of war to save Va. I doubt if this point will be attacked but some flank movement[,] Rappahannock or the Valley (the former, I think)[,] will be tried. We are fifteen miles in front of Gordonsville three miles back of the Rapidan (the West Branch of the Rappahannock) our present line of defense. We occupy the right but Hill's Division & two Brigades of this Division are still farther to our right in the direction of Fredericksburg which is some thirty miles distant. The success of our cause now depends on A. S. Johnston & Beauregard. If they whip Buell [and] retake Tenn, & Kentucky we are safe, if not we shall be compelled to take to

47. Lieutenant Philip Taylor Sutton (1833–1902) served as an aide-de-camp to General Rodes. A native of Hanover County, Va., Sutton attended the College of William and Mary. He was later wounded in action at the Battle of Seven Pines and lost an arm. He never fully recovered and subsequently resigned from the army on 27 December 1862. Sutton became a tobacco merchant in Richmond (Krick, *Staff Officers*, 278).

48. Jackson reported that he had total of 3,087 men present for duty at the Battle of Kernstown, which took place on 23 March—the day after Carter's letter (*OR* 12[1]:383).

the mountains of the Southwest with what res{ults} God only knows.⁴⁹ A. S. Johnston I have no confidence in. Beauregard will do everything that an undaunted & skillful general can do with limited means. We are near Col Taliaferro's at Rapidan Station. It is a sweet place. Do you know them well enough to visit them[?] The passenger train runs I think only to Orange Ct House five miles back of that place. Don't act as hastily as you generally do, but write an answer. There is close by me a fine house belonging to Mrs Taliaferro.⁵⁰ She was a Miss Carter sister to Alfred B. Carter of Mississippi.⁵¹ Uncle Hill & I[,] you recollect[,] stayed with him some time.⁵² Charles Randolph's family is with them at this time. I wish you could board near me. As usual, we are placed in an out of the way position on the right. Your last letter was the 14th [from] Staunton Hill, but doubtless there are others in the P.O. Wm joined us at the Rappahannock Station[,] also Julian. They were run off by the Yankees. Papa with Renshaw[,] Lucy & some of the servants & horses went by way of Staunton to Pampatike. Mama remained alone with two or three servants. I hope she was not molested. She refused to leave. If she had some associates the plan would be a good one but I am uneasy about her alone. The policy of the enemy is obviously to conciliate now that the invasion is begun on so large a scale save as to our negroes, but as they are ours all their efforts at conciliation will be fruitless. The march of our troops backward was a shameful exhibition of want of decency & discipline. Poultry yards were swept, horses impressed also wagons[,] rails burnt, houses & kitchens entered & robbed. These acts were committed by stragglers & the worst of them by the Louisiana Tigers, the Mississippi River scoundrels. One was shot by a citizen. This want of discipline results from the 12 mo[nth]s volunteering instead of the war, & from the elective system. The officers from Cols down are courting popularity to be reelected at the reorga-

49. Brigadier General Don Carlos Buell (1818–98) of Ohio commanded the Union Army of the Ohio (Eicher and Eicher, *High Commands*, 152).

50. Louisa Carter Taliaferro (1815–76) was married to Benjamin F. Taliaferro (d. 1855). The couple lived at Mount Sharon in Orange County, Va. (Hardy, *Colonial Families of the Southern States*, 117). After the war, she operated the Mount Sharon Select School for Young Ladies in Orange County (Minor Family Papers, 1810–1932, VHS).

51. Alfred Ball Carter (1823–1901) of King William County served in the 6th Virginia Cavalry as a first lieutenant and later captain of Company F. He was twice wounded in action and later assigned to services in the reserves in March 1865. Before the war, he had lived in Mississippi, where, like the Carter family, he operated a plantation (Randolph Family Bible records, 1825–1901, VHS; CSR). Alfred's sister was Louisa Carter Taliaferro (see previous note).

52. Hill Carter (b. 1795) was the older brother of Tom Carter's father, Thomas Nelson Carter (McGill, *Beverley Family of Virginia*, 463).

nization & the Generals can do nothing without the cooperation of the subordinate officers. Wm reports that in Jefferson the Yankees behaved well. Many persons have fled before them with their servants & effects. Every servant should be taken back by law. The male can be employed in the army as teamsters[,] cooks & to work on intrenchments. Instead of this their owners procrastinate until too late & the negroes get off in whole families. Ours at Pampatike are in no danger. When the danger arises you might send them to Charlotte. Papa then would have to get some agent to take his to the South. Time enough for this when that country is threatened. My stocks ought to be changed into Confederate bonds. They are in Mr Rose's vault in the Farmers' Bank. Wortham knows all about them. See him. I shall write again in a few days. Papa is now at Pampatike I suppose. They just escaped in time. The Yankee Cavalry reached Funsten's farm the same day he left. I was truly grieved to hear of the death of Dr Turner. He was a sincere friend of mine & has been of invaluable service to me since this war. Poor old gentleman, he died of a broken heart I imagine. This war to his despondent nature must end only in ruin. He was buried by his own request at Pampatike. It is said he pointed out the spot in the graveyard. None will mourn his loss more than I do except his own family.

The messenger is waiting. I must close. Write to me at Orange Ct House. No [post] office at Rapidan Station. Kiss my precious children. Love to Aunt Sarah & Sister.

God bless you darling.

—ᴍ—

Camp Rapidan
March 23rd 1862

My dearest wife

I wrote yesterday & directed the letter to the care of Wortham. I write again today to ask when you come (if you think it proper to visit the Taliaferros) that you will bring several things for me. While waiting at the ford the other day a little son of the Col said the family intended to remain at home [and] that his father was in Jackson's Army but the ladies were at home. If you prefer I can get lodgings I suppose at Orange Ct House five miles distant. I understand the cars run to Rapidan Station. You ought of course to have an escort. If you could bring the children it would be a great comfort, or even Thomas alone. I want my new coat, a cravat[,] my best pair of pants, some red tape or material for stripes on my present uniform, & a box of dye, that I may spruce up for your benefit. I can see you several times a week I hope. The furloughed men report that two of my teams & wagons have been impressed. The burden of war is not equally divided. Eight mules from one estate while others go free is unjust. No one objects to anything that is necessary, but hundreds of teams & hands could have been obtained from the country just abandoned. It is well Papa has gone to Pampatike. These young officers sent to impress take where they can get without regard to the proprieties. My great grandfather spent his whole fortune in the revolution for his country & never a cent was ever repaid to him or his heirs.[53] The payment of taxes will be a fair mode of distributing the burden. I am willing to give half if others are required to do the same, & by the way[,] we may have to give all. Seven of the men are at Yorktown. With a little management & energy, thousands [of mules] might have been hired from the country we have left. Davis & Johnston have been in consultation several days at Gordonsville.[54]

God bless you my precious wife.

—⚬—

Camp Rapidan
April 1st 1862

My darling Wife,

I have but a moment to write by a messenger to Gordonsville. Our mails at this point have been interrupted for some time. On Thursday I was sent to Gordonsville to get ammunition. That night the whole army received orders to march. My Battery was ordered to Richmond by way of Louisa Ct House. They marched nearly to that point before the order was countermanded. I was not with it but at Gordonsville. Johnston is now in Richmond, expected today. I think the question is whether to fight on this line or at the Junction of the Fredericksburg & Central Railroads. The enemy are on our front at the Rappahannock. I don't know in what force. If we fall back to Richmond some step ought to be taken in regard to the servants. They will all go notwithstanding their profession of attachment. This has been the case in our front & in the

53. Carter is referring to Charles Carter (1732–1806).
54. President Davis traveled to General J. E. Johnston's headquarters, where the two discussed the current strategic situation in Virginia (Cooper, *Jefferson Davis*, 403).

Valley I understand. Very large numbers have gone, indeed all that chose to go. Whole families have gone. It is hardly worthwhile to change the stocks. They are probably as safe as any other investment. Wm Taliaferro arrived last night. Reported for duty this morning. Saw you in Richd, he says. I wish I could see you before this engagement comes off, but the trains are under military control & run irregularly, & there is great difficulty between Gordonsville & this place. Wm Taliaferro was delayed somewhat on the route between here & Richmond from Friday till last night. I should not be able to hear from you by mail, so don't rely on that mode to communicate with me. Before you leave Richmond learn if we are moving back. We expect to do so every day [and] are under marching orders all the time with three days rations ahead[,] hard bread & pork.

Give much love to Papa & the Renshaws. I hope you are all comfortable at Pampatike. Mr Lee is wounded, but not dangerously, in the fleshy part of his thigh.[55] Mason's house not burnt nor McDonald's, nor Funstan's—nothing done but to stock[,] servants & forage. If we fall back try & meet me in Richd. I will endeavor to telegraph you through Wortham from Louisa Ct House. God bless you my precious wife & children. Kiss them for me.

In haste
Ever y[ou]r devoted husband.

—w—

Yorktown
April 13th 1862

My precious wife,

I arrived here (or rather at Lebanon Church, four miles distant) the night after I left you. The next morning came to Shield's Farm, Early's Hdqrs, & remained there until yesterday when I was ordered to Wynns Mill & five minutes after ordered to this place.[56] You can not conceive of the loathsome filth of this place. We are encamped within the fortifications & live mixed with infantry & artillery after the most piggish style. My guns are separated from Dan to Beersheba, & all of the artillery of

55. Carter is referring to Lieutenant Richard Henry Lee of the 2nd Virginia Infantry, who was wounded at the Battle of Kernstown (CSR).
56. Wynne's Mill, which Carter misspelled as "Wynns" and Winns" in this letter, was located on the Warwick River and incorporated into Major General John B. Magruder's line of Confederate defenses.

this work under a Major Goode son of Wm O. Goode.[57] My Brigade is close by, Rodes having spent a week or so in getting together his Regiments which were scattered over the Peninsula. Orders are sent to me directly from Magruder without going through Hill[,] Early & Rodes.[58] The two latter seem to have a *big disgust* on them. Rodes is suffering seriously from violent catarrh & can hardly talk.[59] I am much annoyed at the separation from my Brigade. It breaks in upon the esprit de corps. The feeling between the Regts & the Battery is very strong. They boast high on us, & when I went in one of the forts redoubts where the 12th Mississippi was stationed they gave me three hearty cheers. Thompson Brown was anxious I should be at Winns Mill.[60] But for my ear I should have seen him today. I can assure you this earache has annoyed me beyond expression. The pain is not acute except at times but the discharge & deafness & dull aching & unceasing rumbling is distressing indeed. Jack Page syringed it out last night but I thought it more painful in the night.[61] The secretion of a watery waxy fluid is profuse, & I can hardly hear in the open air.

57. John Thomas Goode (1835–1916) of Mecklenburg County, Va., was a graduate of the Virginia Military Institute who served as a lieutenant in the U.S. Artillery from 1855 to 1861. He entered Confederate service as a captain of artillery on 16 March 1861 and was later promoted to major in October 1861 and to lieutenant colonel in late April 1862. At the time of Carter's letter, Goode was serving as chief of artillery and ordnance at Yorktown, Va. (Krick, *Lee's Colonels*, 159; *OR* 11[3]:438). His father, William Osborne Goode (1798–1859), was a lawyer and a politician who served in the Virginia House of Delegates between 1822 and 1852, including three terms as speaker, and in the U.S. House of Representatives in 1841 and from 1853 until his death in 1859 (*Biographical Directory of the United States Congress,* "William Osborne Goode," http://bioguide .congress.gov/scripts/biodisplay.pl?index=G000281 [accessed 30 Sept. 2013]).

58. Major General Daniel Harvey Hill (1821–89) of South Carolina commanded the division that included Rodes's brigade and Carter's battery (CSR).

59. Catarrh is the profuse discharge from the nose and eyes that generally accompanies a common cold.

60. Major John Thompson Brown (1835–64) of Petersburg, Va., enlisted in the 2nd Company of Richmond Howitzers on 21 April 1861. In May he was elected captain, and in September he became a major. Three artillery pieces of the 2nd Richmond Howitzers were in position at Wynn's Mill as part of the Warwick River defenses (CSR; *OR* 11[1]:413).

61. John Randolph Page (1830–1901) was a surgeon in charge of a Confederate general hospital in Yorktown, Va. He was a native of Gloucester County, Va., and graduated with a medical degree from the University of Virginia in 1850. For several years, he studied at clinics in Paris, France, before returning to practice medicine in Gloucester County. On 19 July 1861, Page was appointed assistant surgeon in the Confederate army and served briefly with the 18th Virginia Infantry. In December 1861 he reported to Brigadier General William Nelson Pendleton to serve as assistant surgeon in the artillery corps. The following January, Page was transferred to General John B. Magruder's command at Yorktown, where he directed the "new general hospital." Later in the war, Page served as surgeon at general hospitals in Lynchburg and Richmond. He was paroled at Richmond on 15 April 1865. After the war, Page taught medicine at Louisiana State Seminary in Alexandria, La.; at Washington Medical College in Baltimore, Md.; and at the

I do trust the Yankees will make some movement which will prevent the possibility of summer campaign here. If Beauregard has repulsed Buell's army & killed him & if we can defeat McClellan I hope the end of the war is within sight. We had a very pretty skirmish the evening I reached here.[62] My Battery was not engaged. From the miserable engineering near Redoubt No. 5 a peach orchard & fence had been left standing. Behind the fence rifle pits were dug in the night by the enemy & their sharpshooters placed in them only from 400 to 600 yards from our works & encampments. They have killed & wounded some 8 or 10 in our Brigade & were firing at every head that peeped over a redoubt. This became so annoying that Early threw out skirmishers to dislodge them. From the fort I saw it all. Col. Ward behaved very gallantly with his 2nd Florida Regt.[,] dashing in on horseback & leading his men through the orchard.[63] He was eager to take the enemys battery which was firing in the rear of the orchard. Several of our men were wounded & one or two have mortally. The Yankees ran like clever fellows until they reached their battery. The fence & barn were burned. Last night the remaining houses were burnt & the orchard cut down which should have been done before the enemy came up. It is most remarkable the enemy should have been allowed to come right up on our last line of defence & with their glass examine every work, plant their batteries & throw up works within sight. No advance cor{ps} at all. Men[,] wagons[,] horses fired at on the road to Yorktown. Many balls whistled by me the first day, & they were firing all day at our men. Johnston arrived yesterday. Magruder was very late. He seemed glad Johnston was to come.

I have thought unceasingly of you & the children. Your thousand acts of tenderness & devotion to me my darling are appreciated & treasured

---

University of Virginia. He also served as chief surgeon of the Georgia Pacific Railroad and of the Sloss Iron and Steel Works before failing health forced him to return to Charlottesville, Va., where he died on 11 March 1901 (CSR; 1860 Census, Gloucester County; *OR* 11[3]: 457; Richey, *Memorial History of the John Bowie Strange Camp*, 83–84).

62. Carter is referring to a skirmish on 5 April 1862 in which Brigadier General Jubal Early ordered a sortie against Union troops located in a peach orchard near Redoubt 5 in the Confederate defenses on the Warwick River line. The 2nd Florida Infantry and the 2nd Mississippi Battalion pushed into the orchard and successfully drove the Union force back (*OR* 11[1]:406).

63. Colonel George Taliaferro Ward (1810–62) commanded the 2nd Florida Infantry in Brigadier General Jubal A. Early's brigade. Though a native of Fayette County, Ky., when the war began, Ward was a wealthy planter and banker in Leon County, Fla., worth $130,650 in personal property and $70,000 in real property (1860 Census, Leon County). On 12 July 1861, he became colonel of the 2nd Florida Infantry. Colonel Ward was killed in action at the Battle of Williamsburg and is buried there at Bruton Parish Church (Krick, *Lee's Colonels*, 391; *OR* 11[1]:569).

by me. No man has ever been blessed with a more devoted & true wife than you have been to me. I wish you to remember this if I should fall. I only wish I were worthy of your devotion, but you know my heart beats only for you & my children.

Everyone here has been very kind[,] particularly Wm Nelson[64] of Hanover & Jack Page. There seems some doubt now of a battle here. Can't tell anything about it. Every thing is in confusion here. Johnston will change matters. I have bought a horse & will send Nelson home. I lost my gauntlets. Try to send me a pair by some person. If I am to stay here, I should like my new coat & pants.

Much love to all. God ever bless you dearest & my children.

Y[ou]r own husband
Thos. H. Carter

—m—

Near Yorktown
April 21st 1862

My precious Wife,

I have written twice since my arrival here but I fear from the irregularity of the mails they will be delayed on the route. I have received one from you through Rodes. I know you have written oftener but the letters have been delayed. We are still near Yorktown expecting a battle hourly. If the enemy bring up a fleet & plant a siege train in the woods on our front I have no idea that Yorktown will stand. It is impossible. We know that the best forts of masonry have fallen by dint of heavy firing & the resources of the enemy in this respect are almost boundless. By land we can whip them I think.

I do not know what to advise in regard to the servants at Pampatike. I believe half or three fourths of them will leave when the Yankees approach in foraging & marauding parties. Still I do not believe they

---

64. William Nelson (1807–92) commanded the Hanover Light Artillery, which was stationed near Lee's Mill on the Warwick River defenses. A prewar farmer from Hanover County, Va., Nelson organized the Hanover Light Artillery on 17 May 1861 and served as its first captain. Almost from the start, his stern manner and tendency toward strictness made him unpopular with his men; when the unit reorganized on 20 April 1862, the men did not reelect Captain Nelson. On 26 May he was promoted to major and given command of an artillery battalion. Later in the war, Nelson rose to the rank of colonel and continued to command an artillery battalion (*OR* 11[1]:413; Moore, *Miscellaneous Disbanded Virginia Light Artillery*, 46, 120; Runge, *Four Years in the Confederate Artillery*, xvi–xvii).

(the Yankees) can reach Richmond but as soon as they get Yorktown they have possession of York River & our country will be open to marauders. The Army of course would not molest us as there is nothing they want except forage & our negroes which by the way is a great deal. My opinion is that the enemy are so close to our last line (Yorktown which is in short range of their field & siege Artillery) that in order to hold it we ought to attack them & drive them back & occupy a line a mile or two in front, cleaning away the woods which have afforded entire protection thus far to all their machinations. Such engineering the world never saw[—]to leave a woods which conceals their movements while we are in full view with naked eye. The plan would seem to be when the bombardment begins Johnston should attack on our right & break up their devilish arrangements. Our fortifications with a few exceptions are flimsy enough. I am having bomb proofs made for the cannoneers which will be some protection. The parapet is so low that I would prefer fighting on the field where[,] by changing the position of our guns every few minutes by hand[,] the range of the enemy's guns is broken & ravines & hollows can be used for the caissons. Johnston's whole army[,] except Ewell's Division & three Cavalry Regts[,] is here.[65] Magruder commands the right, Longstreet the center & Hill the left, & G. W. Smith the reserve. Stuart's Cavalry is here. Johnston commands the whole, & the military & naval operations of Norfolk & the Peninsula. Julian[,] Wm Newton[,] Wms Wickham[,] Col. Pendleton's Artillery[,] Washington's Artillery all here—a force between fifty & sixty thousand. There has been some dissatisfaction among the troops relative to the Conscription act. Some wish to leave *now* in the presence of the enemy, showing how little can be trusted to the dear people. Thirty nine of Pryor's Regt. asked for a discharge to join another Regt. near Portsmouth, in which they had re-enlisted.[66] They were put to work in the trenches under guard. If there is much more difficulty in this matter Johnston will make an example—shooting a few. If the Conscription act had not been passed

65. General Richard S. Ewell's division was cooperating with General Thomas J. Jackson's force, then operating in the Shenandoah Valley. In mid-April Ewell's command, which was encamped near Brandy Station in Culpeper County, Va., included, along with his infantry, the 2nd, 6th, and 7th Virginia Cavalry regiments.

66. Colonel Roger Atkinson Pryor (1828–1919) of Virginia commanded the 3rd Virginia Infantry. Originally formed at Portsmouth, Va., on 20 April 1861, the unit reorganized on 27 April 1862. Apparently at that time, several of the men in the unit no longer wanted to serve under Pryor, whom they found to be "too overbearing" (Warner, *Generals in Gray*, 247–48; Wallace, *3rd Virginia Infantry*, 22).

so soon we should have been ruined.[67] Whole regiments would have left in the midst of a battle. Men will not stand this work except by compulsion or from principle[,] Demagogarism to the contrary. Whole Divisions are lying in the trenches night & day[,] in fair & foul weather[,] without cover. If the men who bring on war had to fight as *privates* there would never be another.

I sent my horse by Wm Edwards. Please get my watch from Mr Fontaine. I shall not require the saddle bags. To my watch was attached my class ring. God bless you my own darling. My heart overflows with affection for you. Embrace my sweetest little children.

Ever y[ou]r own husband

———⁓———

Yorktown
April 26th 1862

My precious Wife,

Since I last wrote, two letters from you have been received. The first from Pampatike the last, an old one, from Richmond. I enclose several letters from Orange Ct House—old ones but of interest perhaps to you. I think you have received a later letter from Mama. The one from Pauline to her is of interest also.

We are still awaiting the pleasure of McClellan who is regularly intrenching himself & getting ready for siege operations. Everything is quiet except an occasional fire from the river on Yorktown & on our lines here & a return from our guns on the boats & intrenchments. The pickets are in full view, also their wagons hauling lumber from a steam saw

67. The conscription act that Carter referred to was passed by the Confederate Congress on 16 April 1862. It was the first of three enacted by the government during the war. Simply stated, it drafted into military service all white males between the ages of eighteen and thirty-five for three years or the duration of the war. Those men already in the army would serve a total of three years from their original date of enlistment. Soldiers who joined the army in 1861—the original twelve-month volunteers—qualified for a sixty-day leave of absence and had the right to reorganize their units and elect their officers. New enlistees had the option to volunteer before they could be conscripted, and they could participate in the election of officers or join already-existing units to serve with friends or relatives (Lund, "Conscription," 396–99).

The act also provided exemptions from the draft for the following occupations: Confederate and state officials; war-industry laborers; railroad employees; teachers; ministers; druggists; hospital attendants; and the physically and mentally disabled. Additionally, the act included the "Twenty-Slave Law," which exempted one white male on any farm with more than twenty slaves. To prevent men from avoiding the draft by becoming overseers, the law stipulated that individuals had to have been employed as such before 16 April 1862.

mill. I throw a shell among them now & then & they take to their heels & quickly abscond. When the great struggle will begin no one knows. I fear nothing but their gunboats at Yorktown. If they pass there in any force we must fall back to the Chickahominy which leaves open our country. I have a sort of hope that the Merrimac may keep off the fleet & yet that removal from the James River would be dangerous.[68] I hope however she may be a terror on both sides—the York & the James. I feel much uneasiness as to the result of this conflict. So much depends on it. Our state will be lost if we are defeated. The Fredericksburg Column will make an effort first I think.[69] Ewell[,] Jackson & Field[,] with such reinforcements as Genl. Lee may be able to send from various places[,] will hold the enemy in check unless much stronger than we suppose.[70] On the Infantry line here we can keep back McClellan, but I doubt the water. There was some disturbance in Pryor's Regt. in a Compy whose term had expired, but thirty nine were put in the trenches at work & soon came to their senses & wrote the most penitential letters stating that they misunderstood the Conscript Law. There will be no more trouble except on the score of electioneering. The election of officers will take place in a month & after that we shall have a good army. Tell Lucy with the best love of Wm & myself that her letter was received & we thank her for it. I hope you are all comfortable at Pampatike. Tell Mr Renshaw to run down & see us. We will give him soldier's fare—a real soldiers fare. We have had the hardest time of all in the trenches night & day & it rains incessantly. Without shelter thousands of men sleep in mud & mire & rain. Some of them spread a blanket over a pole on forks & pin down the ends. With the other blanket they wrap themselves & sleep & shiver {remainder of letter missing}

—⁂—

68. The *Merrimack* was a Union screw steamer that was partially burned and scuttled by Federal forces as they evacuated Norfolk, Va., on 20–21 April 1861. Confederates subsequently raised the ship and converted her into an ironclad. Rechristened the CSS *Virginia*, she attacked with ease several Union wooden vessels at Hampton Roads on 8 March 1862. The next day, the *Virginia* fought against the *Monitor* in the first battle between ironclad ships. The contest ended in a draw. After Norfolk fell to the Union on 9 May 1862, the *Virginia*, which could not reach a safe place, was scuttled by her Confederate crew to prevent her capture (Boatner, *Dictionary*, 560–61).

69. Carter is referring to the Union force at Fredericksburg. Under the command of Irvin McDowell, this Department of the Rappahannock consisted of three divisions led by William Buel Franklin (1823–1903), George Archibald McCall (1802–68), and Rufus King (1814–76) (*OR* 5:21, 11[3]:67–68).

70. Brigadier General Charles William Field (1828–92) of Kentucky commanded an infantry brigade in the Confederate Aquia District (Eicher and Eicher, *High Commands*, 234).

My dearest Wife

Mr Dudley has just arrived bringing me the sad intelligence of my darling boy's illness which I fear must terminate fatally.[71] I wish indeed it were in my power to be with you & him but it is utterly useless unless to apply for a furlough of more than 24 hours & even that would not be granted probably. I consulted with Rodes as to the propriety of making application & as to the possibility of getting leave of absence, & he thinks it improper & impossible, in which opinion, however much it wrings my heart, I fully concur. God knows how much I long to go to you both & see him once more but it is impossible. War is the greatest evil that ever befell a nation—it is the aggregate of all evils. My own darling wife you must put your trust in that Heavenly Father who alone can alleviate our sufferings & if our precious child is taken from us our loss is his gain. He will be saved the troubles of this mortal life & soon be introduced into that blissful state which is the only object worth living for. He will leave this miserable world, pure & free from guile & his bright spirit will join our other little darling in Heaven where I hope we shall all be reunited. It almost breaks my heart not to see him. Is there no hope? Write every day. I shall be in such suspense until I hear. The mail comes here but does not return & has to be sent by private hands. I wrote yesterday enclosing a letter from Mama & Papa. What brought on this attack? The overseer says it is Diphtheria. You speak of it as Bronchitis. I fear it is Scarlet Fever or Pneumonia. Has he been well since we parted in Richd? Dear dear little fellow. I cannot help hoping he may be spared to us yet. May not your fears have exaggerated his attack? If I could go to you it would be a great relief to me as well as yourself but we know not what an hour will bring forth. The cannon are firing this morning with regularity bursting shell over Yorktown from the vessels. Last night there was a slight skirmish among the pickets in front of my redoubts. Yet I think the battle may not be fought for some days, until one is fought between Fredericksburg & Richd. Still where death prevails all around the Generals would not hear of my leaving. It is one of the trials of these times. God grant they may soon end. Darling my heart bleeds to think of my

---

71. Carter's son Thomas Nelson survived this unidentified illness and lived until 1917.

sweet little boy dying & I not near him but I can do nothing. I can't leave my post now. Pray to God for help. Write daily. Love to all.

Y[ou]r own devoted husband.

—⁓—

Yorktown
April 29th 1862

My dearest wife,

It was with inexpressible joy that I heard last night by telegraph from Mr Thos Robinson that our precious boy was better. He saw Thomas Gregory & was so kind as to telegraph me at once on his arrival at West Point.[72] Planter is to go home today for Armistead & to return Friday.[73] I send this note by him. Write by him on his return. I feel grateful to God for this great mercy & rejoiced that you have experienced such relief from this severe trial. I am well. My ear is much better & my hearing returns gradually & I trust will not be impaired. My company reorganized yesterday. I was unanimously re-elected but they turned out every one of my Lieutenants—Fontaine[,] Ryland & Hawes much to my regret. Wm Carter was elected 1st Lieutenant[,] Newman 2nd Lieut & Dabney 3rd Lieut. There is some doubt whether the election was valid. Rodes thinks those men who re-enlisted—over 35 & under 18[—]will not be held in service.

Early[,] Genl Lee &c. think they will. The Secretary of War has been telegraphed to know. If they are held to service they are entitled to a vote & the election will be held over. I fear Wm will not be re-elected[,] for in the election yesterday his vote was only 5 more than Ryland's & they adopted the plan of running one for each Lieutenancy & if he failed[,] to drop him. But for this arrangement Wm would stand a chance for 2nd or 3rd Lieutenancy if he missed the 1st Lieut. Still he is very popular & may get one. He came out & told the Company he did not wish to run against Ryland & Hawes but would run for the 3rd Lieutenancy. They ran him notwithstanding. He acted very well about it & Ryland has no hard feelings towards him. No attack yet. The enemy are throwing up breastworks apparently for siege operations. They shell Yorktown every

---

72. Thomas Robinson (b. 1812?) was a farmer from King William County, Va., and a neighbor of Dr. Thomas Gregory (b. 1827?), a local physician (1860 Census, King William County).
73. Planter has not been identified.

night, that is, they throw a dozen or so without much damage—one man killed only. Col. Crump who commands Gloucester Pt. with two or three Regts has undoubted evidence of their intention to land forces on his side.[74] He says no troops have left McClellan's army. On the contrary, large re-inforcements have been sent him. The capture of New Orleans is a heavy blow, cutting of[f] four states.[75] Don't know when the attack will be made here.

Much love to Papa & the Renshaws. Tell Lucy I will answer her letter & am much obliged for it. I am glad the wheat was saved. Dudley deserves credit for it, or Carrington. Armistead Braxton is still here. God bless you & my precious children. Gregory seems to think Thomas out of danger. God grant it. My relief is very great. The telegram came by a courier in the night. Rodes sent it to me.

E[ve]r y[ou]r devoted husband.

—⁂—

May 1st 1862

My dearest wife,

I avail myself of Mr Robins' polite offer to send you a line. Your letter by Pat was received yesterday & I was rejoiced to hear of the continued improvement of Thomas. God be thanked for his mercy in this matter. The saddle bags arrived safely with the contents. The boxes have not arrived but are in the vessel near Yorktown. These vessels are cautious in landing since the establishment of a land Battery which shells them with great accuracy. The Logan Steamboat has to run at night without lights to avoid the fire of this battery. No attack yet. I do not think Yorktown

74. Colonel Charles Alfred Crump (1822–62) of Powhatan County, Va., commanded Confederate defenses at Gloucester Point. He was a graduate of the Virginia Military Institute, a prewar colonel of the Nottoway County militia, and a delegate representing Amelia and Nottoway Counties in the Virginia legislature. Crump began the war as lieutenant colonel in the 16th Virginia Infantry in May 1861. Two months later, he was appointed colonel of the 26th Virginia Infantry but was dropped from the regiment when the unit reorganized in May 1862. On 28 August 1862, Crump rejoined the 16th Virginia as its colonel. Two days later, he was killed at the Battle of Second Bull Run (*OR* 11[3]:470; Krick, *Lee's Colonels*, 104–5; CSR). Crump's command at Gloucester Point consisted of the 26th Virginia Infantry, the 3rd Virginia Cavalry (one company), the 1st Virginia Artillery (one company), the 4th Heavy Artillery Battalion, and the 9th, 21st, and 87th Virginia Militia regiments (*OR*, 9:37). Perhaps Carter was unaware of the presence of the militia units, or he was discounting their usefulness.

75. New Orleans fell to Union naval forces under Admiral David Glasgow Farragut on 25 April 1862 (Boatner, *Dictionary*, 591).

tenable. It will be a repetition of Pulaski, Macon[,] Jackson &c. &c. but they are still sending guns & mounting them.[76] If the rain ever stops & the roads improve Johnston will retire behind the Chickahominy I suppose. Our guns are the old smooth bores that cannot contend with the improved Federal Artillery.[77] We shall lose our servants & teams & forage to a considerable extent, should they fall back.

There was shelling for an hour or so last night & some musketry but no one knows when the great struggle will take place. No answer to the telegraph until today in regard to the re-enlistment [of] men over 35 & under 18. It has come but I have not heard the tenor of it. If the election is held over it is probable Wm will be defeated for 1st Lieutenancy as the popular favor is proverbially fickle & a new class of voters will come in.

I am glad to get the coffee. Should we save the box[?] Tea I prefer in camp. It is better than coffee made hurriedly.

Our defense of forts has become a farce. Better to evacuate before the attack & save the powder[,] other ammunition & the men[,] say nothing of their reputation which surrenders with "Nobody hurt." I hardly know whether to advise you to run or remain should we retire to the Chickahominy. I believe you would be perfectly safe but cut off from me. Still you are really separated now. I trust dear Lucy & the children are well & comfortable. I wish I could be with her & Mr Renshaw at Pampatike. Tell the latter if he has any desire to see the famous Yorktown we will give him the best accommodations the place can afford.

Any contract with Gresham & Dabney which can be made with a fair price for the wheat at the landing had better be done.[78] My own opinion is that the possession of our country by the Yankees is just a question of time—and that a short time. Our only plan is to get them on terra firma & they have never gotten any advantage worthy of mention there. On water they are superior for obvious reasons. Kiss my dear little ones & tell Thomas Papa has thought of him day & night & has been mighty

76. Fort Pulaski (near Savannah), Fort Macon (near Bogue Point, N.C.), and Fort Jackson (on the Mississippi River about seventy miles south of New Orleans) fell to Union forces on 11, 25, and 28 April 1862, respectively.

77. The interior of the barrels of smoothbore cannon were smooth and therefore less effective for long-range firing. The Union army had a large supply of newer rifled artillery that could fire more accurately over a longer range because of the effect that grooves inside the barrel had on the fired shells (Gottfried, *Artillery of Gettysburg*, 13).

78. Carter may be referring to O. S. Gresham, a merchant in King William County (1860 Census, King William County). Dabney is unidentified.

anxious to see him. I wish I had something to send him. God bless him & raise him up to be a useful Christian man. Wms Wickham spent Sunday with me. His Father[,] in his letters[,] is strongly Union & thinks the war will not last long since the border states are captured.[79] Our army can not subsist.

> God bless you my darling wife.
> Ev[er] your own devoted husband.

79. Carter is referring to his uncle William Fanning Wickham (1793–1880), the father of Williams Carter Wickham. William Fanning Wickham was a farmer in Hanover County, Va., whose wife, Anne Butler Carter Wickham, was Carter's aunt (Cashin, "Landscape and Memory," 493; McGill, *Beverley Family of Virginia*, 465).

—m—

To Maryland and Back

13 July–17 December 1862

Three days after writing to his wife on 1 May, Tom Carter and his battery evacuated their position near Yorktown and marched west along muddy roads toward Richmond. After arriving near the capital city a few days later, the King William Artillery settled into camp until the last day of May. On the thirty-first, Carter and his battery experienced their first battle when Johnston ordered a major attack against the one-third of McClellan's army that lay east of Richmond and south of the Chickahominy River. In support of Robert Rodes's brigade, Carter led the King William Artillery and its five guns into the fight along the Williamsburg Road. The battery opened fire on a Union redoubt and helped force its occupants to abandon the position and withdraw. In his official report of the battle, General Rodes reserved special praise for Carter's battery. "The conduct of the King William Artillery," he proclaimed, "has nowhere in the history of the war been equaled for daring, coolness, or efficiency." The fight was a costly one for the unit. The battery lost four men killed or mortally wounded and at least twenty-four wounded. Those numbers, however, were replenished in June, when the unit received more than eighty men from three batteries that had been disbanded.[1]

---

1. Macaluso, *Morris, Orange, and King William Artillery*, 23–25; *OR* 11[1]:975; *RDD*, 3 June 1862. In a brief notation on Rodes's original report, Major General D. H. Hill, Carter's divisional commander, commented on Rodes's words of praise for the battery: "This is a strong expression, and argues that the writer was conversant with the conduct of artillery in all the various actions of the war." In an accompanying endorsement on the report, Hill further challenged Rodes's assessment of the King William Artillery's role in forcing the Union troops to evacuate their redoubt. "The truth is," Hill stated, "[Carter] fired but twice at the redoubts." Instead, argued Hill, it was the fire of another Confederate brigade on the flank of the enemy position that caused the Union soldiers to withdraw (*OR* 11[1]:975–76). Despite this episode, Hill and Carter thought very highly of one another. Later, when Hill was transferred to command in North Carolina in March 1863, he asked Carter to serve as his chief of artillery.

Until the last week of June, Carter and his men rested in the Richmond defenses. On the twenty-sixth, the Confederate army, now under the command of General Robert E. Lee, began a week-long series of attacks against McClellan's army known as the Seven Days Battles. The King William Artillery did not experience heavy service during these clashes. At the battle of Gaines's Mill, the battery unlimbered on the far left of the Confederate line and traded fire with Union guns late in the action. Three days later, at White Oak Swamp, it joined a line of other batteries and engaged enemy artillery. Following the first campaign of Lee's newly dubbed Army of Northern Virginia, Carter and his men once again returned to Richmond to rest. On 24 July Tom Carter's brother Julian, a private in the 4th Virginia Cavalry, was killed in a charge at Malvern Hill. In a letter written later that day to Mary Custis Lee, wife of Robert E. Lee, Tom wrote: "May God soften & bless this sad blow to us all."[2]

The King William Artillery remained in the Richmond area until the end of August, when, on the twenty-sixth, it left Hanover Junction with Hill's division and traveled to Manassas to join the rest of Lee's army following its victory over Major General John Pope's Army of Virginia at the Battle of Second Bull Run. Carter's men arrived in northern Virginia on 3 September and the next day crossed the Potomac River at White's Ferry in the Confederate army's first invasion of the North. His morale was riding high as he made his way into Maryland. Not only was Carter excited at the prospect of what the Confederate army might accomplish there, but he also had great faith in the commanding general. "We all trust in God & Lee," he informed Susan. "He has the entire confidence of the Army."[3]

After resting in Frederick for a few days, Hill's division marched toward Hagerstown on the ninth. On the fourteenth, it defended the passes of the South Mountain range against advance elements of the Army of the Potomac, which had moved west from Washington. Late in the fight at Turner's Gap, Carter's battery supported Robert Rodes's brigade in a desperate action to defend the division's left flank. After stalling the Federals at South Mountain, the Confederates marched to Sharpsburg, where the Army of Northern Virginia planned to reassemble.[4]

Three days later, the King William Artillery took part in the bloody

2. *OR* 11[2]:632; Macaluso, *Morris, Orange, and King William Artillery*, 26–27; THC to Mary Anna Randolph Custis Lee, 24 July 1862, Lee Family Papers, 1732–1892, VHS. In the fight at Gaines's Mill, Carter reported only three men wounded.
3. Macaluso, *Morris, Orange, and King William Artillery*, 27–28; THC to SRC, 7 Sept. 1862.
4. Macaluso, *Morris, Orange, and King William Artillery*, 28; THC to SRC, 4 Oct. 1862.

day-long battle of Antietam. As with many units in Lee's army that day, Carter's battery seemed to be in constant motion from one part of the field to another. Initially posted behind the Confederate center near the Sunken Road early in the morning, the battery withdrew a few hours later in the face of heavy artillery fire to a ridge that ran from the Confederate left near the Dunkard Church south to Sharpsburg. From that position, Carter moved his men in the midafternoon farther to the rear to rearm. Finally, the King William Artillery unlimbered late in the day just east of the village near the Boonsboro Turnpike. There, it supported the dramatic attack on the Union left flank by Major General A. P. Hill's division. At some point during the battle, Carter suffered a slight wound when a spent shell struck his foot and mashed one of his toes. The unit lost six men (two killed, three wounded, and one missing) and several of its horses. On the night of 18 September, Carter's guns acted as rearguard artillery for the army as it crossed the Potomac River back into Virginia.[5]

Lee's army spent most of the next two months bivouacked in the lower Shenandoah Valley between Winchester and Bunker Hill. At the beginning of October, the Army of Northern Virginia reorganized its artillery by reducing the number of batteries and removing ineffective officers. The King William Artillery, replenished with men from the disbanded Turner Artillery from Goochland County, Virginia, now served in a battalion in D. H. Hill's division. Tom Carter, though only a captain, commanded the battalion, which consisted of his former battery (now under his brother William P. P. Carter) and the Morris, Orange, and Jeff Davis Artilleries. On 1 November, Hill named Carter as his chief of artillery. Stonewall Jackson's newly designated 2nd Corps, in which the division served, remained in the valley until 20 November. On that date, it began to move toward Fredericksburg, where Longstreet's 1st Corps had already gone to counter the movement of the Army of the Potomac, now commanded by Major General Ambrose E. Burnside. On 3 December, Carter and the King William Artillery took part in a brief expedition to Port Royal, south of Fredericksburg, where they fired on Union naval vessels. They returned to Jackson's corps on 12 December, the day before the Battle of Fredericksburg. During that day-long conflict, the battalion served as reserve artillery for Jackson's infantry on the southern part of the battlefield. The battle resulted in an overwhelming Confederate victory. Further bolster-

---

5. OR 19[1]:1030–31; Macaluso, *Morris, Orange, and King William Artillery*, 29. For mention of his wounding at Antietam, see THC to SRC, 4 Oct. 1862.

ing Carter's morale, his promotion to major, which he had been waiting for since Hill made him chief of artillery at the beginning of November, finally came through on 12 December.[6]

—ɯ—

Sunday Afternoon
Near Richmond
July 13th 1862

My dearest wife,

It is Sunday but to insure your getting this Tuesday morning by the mail I write now. I have just dined with Rodes & enjoyed a good dinner of vegetables. I shall send James to the City tomorrow to get something of the kind for myself. There is nothing new to relate. We are busily engaged in reorganizing, enforcing camp duties, catching stragglers & deserters &c. &c. Of the latter there are not a few—some four of my old Company & about twenty-five of the two last Companies transferred to me.[7] We know but little of the movements of the two armies. Our principal Divisions & Corps are close to Richd. Jackson is thought to be on the Mechanicsville road but I suppose will return to the Valley as soon as he takes a breathing spell.[8] Indeed he may have it started already. I think we will rest a month or two before another battle, unless the enemy tries another mode of attack by way of Petersburg or the James River obstructions.[9] While I have but little confidence in the intervention of England

6. Macaluso, *Morris, Orange, and King William Artillery*, 31–34; THC to SRC, 1 Nov. 1862; SRC to William Patterson Smith, THCP, 1850–1915, VHS; *OR* 21:36, 633. Carter's promotion to major, which did not officially take place until 12 December, bore a date of rank of 1 November. The reason for the delay of more than a month was because the adjutant and inspector general's office could not find the resignation of D. H. Hill's former chief of artillery, Major Scipio Pierson (D. H. Hill to Samuel Cooper, 5 Dec. 1862, Letters Received by the Confederate Adjutant and Inspector General's Office, NARA; James Alexander Seddon to D. H. Hill, 12 Dec. 1862, Letters Sent by the Confederate Secretary of War, NARA).

7. On three separate occasions in June, Carter's battery accepted transfers from under-strength artillery units that were being disbanded: twenty-five men transferred in from Captain Thomas T. Cropper's Richmond Flying Artillery on 3 June; seventeen men came from Captain William W. Fraser's Hampton Artillery on 14 June; and forty-nine men arrived from Captain Samuel T. Bayley's Company of Virginia Heavy Artillery. Not all of the men who were transferred reported for duty. Some may have considered themselves as having been discharged, while others took the opportunity to quietly leave the army (Wallace, *Military Organizations*, 15; Macaluso, *Morris, Orange, and King William Artillery*, 25).

8. Major General T. J. Jackson received orders on 13 July to lead his and Major General Richard S. Ewell's divisions from Richmond to Louisa Court House and then on to Gordonsville, Va., to oppose Major General John Pope's advancing Army of Virginia (*OR* 12[3]:915).

9. The King William Artillery remained in the Richmond area until early August, at which

& France I can not help indulging a slender hope on the subject. There was a decided tendency towards mediation before the "Seven Pines" battle. Since [then] it has increased & I trust it may eventuate in something substantial this time, but it is folly to rely at all upon it. I hope too for the financial crash which must come soon or late. Gold has steadily advanced notwithstanding the fact that there are no imports of consequence at this time in the North. The foreign capitalists are obviously selling their American stocks to stand from under the crash ahead, & this accounts for the gold now going abroad.

John Edwards is endeavoring to get a substitute. Larkin Garrett is now in Richd, for this purpose.[10] Of course every one will get off who can. He will be required to get a good one. The Brigade including Rodes is much dissatisfied with Hill. His North Carolina troops have behaved badly & this Brigade has in every instance shown the most daring courage. They think they bleed & N. Carolina derives the benefit. Hill is evidently partial to his state troops & officers—indeed it is natural. He has been greatly censured for the charge on the batteries at Malvern Hills. His orders from Jackson were to hold himself in reserve until Armistead from Magruder's Corps flanked the batteries from the lowgrounds.[11] He heard a cheer & immediately ordered a charge. Our Brigade as usual led off in an open field 800 to 1000 yards directly in front of the batteries. They fell like autumn leaves but went up to within 200 yds of the batteries & laid down to await reinforcements. Garland's N. Carolina troops were sent but broke before reaching them.[12] They finally were compelled to leave after losing half the Brigade without accomplishing any thing except the slaughter of hundreds of gallant spirits. Jackson's men say the Yankees down here fight far more obstinately than in the valley. Doubtless they do as they are better disciplined & managed by McClellan. Had Huger & Magruder been efficient generals a large portion of McClellan's

---

time it moved to Hanover Junction. On 26 August the battery, along with the rest of D. H. Hill's division, started north to join the main Confederate army near Manassas. On 3 September, the King William Artillery finally reached Lee's army at Chantilly, Va. (*OR* 12[3]:945; Macaluso, *Morris, Orange, and King William Artillery*, 27–28).

10. Larkin (or Lark) S. Garrett (b. 1823?) was a thirty-nine-year-old farmer from King William County, Va., with a wife and three boys under ten years old. His real estate and personal property were each valued at $6,000 in 1860 (1860 Census, King William County).

11. Brigadier General Lewis Addison Armistead (1817–63) of Virginia commanded a brigade in Benjamin Huger's division and not in John Bankhead Magruder's division as Carter states (*OR* 11[2]:485).

12. Brigadier General Samuel Garland's brigade consisted of the 5th, 12th, 13th, 20th, and 23rd North Carolina Infantry regiments (*OR* 11[2]:485).

army would have been routed & captured. Let us thank God devoutly for what has been done. Had they been routed as [at] Manassas the same fatal lethargy might have been the consequence. Every thing is for the best. I had preaching in the Camp today.

Kiss the dearest little children for me. I have not yet heard from you since you left Richmond. God bless you. Tell me every thing. I want to see you terribly. When will you leave Pampatike[?] Stay until you think there is risk to your health & the children's. Have you heard from Mama? Tell me about H[ickory] Hill.[13]

Y[ou]r own devoted husband.

———w———

Camp near Richmond
August 15th 1862

My dearest Wife,

I arrived here last night & found the Division still in the same Camp. G. W. Smith is now our Division General, much to the annoyance of Ripley who tendered his resignation which was not accepted.[14] From the appointment of G. W. Smith, I should think it probable we will remain here unless absolutely needed with Jackson. Genl. Smith is, I suppose, unfit for field duty, though this is only conjecture on my part. I find my Battery in bad order, between forty & fifty absent without leave, an unusually large number sick & absent with leave[,] so that there are not enough men to man the guns. Phil Fontaine is dead.[15] I mourn his loss almost as I would a brother. He was so noble & brave & the best Sergt I had. James Tuck, wounded at White Oak Swamp, is also dead, & several

---

13. Hickory Hill, located in Hanover County, Va., was the home of the Wickham family. William Fanning Wickham (1793–1880) built the house in 1820 on land owned by his wife, Anne Butler (Carter) Wickham, who was Tom Carter's aunt and his father's older sister (*Old Homes of Hanover County*, 85; McGill, *Beverley Family of Virginia*, 463).

14. Brigadier General Roswell Sabine Ripley (1823–87) of Ohio commanded a brigade in D. H. Hill's division. Ripley, a quarrelsome officer, apparently did not like his temporary assignment to service under Major General Gustavus W. Smith, who was placed in command of the defenses of Richmond on 10 August (Warner, *Generals in Gray*, 257; Eicher and Eicher, *High Commands*, 454; Smith's CSR-Officers).

15. Phillip Aylett Fontaine (1845–62) enlisted as a private in the King William Artillery at Bond's Store on 1 June 1861. On 6 August 1862, he died at home from a fever (*RDD*, 26 Aug. 1862). Though Carter refers to Fontaine as a sergeant, his service records indicate that he held the rank of corporal (CSR). His brother, Patrick Henry Fontaine, had also served in the battery before leaving the unit following its reorganization in May 1862.

others desperately ill.[16] If I can get flies instead of these abominable tents I hope the health of the Company will improve. Two go off daily to the hospital I am told. The horses are good scarecrows. What with flies & want of forage they are miserably poor.

I wish you to write to some friend at the Allegheny Springs & ask that they will send my furlough to me at Richmond[,] Rodes' Brigade.[17] Whiting sent it up yesterday before my arrival. When it comes I may take a few days of it to see you. Were the Battery in good order I would use it all. Nothing new from the lines. France is in my Company. Marylanders are arriving daily in Richd in large numbers. Snowden Andrews [was] killed by the explosion of a shell inside of him.[18] Shirley has been promoted to full Surgeon. Papa[,] Lucy[,] Evelyn & Renshaw reached Annfield safely.[19] Renshaw stayed a few days & returned to Charlottesville to join Willie Randolph's Company.[20] He will not be able to stand it. On his return to Charlottesville he found Wm's letter announcing Julian's death.[21] He forwarded it to Mama by a safe opportunity. Wortham was telegraphed by Robert from Natchez to know where Julian was buried. Therefore a letter would reach him. You must write.

16. James T. Tuck (1840–62), a farmer in King William County, Va., enlisted as a private in the King William Artillery at Bond's Store on 1 June 1861. He was wounded at White Oak Swamp on 1 July 1862 and died exactly one month later. Tuck's service records indicate that he stood five feet, five inches tall and had black eyes, black hair, and a dark complexion. On 12 October 1863, because Private Tuck was unmarried, his father, Charles Tuck, received his son's Confederate pay in the amount of $142.90, which covered five months of military service from 1 March to 1 August 1862 (CSR).

17. Alleghany Springs is located in Montgomery County, Va.

18. Major Richard Snowden Andrews (1830–1903) of Maryland commanded the artillery of Jackson's division at the Battle of Cedar Mountain. During the fight, he was struck in the abdomen by shell fragments and nearly eviscerated. Carter's announcement of his death was premature. Though gravely wounded, Andrews survived. He was wounded for a second time at the Second Battle of Winchester in June 1863 and served in the bureau of ordnance for the remainder of the war. He died in Baltimore in 1903 (CSR; Krick, *Lee's Colonels*, 33).

19. Rosa Evelyn Carter (1846–65), the youngest daughter of Thomas Nelson Carter and Anne Willing (Page) Carter, was Thomas Henry Carter's half sister (McGill, *Beverley Family of Virginia*, 471).

20. Carter is referring to Company C of the 2nd Virginia Infantry, which was commanded by Captain William Wellford Randolph (CSR).

21. Private Julian Carter was killed in a cavalry engagement at Malvern Hill in Henrico County, Va., on 24 July 1862 (CSR). In a letter written later that same day to Mary Custis Lee, wife of Robert E. Lee, Tom Carter related the following: "I have but a moment to write to convey the sad intelligence of Julian's death. He was killed at Malvern Hills this morning at 9 A.M. in a charge upon the enemy's cavalry while a long distance in front of his Company, and while fighting with characteristic courage for every thing that makes life dear to us" (THC to Mary Anna Randolph Custis Lee, 24 July 1862, Lee Family Papers, 1732–1892, VHS).

Much love to Aunt [Cornelia] & Cousin Nannie.[22] Kiss the darling children. God bless you.

Y[ou]r own devoted husband.

Genl. Lee is said to have gone to Gordonsville.[23] Only two Divisions on this side of the James. McLaws & G. W. Smith's[.] Longstreet gone.

Renshaw enclosed a letter to you from Mama. He did not say where to. I suppose to Old Church.

—⁓—

6 1/2 A.M.[24]

Camp near Richmond

Aug 18th 1862

My dearest Wife,

I enclose you letters from Mary & Mama.[25] Lizzie Nicholas has since received one from Dr Buckner asking for the particulars in regard to poor Julian.[26] Lizzie answered & sent it yesterday evening. She can now & then get opportunities to Baltimore & Clarke but you must pay the postage as it is heavy on her to send a mail for all her friends.

We are off this morning to some other clime. At 9 A.M. we form with all the Artillery of G. W. Smith's Division in the Wmsburg road with five days rations. I suppose therefore we are to march to Jackson. Genl. Lee has gone up to the Army. Genl. McLaws Division is the only one left this side of the James. McClellan is thought to be moving his whole army from the Peninsula to Fredericksburg.[27] I have received no letter from you since we parted. Direct to Orange Ct House until further notice.

---

22. Carter is most likely referring to Cornelia C. Gaines Meaux (1810?–85) and her step-daughter Nannie O. Meaux Phillips (b. 1824?). They both lived at Coverley in Amelia County, Va. Cornelia was the younger sister of Carter's mother, Juliet Muse Gaines Carter (1806–34) (Dorman, *Claiborne of Virginia*, 69; 1860 Census, Amelia County).

23. Lee left Richmond for Gordonsville, Va., on 15 August and arrived there later that day (*OR* 11[3]:677–78).

24. THC to SRC, 18 Aug. 1862, Private Collection.

25. Mary has not been identified.

26. Dr. Buckner has not been identified. Carter may be referring to Elizabeth Byrd Nicholas (1830–1901), who lived in Richmond and later served as president of the National Colonial Dames of America (Pacquet du Bellet, *Some Prominent Virginia Families*, 2:329–30).

27. No longer concerned that McClellan's forces at Harrison's Landing on the James River posed a threat to Richmond, Lee concentrated his army in central Virginia for operations against John Pope's Army of Virginia. By 16 August the Army of the Potomac, having begun its evacuation of Harrison's Landing several days before, began arriving at Aquia Landing and Alexandria, Va., from which points it could reinforce Pope's army (Long, *Day by Day*, 251).

I am sorry indeed not to see you & my sweet little ones before I go again to that country but it is perhaps better as it is. Mrs Rodes & Mrs Gordon talk of going up.[28] I think you had better divide your time with Aunts Cornelia & Sarah & Sister. I have not yet answered Sister Ann's letter. Saw Col Rutherfoord yesterday evening. Mrs R. was suffering from attack of Jaundice—all well at R[ock] Castle, Ayletts at Montville.[29] Mama wrote a most grateful note to Mrs Rutherfoord which I took yesterday. I shall have to present my poultry to Cousin Maria this morning.[30] Rodes is sick in R[ichmond] but goes with us today. I enclose a letter from him to me while at the Springs.

My Company is much scattered since I left. Dabney & Hart managed miserably in every way.[31] Hart & Lucien Robinson got off on the plea of recruiting & are now circulating in King Wm.[32] A large number of the old members are absent on one pretext or another & there are not enough to work the guns properly. Much love to Aunt Cornelia & Cousin Nannie. Wm stands Camp well thus far.

God ever bless you my darling & the children. I am very sad at the idea of leaving you so far. ·

Ever y[ou]r devoted husband.

28. Carter is referring to Fanny Rebecca Haralson Gordon, the wife of Colonel John Brown Gordon. She and John were married on 18 September 1854, her seventeenth birthday, at her family's home in La Grange, Ga. Her father—Hugh Anderson Haralson (1805–54), who represented Georgia in the U.S. House of Representatives from 1843 to 1851—died one week later (Eckert, *John Brown Gordon*, 10; *Biographical Dictionary of the United States Congress*, "Hugh Anderson Haralson," http://bioguide.congress.gov/scripts/biodisplay.pl?index=H000178 [accessed 30 Sept. 2013]).

29. Montville was the King William County, Va., home of the Aylett family. Built in 1803 by William Aylett (1775–1847), the house was occupied during the Civil War by his son, William Roane Aylett (1833–1900), colonel of the 53rd Virginia Infantry. Colonel Aylett's brother, Patrick Henry Aylett (1825–70), was married to Emily Ann Rutherfoord Aylett (1830–80), whose brother John Coles Rutherfoord was married to Ann Seddon Roy Rutherfoord, Susan Carter's sister (Clarke, *Old King William Homes and Families*, 18–19).

30. Cousin Maria has not been identified.

31. William E. Hart (1836–82), a schoolteacher from King William County, Va., enlisted as a corporal in the King William Artillery at Bond's Store on 1 June 1861. In 1862 he was elected to second lieutenant (23 June) and later promoted to first lieutenant (1 November). Two years later, on 12 May 1864, Hart, along with most of the battery, was captured near Spotsylvania Court House during the fight at the Bloody Angle. He subsequently joined more than 500 Confederate prisoners of war at Morris Island, S.C., where at one point they were used as human shields against Confederate gunners at Fort Sumter. This group of prisoners became known as the "Immortal Six Hundred." At the time of his release from prison in June 1865, Hart was described as being of light complexion with dark hair and blue eyes and standing five feet, eight inches tall (CSR; 1860 Census, King William County).

32. Lucien Dabney Robinson (1844–1915) enlisted as a private in the King William Artillery at Bond's Store on 1 June 1861. He was promoted to sergeant before 31 October 1862 and to

Wms Wickham has joined his Regt. Did you not forget to put up my gauntlets[?] I can't find them.

—⁂—

"Maryland My Maryland"[33]
3 3/4 miles from Fredericktown
Sept. 7 '62
Sunday night

My precious wife

I have at last, I hope, an opportunity of sending you a line. I wrote you at Gordonsville about ten days since.

I fear you have been uneasy about me but you must believe nothing you hear until confirmed. We missed the battle at Manassas by a day.[34] The battle field gave evidence of terrible slaughter on the Yankee side. They lost apparently ten to one. The ground was covered here & there for miles with their dead & wounded. Some of the latter had been lying out for three days & nights. God help them. At one place our troops were concealed in a railroad cut. The enemy approached within forty or fifty yards when a volley was delivered. The ground was covered with dead. I mentioned this to [D. H.] Hill. He answered that ~~he was~~ although a great admirer of a beautiful woman he never saw so beautiful a sight. Savage is he not! Well we are in "My Maryland." The Brigade crossed the 4th[,] the first that landed on this shore. I crossed the night of the 5th about midnight. The ford is just passable for artillery. Some of the ammunition chest escaped by an inch. What would a rain do on a retreat? The people in this county vary in sentiment but it is said to be one of the most unsound in the state. Some are enthusiastic, some indifferent. Some Union but not insulting. I do not think they are prepared to undergo the privation we are now enduring but we are told that Balti[more] & neighborhood are as sound as Va. In Fredericktown many of the ladies smiled & bowed. The Southerners promise 30,000 or 40,000. I shall be glad to get half. The country from the mouth of Monocacy where we

---

second lieutenant before 2 February 1863 (see Carter's letter dated 15 March 1863 for mention of Robinson's promotion to lieutenant). Following the capture of nearly half of the battery at the Bloody Angle on 12 May 1864, Robinson commanded the King William Artillery for the remainder of the war (CSR).

33. THC to SRC, 7 Sept. 1862, THCP, 1850–1914.

34. Carter is referring to the Battle of Second Bull Run (or Second Manassas), which was fought on 29 and 30 August.

crossed the Potomac to this place is magnificent in soil, cultivation & scenery—equal to Loudon [County] & the valley. The move is the boldest I ever conceived of—our supplies till now hauled in wagons from Rapidan to this place across a country for the most part that is one scene of desolation—not a horse, cow, sheep, fence, corn field, wheat stack, or hay rick to be seen for scores of miles. It seems to me now[,] however[,] we can cut loose from our trains & depend upon this country. Confederate money is taken not always cheerfully but generally so. Beef & flour are plentiful. Beeves have been driven with us thus far. They are very fine. Jackson's column reached here early yesterday. Longstreet came up today. Walker with his Brigade & Ransom's will come tomorrow & our army will be strong in numbers.[35] The straggling exceeds anything ever known—from 10,000 to 20,000 between here & Gordonsville. Lee is taking the most stringent steps to prevent it. He has the entire confidence of the Army but there is no enthusiasm. Jackson on the contrary is idolized by the Army & people. All along the road he is inquired for. Yesterday his horse (a new one just presented) reared & fell on him bruising him badly. He turned over the command to D. H. Hill but resumed it in the evening & continued in com[man]d today. We are in his Corps & will have fighting enough to please even D. H. Hill. A. P. Hill is again under arrest.[36] He was reprimanded by Jackson in consequence of some delay in the movement of his Division at which he took offense & offered his sword. Jackson told him to keep it but to go to the rear under arrest. He marches at the rear of his Division. Tombs was arrested also by Longstreet but relieved in time for the Manassas battle when he is said to have behaved gallantly.[37] The difficulty arose from his relieving a Reg[imen]t

35. Brigadier General John George Walker (1822–93) of Missouri commanded a brigade that consisted of the 3rd Arkansas; the 27th, 46th, and 48th North Carolina; and the 30th Virginia Infantry regiments and the Stafford (Va.) Light Artillery Battery. The brigade of Brigadier General Robert Ransom (1828–92) of North Carolina included the 24th, 25th, 35th, and 49th North Carolina Infantry regiments and Branch's (Va.) Artillery Battery (OR, 19[1]:805).

36. Major General Ambrose Powell Hill (1825–65) of Virginia commanded a division, known as the "Light Division," in Stonewall Jackson's command (later 2nd Corps). Jackson and Hill first clashed a month earlier before the Battle of Cedar Mountain (9 August 1862), when Hill's division did not take its proper place in Jackson's line of march. The second occasion occurred on 4 September, when Hill's men failed to begin their march at the appointed time. Jackson arrested his division commander and ordered the prickly Hill to ride at the rear of his column. In January 1863, R. E. Lee urged Hill to drop the matter because he believed that Hill's infractions, balanced against his worth as a commander, did not warrant a trial (Warner, Generals in Gray, 134–35; OR 19[2]:732).

37. Brigadier General Robert Augustus Toombs (1810–85) of Georgia commanded a brigade in David R. Jones's division of James Longstreet's corps during the Maryland Campaign.

*Thomas J. Jackson
(National Archives and
Records Administration)*

on picket because rations were not sent. I don't believe in his cowardice; his expression contradicts it. Our next step no one can predict. It is rumoured that the enemy are massing at Rockville (30 miles distant & ten from Georgetown). Some suppose we will march into Pennsylvania, others to Balti[more] or to Washington. The splendid bridge here across Monocacy River on the B & O R[ailroad] is being mined. We expect to march tomorrow. This day's rest has been a great pleasure to us. We are prepared to fight everyday, & this day week many a gallant soul may be sleeping his last sleep. Rodes overtook us last night. He regrets not being with the Brigade when it crossed. Hill for a wonder gave it the preference & allowed it to lead. I passed the 12th Miss. (now in Featherston's Brig.)

Toomb's brigade consisted of the 2nd, 15th, 17th, and 20th Georgia Infantry regiments. On 17 August, Toombs was absent from his brigade when Longstreet ordered the Georgian to send two of his regiments to guard Raccoon Ford on the Rapidan River. Toombs's subordinate, Colonel Henry Lewis Benning (1814–75), promptly followed the order. Upon Toombs's return to camp, he angrily countermanded Longstreet's order and had the regiments come back to camp. That night, Union cavalry chose that precise moment to commence a raid across the Rapidan at Raccoon Ford, something they had not done in some time. The next day, when General Longstreet discovered why the ford had been left unguarded, he immediately placed Robert Toombs under arrest for disobeying orders. Not until 30 August, during the Battle of Second Bull Run, did Toombs return to duty (Warner, *Generals in Gray*, 25–26, 306–7; *OR*, 19[1]:804; Hennessy, *Return to Bull Run*, 44–45, 47–48).

on the route. They cheered & recheered me until I felt quite foolish. I am again with the Brigade. They received us with every mark of affection.

The end of this daring movement no one can see. We all trust in God & Lee. A defeat would be the absolute destruction of this army with the Potomac in the rear. Whether it is simply to free Maryland or to invade Penn[sylvania]. I do not know. I believe the former. The draft takes effect the 15th. Meantime *I hope* we shall get a large proportion of the men between 18 & 45, which will supply the place of the stragglers. Lee in a special order urges the men not to excite the hostility of the people by depredations.[38] But of course great damage is done by an army in its passage through the country. I am perfectly well again. I hope not to be wounded so far from you. Kiss my darling little children for me. Dear dear little things. I have not heard from you since we parted but hope when the mail arrives to secure a large batch. I have been romancing with your daguerreotype. Wm. is well & fat. He had a fever a day & night on the road which alarmed me & I started him to Col. Taliaferro's, but he insisted upon remaining. It was only a cold. {Remainder of letter missing}

—⚬—

Camp near Bunker Hill
10 miles above Winchester on Martinsburg Turnpike
Oct. 4th 1862

My dearest wife,

I wrote you last from Fredericktown & received y[ou]r last letter of the 3rd Sept written at Staunton Hill.[39] I omitted writing at Gordonsville because I had mailed a letter from Louisa Ct. H[ouse].

Of course you have heard everything in regard to the Maryland invasion. In a material point of view taking into calculation the capture of Harper's Ferry & the battle of Sharpsburg, we gained advantage; but the retreat rendered necessary by want of supplies & ordnance stores leaves the moral effect with the enemy, & McClellan is enabled to boast of a victory achieved more by adverse circumstances than his own arms. Well we

38. Carter is most likely referring to General Orders No. 102, issued on 4 September, which included General Lee's concern that "excesses committed [by Confederate troops] will exasperate the people [of Maryland], lead to disastrous results, and enlist the populace on the side of the Federal forces in hostility to our own" (*OR* 19[2]:592).

39. Staunton Hill was a Gothic Revival mansion in Charlotte County, Va. It was constructed in 1847–48 by Charles Bruce (1826–96), who lived there with his wife, Sarah Alexander Seddon Bruce (1829–1907), an aunt of Carter's wife (Ailsworth, Keller, Nichols, and Walker, *Charlotte County, Rich Indeed*, 418).

must not despond. It is expecting too much that no disaster shall befall us. At the Blue Ridge Mountains near Boonsborough we were whipped after holding the pass until after dark, simply by overwhelming numbers & bad management.[40] Jackson's whole Corps was across the Potomac in Va. surrounding H Ferry. Also Walkers Division, R. H. Anderson's Division, & McLaws Division were absent aiding in this capture. We had Hill's (D. H.) Division only & the remainder of Longstreet's Corps, to contend with the whole Yankee Army. Still I think with good management we could have held them in check. They succeeded in getting possession of a road across the mountain about a mile to our left which came into the Turnpike about halfway down the mountain on one side & this success won the mountain pass. Our men in many instances behaved very badly. Hills troops are mostly N[orth] Carolinians not our best troops by any means & his men have taken up the impression that he is rash & enter a battle with the idea that they are to be exposed to certain annihilation. Therefore, they fought badly. Longstreets men were fatigued by a march of ten miles from Hagerstown up to the top of the mountain & whole Brigades ran like curs. Rodes' Brigade on the extreme left was flanked by two Divisions coming on the road before described & would have been almost destroyed or captured but for the gallantry of Gordon[,] who kept his Regt under perfect control when every other Regt broke & fled, marching it so skillfully under a terrible fire as to cover the retreat.[41] Had they ordered me up in time I could easily have prevented this movement of the enemy by which they gained the road. As it was[,] by the time I had climbed the mountain some two miles, the enemy had driven back Rodes' & gained the road & came near capturing the battery. Rodes ordered me to reverse above & leave. This was easier said than done on a steep[,] shelving[,] narrow mountain road. Every gun & caisson was unlimbered & the turn made in time so I was not engaged in that battle. From the top of a high peak while my battery was idle I saw a portion of the fight. That night (Sunday the 14th) we retreated to Sharpsburg. Next day, Jackson Captured H Ferry & hastened to our assistance. Monday morning we formed our line of battle in front of Sharpsburg on a high range of hills. The enemy formed on the opposite range sepa-

40. Carter is referring to the Battle of South Mountain, a fight that took place on 14 September 1862, three days before the Battle of Antietam.
41. Colonel John Brown Gordon (1832–1904) of Georgia commanded the 6th Alabama Infantry of Rodes's Brigade at the Battles of South Mountain and Antietam. On 1 November 1862, he was promoted to brigadier general (*OR* 19[1]:808; Eicher and Eicher, *High Commands*, 260).

rated by the valley of a creek. The country was open except on our left. Tuesday at dusk they commenced skirmishing to gain a skirt of woods & Wednesday at daybreak commenced the great struggle which continued with a slight intermission at 2 or 3 P.M. 'till dark. The whole scene beggars all description. Houses, barns, hay & straw ricks on fire, the incessant roar of artillery & bursting shells, the rattling of musketry, the killed & wounded all combined to give as correct an idea of the Lower Regions as I have ever imagined. I fought from daybreak until an hour before sundown with an intermission of two or three hours near midday. But I protected the Battery as far as possible by placing the guns just behind the crest so that they would fire over. In this way the balls of the enemy strike the crest in front[,] ricochet & pass over. I had only one man killed outright (Lewis Pemberton from Kg Wm[42]) & three wounded[,] all by artillery. I fear Dabney will lose his life. His foot was badly crushed by a shell. Three Surgeons advised amputation [and] three thought it might be saved. He is very ill, now at Dr Nelsons[43] (at Smithfield) brother of Hugh [Nelson] of Clarke. Today he is better but has fever all the time I learn & has been delirious several days this week. He has every attention. His mother is expected daily. His constitution is good & I hope he will recover. France was wounded on the knee by a fragment of shell. He is nearly well & is with us. My boot was broken & 2nd toe mashed by a ball from a Spherical case shot. It is entirely well now & I have not been absent from duty at all. This is the third time my right leg has been struck by spent balls of the same description. A more singular coincidence was that five horses at one caisson were killed by solid shot that day at different times & the drivers tell me that no horses have ever been touched at that caisson in previous battles. Pemberton's leg was shot off above the knee by a shell which exploded at the time & tore open his abdomen. He lived a few minutes & spoke several times. It was his first battle. I spent one night at Annfield a few days since. Everything is quiet & sweet there—all well. The country much burnt & suffering for rain. The house is unusually attractive now that all the furniture from Baltimore is in it. Mama has prayers for us morning[,] noon & night literally, & is so anx-

42. Lewis Howard Pemberton (1840?–62) enlisted as a private in the King William Artillery on 1 June 1861 at Bond's Store. He was the only member of the battery killed in action at the Battle of Antietam. In August 1863, Lewis's widowed mother, Ann C. Pemberton, filed a claim for her son's back pay, which she finally received, in the amount of $55.80, on 1 March 1864 (CSR; *OR* 19[1]:1031).

43. Carter may be referring to Dr. Mann Page Nelson (b. 1795?) of Smithfield, Clarke County, Va., an older brother of Hugh Mortimer Nelson (McGill, *Beverley Family of Virginia*, 425).

ious that she looks thin. Surely she is one of the loveliest characters on earth. We ought to feel no fear of our persons in battle with such prayers ascending almost hourly for us. Wm is perfectly well. He spent several days at home. I smuggled him off on business. For myself I have to be most circumspect as Hill imagines a leave of absence another name for an escape from dangers. He is always kind to me however & was again very complementary at Sharpsburg.

Wm imagines himself in love with Lucy Page.[44] She is a lovely girl. Mama thinks them too nearly related. Lucy Carter looks uncommonly well. The youngest child is very sweet & interesting. Renshaw is there looking quite badly & threatened with Camp Fever. They are uneasy lest the Valley should again be left in the hands of the enemy. Our future movements are wrapt in obscurity, & dependent on those of the enemy as we are again on the defensive until they cross the river. I never could understand our ability to invade. A line of communication must be kept open according to all military writers & common sense. What hope had we with a wagon train from Staunton to Baltimore or Phila[?] Then our reinforcements in the shape of conscripts[,] convalescents[,] deserters &c. &c., would never reach us by such a route. Straggling is another great evil we have to contend with & threatens to ruin our cause unless prevented. All these difficulties are not easily overcome with a powerful enemy on our front growing stronger every mile we advance.

I never saw Genl. Lee so anxious as he was at Sharpsburg during the battle. The centre gave way & but for four or five batteries there would have been a rout, & with no infantry we held for hours a half-mile of ground. Again & again the enemy tried to plant a battery & throw out skirmishers but we showered the iron hail upon them & forced them back. And yet we get but little credit for what we do. The loss in Artillery is necessarily smaller than in Infantry—one using long range & the other short range weapons, & there is a habit of estimating the damage done the enemy by the loss of killed & wounded—a foolish standard—for a Regt or Battery may be cut to pieces without injuring the enemy at all. Genl. Lee exposed himself entirely too much. He got down & endeavored to rally some of D. R. Jones' men[,] but in vain.[45] They ran like

44. Lucy Randolph Page (1842–93) was the third daughter of Dr. Robert Powel Page of Briars, Clarke County, Va., and a cousin of Carter's stepmother, Anne Willing Page Carter (McGill, *Beverley Family of Virginia*, 471).

45. Brigadier General David Rumph Jones's six-brigade division, the far right of Lee's line, guarded the lower bridge (later known as Burnside's Bridge) on Antietam Creek and the

hounds. The truth is the men were utterly broken down. They had lived on corn & apples for days. I eat enough for a young colt.

God be praised however[,] we drove them back on the left & right nearly a mile. They gained several hundred yards in the centre. So far as the battle is concerned ~~it~~ we gained a victory, & challenged them all day Thursday which was declined. Thursday night we fell back in a half starved condition to get supplies. The retreat across the river was admirable. Genl Lee & staff worked unremittingly all night. Genl. Pendleton next day managed in the battle of Shepardstown to lose four pieces. We are regularly installed in Jackson's Corps, & no winter quarters for us. I think there may be heavy fighting this month. Mama has written you to come to Clarke. I advise you not to do so. There is no certain means of conveyance to or fro & a week from now this army may be gone north or south. The country here is pretty well exhausted & we can't stay much longer. Our army is sadly in want of shoes & clothes. The wonder is that they fight as they do[,] poor miserable creatures. Wm wants a uniform frock coat[,] artillery regulation in every respect[,] at Biers & Poindexter.[46] You must send . . . {Remainder of letter missing}

—⁓⁓—

Near Bunker Hill
Oct. 8th 1862

My dearest wife,

I wrote you a long letter some days since which you have probably received. There is nothing of interest since. The enemy are on the other side of the Potomac. Our pickets again at Shepardstown. A large force is supposed to be at Harpers Ferry & they are rebuilding the bridge. There may be another great battle this fall but I doubt it. This summers campaign must be nearly closed. We have the usual rumors of foreign intervention & peace.

---

ground between the creek and the town of Sharpsburg on the morning of 17 September. Around 1:00 P.M., Major General Ambrose E. Burnside's IX Corps finally overpowered the Confederate defenders, crossed the bridge, and pushed the Southerners back toward the town. Jones's remaining brigades formed on a ridge just east of Sharpsburg and were in danger of being overwhelmed when Major General A. P. Hill's Light Division arrived from Harpers Ferry and halted the Union advance (*OR* 19[1]:886).

46. Beers & Poindexter was a merchant tailor, operated by William S. Beers and James H. Poindexter and located at 104 Main Street in Richmond (*Richmond City Directory 1860*).

I fear Dabney is dying. The Dr thought he would not survive the night. I am truly sorry for him & his mother. She reached him yesterday & is almost distracted. He had had every attention. His life will have been sacrificed by the attempt to save his leg. I can not help hoping there is some chance for him though the surgeon says not, & told Wm he could not live 'till morning. I saw him Sunday. I thought then he was in great danger but not hopelessly ill.

I have been most unfortunate with my officers.

Twenty batteries have been broken up to fill other batteries. The officers are simply relieved from duty & the men turned over. Leake's Company from Goochland is transferred to me, some forty strong.[47] Many of the officers are mortified but on the whole pleased, as they get out of service. I don't doubt you would have been highly pleased if mine had been broken up, would you not? They will keep me to fight as long as they can, putting every man of political influence over me, & by way of pitching me a crumb of comfort then say openly I am too good a Captain to be promoted. Well I ask nothing of any [of] them, but pursue the path of duty. I saw Ben Harrison yesterday in ~~Richd~~ Winchester.[48] Nothing new. I have received two most affectionate letters from Robert, the latest dated 10th August. Do write to him. He wants photographs of Wm & myself. Your last letter was the 30th September [from] Rock Castle. Kiss my precious little ones. Put your trust in God & may he bless you evermore.

Y[ou]r own husband.

How is Lucy Lindley[?] Shirley wrote she was at the point of death the 7th of September.[49]

—✴—

47. Captain Walter Daniel Leake's company formed in Goochland County, Va., as the Turner Artillery on 29 August 1861. The unit reorganized on 12 May 1862. On 12 September 1862, Leake resigned, and on 4 October the battery officially disbanded. The remaining members of the unit were assigned to the King William Artillery (Wallace, *Virginia Military Organizations*, 25–26).

48. Ben Harrison is possibly Benjamin Harrison (b. 1824?) of Clarke County, Va. He was a physician and a farmer who had a wife, Matilda (1836?), and a three-year-old son, Benjamin. According to the 1860 census, Harrison owned real estate valued at $22,000 and personal property worth $20,000 (1860 Census, Clarke County).

49. Lucy Lindley Braxton Temple died on 25 September 1862 (McGill, *Beverley Family of Virginia*, 494).

King Wm Artillery Camp
Near Bunker Hill
October 18th 1862

My dearest Wife,

We are still here as when I last wrote but expect to move at any moment as we are already packed & have rations cooked for two days ahead. The wagons will probably go to the rear, but we will stand either for battle or a slow retreat. The enemy have crossed the river in large force at Harper's Ferry, Shepardstown & Wmsport & are coming down on us. The bridge at H F has been rebuilt. There was a skirmish at Charlestown day before yesterday between our outpost troops & the enemy in considerable force.[50] Thompson Brown lost one of his Parrot guns & the Capt of the Battery, Smith, lost a foot.[51] We were driven back but they do not seem to have pursued at all. The great battle may be fought near Winchester on the fortified heights or we may draw them farther from their railroad into the interior, which I think would be advisable. Should we fight at Winchester they have greatly the advantage with a railroad in their rear & ample supplies[,] while we must depend on the mills around & a wagon train to Staunton. Reinforcements would reach us after several days marching. With them[,] they would pour in by rail. Lee says we fought them with less than a third their number at Sharpsburg.[52] The proportion must be still the same. There we lived on roasting ears

50. On 16 October, Major General George B. McClellan sent two Federal forces on reconnaissance missions. The first marched from Sharpsburg, Md., to Smithfield, Va. The second force moved from Harpers Ferry to Charles Town, Va., where it skirmished with Confederate cavalry and artillery under Colonel Thomas T. Munford (*OR* 19[2]:96–97).

51. On 16 October, Captain Benjamin Hodges Smith Jr. of the 3rd Richmond Howitzers was wounded in the left foot during a fight near Charles Town, Va. (*OR* 19[2]:97). After his wounding, he was captured by the enemy and immediately exchanged. Smith had enlisted as a private in the 3rd Company of Richmond Howitzers on 21 April 1861. By 24 June he had risen in rank to second lieutenant. Later in 1861, he became a first lieutenant, a rank he held until his promotion to captain on 22 June 1862. Smith's wounding in October resulted in the amputation of his left foot. Following a period of recuperation, during which time he detailed to the ordnance department in Richmond, Smith returned to the battery in the summer of 1863. Questions about his conduct at the Battle of Gettysburg culminated in the convening of a court-martial on 30 January 1864. Smith was acquitted, but his reputation suffered. On 10 May 1864, he was captured at Spotsylvania Court House and eventually imprisoned at Fort Delaware, where he remained until his parole on 14 September. Smith returned to the army, and in January/February 1865 he commanded an artillery battalion. Two months later, he surrendered with the rest of Lee's army at Appomattox Court House (CSR; Wallace, *Richmond Howitzers*, 157).

52. In his official report, Robert E. Lee stated that his army fought with less than 40,000 men at Antietam (*OR* 19[1]:151). George McClellan's estimate placed the Confederate army's total at 97,445—an overinflated figure from a commander who tended to exaggerate his opponents'

[of corn] & apples. This source even is not left us now & it is impossible to forage with a powerful enemy close in front. By the way[,] there is but little to get. Wheat can be found but it is usually unthreshed. The corn crop is short from the drought & heavy drafts have been already made on it for the army. We are sending to Clarke[,] Fauquier & Loudoun [Counties] now. The trains have exhausted the valley where corn was never a staple. The disadvantages under which we fight will never be known. On the gigantic scale we now wage war it is absolutely necessary that a railroad shall be our line of communication. Wagon trains may answer for an army of 5000, but not for 50,000. Our poor old state. North of James River is for the time utterly devastated & ruined. We will move forward today, I have just heard, towards Martinsburg. Some of the Divisions are already moving to execute another flank movement I suppose. The main force of the enemy is reported to be midway between Martinsburg & the Winchester Railroad. Your last letter was dated the 10th Oct. [from] Pampatike. I have not written regularly because I was ignorant of your whereabouts. Now that you are at home I hope to write regularly except when marching. I wrote you a long letter early in this month (3rd or 4th) & another short note by Col. Johnson, both of which I suppose you have received ere this. I was truly distressed to hear of the death of dear Lucy. Outside of my family she was the best friend I had. I trust she is happy in heaven now & free from all pain & trouble. It seems to me everyone is dying. In every battle many of my acquaintances & friends are killed & should this war continue God only knows who will escape.

Two days ago Genl. Early offered me the position of Chief of Artillery in his Division with the rank of Major. He has put Courtenay under arrest & offered him the choice of resigning or being Court Martialed. He agreed to resign but yesterday determined to stand the Ct Martial.[53]

---

strength (*OR* 19[1]:67). Modern sources range in their estimates. Stephen Sears claimed that the Union army fought with 71,500 men against between 32,800 and 38,000 Confederates (Sears, *Landscape Turned Red*, 173, 304, 389). James Murfin agreed with McClellan's figure for the Union army at 87,164 present for battle and stated that Lee commanded 35,255 soldiers in the fight (Murfin, *Gleam of Bayonets*, 198). The National Park Service's figures are much smaller for both armies. Its totals for soldiers actually engaged on the day of the battle are 47,400 Union troops against 34,050 Confederate (*Antietam National Battlefield*, http://www.nps.gov/anti/history culture/casualties.htm [accessed 30 Sept. 2013]). Clearly, there are many differences in the numbers. Lee's figure of less than 40,000 does agree with all but McClellan's estimate; Lee's claim, as reported by Carter, that his army fought with less than a third the strength of the Union army is an exaggeration. Perhaps he was still coming to grips with having not succeeded in Maryland and was looking for one way to explain the battle's disappointing outcome.

53. Alfred Ranson Courtney (1833–1914) enlisted as captain of the Henrico Artillery on 14 July 1861. In August 1862 he earned promotion to the rank of major and served as Richard

Early says he has never been under fire since he (Early) took charge of Ewell's Division from Cedar Run to this time, that he left for Richd after the surrender of Harper's Ferry & has just returned. Genl. Early is a man of excellent sense & one of our best fighters but I feel great reluctance in leaving my battery[,] brigade & Rodes. I told Genl. Early I would take a day to consider & felt relieved yesterday when he wrote me that there was a balk in the matter at present as Courtenay would stand the Ct Martial. There are five very good batteries in his Division.[54] Wm would be promoted to a Captaincy. Under Rodes he will do very well, having had a large experience in the management of a battery in camp & on the field. I should be sorry to leave him & break up our mess & separate servants &c., but everyone thinks I ought to accept if there is an opening. My social intercourse would not be as pleasant as here. I hope Rodes may yet be made Maj Genl. I know you would prefer me to accept. Hill has made his report of the battle of "Seven Pines." He mentions me very favorably but his praise is so general, including troops that did nothing, that I do not attach much importance to his report. He has not done Rodes justice at all. His brigade charged through to the abattis[,] across an open field[,] shoe-deep in mud[,] up to the redoubt & rifle pits taking almost all the earthworks in the field & yet he gives him no especial notice. Rains did nothing in the woods on our right with his Brigade except to fire with a small portion of his command occasionally & yet he (Hill) fancies he made a great flank movement by which Rodes succeeded in the front attack. Every Col in Rains' Brigade denies this & complains that he refused to advance without orders. Well what does it matter, the army understands pretty well who did the fighting.

I do not agree with you about the Southern Servants. They had better remain there. None have left thus far, & Va. is more unsafe than La.[55]

Ewell's and then Jubal Early's chief of artillery. Early brought Courtney up on charges of misconduct during the 1862 Maryland Campaign. On 20 April 1863, Courtney, at his own request, was relieved of duty under Early following the court-martial. Courtney commanded an artillery battalion in the Army of Tennessee from July 1863 to 1865 (Krick, *Staff Officers*, 104).

54. As of the date of Carter's letter, Early's division contained the following batteries: Charlottesville Artillery, Chesapeake (Maryland) Artillery, Courtney Artillery, Louisiana Guard Artillery, 1st Maryland Battery, and Staunton Artillery (*OR* 19[1]:807).

55. Carter is referring to slaves that he, his father, and his brother William sent to Louisiana in 1859 after the three men had purchased 1,027 acres of land in that state in March 1858. Tom and William Page Carter paid for the shipment to Louisiana of twenty-three slaves from Pampatike and seventeen from Annandale in Clarke County. (For a complete list of the slaves sent south and records of the purchase of the Louisiana property, see Thomas Henry Carter Account Book, 1859–88, VHS).

Write to Robert & tell him so if you please. The expense would be heavy & I don't know where the money is to come from. Before you take such important steps do consult with me in [the] future.

Nothing new here. Shirley is anxious to marry this fall. I advise against it. Wm Randolph is to be married soon, that is if he is not killed meantime. He is the Capt of four men in Jackson's old brigade.

We have been most pleasantly encamped here for some weeks but have suffered for vegetables & other good things. I have seen no one from Clarke lately. All well I suppose. My Compy has been increased by Leake's Co—about 61 men total but only 30 received thus far, 16 more expected daily.

You will have to buy mules. After sowing wheat you will send off the old crops I suppose as fast as possible. It would be well to start the lighter as soon as completed. I hope it is sound & safe. Wheat is selling at fabulous prices I hear. You have done admirably with the leather. Is there much winter clothing made[?] Take care of the colts this winter. Do tell me all about the children. God bless their little heads. I think so constantly of you all & long so earnestly for a reunion with you. We are all so tired of this war. Nothing but blood[,] blood & absence from home & all that is precious to us. I have been much troubled with diarrhea for three weeks past, but am perfectly well again with a fine appetite when there is any thing to eat. The scarcity here is most unusual in consequence of drought & the presence of the army. Give a great deal of love to all for me[:] Sister Ann[,] Aunt Sally & the Seddons, all in our neighborhood. I will write to Cousin Nora when I get time.[56] I sent you letters from Robert. He is anxious to hear from us. Do write. Wm is well. God forever bless you my darling.

Ever y[ou]r devoted husband

—⁓—

Sunday morning
[October 19th, 1862]

My darling Sue,

I open this letter to add a line stating that the order to march on the enemy was countermanded after the letter was closed yesterday. We are

56. Cousin Nora is likely Nora Crena Braxton Macon (1824–92). She was the oldest of the seven daughters of Carter and Mary Grymes Sayre Braxton of Ingleside, Hanover County, Va. (Braxton Family Bible Records, 1789–1941, VHS; Colvin, *On Deep Water*, 27).

again quietly encamped at the same place. Early's Division[,] Jacksons old Divi & A. P. Hill's moved towards Martinsburg to destroy the Railroad, it is said—a large force [of Union troops] being sent to prevent interference. The enemy has retired across the river. It is therefore probable that the force represented to be on this side was greatly exaggerated, probably several Divisions only, making a reconnaissance.

Nothing new. I hope you have received my letters herein mentioned. Mr Wm Turner will aid you in any way.[57] He has been truly kind & I am grateful for it. He is [a] good man of real sterling worth. James & Martin are well. Martin is the best boy I have ever seen. James is at times trifling but as he is attached to us I put up with a good deal. Both could have escaped when the Yankees attacked the wagon train on the Wmsport Road in M[aryland] but they were greatly alarmed & made tracks saving my mare they were then leading. James came to us on the battle field under a smart fire of Sharpshooters to bring us food, the day after the battle. The sound of the minnies buzzing near his ears had quite an amusing effect. Do write to Mama. They were all so affectionate about you & all of us. Poor Mama is wretched about Wm & myself, has prayers three times daily for us. Every thing there is so comfortable. They think Pampatike most unhealthy since their trial of it this summer, & so it is. Lewis has improved greatly since his return to Clarke.

God bless you ever

—⁋—

Camp near Bunker Hill
Oct. 23rd 1862

My precious wife,

We are still, you see, in status quo with the prospect, so far as I can see, of a quiet time for the rest of the fall. However this is mere conjecture for we know not what a day may bring forth. Jackson is still engaged with his corps[,] except D. H. Hill's Division[,] in destroying the B. & O. R[ailroad] & the Canal I hope. The latter I have not heard. He wrote to Genl Hill a few days since to be ready for a move at any moment as his division might be required. Up to this time we have received no orders & I hope will receive none as we are comfortably situated here

57. William Turner has not been identified.

on excellent ground. Forage is becoming extremely scarce. The wagon teams go from 25 to 30 miles for hay & nearly 40 for corn. I am much better supplied with vegetables & fowls than when I last wrote. I make the Quartermaster Leigh buy such things on his foraging expeditions.[58] Consequently we live well now. Every thing is at famine rates—butter some times 75 cts. to 1.00[,] ducks 1.00, turkeys $2 to $3 apiece. The men speculate largely, buy honey at 50 cts. per pound & sell at $2. A hive was retailed at $71. A bag of small apples retailed at $61 & miserably small at that. I shall stop it. The spirit is a mean one. The men ought to have such articles at cost price. Since I began this I have heard of the return of Jackson & the probability of our moving camp in a day or two, towards the Shenandoah it is thought. We get papers regularly, two days old. Bragg's victory is dwindling to a long retreat to Cumberland Gap.[59] Still the battle may have been a success & the retreat occasioned by the overwhelming forces which the Yankees brought up & can always bring against us. I am glad to see Penn, Ohio & Indiana have gone for the Democrats. The vote is doubtless in the main for war but it is the conservative element & will be the peace element when strong enough to show their hand. This is a step in the right direction & looks to peace I trust, however remote the prospect.[60] A year ago such a vote could not have been polled. New York may vote the same ticket on the 4th proximo. Nothing from Clarke since I last wrote. We are unable to get there although only 20 miles from home. I wrote you a letter some four days since. Your last letter was the 10th inst. It is quite cold now, but Rodes has lent me a fine Yankee tent which enables us to keep comfortable. I have occasional returns of diarrhea but am better than I have been. Aunt Cornelia wrote on the 30th Sept. that you had gone to Mrs Cocke's in her carriage. How did you like

58. Possibly Captain Chapman Johnson Leigh (1826?–1911), who served as an assistant quartermaster and later as a paymaster in Richmond (Krick, *Staff Officers*, 200).

59. Carter is referring to General Braxton Bragg's invasion of Kentucky, which began in early September at the same time that Lee's army crossed into Maryland. Bragg's advance was halted on 8 October at the Battle of Perryville, where a confused fight resulted in a narrow Union victory. On 23 October, the date of Carter's letter, Bragg's army passed through Cumberland Gap back into Tennessee, thus ending the second Confederate invasion of Northern territory in 1862 (Long, *Day by Day*, 276, 281).

60. In U.S. congressional elections held in October 1862, the Democratic Party captured a majority of the House seats in Ohio, Indiana, and Pennsylvania. The Emancipation Proclamation, announced by Lincoln on 22 September, convinced many in those states to elect more-conservative Democratic candidates, while voters in New England overwhelmingly supported Republican candidates. By far, the main reason for dissatisfaction among northerners with the Lincoln administration was its failure to bring the bloody war to an end (Long, *Day by Day*, 278; Nevins, *War for the Union*, 2:318–22).

the trip & what was the distance? Did you stop at your Uncle's on your return[?]

I fear you must be lonely at Pampatike. I pray for peace, that we may once more enjoy each other's society. At times I am sick to loathing of this life, separated from you with no hope of early reunion. When together the time is only long enough to tantalize. Well God's will be done. We must submit patiently & with a Christian spirit knowing that these earthly trials are for our eternal good. I think so often of poor Lucy—so young & bright last year & now mouldering in the grave.[61] Our hope ought to be only in heaven, where are joys forever. Gordon has been at death's door in Staunton & is still very low though somewhat better.[62] Rodes has written a most handsome letter to the Secretary of War strongly endorsed by Genl Hill, recommending him for the position of Brigadier General. His five wounds are still discharging & he suffers in addition to these evils from chills & fevers. I fear he will hardly recover. Genl. Anderson of this Division who commanded a N. Carolina Brigade, is dead. He was shot through the instep with a Minnie ball & amputation not being performed he died, as in the case of Dabney.[63] His poor wife I deeply pity. She was perfectly devoted to him. I met her at Gordonsville last spring. She has one child, an infant.

We have no idea of the programme for the winter. I suppose we shall get near some railroad probably on the Rappahannock. I have heard nothing more from Early in regard to the position he offered me. The Court Martial of Courtenay will require much time & I doubt if Early can have him displaced for want of proof. I care but little. As a matter of pride I should be gratified, but in other respects I prefer my present position. It is possible that Rodes will be promoted & I should much prefer a position on his staff as Chief of Artillery.

As the mail does not leave until tomorrow morning I will leave this

61. Carter's cousin Lucy Lindley Braxton Temple died on 25 September 1862.

62. Colonel John Brown Gordon was wounded five times during the Battle of Antietam—twice in his right leg, and once each in his left arm, left shoulder, and face. The final wound almost proved fatal when he fell unconscious to the ground with his face in his cap and nearly drowned in his own blood. Gordon's wife came to Staunton to take care of her husband (Welsh, *Medical Histories of Confederate Generals*, 83).

63. General Brigadier George Burgwyn Anderson (1831–62) of North Carolina commanded a brigade in D. H. Hill's division. Anderson was struck by a minié ball in the ankle while overseeing his brigade's defense of the Sunken Road at Antietam. After an agonizing journey by train to Raleigh, N.C., during which time the wound had become infected, Anderson had his foot amputated by the family physician. On 16 October, shortly after the surgery, Anderson died.

letter open in case there should be an order to move—or any other news you might like to hear. My Company is filling up rapidly[,] 114 present for duty & more expected daily. Kiss my own dear little ones for me. I love to think of you all. I hope things are getting on more favorably. Make Henry take care of the carriage horses. This is the season to fatten everything before the cold & hard weather puts in. Have you been able to buy mules[?]

[line added on Oct. 24th] Nothing new this morning. There is smallpox in the army, cases appearing in Ripley's Brigade & a number in Winchester.[64]

God bless you always my darling
Y[ou]r devoted husband,
Thos. H. Carter

—⁓—

Camp midway between Paris & Upperville
November 1st 1862

My dearest Mama,[65]

We arrived here early yesterday after a short march from beyond the river. We found Walker's Division at Paris. It has gone in the direction of Salem, how far I do not know. Stuarts Cavalry had a skirmish at or near Aldie yesterday[.] Captured some sixty prisoners. Our cavalry behaved very badly a day or two since at Upperville. Some 200 were put to flight by 26 Yankee Cavalry.[66] It is said Genl. [D. H.] Hill has sent back the Captain (Gibson) in disgrace.[67] We hear many rumors. A large force is thought to be at Manassas[,] Centreville & Lovettsville. The latter place is about eight miles below Harpers Ferry, in Loudon. Jackson is still about Weehaw, & we are yet uncertain whether we are attached to his

64. Brigadier General Roswell S. Ripley's brigade consisted of the 4th and 44th Georgia and the 1st and 3rd North Carolina Infantry regiments (*OR* 19[1]:808).

65. Carter wrote this letter to his stepmother, Anne Willing Page Carter.

66. These skirmishes in Loudoun County, Va., took place when Jeb Stuart's cavalry moved east of the Blue Ridge Mountains to screen Lee's army from advancing Union forces, which had crossed the Potomac into Virginia on 26 October. Thomas J. Jackson's command remained in the Shenandoah Valley, while James Longstreet's men moved toward Culpeper to prevent McClellan's army from flanking the Confederates (*OR* 19[2]:141).

67. Carter is most likely referring to Captain Bruce Gibson (1830–1901), the commander of Company A of the 6th Virginia Cavalry, whose men had skirmished with Union cavalry at Upperville, Va., on 17 October. Gibson, a native of Loudoun County, Va., enlisted as a sergeant in the 6th Virginia on 24 July 1861. He was promoted to first lieutenant on 14 November 1861. His service records indicate that beginning in the early spring of 1862, he commanded Company

Corps or not. I think we will join Longstreet after a while. McLaws' Division left the neighborhood of Winchester yesterday morning for Front Royal & we hear that the wagon trains are making for Culpeper. I have seen the papers of the 29th. I send one by Joe Jones who will take this to you. Nothing particularly new. There is evidently a tremendous pressure upon McClellan to advance. Whether he will be influenced by it no one can tell. He obviously would prefer to avoid it, his recollection of Sharpsburg is a wholesome check to his ambition. Lee will certainly give battle if McC[lellan] advances. I know you will be pleased to hear that Genl Hill offered me today the position of Chief of Artillery of his Division. I accepted it & Wm is now Captain of my old battery. Jones has behaved most generously. He told Genl. Hill that he had but one objection to the arrangement & that was, a fear that my promotion over him might be misconstrued into a slur on his standing as an officer.[68] Hill told him he thought not. Hill has written a most complimentary letter to Genl Lee of all of his officers of artillery in which I fear he has greatly overrated me. Well I can only do my best which I have always done & trust in Providence to give me his favor as has been granted so signally thus far. Wm will make a good officer. He is very conscientious in the discharge of his duties, & as cool & brave in danger on the field as any one can be. I do not apprehend a battle immediately, if so I trust God will grant us a great victory & cover our heads in the day of battle.

"But how can man die better
Than facing fearful odds
For the ashes of his Fathers
& the temples of his gods."

God bless you all.
Ev[e]r y[ou]rs most aff[ec]t[ionate]ly,
Thos. H. Carter

—⚬—

A of the regiment. Muster rolls and other records from September 1862 forward refer to him as captain of the unit. Gibson served with the 6th Virginia until he was captured at the Battle of Yellow Tavern on 11 May 1864. He spent the remainder of the war as a prisoner and took the oath of allegiance at Fort Delaware on 30 May 1865 (CSR; Musick, *6th Virginia Cavalry*, 26).

68. Hilary Pollard Jones (1833–1913), a prewar teacher, entered Confederate service in August 1861 as a first lieutenant in the Morris (Virginia) Artillery. After briefly commanding the Jeff Davis Artillery in April 1862, he was promoted to major on 28 May. During the Seven Days Battles and the Maryland Campaign, Jones commanded a battalion of reserve artillery, often

My dearest Wife,

Your last letter of the 4th inst was received yesterday. I am sorry to hear of your sickness but trust you are entirely restored to health now. There is no necessity for you to risk your health at this time particularly, when overexertion might be productive of serious if not fatal injury. I am glad to hear that your efforts with the wheat have resulted so favorably. It ought to be kept 'till the last & until it is thoroughly dry. The remainder of the wheat & corn could be shipped meantime. You will find it useless to seed in the lowgrounds after the middle or 20th of this month. The land will reject the wheat in freezing & thawing even if you should secure a stand[,] unless it is the old part & the fall should be mild, in that event you might sow 'till the 25th. It will make a half crop under favorable circumstances. The water furrows & ditches in the lowgrounds have to be well opened & kept open during the winter[,] for where water stands wheat will not grow. The front field will be much improved by standing two summers in clover. I advise that you leave it next summer & that you will not put it in corn next spring. The force will be too small to cultivate a large surface in corn. Have you heard from y[ou]r Uncle Smith in regard to the mules?[69] Such mules as he would buy you would be worth a half dozen of those furnished you by Wortham. Were you paid for the three mules never returned as well as for the services of the 12 mules, wagons & servants? In justice the government ought to pay for the three distempered animals sent down & estimated at $140 or $150 apiece but doubtless it would be impossible to get this money. You did right to half load only the boat on this trip. It would have saved trouble if you had done this in the beginning. Where is Dudley's tug boat to come from? He must expect to construct it on the Pamunkey. I hear the Yankees have landed at West Point & have destroyed the earthworks there. I trust you will hear nothing further from them. They are said

---

serving with D. H. Hill's division. Hill's choice of Tom Carter to command his divisional artillery was somewhat unorthodox in that Jones, a major, outranked Carter. This was remedied when Carter's promotion to major, which came officially on 12 December, bore a rank date of 1 November 1862 (CSR; *OR* 11[2]:489, 19[1]:809).

69. Carter is referring to William Patterson Smith (1796–1878), who was Susan Carter's uncle by marriage to her mother's sister Marian (or Marion) Seddon. William Smith and his wife lived at Glen Roy in Gloucester County, Va. (Lancaster, *Historic Virginia Homes*, 244).

now to sweep everything before them in the way of stock[,] servants[,] forage[,] poultry &c. &c. I pray they may never visit our county again but think it extremely probable. The river approach is the best one to Richmond, unless they try the Suffolk route, with the view of cutting our communications with the South & ultimately starve us out.

Genl. Hill told me this morning that McClellan has been superceded. He saw it in a Yankee paper. Burnside I suppose has succeeded him.[70] I am glad of it. McC[lellan] is by far the best man they have & therefore the most dangerous to our cause.

Since I last wrote we have moved twelve or fourteen miles. We marched from Front Royal to Strausburg & thence to this place five miles distant & nearer to Winchester. Our pickets were fired into at Charles-town & for a day or two we expected an advance from that direction where Porter & Franklin are reported to command, but all is quiet.[71] Longstreet is still, so far as I know, at Culpeper Ct H, & Jackson likely to remain in the Valley with his whole corps, higher up in Shenandoah & Page[,] I presume[,] where forage & provisions can be obtained. There is nothing here. The country is almost entirely exhausted. The people have not enough in many instances to subsist on. I wish we could be located on some Railroad. Longstreet always gets his Corps into some comfort-able quarters. While Jackson prefers the bleak outdoors.

I have not yet received my Commission & do not yet know what my rank will be. Jones has acted most kindly in the matter but he is very ambitious & dislikes Hill most cordially & rather chafes at his present position although he endeavors to conceal the real cause. He is much opposed too to remaining in the valley [and] wishes to be in Longstreet's Army in Picket's Division or Hood's.[72] The two last named men have been promoted to Maj Genls. Nothing of the promotion of Rodes or Early. It is rumored now & then that Rodes has been promoted & placed

70. Major General Ambrose Everett Burnside, who had been in charge of the defenses at Harpers Ferry, Va., throughout October, took command of the Army of the Potomac on 7 November 1862 (*OR* 19[2]:420, 551).

71. Major General Fitz John Porter (1822–92) of New Hampshire commanded the V Corps of the Army of the Potomac (Warner, *Generals in Blue*, 378–80). Major General William Buel Franklin (1823–1903) of Pennsylvania commanded the VI Corps of the Army of the Potomac (Eicher and Eicher, *High Commands*, 243).

72. Major Generals George Edward Pickett (1825–75) of Virginia and John Bell Hood (1831–79) of Kentucky commanded divisions in Lieutenant General James Longstreet's newly desig-nated 1st Corps of the Army of Northern Virginia. Both Pickett's and Hood's promotions bore a date of rank of 10 October 1862 (Warner, *Generals in Gray*, 142–43, 239–40).

in command of the Alabama troops in that state, but the rumors are never confirmed.

Doles,[73] a Col. in Ripley's Brigade, has been promoted to Brig Genl. Ripley transferred I presume to S. Carolina at his own request.[74] Colquit has been made Brigadier.[75] Col Iverson also to command Garlands old Brigade.[76] McRae s[enio]r Col. overslaughed.[77] Ramseur Brigadier to command Anderson's Brigade.[78]

Hill is in a rage at this time[,] & very justly, at the way the Artillery has been treated in his Division. He has written as I told you in my last, to Genl Lee & the whole matter was referred to Genl. Pendleton. He now writes to the Secretary of War. He tells him that of the 59 pieces captured around Richmond he has not received one. In this he has made a small mistake. I did secure one after much effort. He says that of the 72 captured at Harper's Ferry not one was given to this Division & yet the Capture was effected by the delay of McClellan's Army at South Mountain by his Division. Of the eight guns captured at Seven Pines by the blood

73. George Pierce Doles (1830–64) of Georgia was promoted to the rank of brigadier general on 1 November 1862 (Warner, *Generals in Gray*, 74).

74. Brigadier General Roswell S. Ripley had been transferred to Charleston, S.C., on 10 October. There, he commanded the harbor defenses until early in 1865 (*OR* 19[2]:684, 699).

75. Alfred Holt Colquitt (1824–94) of Georgia was promoted from the rank of colonel to brigadier general on 1 September 1862. He commanded a brigade in D. H. Hill's division (Eicher and Eicher, *High Commands*, 180). For letters written by several Confederate officers recommending Colquitt for promotion to brigadier, see his CSR.

76. Colonel Alfred Iverson (1829–1911) of Georgia commanded the 20th North Carolina Infantry in Brigadier General Samuel Garland's brigade. In the fall of 1862, General Lee sought to fill vacancies at various levels in the army that had resulted from the campaigns of the summer. On 1 November 1862, Iverson was promoted to the rank of brigadier general, and five days later, he was given command of the brigade in place of Garland, who been killed at the Battle of South Mountain (Warner, *Generals in Gray*, 147–48; CSR; *OR* 19[2]:684, 699).

77. Lieutenant Colonel William MacRae (1834–82) commanded the 15th North Carolina Infantry in Brigadier General Howell Cobb's brigade. When Cobb fell wounded during the Battle of Antietam, MacRae led the brigade for the remainder of the fight. On 26 November 1862, MacRae's regiment was transferred to Brigadier General John R. Cooke's brigade. Three months later, on 27 February 1863, MacRae earned promotion to colonel. After Brigadier General William W. Kirkland suffered a severe wound during the Battle of Cold Harbor, Lee promoted MacRae to the temporary rank of brigadier general and gave him command of Kirkland's brigade. William MacRae's official appointment as brigadier general came on 4 November 1864 (Warner, *Generals in Gray*, 206–7; Sommers, "William MacRae," 136–37; CSR). "Overslaughed" means "to pass over, skip, or remit the ordinary turn of duty of an officer, a company, etc., in consideration of his (or its) being detailed on that day for a duty which takes precedence" (*Oxford English Dictionary*).

78. Stephen Dodson Ramseur (1837–64) of North Carolina, promoted to brigadier general on 1 November 1862, took command of the brigade formerly commanded by Brigadier General George Burgwyn Anderson (1831–62), who was mortally wounded at the Battle of Antietam (CSR; *OR* 19[2]:699; Warner, *Generals in Gray*, 5–6).

of his Division without the aid of a solitary musket besides[,] we received not one. He states that he had been put off from time to time on one pretext & another & now he makes a distinct issue that unless these guns are assigned he had best be relieved from his command—that the "brave Artillerists of his Division are suffering from prejudice to him or want of Confidence in him." I don't know what will be the consequence.

I have been under fire once or twice lately with the pickets, both artillery & musket fire. The Yankees were near getting me. I was with the extreme videttes watching from a point on the mountain the skirmish below between Rosser in Command of Fitz Lee's Cavalry & the enemy.[79] I saw their Cavalry within a few hundred yards but supposed they were too much engrossed in the fight to turn aside to take Manassas gap, which we were picketing. Suddenly a body of cavalry burst into view at full speed on the road about 150 yds ahead. I had to regain the road from my position & this distance was so much time lost. Fortunately I had just mounted my mare or I should have been captured. Both sides plied the spurs vigorously. I gained the road ahead & they ran me to the reserve picket where I pulled up & tried to gather them together to make a stand. They had squandered in every direction but with the aid of a gallant lieutenant they were gotten together behind a fence & some trees & delivered a very steady fire. The Yankees pulled up[,] dismounted & returned the fire & fell back. No harm done on either side—all parties being too much excited to aim at all. I do not think there will be fighting this fall unless Jackson brings it on. Possibly if the report of the promotion of Burnside be true he may deem it his duty to advance. If we winter in the Valley I shall see nothing of you I fear. I may be allowed to go to Richmond on business but officers are required to set the men an example. I wish we had not been guilty of the little indiscretion which will keep you at home so closely this winter, but every thing is for the best. I pray most earnestly every day that this war may end, & I can not help indulging the hope the united prayers of the people of the South must bring about this blessed result. And if it should my darling how thankful we ought to be & how earnestly we should try to be content with our lot in life. I recollect so often my desire for change & a better condition at Pampatike before the war, & now those times seem as a pleasant dream

79. Colonel Thomas Lafayette Rosser (1836–1910) commanded the 5th Virginia Cavalry. He was promoted to brigadier general on 28 September 1863 and to major general on 1 November 1864. Rosser commanded Jubal Early's cavalry in the 1864 Shenandoah Valley Campaign (Warner, *Generals in Gray*, 264–65).

that I would give all I possess to enjoy once more. There is no perfect happiness in this life. We should do our duty & look to the life eternal which gives the only joy & peace that remaineth. All here is so transient & evanescent. These thoughts occur to me frequently in the service where friends & familiar faces are laid low in every engagement, & where I think too, often of many in our neighborhood who were true to me & mine that are forever gone from this world. Bring our dear little ones up to realize the importance of these things. I know you will my darling.

God forever bless you & them.
Y[ou]r devoted husband.

—ꟿ—

Camp near Gordonsville
Nov. 27 1862

My dearest Wife,

Your last most acceptable letter of the 18th inst was received yesterday evening. I sent word yesterday by Johnson of King Wm that I was at this point, but so uncertain of the length of stay that it would be useless to write here. Your manner of directing my letters, however, insures their safe delivery, it matters not where we may be. I find { . . . } more certain than naming the place which often sends a letter to that point without regard to the movements of the army. Therefore you can continue to write & direct as you have done. There will be some delay in the reception of course, but not much, as the mail follows the army. We left Middletown on Friday the 21st. much to our surprise as there was every indication of wintering there. Jackson had taken a house in Winchester & it is said his wife was with him.[80] (By the way[,] she has just presented him with a boy.) We marched rapidly to this place averaging a little over 19 miles per day with one Division. We came to New Market & then across the Massanutton & Blue Ridge by a turnpike leading to Gordonsville. The passage of the Blue Ridge is exceedingly difficult & tortuous by a road at heavy grade 12 miles across (& not more than three by air line). There is no gap. The road has been made at great expense for convenience as there is no gap near. We reached here Tuesday night. Early is a few miles behind, near Liberty Mills. Jackson's Division [is]

---

80. Carter is referring to Mary Anna Morison Jackson (1831–1915). On 23 November she gave birth to their daughter Julia Laura Jackson (Robertson, *Stonewall Jackson*, 645).

near Madison Ct House, about 16 miles distant & A. P. Hills I suppose [is] near the same place. We had orders & were about to start for the Junction (Hanover) but they were countermanded, Burnside's movements probably being still uncertain. I am a little doubtful whether he will try the Fredericksburg route to Richmond, or the Suffolk. Many think the latter. If so it will cause the abandonment of upper Va. entirely with the exception of cavalry & small bodies like the army of Loring & would also endanger Petersburg & our great Southern states.[81] This would be a serious blow but I think the best route to Richmond is from Fredericksburg—that is, if they wish to take it immediately & have the force to do so. The other route would do us more damage but would be the longest, I think. With their water facilities & other resources what an enormous advantage they have. Genl Lee however is anxious to give battle & I hear is confident of victory. My faith during the engagement is often shaken but I am glad to say that I have never fought in a battle which has ended in defeat. I have witnessed one however at South Mountain, if a fight against such odds could be called a defeat, where delay was aimed at & accomplished. There is no other news. We know nothing but what you see in the papers & I suppose Burnside's movements will decide ours. Everything is being moved from Gordonsville to Lynchburg or Richd, as if we should retire to the Junction or to the Southside. In either event I will notify you so that I can see you at H[ickory] Hill or Richd. I hope this letter will go straight through & reach you tomorrow morning though I doubt it. The mails are uncertain. I saw Dr Randolph yesterday just up from Clarke. All quiet since our departure. A Brigade of Cavalry [is] left up there. A small force of Yankees [is] at H Ferry.

You will do well to get all your salt from Mathews. It ought to be cheap there. A fine salt mine has been discovered in Alabama & Gov Pickens of S. Carolina has received an offer of a supply for the state at $5 per bushel.[82] I shall write to Robert about a servant. Certainly that purchase has been unfortunate. I hardly know what will be done with the servants unless they are moved to Texas, where they can be fed on beef. I am glad to see your Uncle Alexander has been appointed Sec.

---

81. Major General William Wing Loring (1818–86) of North Carolina commanded the Confederate Department of Western Virginia. On the day that Carter wrote this letter, Loring was, at his own request, relieved from his command in western Virginia and assigned to lead a division in the Army of Mississippi (Warner, *Generals in Gray*, 193–94; *OR* 21:1036).

82. Francis Wilkinson Pickens (1807–69) was governor of South Carolina from December 1860 to December 1862 (Edmunds, "Francis Wilkinson Pickens," 470–72).

of War. I hope he gives as much satisfaction as Randolph—he has been signally successful.[83] Do you know why he resigned?

I wish you would drive about & enjoy yourself more. Go to see your friends & attend to business too. It will do you good. I am glad to hear that the Chesapeake debt will be paid off. I write in great haste. God bless you & the precious little things.

Ever y[ou]r own devoted husband.

[I] have not yet received my promotion—expect the commission soon.[84] Direct [your letters] still to me as Captain. I am acting Chief of Artillery until promoted. There are guns enough to entitle me to a Lt Colonelcy but I think Genl Hill has applied only for a Majority.

—⁓⁓—

Camp near Grace Church,
6 miles from Fredericksburg
Bowling Green Road
Dec. 17th 1862

{W}e have again to thank God, my dearest Wife, for anot{her} {vi}ctory & the safety of Wm & myself after a hard fough{t} battle near Fredericksburg. Genl. Hill's Div. was ordered up from Port Royal on Friday evening. The march continued most of the night. My battery marched all night & arrived on the field about 9 A.M. I went to the front {to} learn the nature of the ground with the view of plac{ing} {t}he batteries. A. P. Hill occupied the whole of Jacks{on's} {f}ront. Ewell's Div. (com[mande]d by Early) & Jackson's Div. (com[mande]d by Taliaferro) formed the second line about 200 or 300 yds in rear & D.H. Hill for once in this life was placed in reserve. When I reached the front the battle had not yet begun. We occupied the high ground for about a mile & Longstreet joining on our left extended up to Fre{der}icksburg. Our

83. George Wythe Randolph (1818–67), the maternal grandson of Thomas Jefferson, was the Confederate secretary of war from 22 March to 15 November 1862. Earlier in the war, he had served as the first commander of the Richmond Howitzers and as chief of artillery for John Bankhead Magruder. On 12 February 1862, Randolph was commissioned brigadier general but accepted the post of secretary of war a month later. After his term on the cabinet, Randolph returned to field command, but tuberculosis forced him to leave the army and travel to France for recuperation. He officially resigned his commission on 18 December 1864. Randolph died on 3 April 1867 and was buried at Monticello, the home of his grandfather in Albemarle County, Va. (Warner, *Generals in Gray*, 252–53).

84. Carter's promotion to major became official on 12 December 1863. His new rank dated from 1 November, the day that D. H. Hill asked Carter to serve as his chief of artillery (CSR).

ground was in woods, theirs (the ene{my)} on {the} flats in front of Mr Bernard's house & stretching up to the town.[85] The pontoon bridge just back of Mr Bernard's. Their siege guns opposite F[redericksburg]. Their field guns of longest range opposite us on the Stafford shore. Our position was very strong for defence {no}t good for offensive operations, on account of {t}he heavy ditch banks on the road from F[redericksburg] to Port Roy{al}. These embankments made for wattling fences were admirable breastworks, through which embrasures were cut for their guns. A. P. Hill's artillery was on the right, none in the centre as the woods were too dense for its use. This was our weak point & they knew it. The enemy opened from a long arc of guns & then their troops were drawn up all along our front, about a 1000 yds to the front line. The other lines were a few hund{red} {y}ds apart all parallel & stretching up throug{h} {t}he mist towards the town as far as the eye cou{ld} {re}ach. They made a feint at our right after some maneuvering & then formed in six or seven lines opposite our centre & charged. The whole scene was grand. Their troops superbly drilled, coming on with flying colours & marched boldly across the plains to the woods & gained it notwithstanding the fire of the artillery. They broke through Archer's Brig.[86] & Gregg's,[87] but were repulsed by Holk's & Lawton's Brig. {o}f Early's Div. on the 2nd line, & driven entirely bac{k} {to} the cedar wattling.[88] Dead bodies covered

85. Arthur Bernard's house, known as Mannsfield, was located south of Fredericksburg near the Rappahannock River. It was a two-story stone structure built by 1766. The Bernard property consisted of 1,800 acres and included several outbuildings. Mannsfield was used as a Union field hospital during the Battle of Fredericksburg (Harrison, *Fredericksburg Civil War Sites*, 2:76–82).

86. Archer's brigade at Fredericksburg consisted of the 5th Alabama Infantry Battalion; the 19th Georgia Infantry; and the 1st, 7th, and 14th Tennessee Infantry regiments (*OR* 21:542). Brigadier General James Jay Archer (1817–64) of Maryland commanded the brigade.

87. Gregg's brigade included the 1st South Carolina Rifles and the 1st, 12th, 13th, and 14th South Carolina Infantry regiments (*OR* 21:542). Brigadier General Maxcy Gregg (1814–62) of South Carolina commanded the brigade and was killed during the battle (Warner, *Generals in Grey*, 119–20).

88. Carter is referring to the brigades of Brigadier Generals Isaac Ridgeway Trimble (1802–88) of Virginia and Alexander Robert Lawton (1818–96) of South Carolina. Trimble had been severely wounded at the Battle of Second Bull Run; thus Colonel (later Major General) Robert Frederick Hoke (1837–1912) of the 21st North Carolina commanded the brigade, which consisted of the 15th Alabama Infantry, the 12th and 21st Georgia Infantry, the 21st North Carolina Infantry, and the 1st North Carolina Infantry Battalion. General Lawton was badly wounded at the Battle of Antietam, and command of his brigade fell initially to Colonel Edmund Nathan Atkinson (1834–84) of the 26th Georgia Infantry. During the Battle of Fredericksburg, however, Atkinson was wounded in the elbow, and Colonel Clement Anselm Evans (1833–1911) of the 31st Georgia Infantry took command of the brigade. Lawton's brigade included the 13th, 26th, 31st, 38th, 60th, and 61st Georgia Infantry regiments (*OR* 21:543, 670–71; Warner, *Generals in Gray*, 83, 140–41, 175–76, 310–11; Krick, *Lee's Colonels*, 36).

the grou{nd.} A. P. Hill's Artillery having been pretty much knocked to pieces I ordered up five rifle pieces & Brown sent up a large number.[89] Only one piece of my old battery came up, the Parrot, commanded by Wm. He behaved as he always does[,] most gallantly fighting side by side with Pegram[90] & when Jackson ordered the Artillery to advance on the plains below & volunteers were called for[,] he offered to go with anyone although nearly half of his detachment had been killed & wounded. It was the mos{t} {de}structive Artillery fire of the war—horses & me{n} {p}iled up by scores in some two hundred yds. A general charge was ordered at sundown. I took fourteen pieces on A. P. Hill's left & reported to him but was pleased to hear that Jackson had left it discretionary with him to advance or not, & he thought it too late. As I looked across the wide open flat at the long line of Artillery & infantry growing more {o}bscure as darkness approached & heard the bullet{s} {w}histling by me all the time I felt much pleased {t}o give up the charge at that hour, for I knew n{oth}ing of the ground & a single ditch might have brought the guns to a halt under a murderous fire. Well thank God we won a great victory which I trust may have a powerful moral effect.

I wr{ite} in haste {to} relieve your {an}xiety. I cannot tell you my darling how much I wish to see you & the precious children. I hope to get off for a day or two when the campaign is ended, which I hope is now near at hand. Your last [letter] is the 6th Dec. God forever bless you.

Y[ou]r devoted husband.

D. H. Hill's Division was not engaged. Eight pieces only engaged, all lost heavily. The man killed at Wm's gun was Duke of Goochland from Leake's Co.[91]

---

89. Colonel John Thompson Brown commanded a battalion in the reserve artillery at the Battle of Fredericksburg (*OR* 21:544).

90. Captain William Ransom Johnson Pegram (1841–65) commanded the Purcell Artillery at the Battle of Fredericksburg (*OR* 21:542; Krick, *Lee's Colonels*, 302).

91. James M. Duke (d. 1862) enlisted in Goochland County, Va., as a private in the Turner Artillery on 29 August 1861. The Turner battery disbanded on 4 October 1862. Four days later, Duke and the other members of the unit transferred into the King William Artillery. He was killed at the Battle of Fredericksburg (CSR).

CHAPTER FIVE

Winter Quarters
20 January–25 June 1863

Following the Battle of Fredericksburg, the opposing armies settled into winter camps on opposite sides of the Rappahannock River. On 24 December General Lee tried to remedy the lack of forage for his army by dispersing more than half of the artillery into counties south of Fredericksburg. Batteries could find food for their horses there and still be within easy marching distance in case the army needed to reassemble quickly. Jackson's 2nd Corps artillery encamped in Caroline County. Major Tom Carter's men set up their winter camp near Grace Church, a few miles south of Fredericksburg. At the end of January 1863, it relocated farther south to Milford Depot.[1]

Carter and his artillery experienced important changes in the first half of February. His former division commander, Major General D. H. Hill, who had left the army in mid-January, assumed command of Confederate forces in North Carolina on 7 February. Carter's close friend, Brigadier General Robert E. Rodes, became the temporary commander of the division. More significantly, on 15 February Brigadier General William Nelson Pendleton reorganized the artillery of the Army of Northern Virginia. Hoping to increase its efficiency and ensure better concentration of fire in battle, he organized the various batteries into battalions and assigned one battalion to each infantry division and two to both corps as an artillery reserve. Carter's battalion, one of the few that preexisted the reorganization, was formally assigned to D. H. Hill's division. In the midst of all this activity, Colonel Stapleton Crutchfield, Stonewall Jackson's chief of ar-

---

1. *OR* 21:1077. Carter's letters written before 27 January are dated from Grace Church. From that date until the beginning of the Chancellorsville Campaign in late April, they are addressed from Milford Depot.

tillery, recommended Carter for promotion to lieutenant colonel, a rank more fitting for a battalion commander.[2]

That recommendation played an important part in a difficult decision that Carter faced in March. After General Hill settled into his new command in North Carolina, he wrote to Carter and asked him to serve as his artillery chief. The position guaranteed a promotion and significantly larger command responsibilities. Carter shared the request with Rodes. His friend advised him "to consider Hill's offer seriously before refusing it." Sometime before 22 March, Carter made up his mind to remain with the army in Virginia. On that date, Rodes sent Hill a letter explaining that Carter had decided against accepting the offer because he expected to receive his promotion to lieutenant colonel shortly. The new commission did, in fact, come through on 4 April. Another reason no doubt played an important part in Tom's decision: on 4 March Susan had given birth to their third child. They named the baby girl Anne Willing after his stepmother.[3]

Carter's battalion remained at Milford Depot until 29 April, when it left its camps for Fredericksburg. The next day, it marched west toward Chancellorsville. Lee's army was reacting to movements by the Army of the Potomac, now under Major General Joseph Hooker. A large portion of the Union army had marched on roads north of the Rapidan River and crossed several miles west of Fredericksburg, intending to attack Lee's army from the rear. The initial confrontation of what became the Battle of Chancellorsville took place on the Orange Turnpike on 1 May. The next day, Stonewall Jackson's 2nd Corps, with Rodes's division in the lead, executed a march of at least a dozen miles that placed it on the exposed right flank of Hooker's army. At 5:15 P.M. Jackson ordered Rodes to begin the planned attack. Carter's battalion, which initially took position in a field just south of the Orange Turnpike, shifted to the road to support Rodes's assault. Jackson's attack overwhelmed Hooker's right flank, the XI Corps, and pushed it back toward the Union center at Chancellorsville. Carter's guns, which were restricted to the turnpike by dense woods on either side, got to within 1,000 yards of the small hamlet. There, the large concentration of Union artillery in the fields around Chancellorsville prevented the battalion from continuing the fight. On the morning of the third, Carter

2. *OR* 18:872; 21:1093; 25[2]:614, 625–26, 655.
3. Robert E. Rodes to THC, 10 Mar. 1863, THCP, 1861–1896, VHS; Robert E. Rodes to D. H. Hill, 22 Mar. 1863, Daniel Harvey Hill Papers, North Carolina Division of Archives and History; Carter's CSR. Carter's new commission bore the date of rank of 2 March.

moved some of his guns south of the turnpike to an abandoned Union position at Hazel Grove. From there, his battalion, along with several other batteries, supported Confederate infantry attacks by pounding the Union lines southwest of Chancellorsville. By noon the battle had ended, and Hooker's army had pulled back to hastily constructed defenses near United States Ford on the Rapidan River. Carter reported losses in his battalion of nine men killed and thirty-seven wounded.[4]

Two weeks after his great victory at the Battle of Chancellorsville, Robert E. Lee decided to build on the momentum and invade the North a second time. Before beginning the next campaign, however, the commanding general once more reorganized his army. On 30 May, partly as a consequence of Stonewall Jackson's death after Chancellorsville, Lee rearranged the army into three corps with three divisions each. The artillery maintained its organization of one battalion per infantry division and two battalions in reserve in each corps. Robert Rodes's division and Tom Carter's battalion remained in the 2nd Corps, now commanded by Lieutenant General Richard S. Ewell.[5]

The Army of Northern Virginia began moving north from Fredericksburg at the beginning of June. On 4 June Carter's battalion left its camps below the town and marched toward Culpeper Court House, where it arrived three days later. On the tenth, it continued toward the Shenandoah valley. Two days later, the three divisions of the 2nd Corps routed Union general Robert H. Milroy's troops at Winchester and Martinsburg, thus opening the way for the rest of Lee's army to follow. Rodes's division continued north and crossed the Potomac River at Williamsport, Maryland, on 15 June. The division, with Carter's battalion following, made its way from there to Chambersburg, Pennsylvania, where it arrived on the twenty-fourth. Three days earlier, General Lee had issued explicit orders for the men to refrain from taking or destroying private property during the invasion. This command frustrated Carter and many others in the army. "I know this humane & magnanimous course is right & that we shall be rewarded in some way," he wrote to Susan on the twenty-fifth, "but it is hard to practice when one recollects the barren & devastated waste between the Potomac & the Rappahannock & all the privations our grand

4. *OR* 25[1]:939, 998–1000.
5. *OR* 25[2]:850. Robert Rodes took permanent command of D. H. Hill's division on 8 May 1863 (*OR* 25[2]:787). His promotion to major general, which came through the day before, was dated to 2 May in recognition of his leadership during Stonewall Jackson's flank attack at Chancellorsville (Krick, "'We Have Never Suffered a Greater Loss Save in the Great Jackson,'" 130).

old state has undergone." In the same letter, Carter admitted to his wife that he did not know "the full object of the invasion."[6]

—⟋⟍—

Near Grace Church
Jan 20th 1863

My precious Wife,

I reached here on Sunday & took up my abode with William for two nights. Thanks to your large bed tick, I have slept most comfortably. Today at Genl. Rodes' request I have taken quarters with him & mess with himself & staff. I think of you constantly & most tenderly my darling & look forward to our reunion in peace as the greatest earthly happiness that can ever befall me. I have looked over our lines hastily & have come to the conclusion that whatever the enemy may do in [the] future, it is not their intention to cross on our front immediately. The preparations are inadequate as yet to an effectual crossing. They are still intrenching on a small scale opposite to Wm P. Taylor's. The causeway, constructed to the old ferry landing at Snowden, is a narrow insignificant concern entirely unfit for the purpose of crossing a large army.[7] They may cross above Fredericksburg at Richard's Ford, where they have cut a road.[8] I hear that Longstreet[,] Jackson & Genl Lee expect a cross-

6. Macaluso, *Morris, Orange, and King William Artillery*, 44; Boatner, *Dictionary*, 332; *OR* 27[3]:912; THC to SRC, 25 June 1863. In spite of Lee's orders, the Confederates confiscated a great deal of private property while on the march in Maryland and Pennsylvania. A modern study of the campaign estimates the army "seized between 45,000 and 50,000 head of cattle, about 35,000 head of sheep, and thousands of hogs" (Brown, *Retreat from Gettysburg*, 28).

7. Snowden was located in Stafford County, Va., on the north side of the Rappahannock River about seven miles southeast of Fredericksburg on the River Road (modern Route 3). At the time of Carter's letter, the home was owned by John Seddon (1826–63), the younger brother of Confederate secretary of war James Alexander Seddon. John had served as a lieutenant of infantry during the Mexican War and represented King George and Stafford Counties in the Virginia House of Delegates from 1855 to 1861. On 14 May 1861, he enlisted as the captain of Company D of the 1st Virginia Infantry Battalion. Following brief service as acting assistant adjutant general on the staff of Brigadier General Daniel Ruggles (1810–97) in the summer of 1861, Seddon returned to duty with the battalion. His promotion to major came on 20 May 1862, followed by his resignation for poor health in October of that year. John Seddon returned to Snowden, where he died on 3 December 1863 (Moncure, "The Destruction of Snowden," 1; Leonard, *General Assembly of Virginia*, 460, 465, 470; Krick, *Staff Officers*, 262; Krick, *Lee's Colonels*, 340).

8. Richard's (or Richards') Ford was located on the Rappahannock River about a mile north of where the Rapidan River met the Rappahannock. At the end of December 1862, a Union expedition crossed at the ford, which may have brought that particular crossing to Carter's mind (*OR* 21:742).

ing, but this may be a rumor. Our lines are being made very strong & a great deal of dirt work has been done. Rodes is commanding the Division as Senior Brigadier since the departure of Hill.[9] It is said that he first offered his resignation on the plea of ill health which was refused. He then applied for a transfer to the South. The result is not known except that he was ordered to Richmond. He expected to succeed in one way or another to escape this position, & seemed determined on it. He sold his extra horses & made all preparations for a final leave.

We are much pleased with Rodes & hope his chance is good for promotion to the command of the Division. Early has just received notice of his promotion. He deserves it & has the consciousness of having won it without fear or favor [but] by hard fighting. Today, there has been a review of Rooney Lee's Brigade[10] on the bottom between Wm P. Taylor's & Morse Neck house.[11] Genls Lee[,] ~~Longstreet~~ Jackson[,] Stuart & Hill (A. P.) were present & many of the lesser lights. Ladies in carriages[,] ambulances & on horseback & in wagons were present. Genl. Lee asked after you very kindly. Charlotte is with Rooney & Genl. Lee says Cousin Lucy Wickham was anxious to join W[illia]ms but the latter had gone off so far that he feared she could not do so.[12] I don't know where it is but suppose about Mangohick Church.[13] Do write me of everything at

9. On 14 January 1863, General Hill left the army and reported to Richmond, where he remained until 7 February, when he assumed command of what later became the Department of North Carolina (*OR* 18:847, 872, 953).

10. Brigadier General W. H. F. "Rooney" Lee's brigade consisted of the 2nd North Carolina Cavalry and the 9th, 10th, 13th, and 15th Virginia Cavalry (*OR* 21:544).

11. William P. Taylor's house, called Hayfield, was located in Caroline County, Va., near the Rappahannock River, approximately ten miles south of Fredericksburg. The prosperous Taylor family owned 158 slaves and $140,000 in real estate in 1860 (*Official Atlas of the Civil War*, plate XXXIX, maps 2 and 3; 1860 Census, Caroline County; 1860 Census, Caroline County, Slave Schedules). A little farther south was Moss Neck (not "Morse" as Carter mistakenly wrote), the home of the Corbin family. Richard and his wife, Roberta, and their five-year-old daughter, Jane, lived in the 250-foot-long brick house on the 1,600-acre plantation (valued at $25,000). In the winter of 1863, Stonewall Jackson pitched his headquarters tent in the yard of Moss Neck (1860 Census, Caroline County; 1860 Census, Caroline County, Slave Schedules; Robertson, *Stonewall Jackson*, 667).

12. Lucy Penn Taylor Wickham (1830–1913) was the wife of Colonel Williams Carter Wickham (1820–80), commander of the 4th Virginia Cavalry (McGill, *Beverley Family of Virginia*, 465).

13. Mangohick Church was built around 1730 in King William County, Va., not far from the county's western border. Constructed in the Flemish-bond brick style common among many of Virginia's colonial churches, Mangohick was an Anglican church that became a "free church" after the disestablishment of the Anglican Church in Virginia following the American Revolution. After the Civil War, Mangohick Church was deeded to a black Baptist congregation ("Mangohick Church, c. 1730, King William County," 207–8).

Pampatike. I feel much more interest since I have seen you in everything there. Hart has not gone yet. His furlough has not yet returned but is on the way. Wm has applied for a detail of one Lieutenant & several men to arrest absentees & you may have an opportunity to send my collars & cravats by him. A very small trunk or large valise would do for me. I find I have not many clothes. They seem lost in your large trunk which is about one fourth full with all my clothes in it. Tell me what you did about the stocks. Had you time to the interest? What balance have you at Wortham's? Above all tell me about the precious children. God bless you darling. Love to all. Let me know what you decide upon in regard to the parsonage. I shall try to be with you.

Ever your own devoted husband.

Jan. 22nd. I kept this letter with the expectation of sending it by private hands yesterday but the weather was so inclement that the person did not go.

I open it to tell you there is nothing new except this long storm of rain. I fear you had an uncomfortable ride home. Do tell me everything. I miss you more than I have ever done. Genl Hill is in North Carolina. Nothing is known of his resignation. There is a rumour that it will be accepted in a few weeks & is delayed because [it is] not prudent to grant it at this time. Don't know why unless [there is] a fear of giving the impression of dissension in our ranks, for he stands high with the enemy. When you can send anything, please send collars & cravat[,] handkerchiefs & cotton socks all marked [and] any eatables that you can spare conveniently. You need not deprive yourself at all because in the mess we make a [unreadable word] business at the end of the month & of course I get nothing & would accept nothing for the things you send. Where did you get the whiskey you brought me & what did it cost? We are very fond of catsups of every kind—tomato or walnut &c. Hart has not yet left. All furloughs have been kept at general hdquarters probably on account of the alarm here.

Kiss the darling children. I hope you took them something for their dear Papa who loves them more than tongue can tell or words express.

Ever y[ou]r own husband.

—w—

Camp near Grace Church
Jan. 24th 1863

My precious Wife,

The time for my second letter has again rolled around. I wish to write by every mail but you must feel no uneasiness should you fail to receive my letters. The mails are extremely irregular on account of the heavy business of the army. We are totally engaged day & night fortifying our front for infantry & artillery. The line first adopted, which was the road from Fred[ericksbur]g to Port Royal, has been abandoned & the heights this side of the flats are now being intrenched. Very heavy works are going up just around Basil Gordon's house & in front of Sam Gordons.[14] The former has moved his family, the latter has considered moving his also. At the foot of these hills are the rifle pits for the infantry. The works on top are for Artillery. The corduroy road, you heard had been built by the enemy, extends to the old ferry landing just below Snowden house. The enemy have thrown up earthworks opposite to Wm P. Taylors & we thought we discovered a redoubt today in the pines to *our* left of Snowden, say three or four hundred yds from { . . . } a body of Cavalry figured around the grounds but this is no unusual sight, as they picket the shore all along to P. Royal. The smoke could be seen for the first time (by myself) coming from the chimneys. I felt sorry for the dear little woman that everyone seems to love as I thought of her alone with her children in the midst of those villainous Yankees. I sometimes doubt if she is there. I never see the children in the yard or porch. What a lonely life she must lead. Genl Lee wrote to Genl Jackson stating that all his information went to show that the enemy had collected their pontoons & artillery back of Snowden & yesterday he ordered the working parties to be kept on at night & all the extra baggage to the rear. Still my own impression is that they will make a feint here with Artillery & cross above

14. The homes of Bazil and Samuel Gordon were located in Caroline County on a ridge overlooking a plain that stretched to the Rappahannock River. West of the Gordon homes was Grace Church, where Carter's camp was located. Bazil Gordon was listed in the 1860 census as being fifty-two years old with a wife and five children. He owned real estate valued at $61,000 and real property worth $71,000, which included sixty-one slaves. Samuel Gordon, fifty-six in 1860, had a wife and six children and owned real estate valued at $86,500 and real property worth $110,738, which included forty-four slaves (Gilmer, "Map of Caroline County," 1864, Jeremy Francis Gilmer Collection, VHS; 1860 Census, Caroline County; 1860 Census, Caroline County, Slave Schedules).

Fred[ericksburg]. This is their best plan. In this manner they could turn our line of works & force us to fight on equal terms, just as we managed them from Mechanicsville to White Oak Swamp. Let them come as they may[,] their route is beset with difficulties. Our position here is strong as could be desired or rather will be when finished. It must be sometime before they are ready to cross here. Their preparations are incomplete at this time.

I begin to fear there is little chance for my furlough unless all these alarms subside. I shall not despair however for a fortnight. If it should be impossible for me to leave, do, my darling, think of the parsonage plan. It is so painful to think of you alone at Pampatike. Affairs would not prosper as they do now under your management but probably you would be happier at the parsonage. I can not express to you the desire I have for your society. My admiration & love for you increase with my years & I pine for the welfare of my sweet little children. God only knows how I long to be with you all. I trust that the next campaign will end the war & that peace & independence will again bless us, & then, if that kind Providence who has so mercifully & miraculously watched over me thus far in all dangers, should continue his gracious care & spare my life, we will indeed enjoy sweet companionship together. You will be glad to hear that your Uncle Alex is giving entire satisfaction in the discharge of his duties. He attends to business I understand with his usual ability & with dispatch. I had feared that in the latter respect his health & extreme amiability & urbanity would prove an obstacle but I hear in the army that it is not so. I enclose you a note from Mama to Shirley. Nothing new. Wm is well. The money for his coat was not sent Shirley. He will pay me, how much was it? Do you want it? Hart went down today & will return Tuesday—too soon for you to send the things. I got today a most excellent army overcoat. It is genuine English cloth with no cotton in it[,] of a bluish gray. I will send it to you to line by the first opportunity. It cost only $18—government price. I wish to write to Mama soon. Do you know what amount is to their credit at Wortham's[?]

It is thought Genl Hill's resignation has been accepted on account of his health but will not be made public for reasons of policy for a few weeks. I hope sincerely Rodes will get his place. His chance is said to be good. The work he has done on his front is very creditable to his energy & military talent. We will be in front this time & with God's help we hope not only to defeat them but to utterly rout them. There is to be an entire reorganization of the Artillery in the Spring. I hope to get an independent command whether large or small. I have had my own way so long it is hard to submit to some of the boobies who will be high in rank.

Good night, darling. God bless you all.

Ever y[ou]r own husband.

The signs of peace are growing brighter. The sentiment at the North is undergoing a change & dissension obviously on the rise.

—ᨑ—

Camp near Milford Depot
Jan. 27th 1863

Well my darling here we are again much to the surprise of all parties. All orders rec[eive]d up to the time of the one to march to this place were decidedly belligerent. Working parties put on at night as well as day, superfluous baggage to the rear &c.[,] looked like stern work ahead but on Sunday we were ordered to be in readiness to march back at 8 A.M. Monday. I am much pleased consequently at the prospect of being with you during your confinement, unless the prospect is removed by some alarms similar to the one calling us to the front.[15] The New York Tribune gives an account in yesterday's paper which looks as if they really intended to cross last Tuesday or Monday. Possibly the storm about that time prevented the attack. It seems probable now that the heavy rains recently will prevent operations on our front immediately & the Yankees may try the N Carolina water Campaign. I do not mean that this army on our front will be entirely removed & perhaps very partially if at all removed but their gunboats & N.C. army already there may do something. If the soil there is like that here the land forces can do nothing & I imagine the soil is even worse.

I went immediately on my arrival yesterday to Dr Baylor's & spent the night.[16] They were exceedingly kind & hospitable. They are most urgent in their requests for me to spend all my nights with them. This I

15. Carter's wife was carrying their third child at the time of this letter. She gave birth to their second daughter on 4 March 1863. They named her Anne Willing after Tom Carter's stepmother.

16. Dr. John Roy Baylor (1821–97) lived at nearby Newmarket, the Baylor family home in Caroline County (Wingfield, *History of Caroline County*, 377).

cannot of course do but I promised to return tonight. I found my things there which you so kindly & thoughtfully sent me. They are very nice. The knife I will contrive to get soon. I felt very sad without you & was glad they put me in the other room upstairs[,] otherwise I should have mourned all night. Dr Palmer has written Dr Baylor that he has heard news of the highest importance to our affairs but is not at liberty to tell, but it is much more important than mediation.[17] This much he would say[,] that Dr Baylor ought at once to sell his N. Car[olina] stock & buy C[onfederate] stock. The legislation in our Congress, however (I see by the Whig today) [it] is thought will so reduce the amount of currency in circulation, say to 150 millions, that the Editor thinks stocks will decline. If so it would be best to hold on before purchasing. I suppose when the redundancy in our currency is diminished that everything will fall in price, grain among the rest, but really I know but little about the intricate laws of currency. I know forage is more & more scarce but if you have anything to sell I should get it off as opportunity offers without sacrifice. I am sorry H. Tomlin got the boat but feared Mr Duling would be afraid to continue shipping after the alarm at the White H[ouse]. I suppose it was at that time Tomlin secured it.

What do you think of my getting myself into a scrape of buying a coat at $120.00[?] Genl. Rodes rec[eive]d a most beautiful coat, which was too small for him. It fits me admirably & supposing as it was made in Charleston of cloth at government price, though of the finest quality, that it would be particularly cheap. I told him I would take it, although the trimmings are not suitable[,] intending to have them altered. To my surprise, the price is $120. The collar alone cost $15. I think I shall send it to Biers & Poindexter or to Schafer & tell them to sell it at cost which I don't doubt they can do as the cloth is of beautiful color & quality & it is made by Schafer's measure & the most stylish cut I have seen. I bought it simply because I expected to get an excellent coat at a low price—not that I needed it at all. Let this be a lesson to you as well as to myself never to buy what is not wanted.

My mess was soon broken up with Genl Rodes by this movement backwards one week only. I am sorry too to add that my mess with Wm

17. Carter may be referring to Dr. William P. Palmer, a Confederate surgeon who was in charge of the post hospital at Camp Lee near Richmond, Va. (CSR).

is also broken. The Captains, except Hardaway who was ordered to remain, decided by lot who should stay & it fell on Wm.[18] He was most anxious to come. They let Bondurant off from the lottery as his wife had just arrived at Milford.[19] Wm's men were much chagrined. Two batteries remained on the front with each Division. I fear the forage subject is to give great trouble. The roads are becoming worse every day & the horses are falling off daily. France & Bob came down with me & we are encamped at the same place in the woods where you left us last. Maria Tompkins will write in a day or two[,] possibly today.[20] They have very kindly hemmed the handkerchiefs for me. No one outside of that family seems to have the least idea you are enceinte.[21] All ask when you will return & why you don't return. Nothing new from the front today. I r[eceive]d y[ou]r letter from Pampatike & am glad things are not worse.

I hope you took the children something from their Papa. Tell me about them in every letter. I love to see their names even.

> God ever bless you darling.
> E[ve]r y[ou]r devoted husband

The Dr (Baylor) I think is more in favor of stocks now than grazing lands. I must have a talk with him on the subject. Something must be done. Considering the precarious life I lead possibly stocks would be best for you. Got some kind messages day before yesterday from Dr Temple. He is at Guineas'. I have written to you 3 times now.

—⁓—

18. Robert Archelaus Hardaway (1829–99) of Georgia served as captain of the Hardaway (Ala.) Artillery from 1 May 1861 until his promotion to major on 10 January 1863 (to rank from 3 December 1862). His new rank, however, was not confirmed until 1 May 1863. At the Battle of Chancellorsville, Hardaway was acting chief of artillery of Richard H. Anderson's division. On 27 February 1864, Hardaway was promoted to lieutenant colonel (CSR).

19. Captain James William Bondurant (1835–67) of Buckingham County, Va., commanded the Jeff Davis (Ala.) Artillery (Krick, *Lee's Colonels*, 57).

20. Carter may be referring to Maria M. Tompkins (b. 1831?) of Richmond, Va., who is listed in the 1860 census as a twenty-nine-year-old resident of the city. In the spring of 1862, she was staying at Newmarket, the Caroline County, Va., home of Dr. John Baylor (1860 Census, 2nd Ward City of Richmond; see Carter's letter of 4 April 1863 for a reference to Maria Tompkins's residence at Newmarket).

21. Enceinte is a French word meaning pregnant.

Artillery Camp near Milford Depot
Feb. 6th 1863

My dear Sir,[22]

I owe you an apology for my long delay in answering your letter in regard to the young Turners.[23] It reached me on the battlefield at Fredericksburg nearly two months ago. Although I have not answered the letter I have given the subject my attention. My brother now commands my old battery & I find on inquiry [he] has done what he could for these young gentlemen.[24] When Leake's men were transferred to me[,] my company organization was complete & it was therefore impossible to give, as I wished to do, any position to his noncommissioned officers. Several sergeants & corporals being absent, one or two of these noncommissioned offi[cers] were allowed to serve in their places, but this arrangement was only temporary of course & they had to return to ranks afterwards. It is natural this company should be dissatisfied with an arrangement which disbanded their old organization & threw them into a new Comp'y with new officers & new associates & without officers of their own choice, but the good of the service required this change however hard it might fall upon some cases, & it was done. The Goochland men have however behaved in a most unexceptionable manner & I hope are entirely satisfied. I have seen Mr Turner, the father of these gentlemen, since his letter to you was written & he assured me that their present position was satisfactory to him.

We are knee deep in mud here & in every direction for twenty or thirty miles around with the pleasure of knowing that the Yankees are still deeper, & that too in the worst soil for roads in this state. They can

22. Carter wrote this letter to John Coles Rutherfoord (1825–66) of Rock Castle in Goochland County, Va., who was married to Ann Seddon Roy Rutherfoord, Carter's wife's sister. John Rutherfoord represented Goochland County in the House of Delegates (Leonard, *General Assembly of Virginia*, 479).

23. Carter is probably referring to the following members of Captain Walter D. Leake's artillery battery, who were assigned to the King William Artillery after their unit disbanded on 4 October 1862: Private Charles W. Turner (1840?–1905), Private Joseph Wilmer Turner (b. 1845?), and Corporal William Argyle Turner. All three reported for duty with Carter's battery on 8 October 1862. Charles and Joseph Turner were the sons of George W. Turner (b. 1814?), a farmer from Goochland County, Va. (CSR; 1860 Census, Goochland County).

24. There is no mention in William P. Carter's service record of when he officially took command of the King William Artillery. Most likely, he had been acting in that capacity since early November 1862, after his brother Thomas became D. H. Hill's artillery chief. Hill mentions William Carter in his report of the Battle of Fredericksburg as one of several who "brought out their batteries," suggesting that Carter was in command of the battery by 13 December (*OR* 21:643).

not advance until the ground becomes firm & with the weather usual to this season. That will not be until the drying winds of March. As soon as possible they must give battle. The outside pressure, produced by their want of success[,] the state of their finances & the dissension at home & the near approach of the time for disbandment of a large portion of their troops, will force an advance at the earliest practicable moment— whether Hooker in a military point of view thinks it desirable or not.[25] The result, with the help of God, is not doubtful. We, of the Army of the Potomac, have the vanity to believe that we can't be whipped.[26] There is reason to believe too that their army is much demoralized & opposed to crossing the Rappahannock under any circumstances. They have also lost their best officers[:] McClellan[,] Porter[,] Kearney[,] Sumner & Franklin.[27] There is hardly a man of note among their commanders at this time.

I feel far more uneasiness concerning the Western campaign & our Southern Coast. Every effort will certainly be made to open the navigation of the Mississippi River by way of pacifying the Northwest which is fast becoming unruly. Yet I cannot believe that they will succeed in keeping open a river averaging less than a mile in width commanded by high bluffs at many points & traversing hundreds of miles of our country subjecting its trade to the dangers of light & heavy Artillery. Ironclad

25. Major General Joseph Hooker (1814–79) of Massachusetts, a Union division commander with a solid combat reputation, replaced Major General Ambrose Burnside as commander of the Army of the Potomac on 26 January 1863 (Warner, *Generals in Blue*, 233–35; *OR* 25[2]:4–5).

26. Why Carter referred to the Confederate army as the "Army of the Potomac" here is a mystery. The main Southern army in Virginia had not been called that since the fall/winter of 1861/62. Perhaps he was confused because he had just been writing about the Union Army of the Potomac in the previous sentences.

27. Major General George B. McClellan was relieved of command of the Army of the Potomac on 7 November 1862. In the presidential election of 1864, he opposed Lincoln as the Democratic Party candidate (Warner, *Generals in Blue*, 292). In November 1862, Major General Fitz John Porter was tried in a court-martial and found guilty of disloyalty, disobedience, and misconduct in the face of the enemy during the Battle of Second Bull Run. He was dismissed from the service on 21 January 1863 (Warner, *Generals in Blue*, 379). Major General Philip Kearny (1815–62) of New York was killed at the Battle of Chantilly (or Ox Hill) on 1 September 1862 (Warner, *Generals in Blue*, 258–59). Major General Edwin Vose Sumner (1797–1863) of Massachusetts commanded the II Corps of the Army of the Potomac. Following John Pope's appointment to command of the Army of Virginia, Sumner requested to be relieved of duty. He was reassigned to the Department of Missouri but died on 21 March 1863 while en route (Warner, *Generals in Blue*, 489–90). After the disastrous Battle of Fredericksburg, Ambrose Burnside claimed that Major General William B. Franklin, who had commanded the Left Grand Division of the army, had disobeyed orders and was partially to blame for the Union army's defeat. Burnside subsequently called for Franklin's removal. Although President Lincoln did not officially cashier Franklin, he never again served in the Army of the Potomac. In the summer of 1863, William Franklin was transferred to the Department of the Gulf, where he commanded the XIX Corps (Warner, *Generals in Blue*, 159–60).

gunboats may pass anywhere but no trade should be allowed on the river. Rosecrans too I hope is at the end of his invasion.[28] His line of communication is long & exposed & our cavalry out there bold & active. Success everywhere is so necessary to our cause & to the hope of an early peace that we cannot but feel anxious even where there is no cause for alarm. A single serious reverse would prolong the war.

I am glad to hear from Sue that Sister Ann is doing so well since the advent of Miss Helen Coles.[29] I should have written to her lately but have behaved so shabbily in return for her kindness ~~that~~ in writing to me on several occasions that I have been ashamed to do so. However I shall throw myself on her charitable & generous nature & write soon. I hope dear little Nannie[30] & Master John are as well as when I last saw them.[31] Present me most kindly to your father's family. My Brother & our whole family will always remember with deep gratitude their kindness to him when wounded. He seems entirely restored to health although he complains occasionally of pain in the chest. I trust it is only nervous & that the ball is not still in the thorax.

With love to Sister Ann I am most truly y[ou]rs
Thos. H. Carter

—◊—

Milford Depot
Feb. 12th 1863

My precious Wife,

Your letter of Tuesday is just rec[eive]d & I am sorry to find that you failed to receive my letter of Monday. The mails are too badly managed to calculate on a letter going straight through & I must abandon the plan. I fear you will not receive this tomorrow as you ought to do. The mail from here reaches Richmond early this evening & I don't understand why the letters fail to go out in the stage in the morning. Hereafter I shall give two or three days grace. There is nothing new save several

28. Carter is referring to the current stalemate in Tennessee that existed between the opposing armies of Generals William S. Rosecrans and Braxton Bragg that followed the Union victory at the Battle of Stones River (or Murfreesboro).

29. Helen Coles Rutherfoord (1863–1944) was the daughter of John and Ann Seddon Roy Rutherfoord.

30. Nannie has not been identified.

31. Carter is referring to John Rutherfoord (1861–1942), the son of John and Ann Seddon Roy Rutherfoord.

rumors about our moving with the reserve Artillery to Hanover Ct House & another rumor of moving the horses back without the guns on account of forage. Wm has a hard time getting forage for his teams but they keep up wonderfully & are the best horses in the Division Artillery notwithstanding he has less transportation & farther to haul. He is making efforts to get another wagon or more mules. Andrew Davis returned last night without the box but your note explained it today.[32] If I get my furlough I intend to fit up in the way of eatables & tables[,] plates[,] cups[,] saucers &c. I have a prospect now of getting a wagon when I shall be more comfortable.

Dr Baylor has made his long talked-of trip to Fred[ericksbur]g to attend to the waterworks which have been injured by some military works. Nothing could be done as the works were a military necessity. A large piece of lowgrounds has been flooded by four feet of water to prevent the enemy from landing except under our guns. They are still intrenching in the streets of Fred[ericksbur]g. The Dr thinks had he been landed blindfolded in the town he should not have known it. John Scott at whose house he stayed has lost nothing but on the whole made money.[33] He remained in his house all the time & was in no danger. In no case did the shells penetrate the second wall. He sold $30,000 worth of anthracite coal left by the Yankees on some former occasion also several hundred tons of pig iron.[34] He must be a Scotchman or Yankee. He knows how to make money. The Dr found several families in great comfort & enjoying themselves highly. The main part of the population must suffer though. However[,] a large am[oun]t of money has been subscribed.[35] There is

32. Andrew Davis has not been identified.

33. Carter is referring to John F. Scott (b. 1804) of Fredericksburg, the owner of Hope Foundry in the city. In the 1860 census, Scott lived with his wife, Martha, and their six children and owned real estate valued at $16,000. In March 1863 his name appeared in the *Richmond Daily Dispatch* as one of several who had been elected common councilmen for the city of Fredericksburg (1860 Census, Spotsylvania County; *RDD*, 18 Mar. 1863).

34. Scott's foundry was confiscated by Union authorities when the U.S. army occupied Fredericksburg in the spring of 1862. The facility continued to operate until the Federals withdrew from the town in August, at which time they destroyed the foundry. In late October, Scott advertised for sale as much material from the site as he could salvage, including coal, cast and wrought iron, lumber, and tools and equipment (Harrison, *Fredericksburg Civil War Sites*, 1:36–38).

35. Carter is referring to money raised by the army for the relief of citizens of Fredericksburg. Jedediah Hotchkiss, Stonewall Jackson's mapmaker, claimed that A. P. Hill's Light Division gave $10,000 to the Fredericksburg fund (McDonald, *Map Me a Map*, 107). The amount of money raised by soldiers and civilians totaled $170,000 (Rable, *Fredericksburg! Fredericksburg!*, 429).

not a tree in sight on the opposite side. While he was there the Yankees cut down the last poplar tree at Lacy's house.[36] Lacy sent over under a flag of truce to ask that they would burn the timbers of the houses & spare the trees, without avail. Dr B. could see the house of his Uncle Walker formerly obscured by a large body of woods.[37]

I am sorry to tell you one bad piece of news which you had best not mention on acc[oun]t of the servants. Six of the young men have gone off from the Yensas place: Harry, Claiborne, Jim, Wm, Albert & Robert {remainder of letter missing}

—⁓—

Camp near Milford Depot
Feb. 19th 1863

My precious Wife,

I have waited until the last moment hoping your letter of yesterday would reach me as they sometimes do the day after they leave Old Church but it did not arrive by the mail this morning & I hasten to write by the return mail today so that my letter may go out tomorrow.

Nothing yet of my furlough. I am thinking of putting in another [request] for a longer time—it is possible that the other [could] maybe have been lost, as these papers sometimes meander about the official channels until they get lost in the intricate labyrinth. I am really distressed about it because the time of your confinement is at hand & I know you want me with you. It may come today or tomorrow. In some of the offices they are very careless about papers. I shall continue to hope to the last. From my not rec[eivin]g a letter today it is possible you may have been already confined. Still the mails are irregular & this may account for the non receipt of y[ou]r letter today. I read a letter from Robert to Wm yesterday. He is at Natchez but in fear & trembling lest every thing he has may fall

36. Lacy's house, also known as Chatham, was the two-story brick home of James Lacy. It was located in Stafford County across the Rappahannock River opposite the northern section of Fredericksburg. The house was constructed between 1768 and 1771 by William Fitzhugh, whose mother, Lucy Carter Fitzhugh, was a daughter of Robert "King" Carter and thus a distant relative of Tom Carter. During the Battle of Fredericksburg, the Union army used Chatham as a field hospital, mostly for soldiers of the 1st and 2nd divisions of the II Corps of the Army of the Potomac (Harrison, *Fredericksburg Civil War Sites*, 1:102–5).

37. Walker Roy (b. 1784) of Stafford County, Va., was the older brother of Maria Roy (1790–1850), who married John Baylor of Newmarket, Caroline County, Va., on 6 May 1819. Dr. John Roy Baylor was their son (1860 Census, Stafford County; "Historical and Genealogical Notes and Queries," 331). Maria Roy Baylor was the aunt of William Henry Roy (1799?–1859), Carter's father-in-law (Williams and Johnson, *Roy Genealogy*, 17).

into the hands of the enemy. He feared too that he would be drafted in Miss. after furnishing a substitute in Louisiana. All well. He thought the negroes from Lombardy would return, as Bott had informed him that they had said to the neighboring negroes "that they intended to go to Mass Robert if the overseer attempted to take them to Mason Bayou." They are off to the Yankees in my opinion, never to return. His letter was dated 1st February, showing that the mails must run through with considerable regularity. All well here. Wm has still to haul forage from King Wm which I have most earnestly protested against. We are now getting both hay & corn by the cars while the batteries on the front 16 to 18 miles farther from the forage districts have to haul it, & over worse roads. They too are doing picket duty & are without stables.

All well at Dr Baylor's. I shall send the donkey by the first opportunity. Nothing new, & it is time to close this letter in order to get it mailed today. Kiss the precious little ones & keep up your spirits. My furlough may come at any time. God always bless you my darling. Love to all my friends.

Ever y[ou]r devoted husband

—ᘏᘏ—

Hd. Qrs., Carter's Arty Battalion

March 15th 1863

Your note, my precious wife, was received last evening. Nat & Martin with the things arrived safely & the eatables are much enjoyed by all, particularly poor France. Nat starts back this morning & I shall accompany him as far as Dr Baylors to see what can be done about the donkey. But for the condition of the roads there would be no difficulty. Nat will stay at Uncle's tonight & reach you tomorrow. I am trying to get my staff together. My Lieut of Ordnance has just arrived. His name is Osborne.[38] He is a nephew of Dr Osborne who lives near Brandon.[39] He is gentlemanly & intelligent. From Petersburg.

38. Lieutenant Nathaniel Montgomery Osborne Jr. (b. 1842) of Petersburg, Va., enlisted as a private in the 12th Virginia Infantry on 1 May 1861. On 27 February 1863, he was discharged from the 12th Virginia, promoted to acting first lieutenant, and assigned to duty as an ordnance officer on Carter's battalion staff. Osborne reported for his new duty on 9 March 1863 (Krick, *Staff Officers*, 234; CSR).

39. Carter is possibly referring to Dr. N. M. Osborne of Prince George County, Va., who was a lay delegate to the annual convention of the Protestant Episcopal Church in Virginia, held in Richmond on 16 and 17 May 1861 (*Journal of the Sixty-Sixth Annual Convention*, 12).

France I shall keep but we are not allowed to have our adjutants commissioned. I am sorry for it as he deserves some good place. We are ordered to detail a Lieut from a Battery as adjutant—a bad arrangement as they cannot be spared. Lucien Robinson was elected Lieut in Wm's Battery a short time since. He will do tolerably. Crutchfield answered Woodsons letter to the President in my absence.[40] He says it was full of misstatements. The President had endorsed it with some discourteous remarks to me—founded on the lies of Woodson. Crutchfield disabused his mind. But it was most unfair to censure me on the ex parte statements of a disgraced Lieutenant without hearing my side of the question.

I have just received a flattering invitation from Genl Hill to join him in N. Carolina. He promises the rank of Lt Col. Rodes thinks I ought to consider the matter well before declining. I enclose you Rodes' letter. But I object to leaving my old Motherland. There is one argument in favor of an acceptance. There will be more prospect of distinction on less fighting there. Hill will fight as long as any are left in the state but I think there are but few there & his fighting must soon come to [an] end. The climate however would not suit me. I shall not accept I think[,] certainly not before consulting your wishes. I should be Chief of Artillery of a whole Department there. Let me hear from you at once. I hope to go to Richd tomorrow & return in the evening, although I may stay all night. I wish to secure my Quartermaster before some worthless character is assigned to me of which there is some talk. They have a lot of cast off officers floating about without command, & as there is a mania now in R[ichmon]d on the subject of the number of officers in the Army they will be palmed off on the Artillery. There is much doubt of our promotion. Much love to Sister Ann & to all my friends. Kiss the children.

In great haste God bless you my darling.

Ever y[ou]r devoted husband

—⁓⁓⁓—

40. Colonel Stapleton Crutchfield (1835–65) was chief of artillery of the 2nd Corps of the Army of Northern Virginia (CSR). Carter is referring to an ongoing incident involving a dispute over the appointment of a first lieutenant in the King William Artillery between Lieutenant William Wade Woodson and Sergeant Festus King. (For a more thorough discussion of the controversy, see the note for Festus King in Carter's letter dated 23 September 1863.)

Camp near Milford Depot
March 19th 1863

My precious Wife

I have waited until the last moment with the hope that your letter would arrive with news from you & the little ones but I presume the cars are bringing troops to Chesterfield Depot (as they were doing yesterday) & there is some doubt of their coming today.[41] I trust they will come & return, otherwise you will not receive this letter tomorrow & you may be uneasy about me.

Yesterday we rec[eive]d orders to march with despatch to Hamilton's crossing but before a start was made the order was countermanded. Genl Lee was in R[ichmon]d & Chilton & Jackson are fond of alarms.[42] Lee ret[urne]d yesterday. He is never stampeded & when he draws up in line of battle there is a fight on hand. He was absent when the Artillery was ordered to the front after Xmas. It is said he went to R[ichmon]d on this occasion to get Hood & Picket back & that these troops are now put off at Chesterfield & march to the front.[43]

Your sweet letter has this moment arrived & I am thankful to God that you are doing so well. I have pretty much decided not to accept Hill's invitation. He made application to the Sec of War for me provided I was willing to come. I returned from a 24 hours absence at R[ichmon]d on Tuesday evening. I longed to ride down & return in the night but my whole time was occupied. Your Uncle Alex advised me not to accept as I would gain nothing in rank (our promotion will soon be granted) & of

41. Chesterfield Depot (or Station) was a stop on the Richmond, Fredericksburg & Potomac Railroad (RF&P) located south of Milford Depot in Caroline County, Va. When the railroad line reached the county in 1836, the superintendant of the RF&P changed the village's name from Chesterfield Station to Ruther Glen to avoid confusing it with Chesterfield Court House, the town located south of the James River (Fall, *People, Postoffices, and Communities*, 323; Wingfield, *History of Caroline County*, 34–35).

42. Colonel Robert Hall Chilton (1815–79) served as assistant adjutant general on the staff of Robert E. Lee. He entered Confederate service as a lieutenant colonel in May 1861 (to rank from 16 March) and was promoted to colonel on 13 October 1862. A week later, Chilton was promoted to the rank of brigadier general, but the Confederate Senate rejected the nomination on 11 April 1863. On 16 February 1864, Chilton was again appointed brigadier general (to rank from 21 December 1863), but he resigned his commission and reverted to the rank of colonel and served as the assistant adjutant and inspector general of the Army of Northern Virginia. He was paroled in Greensboro, N.C., around 1 May 1865 (CSR).

43. The rumored arrival of Pickett's and Hood's divisions proved untrue. Both divisions had been sent to Southside Virginia on detached duty in February and would not return to Lee's army until after the Battle of Chancellorsville (*OR* 25[1]:795).

course I prefer to fight in Va. Every body gives the same advice. I have not yet seen Rodes but wish to do so this evening.

We will not be allowed a Quartermaster or Adjutant except by detail from the batteries which is very objectionable. These Battalions are larger than Infantry Regts which are allowed these officers & many more. And our horses give more trouble than a half dozen times the number of men. But they have a horror of multiplying officers, which is an evil no doubt but not so great an evil as inefficient Artillery. Genl Pendleton tells me that Crutchfield was mistaken in regarding the endorsation of the President as discourteous. That he simply wrote, "The Comdg Genl will see that justice is done" & justice might & did require his (Woodson's) removal. Tell dear Sister Ann with love that I saw Mr Aylett in R[ichmon]d.[44] They had heard nothing of her arrival at the Parsonage & were somewhat uneasy. I told him she had reached there safely. I have no objection to the investment of $5000 with Sayre.[45] Ben Ficklin, my old classmate[,] is making a fortune by running the Blockade at Charleston.[46] I would not do this with the Yankees but with the English it is an assistance to our country & if lost will be lost in a good cause. Besides I do not know what to do with it. If Sayre will manage the matter in person I have but little doubt of its success. You had better have some papers to show the investment with Sayre in the event of his death. I am truly sorry to hear of the death of Pelham day before yesterday by a shell.[47] He was a noble & gallant little fellow. So we go, one after another.

Yesterday, Genl Jackson sent orders to us to prepare for attack, as a body of Cavalry had crossed high up. I had Milford to guard & the

44. Mr. Aylett has not been identified. The Ayletts, however, were a prominent King William County, Va., family.

45. Carter is most likely referring to William Sayre (1814–83), the son-in-law of the noted agronomist and southern nationalist Edmund Ruffin (1794–1865) by virtue of his marriage to Ruffin's daughter Elizabeth (1824–60). Sayre lived at Marlbourne, Ruffin's Hanover County, Va., plantation, and managed the property (Ruffin, *Diary of Edmund Ruffin*, 1:6).

46. Benjamin Franklin Ficklin (1827–71) was a classmate of Carter's at the Virginia Military Institute, a Mexican War veteran, and one of the founders of the Pony Express. During the Civil War, Ficklin served as a captain in the Confederate Quartermasters Department, as a blockade-runner (aboard the ships *Virginia*, *Coquette*, and *Giraffe*), and as a Confederate purchasing agent in Europe (*VMI Archives Online*, www.vmi.edu/archives.aspx?id=5269 [accessed 30 Sept. 2013]).

47. Major John Pelham (1838–63) was mortally wounded at the Battle of Kelly's Ford on 17 March 1863. He commanded the Stuart Horse Artillery, which was not present, and happened to be near the fight when it began. The dashing twenty-four-year-old artillerist took part in the action, and while rallying Confederate cavalry, he was struck in the back of the head by a shell fragment. Pelham was carried to Culpeper Court House, Va., where he died early the next day (Krick, *Staff Officers*, 240; Hassler, *John Pelham*, 164–66).

Mattaponi bridge just beyond. It was all bosh, & the men had to sleep out in the cold all night.

I see by the papers Stuart drove them back. I cannot describe to you the comfort your things have been to us. The hog tongues are delicious when cold. I will gather up all your jars & send them to you. I got my wagon in R[ichmon]d. It is on the way now. It ought to have arrived last night. I don't know what is to become of our horses—no more corn from R[ichmon]d the Quartermaster General says. We are now feeding on wheat. Have not seen Wm, but saw Ben Harrison in R[ichmon]d. He is on his way to his Brother's in Sussex. He will return to Clarke in April I think. He thinks Milroy no worse than the other Yankee Genls & the accounts of him exaggerated.[48] Papa had lost two horses but they were stolen by negroes.

Ben says Wm had many private interviews with the fair Lucy Page. He knew nothing of his progress in her affections. John Page is there still afraid to move lest he should be taken up as a conscript.

I think we will go up soon to the front. Genl Lee says there is no doubt that Hooker will attempt to cross the Rappahannock, that he has rec[eive]d orders to cross when the roads will permit a move. For that reason he desired to get back his two Divisions. Their numbers are not diminished but much intermixed with conscripts. I am pleased to hear Thos is so much pleased with the donkey. Was the harness sent with him[?] Dr Baylor has gone to Albermarle on a wedding frolick. A Miss Bowen is the lady.[49] The Dr is to return Friday. Several Holidays & Bowdens are staying at his house. Dote on my precious children for me & give much love to Sister & her little ones.

God forever bless you

Y[ou]r own devoted husband

—⁓—

48. Major General Robert Huston Milroy (1816–90) of Indiana commanded a division in the Union VIII Corps. His particular responsibility was to defend the area around Harpers Ferry and Winchester, Va. (Eicher and Eicher, *High Commands*, 391; Boatner, *Dictionary*, 549).

49. Mary Eliza Bowen (b. 1837?) married John J. Grantham (b. 1828?) on 18 March 1863. She was a cousin of Dr. John Baylor's wife, Ann Bowen Baylor. Ann's father, James Marshall Bowen (1793?–1880), and Mary Eliza's father, Thomas C. Bowen (1802?–86), were brothers (Norford, *Marriages of Albemarle County*, 76; Woods, *Albemarle County in Virginia*, 147–48; 1860 Census, Jefferson County).

Richmond
March 23rd 1863

My precious Wife,

I am here for a few hours only—leave at 3 1/4 P.M. & recollecting that it is my day to write I drop you a line to tell you that there is nothing new, & I am well &c. I ran down this morning to get my Quartermaster & have at last succeeded in getting him, & leave in an hour. I wish most sincerely I could run out & see you. Have just seen Tom Temple who will see you tomorrow. He goes out by the cars. He is out of the service in consequence of his refusal to stand the examination. Your letter of Saturday failed to reach me yesterday but probably got to Camp today. Dr Baylor had not returned yesterday.

I dined at New Market yesterday[,] all well. Mrs Baylor [is] a little uneasy & restless about the Dr's absence—probably detained by the trains on the Central not running regularly. Some 500 troops went up last week to Gordonsville. Hood started up but returned to his Camp. Picket at Petersburg. Our army is massing up the river. Genl Lee has no doubt of the enemy's intention to fight on that line. Too wet for it now. Poor Lewis Coleman died on Saturday.[50] Braxton is my Major, a first-rate man.[51] My Ordnance Officer is a capital appointment—could not have selected better. Kiss my sweetest little ones. Much love to Sister. I wrote to Genl Hill declining his offer. He hinted Bondurant in the event that I declined which he evidently expected. I saw your uncle Alex this morning looking the same as usual. He told me Genl Hill had applied for me.

50. Lewis Minor Coleman (1827–63) died from wounds he suffered at the Battle of Fredericksburg. Coleman graduated from the University of Virginia in 1846, taught Latin at the college, and eventually served as the principal of Hanover Academy in Hanover County, Va. On 27 July 1861, he enlisted in the Morris Artillery and became its captain on 1 August. When the battery reorganized in the middle of May 1862, he resigned his command and accepted appointment to the rank of major of artillery. On 6 June 1862, he was promoted to lieutenant colonel and served in the 1st Virginia Artillery (CSR; "Honor Roll of the University of Virginia," 46). In a postwar sermon, the Reverend J. B. Hawthorne recalled the death of Lewis Coleman. The Baptist minister remembered that among his last words, Coleman said the following: "Tell Gen. Lee and Gen. Jackson they know how Christian soldiers can fight, but I wish they could be here that they might see how one of them can die" (Hawthorne, "Sermon before the Reunion," 411).

51. Carter Moore Braxton (1836–98) was born in Norfolk but grew up in King and Queen County, Va. Before the war, he was a civil engineer in charge of construction for the Fredericksburg and Gordonsville Railroad. Braxton began his Confederate service as captain of the Fredericksburg Artillery. On 4 April 1863, he was promoted to major, to rank from 2 March, and served on Carter's staff. A year later, on 14 March 1864, he earned a promotion to lieutenant colonel. After the war, Braxton resumed his career as a civil engineer (Lane, "Carter Moore Braxton," 201–2; CSR).

God bless you dearest. I think of you with the tenderest affection & would regard it my greatest happiness to be always with you & the dear little ones. Wortham seems to think well of the Cotton speculation if Sayre is a good manager of such matters. He advises me to buy Confed bonds. Says the money is now in those bonds, as is everything of his & not gaining by interest. In the greatest haste

Ever y[ou]rs most devotedly
Thos. H. Carter

—m—

Camp near Milford Depot
April 2nd 1863

My precious wife,

I expect your letter in an hour but as the time between its reception & the closing of the mail is so short I have determined to begin in time. Your letter has just arrived. I was interrupted in writing the first sentence. Nothing new here. Maria Tompkins is still at Ne{w} Market. The soldiers lately have {a}nnoyed Dr Baylor considerably; so much so, that he has obtained a guard. It consists of young Boyden Holliday & Wash who stay at his house.[52] Also a Mr Davis stays there who has been sick. I can hardly advise you what to do. My time is much occupied by this Board or it rather will be occupied. It is intended as a powerful machine for ridding the Army of all incompetent officers & our instructions from the War Department & from Genl Lee are very ~~full~~ rigid, but not as full as I could wish. I dare say the joint stock company would be the best enterprise of the two. If so you might inform Mr Sayre before he accepts your proposal, or do you wish to carry on both[?] I think the joint stock would be the safest, but you will of course find out all about it. Mr Carraway has very good notions about financing & could ascertain all about it for you in Richmond.[53] Th{e} last things you sent me are not ye{t} exhausted. I started James on foot. Nelly is still lame but getting better.[54] I spent [the] night before last with Dr Baylor. They are very kind. The weather is bright & windy today. Nothing of a movement yet but we

---

52. Boyden Holliday and Wash have not been identified.

53. Carter may be referring to the Reverend George Carraway, the rector of Immanuel Episcopal Church in Old Church, Hanover County, Va.

54. Nelly was one of Carter's horses.

know not when the order may come as we reduced baggage sometime since. The four mules last rec[eive]d are very good & my wagon is excellent so that I hope to have no difficulty in moving now. My staff is filling up. Westcott has arrived & is acting Quartermaster, but { . . . } not yet bonded.[55]

Mr Friend was at Dr Baylor's but left yesterday.[56] I took Communion on Sunday for the first time since I have been in the service. France also took the sacrament. The sermon was good, but n{o}t equal to his usual efforts. I have heard nothing of { . . . } Coffman & his courtship & am inclined to doubt it. Do the children still fancy the donkey[?] You must not decide on the name of the little lady if you prefer the Willing until you hear from Mama. Most people prefer the Page. Dr Baylor greatly prefers it. He says Sweet Ann Page should be by all means retained. Lucy's child has the Renshaw appendix which makes a sufficient distinction.[57]

I have read with much pleasure the account of the marriage of the Prince & Princess Alexandria. What a noble woman Victoria is.[58] A virtuous & noble woman is beyond all doubt man's best blessing. Nothing is so disinterested & self sacrificing as their love which endures constant when all other ties are broken. If I live through this war I shall know how to appreciate you my darling—not that I have not always loved you devotedly, but I have never so fully as now understood the {v}oid in a man's heart when there is no one in whom he can repose entire confidence & to whom he can tell the inmost secrets of his heart. I am as happy as I can be away from you & the children but I long for a chat with you & a little doting from you & the little chicks. I find myself making love to you which at our age would be regarded as unpardonable so I must hold it. May God ever bless you all.

Y[ou]r devoted husband.

55. Captain Gideon Granger Westcott (1836–1907/8) joined Carter's staff as assistant quartermaster on 23 March 1863. He had originally enlisted as a corporal in the 5th Alabama Infantry at Greensboro, Ala., on 13 April 1861. In October 1862 Private Westcott served as commissary clerk of Robert Rodes's brigade. During the retreat from Gettysburg, Captain Westcott was captured at Jack's Mountain on 5 July 1863 (CSR; Krick, *Staff Officers*, 299–300).

56. Mr. Friend has not been identified.

57. Carter is referring to Annie Page Renshaw (1861–63), the daughter of his half sister, Lucy Carter Renshaw.

58. Prince Albert Edward married the Princess Alexandra of Denmark on 10 March 1863. He was the oldest son of Queen Victoria of England and would reign after her as King Edward VII.

What do you mean by Mary not having a baby[?] I thought it was announced long ago.

—⚏—

Camp near Milford Depot
April 9th 1863

My precious Wife,

Your letter of April *10th* (*tomorrow*) was rec[eive]d a few minutes since. You seem to keep no note of time from the date. We are still inactive you see & the roads are quite bad yet but our movements are of course dependent on those of the enemy. The weather has been unsettled but a few windy & bright days dry the ground quickly at this season of the year. I wish from the bottom of my heart you could visit me but I do not see how it is to be managed. Dr Baylor's house is full & he has been a good deal annoyed by soldiers & I am kept much occupied by the duties of my position. In regard to the various speculations you have on hand I think you had better be satisfied with the one you have engaged in with Mr Sayre & invest the balance in Confederate 8 per cent stock. I do not understand exactly the arrangements you have made. Do you mean that Mr Sayre will give you half of the net percentage made on the $5,000 & you run all the {r}isk of losing the $5000, or does he engage to secure the $5000 to you & give you half the interest he makes? You know the use of capital is a great advantage & it seems to me after paying all necessary expenses you are entitled to your share of the net profits. For instance if you put in $5000 & he puts in $10,000 & the *net profits* on the whole amount ($15,000) are 10 per cent[,] in my opinion you are entitled to 10 per cent, provided you run the risks of loss &c.

If on the other hand he engages to secure the $5,000 to you, for that consideration you might pay whatever percentage is usual in such cases.

I don't know much about these things never having engaged in a joint stock or partnership concern but I think a silent partner who takes all the risks is entitled to his *proportion* of the *net proceeds*. Their (the other partners') labor & expenses are repaid ~~by~~ under necessary expenses & by the use of the capital. But before you take any steps you had better consult someone who knows more about the matter than I do. Wortham could tell you or probably Mr Carraway. I am truly grateful to God for the success so far at Charleston. I trust & pray it may continue along the whole line from East to West.⁵⁹ The Mississippi expedition seems a fail{ure} thus far,⁶⁰ & gold is again on the rise.

If you can get the butter you have for me to Wortham's I can get it here. A L[ieutenan]t goes daily on the accommodation train in charge of a guard & as he is from my command there will be no difficulty in getting it. Today I sent your jars to Wortham's. Three large stone jars & two small yellow {j}ars. I think I will send my citizen greatcoat also to Wortham's. Wm also has one or two glass jars I think & possibly others. When you send the butter you had better have it put in a wooden pail or firkin such as one of the carpenters can make as there is no probability of returning your jars in [the] future. The lard you sent me I have put in a wooden bucket which cost $4.00, & the pickle we have also. There is enough lard to last some time. If we have moved from here when you have ~~send~~ the butter ready it will be useless to send it. Don't send to R[ichmon]d particularly on this account but you may find opportunities from the parsonage. Genl Lee is not seriously sick you can tell Agnes.⁶¹ Genl Chilton told me on Monday that he had complained of pain across his chest & camp fever was apprehended but at that time he was not confined to his bed & was performing office duties.⁶² He has grown rapidly in the confidence & affection of the men as was shown by their extravagant expressions of his value at the time that his sickness was rumored. Camp fever even if he should have it is not usually dangerous, & there is no certainty that he will have it. God grant that he may not. James returned much delighted with his visit. It so happened that he was at home at East{er.} In his absence Bondurant lent me a servant who got on quite

59. Carter is referring to the successful repulse of Union naval attacks on 7 April by Confederates occupying Fort Sumter in Charleston Harbor. Southern artillery fire from the fort forced the ironclads under the command of Rear Admiral Samuel F. Du Pont to withdraw. Du Pont lost his command as a result of the failed attack (Melton, "Charleston, S.C.," 131).

60. Carter is referring to Major General Ulysses S. Grant's frustrated efforts to capture the city of Vicksburg during February and March 1863. Once Grant successfully transferred his army to the east bank of the Mississippi River south of Vicksburg at the end of March, he was able to move against Confederate forces and eventually cut off and capture the city on 4 July 1863.

61. Agnes Lee (1841–73) was General Robert E. Lee's fifth child and third daughter.

62. According to Douglas Southall Freeman, Lee's biographer, in the first week of April, "[f]or the first time during the war . . . Lee fell ill. He had not been sleeping well, and in some way he contracted a serious throat infection which settled into what seems to have been a pericarditis. His arm, his chest, and his back were attacked with sharp paroxysms of pain that suggest even the possibility of an angina." Doctors treated the general with quinine and constant attention. By 16 April he felt better and returned to duty (Freeman, *Lee*, 2:503; Welch, *Medical Histories of Confederate Generals*, 134–35).

well. I should not be surprised if William is engaged to Lucy Page.[63] He is looking remarkably well. I wonder how those youths[,] Shirley & himself[,] propose to support their wives [during] these starvation times unless indeed the young lasses have the wherewithal. By the end of the war it is hard to tell whether we shall have anything even at Pampatike, for we now & then hear rumours of the enemy attempting the Tappahannock route, & the old standby would be ruined in that event. I think the route will be higher up possibly far above Fredericksburg. I am much amused at your notion that Ann Willing already shows intelligence. It must be your mother's heart & eyes that give that impression. I see Jno Pegram has been whipped in the West.[64] He is said to be engaged to Miss Hetty Cary.[65] Kiss the precious little ones & may God forever bless you all. Love to all at Ingleside.

Ev[e]r y[ou]r devoted

—⚋—

Camp near Milford
April 13th 1863

My precious Wife,

Your usual letter was not rec[eive]d yesterday or today I suppose on account of some irregularity in the mail. I have only a moment to write. The Board of Examination meets at 12 M., & it is nearly that now. Nothing particularly new. I have just heard that an order has been issued prohibiting all trunks from being carried. I shall therefore have to send mine back & get a large carpet bag, double if possible. I will send all such things to Worthams. This morning I sent my citizen greatcoat & gown there. Our promotions have been confirmed & we will receive

63. William Page Carter married Lucy Randolph Page on 28 February 1867 (McGill, *Beverley Family of Virginia*, 471).

64. Brigadier General John Pegram (1832–65) of Virginia commanded a cavalry brigade in the Army of Tennessee (Eicher and Eicher, *High Commands*, 422). Pegram received orders on 20 August 1863 assigning him to the Army of Northern Virginia. On 11 October he took command of an infantry brigade in the 2nd Corps (*OR* 29[2]:659, 783).

65. Hetty Cary (1836–92), though born in Baltimore County, Md., was from a prominent Virginia family. Throughout the Civil War, she held strong southern sympathies and lived in Richmond, where her beauty and popularity made her the foremost belle of the city. On 19 January 1865 she married Confederate general John Pegram, but just eighteen days later, John was killed near Petersburg during the Battle of Hatcher's Run. Exactly three weeks after his wedding ceremony at St. Paul's Episcopal Church in Richmond, Pegram's funeral service took place there, presided over by the same priest (Wert, "The Confederate Belle," 20–27; Warner, *Generals in Gray*, 232).

our commissions in a day or two.[66] All well at Dr Baylor's. The man to be examined is from Bourdurant's Battery. ~~All well at Dr Baylor's~~ Mr Friend delivered a most excellent sermon yesterday.

Everything is budding out at Dr Baylor's & the wheat looking well. It is rumored that Crutchfield is to be made a Brigadier of Infantry as there will be no more Genls of Arty.[67] I have not time to write more. Kiss the dearest children for their Papa & may God always bless you my darlings.

E[ve]r y[ou]r devoted husband

Don't know when we shall move. Getting horses for guns &c. ready for the campaign.

—∿—

Camp near Milford Depot
April 16th 1863

My precious Wife,

I expect every minute to receive your letter of yesterday & of Saturday. I wrote on Monday in great haste, as I had to attend a meeting of the board at 12 M. I am happy to know that one more case is dispensed with. I was kept until 9 P.M. in a tired & hungry state on the case of a L[ieutenan]t from Boudurant's Battery. Nothing new with us except that transportation is being diligently inspected & superfluous baggage ordered back. I shall miss my trunk greatly. I have sent for a carpet bag by Lt Coleman who travels on the Railroad in command of a guard.[68] Do you recollect what became of my valise? I should like to have that if you can send it conveniently to R[ichmon]d. Send it to Wortham's if convenient. Mrs Baylor has gone to her father's to see her sister who was ill at the time the letter was written to Mrs B. Dr Baylor[,] Maria & the guard remained at New Market. Have not heard from the Dr since

---

66. Carter's promotion to lieutenant colonel, to rank from 2 March 1863, had been confirmed on 4 April (CSR).

67. Stapleton Crutchfield had been recommended for promotion to the rank of brigadier general, but he was passed over and remained a colonel for the remainder of the war. In a letter recommending Crutchfield, General Thomas J. Jackson stated that he "discharged his duty with great ability and fidelity" (CSR; Dozier, "Stapleton Crutchfield," 593; Thomas Jonathan Jackson to Samuel Cooper, 14 Apr. 1863, in Crutchfield's CSR).

68. Charles Lloyd Coleman enlisted as a sergeant in the Morris Artillery on 15 October 1861. On 14 May 1862, Coleman was elected to the rank of second lieutenant when the unit reorganized. He served in the battery until his capture on 12 May 1864 at the Battle of Spotsylvania Court House (CSR).

Monday. The rain yesterday prevented his usual trip to us. Your letter of yesterday is just to hand. I am relieved to hear sweet little Julie is better again. Sorry Aunt Cornelia missed the carriage. I think Shirley had better consult with Mama before he marries. It is due to her & it seems to me his marriage now would be premature & without proper arrangement & forethought.

I can carry my trunk but it is expressly against orders. Therefore I must resort to valise & carpet bag. Have you a written contract with Mr Sayre? You ought to have one of course. Suppose he should die. I hope you were most particular in what you said in answer to Rosa.[69] I should not like to seem unkind or opposed to her coming into the family. I hope she is a fine woman. If she has anything to support herself with it might be well enough to marry but I think they had better consult Mama before acting so hastily. Probably you would like a companion. Poor old Pampatike. We are like chickens coming to roost at home. You & I must try & cut loose if I live through this war. For Renshaw[,] Shirley & Wm will all at one time or another be dependent on it for support. Burn this letter at once & show it to *no one*. If Mama favors the marriage you had better let it come off. Opposition then would do no good & probably make you her enemy. Send me Rosa's letter. I can't tell whether Wm is engaged or not. Lucy is a fine woman & if they have anything to live on the match would suit well enough. They are a little too nearly related, but not much. Has Sayre started for Texas? When does he expect to get fairly under way with his enterprise[?] I hope to get your things from R[ichmon]d today or tomorrow. Will Harry Tomlin go out with Sayre[?] Have not yet rec[eive]d my commission. Gone to Hd Qrs I believe.

Have you rec[eive]d your jars[,] my greatcoat & my gown[?] I shall send my trunk as soon as possible. I hope to be able to carry every thing in the valise & carpet bag. I have sent for a carpet bag. Kiss my precious little ones for me. God bless you darling. I want to see you terribly.

Ever your devoted husband

69. Rosa Evelyn Carter (1846–65) was the youngest child of Thomas Nelson Carter and Anne Willing Page Carter and Tom Carter's half sister (McGill, *Beverley Family of Virginia*, 471). Carter is most likely discussing the engagement of his half brother William to Lucy Randolph Page (1842–93). Lucy's younger brother, Robert Powel Page, served as a courier on Carter's staff during the war.

Camp near Milford Depot
April 23rd 1863

My precious Wife,

Your welcome letter of yesterday was rec[eive]d a few moments ago
& I hasten to answer by today's mail. I am glad to hear all about the trans-
action with Mr Sayre & the other gentlemen with whom you have consulted. Think half of the net proceeds with the risks a fair share for you?
How would it have been in the joint stock enterprise? My only objection
to that was on general principles. It may be a good investment but it will
be an exception if it is. Was the stock (Confederate) you bought with
$9000 eight per c[en]t or seven per cent? Did Harry Tomlin go with Mr
Sayre or invest with him[?] Tell me the exact nature of the enterprise.

Your uneasiness about the Yankees is uncalled for at this time so far
as we can see now. I will keep you informed as far as possible. I am truly
sorry to hear about Bob Tomlin. How did it happen? I have heard nothing of any skirmish down there in which he could have lost his leg. My
sweet little daughter, Mama, what can be the matter with her? Don't
dose her too much. I doubt if she has more worms than all children have.
I am pleased to hear such good accounts of Miss Ann Willing. May she
equal her namesake in all that is noble & lovely. I forgot to tell you in my
last [letter] that I have rec[eive]d my commission as Lt Colonel. I have
had a good deal of trouble in the distribution of guns. The Captains are
hard to satisfy & the life in the Army renders men intensely selfish. It is
such a grab game all through. I humored them a while trying to please
all but have abandoned that & simply issue orders. When one strives to
be impartial & strictly just as I do even to my own loss it is hard to be
suspected of partiality. But no one ever lost anything by doing what he
believed to be right & fair.

You need not send anything to me yet. The cart load you sent me has
not yet been exhausted. The tin vessel of butter & the bag of tongues
arrived last night & I am much obliged to you for them. I am glad to
hear you got four jars. I sent five jars to you—three stone & two yellow.
The third stone jar must have been lost. I regret it because they are
difficult to get. I am sorry you think of getting a Carpet bag & valise in
Richmond. They are enormously high [in price] & fit for nothing. The
valises are wooden boxes covered. My old valise is worth a dozen of them
if repaired. Richard could fix it & a new lock could be added. The price
of an oil cloth carpet bag is $35 dollars. Major Braxton has moved over

& now messes with us. He is intelligent & gentlemanly & said to be a good officer. A heavy rain is now falling. I am afraid the lowgrounds will be overflowed & injure the oats. We will stay here some time yet if this weather continues. The farmers are very late in consequence of the rains. Remember me most kindly to Mrs Ellerson. Kiss the sweet children. God bless you all.

—⚯—

Culpepper Ct House
June 8th 1863

My precious Wife,

I reached here yesterday with my Battalion after a four days march from Fr[e]d[ericksbur]g. One day was lost on the road in consequence of an alarm at Fre[dericksbur]g. The Yankees made a demonstration with a large force on the opposite side [of the Rappahannock] & crossed over a small force. They opened a heavy fire of Artillery on our skirmishers from the Stafford heights but crossed over no Artillery. Thinking it might be a general attack on that line we were halted to await the development of their plans. Next day we marched on & reached here yesterday evening. I am connected with Rodes' Division but report to nobody except in a general way. Thompson Brown is still acting Chief [of] Artillery [of the] 2nd Corps which is Ewell's Corps. Lindsay Walker is Chief [of] Arty [of] A. P. Hill's Corps (3rd).[70]

I saw Genl Ewell yesterday. The old fellow looks thin & pale but rides with ease & on horse back no one can tell the wooden leg. He inspected my Arty, seemed to be pleased, but like all Cavalry officers knows but little of Artillery. I hope his health may last, but he looks feeble. His son-in-law Campbell Brown is on his staff[,] also Sandy Pendleton[,] Jackson['] s Adjutant.[71] I think we are going to the valley (I mean the whole Army)

70. Colonel Reuben Lindsay Walker (1827–90) was the chief of artillery of the 3rd Corps of the Army of Northern Virginia. He remained a colonel until commissioned a brigadier general on 1 March 1865 (Warner, Generals in Gray, 322–23; CSR).

71. Major Alexander Swift "Sandie" Pendleton (1840–64) was a newly appointed assistant adjutant general on Lieutenant General Richard S. Ewell's staff in June 1863. The son of Lee's artillery chief, Brigadier General William Nelson Pendleton, Sandie Pendleton had begun the war as a lieutenant and acting ordnance officer on Brigadier General Thomas J. Jackson's staff. Pendleton rose to the rank of major and served as assistant adjutant general with Jackson until the general's death in May 1863. Sandie Pendleton was promoted to lieutenant colonel on 23 July 1863 and served as Ewell's assistant adjutant general until Pendleton was mortally wounded on 22 September 1864 at the Battle of Fisher's Hill. He died the next day (Krick, Staff Officers, 240).

& on to Maryland possibly, but know nothing of the plans. We go in the direction of Sperryville tomorrow, which is the best route to the valley.

We take on six days rations of provisions & forage. I do not know where or when the great battle will be fought. All sorts of rumours prevail, one is that Hooker is fortifying at Centreville. We have drawn him off from Fred[ericksbur]g & [he] must follow where we lead.

I am devoutly thankful to God that you are relieved of the Yankees. I saw some report of a raid the day before I started here & have been uneasy on that score. My mind is greatly easier since the receipt of the cheering news that the Yankees had left. I suppose Papa's horses can be brought back from Aunt Cornelia's. I hope now you can go on with your farming operations. I have an old letter from Mrs Ellerson [of] May 28th in which Dr E. speaks of the pressing machine. The hay crop will be enormously valuable & needful to the army.

I hope you had not sold too many of the cattle before you heard of the departure of the Yankees, but fear the good news came too late. Is Picket still at the Junction? I left your jars at Mr Gordon's having no means of taking them. I think there were three. Mrs Rodes insisted on giving the Genl one although he opposed it. I suppose it was the one with the lard. I took nothing of the things. Mrs R. offered but I thought it best to let them remain. By the way[,] I did get the fish. I think I shall see them in Clarke soon. Direct my letters to the care of Rodes (R. E. Rodes). We leave tomorrow morning for Sperryville[,] Luray &c.

I shall write whenever I can. Keep up your spirits. Trust in God & may he bless you & my dearest children always.

Remember me to all the servants.

Ever y[ou]r devoted husband

—⚮—

Camp near Chambersburg
June 25th 1863

My precious Wife,

I take advantage of another pa{use} in our onward movement to write, although in doubt of your whereabouts & the probability of the receipt of this. I wrote last from Hagerstown the 22nd inst & also from W{illiams}port on the 16th. I hope you have rec[eive]d some of these. We are moving on most leisurely at the rate of ten mi{les} every other day resting the intermediate day & someti{mes} longer, so that the above rate is rather high.

The object is to keep the Army closed up & to keep the soldiers in health & spoils. They have recovered fro{m} the footsoreness & the fatigue occasioned by the rapid march from Culpeper to the Potomac & are now luxuria{ting} on fresh beef[,] onions, eggs, chickens & other good things of this most abundant region. It is indeed a sple{n}did country. The soil is a rich clay similar to {that} of the valley & most productive. It is densely {pop}ulated by Dutch families who make every {use?} of land available. The fields average 12 or { . . . } acres & are all admirably enclosed. Magnifi{cent} barns & small houses comparatively are the { . . . }. The people are a miserable, unintellectual {and} unrefined set & I have not seen a single gen{tle}man or lady since our army crossed the border. With all their material prosperity they are poor indeed compared with our people on the barren soil of many parts of Virginia. The finest houses are inhabited by {j}abbering[,] slovenly Dutch women (in nine cases {ou}t of ten in the family-way) & men who labor on & { . . . } farms. Their hostility to us is strong & open { . . . } furious at the invasion. The kind treatment we extend {to} {t}hem has lulled the terror first excited & they are loud { . . . } threats of what we are to encounter & the terrible end {we} are to meet &c. All of which sounds well enough until the day of battle comes when the first boom {of} the cannon throws them back on the courage Providence has given them which is nothing to boast of.

We are not allowed to injure or destroy property of any kind. Public property is destroyed by order & all things { . . . }eded by the army or by our government are taken {a}t market value by our Quartermasters & Commissaries {and} paid for in Conf[ederate] money. Those refusing to ~~furnish~~ {acce}pt our money are furnished with a certificate that { . . . } property has been taken by our authorities & I presume { . . . } hope to be indemnified by the U.S.[72] Most of them { . . . } the Conf money. In Hagerstown C[onfederate] money was {wi}llingly received at two for one. They say in Balti { . . . } money is taken at that rate & Conf money at three for { . . . }. Of course this discount is made in private purchases

72. On 21 June General Robert E. Lee's headquarters issued orders stating that "no private property shall be injured or destroyed by any person belonging to or connected with the army." The orders also described the methods by which supplies would be confiscated, including payment with Confederate money or the issuance of receipts bearing the market value of the goods taken (OR 27[3]:912–13).

{...} government officials pay for articles with C[onfederate] notes at par value. {An}y beeves[,] horses & sheep are sent back. Lead[,] tin & {a}rticles of this kind are also taken at market value & ret[urne]d {to} Va. The horses & beeves are bought as well as other articles.

I know this humane & magnanimous course is right & that we shall be rewarded in some way but it is hard to practice when one recollects the barren & devastated waste between the Potomac & the Rappahannock & all the privations our grand old state has undergone. These people may well be defiant. They know nothing of war. I never saw greater evidence of thrift & prosperity—everything from a house to a hogpen untouched & looking like the smiling day of peace. The orders in reference to marauding are more rigid of anything than when in Va.

I have seen no evidence of a desire for peace. Now & then some democrat will express the opinion that they had as well let the South go & end the war, but most of the people are for war. No wonder—they are making money out of it & the death of a son or brother is a small matter compared with the almighty dollar in the Yankee's estimation. I do not know the full object of the invasion. It is mainly no doubt to live on the enemy & damage them as much as possible. Many persons apprehend an uprising of the whole population, but the effect is rather the reverse. {...} seems to arrest the enrolling {...} and gets up {three lines damaged}

The men desire {...} Harrisburg on a sort of a {...}ck, stay as long as it may be agreeable & return home. They are afraid to trust their own rulers on the "emergency" or 6 months plan. The "emergency" may last for the rest of the war. I hear that thousands of militia who have offered themselves have been in this way deterred from entering the service & have returned home.

I think we will bear across to the Northern Central [Railroad] & damage it as much as we can. Where the two grand armies will come together in the grand battle I do not know. The great trouble is ammunition & the distance to our railroads is great making it difficult to communicate with R[ichmon]d. Still I trust & pray & believe all will go well. If we can remain here several months it will be a great relief to our country. I have not yet heard from you, because we have no mail. I pray God all may be well with you. Write from time to time. May God bless you & our sweet little ones now & forever.

Your devoted husband

CHAPTER SIX

Guarding the Rapidan

18 September–27 December 1863

Early on 26 June, Lieutenant Colonel Tom Carter and his battalion left Chambersburg, Pennsylvania, with orders to march up the lush Cumberland Valley toward the town of Carlisle. From there, Major General Robert Rodes's division intended to make its way to Harrisburg. Once the Confederates reached Carlisle on the twenty-seventh, however, they remained there for only two days before General Lee recalled them to the Gettysburg area. A southern spy had revealed to Lee on the night of the twenty-eighth that the Union army, now under Major General George Gordon Meade, was north of the Potomac River and moving through Maryland toward the Confederate army. On 30 June Rodes's division marched due south for twenty-two miles until it reached the hamlet of Heidlersburg, where it bivouacked for the night. Gettysburg was still ten miles away.[1]

By 1:00 P.M. on 1 July, the first day of the Battle of Gettysburg, the division reached a point a few miles north of the town. Rodes, following the sounds of battle off to his right front, established his brigades in a line anchored on a piece of high ground known as Oak Hill. On the bare, forward slope of the hill, Tom Carter unlimbered his battalion of artillery in front of Rodes's infantry. While the division commander was still forming his lines, Carter's guns opened "with very decided effect" on the exposed right flank of Union brigades as they were being pushed from the west by Confederates from A. P. Hill's 3rd Corps. After about an hour, Union guns arrived on the scene to contest the Confederates on Oak Hill. Their fire forced Carter to relocate his batteries toward the far left of Rodes's line. At one point, the Morris Artillery took so much enemy fire that its commander reported to Carter that it needed relief. Carter, as "mad as a hornet" over its vulnerable position, rode up to General Rodes and demanded

---

1. Macaluso, *Morris, Orange, and King William Artillery*, 44; *OR* 27[2]:552.

to know "[w]hat fool put that Battery yonder?" After an awkward pause, Rodes responded, "You had better take it away Carter." Not long after, the Confederates on the northern part of the battlefield, now bolstered by the arrival of Jubal Early's division, drove the Union I and XI Corps through the town and onto Cemetery Hill. Carter's guns fired "from time to time" at the retreating Federals to prevent them from organizing any resistance. That action ended Carter's major participation in the battle. On 1 July the battalion lost eight men killed and thirty-three wounded. The Morris Artillery alone lost seventeen horses. The next day, Carter's men rested as the action shifted mainly to the southern end of the battlefield. On 3 July Carter placed his rifled guns near the Lutheran seminary and opened fire on Union artillery on Cemetery Hill to divert them from bombarding Pickett's and Pettigrew's divisions during their doomed attack against the Union center on Cemetery Ridge. During the Confederate retreat from Gettysburg, Carter's battalion crossed the Potomac River at Falling Waters, West Virginia, on 14 July and protected the pontoon bridge from advancing Federals. Once back in the Shenandoah valley, two of Carter's batteries helped defend Manassas Gap against Union cavalry in a small action on 24 July.[2]

By the end of July, the bulk of Lee's army was located in Orange and Culpeper Counties. Carter and his men remained encamped at Liberty Mills in Orange County from then until the early part of September. On the fourteenth, Carter's battalion participated in a heavy skirmish against a mixed force of Union cavalry and artillery that attempted to cross Somerville Ford on the Rapidan River. The Confederates managed to hold the ford. Federal losses amounted to eight killed and forty wounded, while Carter reported six killed and seventeen wounded in the battalion. In the middle of October, Rodes's division and Carter's battalion marched across the Rappahannock River in the Bristoe Campaign, which was R. E. Lee's attempt to get his army between Meade's and Washington, D.C. Carter's men engaged the enemy near Auburn Mills in Fauquier County on the fourteenth. After A. P. Hill's disastrous fight at nearby Bristoe Station on the same day, Lee withdrew the bulk of his army to the west bank of the Rappahannock River. There it remained until the Federals forced a crossing at Rappahannock Station and Kelly's Ford on 7 November. The Confederates now moved south of the Rapidan River and guarded its various

2. *OR* 27[2]:602–4; THC to Daniel Harvey Hill, 1 July 1885, Lee Family Papers, 1732–1892, VHS.

crossings. Carter's battalion set up camp near Morton's Ford in Orange County. At the end of November, the Confederate army established a strong position along nearby Mine Run, a north-south stream that emptied into the Rapidan. General Meade sent several corps of his army across the Rapidan to attack Lee but wisely decided against it when he considered the cost of assaulting the daunting Confederate fortifications. Once the opposing armies ceased hostilities for the year, the Army of Northern Virginia went into winter quarters. As he had done in the early months of 1863, Lee sent his artillery to distant locations to find fodder. Most of the 2nd Corps artillery encamped in Louisa County along the Virginia Central Railroad. Carter's battalion arrived at Frederick's Hall, thirty-four miles south of the Rapidan River, on 18 December.[3]

—⁓—

Camp near Morton's Ford
Sept. 18th 1863

My precious Wife,

I wrote you a note on the 16th to say that Wm & myself were safe after a smart artillery fight at Somerville Ford.[4] My Battalion remained there in position 'till this morning when I was ordered to this point, a ford about 4 miles below Somerville & two below Raccoon Ford. A deserter last night from Slocum's Corps states that it is opposite to us & about 13000 strong. That their army is 96,000 in number, one fifth of which are conscripts. The conscripts he reports to be much disaffected. So much so that they are guarded. He professes to be a Baltimorean & Southern in sentiment. He also says that Slocum made a speech to his Corps yesterday evening & expressed his intention to cross today at Raccoon Ford. The day has passed & he has not crossed, but it may have been prevented by a heavy rain which has caused the river to rise. We place but little credit in anything from a deserter for they have no means of knowing but I am inclined to believe that Meades army is about to give battle.[5]

3. *OR* 29[1]:422–23; THC to SRC, 19 Dec. 1863.

4. On 14 September Carter's battalion supported Confederate infantry in a heavy skirmish against a mixed force of Union cavalry and artillery that attempted to cross Somerville Ford on the Rapidan River. The Confederates managed to hold the ford. Federal losses amounted to eight killed and forty wounded, while Carter reported six killed and seventeen wounded in the battalion (*OR* 29[1]:422).

5. Major General George Gordon Meade (1815–72) of Pennsylvania commanded the Army of the Potomac (Warner, *Generals in Blue*, 315–17).

It seems to be their policy to do so. They are well aware that Longstreet has gone to the West & that they outnumber us two or three to one.[6] The hot weather is past & it is time for Meade to do something. Then too he has a better chance of success than any of his predecessors although I believe he will be repulsed. If they should be too strong for us I suppose we will retire in the direction of Richd. But it is time enough to talk about that when they defeat us. I have no great faith in our Corps commanders. They are both mediocre. My faith is in Providence, the troops & Genl Lee. I hope the Genl will control the movements of the troops more than has been his habit. When Jackson & Longstreet were his Corps commanders general arrangements only were necessary[,] now he should attend to the minutiae. On a long line it is almost impossible to do so.

I do not yet know whether you have left Goss' house.[7] I presume you have. I shall send this letter to Renshaw who will forward it to you. Our sweet intercourse was very unexpectedly broken up & I have been in the dumps ever since. Well such is a soldiers life. We never know what an hour will bring forth. I think of you & the sweet little ones with the most devoted affection. We were delightfully fixed at Goss' house. I wish you would write & thank her & Mr G. for me for their kindness. I enclose some letters which have reached me for you. The crop of wheat is small at Pampatike, but the hay & oats & corn will make it up. I hope when the fall campaign is over we may again meet in safety. If the enemy is repulsed here probably you can come again before we go into winter quarters. Kiss my precious children for me & may God bless you all for Christ sake.

Ever y[ou]r devoted husband

6. Lieutenant General James Longstreet and two divisions of his 1st Corps were temporarily transferred to General Braxton Bragg's Army of Tennessee, which was then located south of Chattanooga, Tenn. John B. Hood and Lafayette McLaws's divisions left Lee's army on 9 September and arrived in Tennessee just in time to play an important role in the Confederate victory at the two-day Battle of Chickamauga (Wert, *James Longstreet*, 303).

7. Carter is referring to the Orange County, Va., home of Ebenezer (b. 1820?) and Ann Goss (b. 1826?). The Gosses and their four daughters lived about seven miles west of Orange Court House, which was nearly twenty miles from Carter's camp near Morton's Ford. The 1860 census lists Ebenezer Goss as a farmer who owned $42,000 worth of real estate and personal property valued at $25,165, including twenty slaves (1860 Census, Orange County).

Camp on Morton's Farm
Sept. 23rd 1863

My precious Wife,

I have written three letters to you since we parted & am inclined to believe you have rec[eive]d none. Yesterday Nine Southall told me you had gone with Mrs Brown to Charlottesville & I shall direct this letter to that place with the hope that it may reach you.[8] The first I sent to Renshaw with the request that he would forward it as speedily as possible. The second—enclosing one from Mrs Bruce,[9] one from Mr Duling,[10] & one from Sister Ann—was directed to Wortham's care [in] R[ichmon]d. The third was directed to Somerset. I am in daily expectation of a scold from you in regard to the non arrival of a letter. You will see I am not to blame. Your note by Henry Hunt[,] the ambulance driver[,] was rec[eive]d.[11] Also one two days ago by Capt. Marye dated Wednesday 16th. No others have reached me.

Nothing new here on our front. Yesterday Stuart fought the Yankee cavalry near Madison Ct House. The result is not known here. From Clarke's Mountain the Signal Corps reported that the firing came South of Madison Ct House three or four miles.[12] I suppose from this report that Stuart was forced back for a time[,] but Wilcoxe's Division was ordered to his support & they probably drove back the enemy towards the last of the evening.[13] The firing seemed to recede a short time before

8. Lieutenant Stephen Valentine Southall (1830–1913) was acting assistant adjutant general to Brigadier General Armistead Lindsay Long. "Nine" Southall was a graduate of the University of Virginia and a lawyer from Charlottesville. Before joining Long's staff, he had served as an adjutant in the 1st Virginia Artillery and then as acting assistant adjutant general on the staff of Colonel J. Thompson Brown (Krick, *Staff Officers*, 272).

9. Mrs. Bruce has not been identified.

10. Most likely Henry Duling (b. 1815?), a forty-eight-year-old overseer in King William County (1860 Census, King William County).

11. Henry Thomas Hunt enlisted in the Jeff Davis Artillery on 1 May 1863 at Franklin, Ala. Carter transferred Hunt to the Orange Artillery on 16 June 1863. In January and February 1864, he was detailed to the battalion medical department as an ambulance driver. Hunt's service records indicate that he was still acting as a driver on 1 March 1865 (CSR).

12. Clarke's Mountain was located south of the Rapidan River in Orange County, Va. The Confederates established a signal station there because it offered an excellent vantage point from which to watch any movement by the Union army, which was then encamped north of the Rapidan in Culpeper County, Va.

13. The 3rd Corps division of Major General Cadmus Marcellus Wilcox (1824–90) of North Carolina consisted of brigades commanded by Brigadier Generals James Henry Lane (1833–1907) of Virginia, Samuel McGowan (1819–97) of South Carolina, Alfred Moore Scales (1827–92) of North Carolina, and Edward Lloyd Thomas (1825–98) of Georgia (*OR* 29[2]:686; Warner, *Generals in Gray*, 172–73, 201–2, 235, 268–69, 305–6, 337–38). Two days before Carter wrote this

it ended. Stuart thought it an attempted raid on Gordonsville.[14] We are still on the line here ready for battle which may take place at any time though the enemy are slow in advancing.

If they advance they will probably turn our line below. It would be folly to attempt to force a fortified line when a detour of a short distance will turn it. Still this detour gives us a considerable advantage.

I have heard today from King Wm through Lt King.[15] He reports everything quiet but the people uneasy in regard to Yankee raids. The crops are small. Duling states that only 900 to 1000 bushels of wheat were made at Pampatike. The hay & oats & corn may help out. I hope you have written to Mama since we parted.

The testaments[,] tracts &c. at last reached us on Monday. All English. The Periodicals are quite interesting for children & even grown persons. The Leisure Hour & the ~~Home Journal~~ Sunday at Home are illustrated.[16]

---

letter, Brigadier General Abner Monroe Perrin (1827–64) of South Carolina had been placed in temporary command of McGowan's brigade while McGowan continued to recuperate from a wound suffered at the Battle of Chancellorsville (*OR* 29[2]:739–40; Welsh, *Medical Histories of Confederate Generals*, 148).

14. The cavalry engagements near Madison Court House and Liberty Mills, Va., on 22 and 23 September ended with the Federals withdrawing across the Rappahannock River (Wert, *Cavalryman of the Lost Cause*, 310–12).

15. Carter is referring to Festus King, who had enlisted as a private in the King William Artillery on 1 June 1861 and had been promoted to sergeant sometime before January 1863. On 5 January 1863, Carter, by special order of Brigadier General William N. Pendleton, nominated King to act as first lieutenant of the King William Artillery. This action offended Second Lieutenant William W. Woodson of the battery because he had been passed over by Sergeant King, a man who held lesser rank. Woodson later resigned on 31 March 1863. In the meantime, the secretary of war declared King's promotion illegal on the grounds that only the president had the power of appointment. In response to the secretary of war, the battery commander, Captain William P. P. Carter, stated that King had been acting as first lieutenant "with fidelity, and to my entire satisfaction," as compared to Woodson, whom Captain Carter declared "was entirely unfitted for the position, being altogether unqualified in the management of men." On 30 March Tom Carter wrote the adjutant and inspector general and requested that Sergeant King's appointment be confirmed. There the matter stood for nearly a year, during which time King performed the duties of a first lieutenant. In mid-March 1864, Carter sent a letter to the adjutant and inspector general in which he detailed the "special skill & valor" that King displayed at the Battles of Seven Pines and Antietam as justification for his promotion. On 9 April, having still not heard anything, Carter wrote the secretary of war—his Uncle Alex—and asked him if he could look into the matter. Finally, Festus King's appointment to the rank of second lieutenant (as of 11 April 1864) came through on 20 April. King did not serve for long in his official capacity. On 12 May he was captured in the attack on the Bloody Angle at Spotsylvania Court House and spent the remainder of the war as a prisoner at Fort Delaware, Del., and Hilton Head, S.C. He was finally released on 16 June 1865 (CSR).

16. *The Leisure Hour* (published weekly from 1852 to 1905) and *Sunday at Home* (published weekly from 1854 to 1894, then monthly until 1940) were British periodicals published by the Religious Tract Society. *The Leisure Hour*, which was directed at families, contained fiction, poetry, and biography, as well as articles on English history and institutions, science and discov-

We are grateful to God for the success in the West.[17] I trust it may not be the usual precursor to evil tidings in the end. We are acting on the defensive here although Genl Lee spoke of going around & stirring them up when riding over the lines a day or two since. I think this remark was intended to encourage us. Long says we are to be reinforced[,] by whom he did not state.[18] The enemy is not supposed to be very strong in numbers—about 56000 we hear. I think we shall whip them. Lee is anxious they should attack.

Thompson is sick. I have not seen him since his indisposition but will go up this evening. He is not confined to the tent but suffers with pain in his knees which he regards as rheumatism. Andrews acts as Chf Arty.

I long to see the same state of things again at Mr Goss'. What a pleasant party & time we had there. Kiss & embrace the sweetest little children. Have not seen Capt. Marye.[19] Peyton is well & anxious to return to Major Lee's. We are tired of the line of battle & prefer the civil scenes. Love to the ladies.

God bless you always.
Y[ou]r devoted husband

—⁓—

Camp near Morton's Ford
Sept. 24th 1863

My precious Wife,

Your letter from Charlottesville was rec[eive]d yesterday & contained as I expected the long dreaded scold. "There is luck in odd numbers" says bold Rory O'Moore & therefore I send forth my fifth letter in search

---

ery, and women's interests. The *Sunday at Home* journal consisted of poetry, biography, religious devotions, and fiction.

17. Carter is referring to the Battle of Chickamauga, fought on 19 and 20 September, in which the Confederate Army of Tennessee defeated the Union Army of the Cumberland.

18. Carter is referring to Brigadier General Armistead Lindsay Long (1825–91) of Virginia. Two days before Carter wrote this letter, Long, who had been Robert E. Lee's military secretary, received his commission as brigadier general and assumed command of the 2nd Corps artillery (Warner, *Generals in Gray*, 191–92).

19. Captain Edward Avenmore "Ned" Marye (1835–64) commanded the Fredericksburg Artillery. He enlisted as a lieutenant on 13 May 1861 and was promoted to captain on 2 March 1863. Marye died of disease on 5 October 1864. His older brother, Colonel Morton Marye, commanded the 17th Virginia Infantry. According to another member of the Fredericksburg Artillery, Ned Marye was "neither a good officer or much of a gentleman" (CSR; Krick, *Fredericksburg Artillery*, 106; quotation from Fleet, *Green Mount*, 233).

of your ladyship.[20] I have nothing new to relate on our front. Yesterday there was a cavalry engagement near Liberty Mills, with what result I have not heard. A part of Ramseur's Brigade was sent this morning to Ge{r}mana Ford some 10 or 12 miles below by the road.[21] Wm's Battery went with it. I have some fear they may be gobbled up down there as they are quite distant.

Another camp has been discovered from Clarke's Mountain somewhat in the direction of that ford & several officers were observed to examine the ground very closely. The force there could only check them a while & give notice of the approach of the enemy. I am sorry the Battery is separated from the Batt'n.

We are rejoicing in the success of Bragg but rejoicing with fear & trembling. If he succeeds in driving Rosecrans from Chattanooga & East Tennessee then indeed will it be a great & glorious victory. Tennessee is necessary to us for meat, nitre[,] iron[,] coal &c. to say nothing of its importance strategically. The death of the brave Hood is a national calamity. He was regarded one of the most rising men in the service.[22] The papers seem to glory in tidings of a battle & are impatient unless one is fought once a fortnight. Even in the midst of victory, it makes me sad to hear of one, so many noble spirits are taken away & so much suffering produced. In this miserable little Artillery duel at Somerville the wounds were unusually serious. One man had his lower jaw & part of his upper carried away leaving his tongue hanging down. He was living when last heard from & doing very well. He is fed with beef[,] tea[,] gruel &c. [and] cannot talk at all but expresses his wants by writing & signs. Ben Davis of Wm's Co was a brother of John Davis once engaged as overseer at Pampatike by Dr Turner, a good & faithful soldier.[23] One of my old

20. Carter is paraphrasing from a Civil War–era song called "Rory O'Moore." The final line in the song is "'For there's no luck to odd numbers' says Rory O'Moore."

21. Brigadier General Stephen D. Ramseur's brigade consisted of the 2nd, 4th, 14th, and 30th North Carolina Infantry regiments (OR 29[2]:683).

22. Carter's report of Major General John B. Hood's death was premature. On 20 September, during the Battle of Chickamauga, he suffered a severe wound to his right thigh and was carried from the field to a nearby hospital, where his leg was amputated. After a long period of recovery, Hood returned to active service in the Army of Tennessee. John Bell Hood died of yellow fever in New Orleans on 30 August 1879 (Welsh, Medical Histories of Confederate Generals, 105; Warner, Generals in Gray, 143).

23. Benjamin F. Davis (d. 1863) enlisted as a private in the King William Artillery at Bond's Store on 1 June 1861 and served with the unit until he was mortally wounded during a skirmish at Somerville Ford on 14 September 1863. His service record indicates that he was absent without leave from 1 June to 31 October 1862 (CSR).

favorites was very badly wounded[,] Jim Allen of King Wm[,] who always acts as loader.[24] He has been in every battle with me & is one of the steadiest men under fire I have ever seen—poor fellow he is ignorant but honest & knows nothing but obedience to orders. I trust he will recover though he is lost to the service[,] his leg having been amputated.

Genl Rodes was not in command as you suppose of Early's Division. Early commanded it himself. Rodes was on the ground with Genls Ewell & Early giving any assistance in his power. Ewell had as well be absent. He does nothing whatever except by the advice of Early or Rodes. I think Rodes is his favorite.

We hear Yankee drums in numbers this morning. They may mean a trick of some kind. I saw Thompson yesterday evening. He is better—had no fever & was in excellent spirits. I was mistaken in saying he was not confined to his tent. He lies down on account of the pain in his leg. The pain is now more in the hip joint than the knees. He will be better doubtless in a few days.

He is very kind about you & says you & the Children must stay with Mrs B. until everything becomes quiet. You must do what you think proper. It is impossible to know what will be done on this line but I should think that there must be fighting this fall. The weather is fine—our army reduced by one Corps & I imagine Meade has no option in the matter but will be ordered by Lincoln to advance. However I trust in God we will be victorious & then have a quiet time until next spring. May he preserve Wm & myself as he has done so wonderfully in times past!

I am really touched by the kindness of the Gosses. Of course you must deposit the money at the bank in Charlottesville. Major Braxton says at Mrs Ball's in Orange Ct House the board last month was fifty dollars.[25] I believe at Hiden's it was sixty. At Routt's it was seventy five Thompson told me & Mrs Peyton can tell you what she paid at Major Lee's. So with these lights before you[,] you can deposit what is right. Find out what should be paid for the children & servants.

24. Private James W. Allen (b. 1842) of the King William Artillery had served with the unit since its formation in 1861. In the action at Somerville Ford on 14 September, he suffered a wound to his leg. On 23 September Allen had his leg amputated at a Richmond hospital. The following April he was discharged from the army (CSR).

25. Possibly Sarah W. Ball (b. 1815?), who lived in Orange Court House, Va., with several of her daughters and owned $4,000 worth of real estate and $3,300 in personal property (1860 Census, Orange County).

Tell Mrs Brown with love that [the] long epistle to her Lord was duly enclosed in a large envelope & forwarded. I have not seen Capt Marye but he is not far from here I think.

Henry (Thompson's servant) started this morning I presume & you will receive my letter by him. If you wish to see the letters sent to the care of Wortham & Co. write & he will forward them.

Troops are arriving daily by the cars[,] convalescents & conscripts I suppose. Osborne thinks 600 a day. He reached here late last night. I am glad of his return—he is my right arm in a battle. He brought a most suitable & convenient present—a knife[,] pen & pencil (with leads) all in one. English. I am writing with it now.

Recollect not to scold me in your next letter. This letter is the fifth I have written & sent off to you.

You must feel every confidence in my affection. I cannot love you more than I do. Kiss my own sweet children. How I long to hug them all around. How heartily tired I am of this abominable & cruel war. I wonder if I shall ever enjoy the pleasures of peace again. Remember [me] most kindly to Mrs Rodes. When will her troubles be over[?]

Mr Duling ought to sow as much wheat as possible in the early part of October. He has bought 260 bushels from V. Croreton. You will therefore sell only some 700 bushels. I hope you will be able to get off your oats & hay early.

There is always danger of a raid. King tells me that the Yankees destroy grain now under the pretense that it is the government tenth & therefore public property.

Wm has been a little sick but is well again. Could you contrive to get Papa's great coat from Hickory Hill for him[?] Mama says he can take it & that Papa consented.

May God bless you & the little ones now & forever.

Y[ou]r own devoted husband

—⁊⁊—

Camp near Morton's Ford
Oct. 5th 1863

My dearest Wife,
I have rec[eive]d no letter from you since you left Charlottesville a week ago, & have felt some uneasiness about the baby as Genl Rodes

brought the intelligence that she was unwell. Probably you were prevented from writing by your trip to R[ichmon]d.

We have just rec[eive]d orders to harness & be in readiness to move at a moment's notice as the enemy is advancing in heavy force on Early's left, just above Somerville Ford. Don't know whether it is a g{en}uine attack or a feint to {co}ver a withdrawal of Meade's forces. In any event I am glad of it as I am sure from the signs that we should have crossed & attacked him in a few days.

As we are prepared for them & as battle is inevitable this fall the sooner the better.

I trust in God we may gain a decisive victory, but unless his favor is most signally shown we can not hope to accomplish much. Our army is about 40,000 strong & in fine health & spirits. The enemy about 50[,000] to 60,000.[26] With Corps commanders like Jackson & Longstreet we might reasonably hope to give the enemy a decent thrashing. Ewell & Hill are poor concerns. Still I have great confidence in our troops, some of our leaders & in Providence & I believe we will drive them back, & possibly strike them a heavy blow.

I have no idea where to direct this letter. It will be safe to send it to Wortham's who will know y[ou]r whereabouts.

Nothing new here except the abovementioned fact. Wm is still at Germanna Ford with his battery. I have a hope that he may escape this battle as he is 10 or 12 miles off, & there is Artillery in reserve at Pisgah Church.[27] His battery is always so heavily engaged that I should be glad if it could be spared. My Batteries are again well filled & well equipped in every respect. One battle may put them out of order again.

Long gives entire satisfaction to the Artillery of this command, so far as I know. He is a perfect gentleman & a man of decided force of character. I hope he may succeed as well on the field. It is rumored that Genl Lee will ultimately place him in the position occupied by Genl Pendleton. It would be an advantage to the Artillery of this Army should he do so. Did you receive the letters sent to Wortham's care? I shall have to bring charges against you for delinquency in the matter of cor-

26. Returns for the month of September state that the Army of Northern Virginia had 44,362 men present; the Army of the Potomac had 77,947 present for duty (*OR* 29[2]:239, 764).

27. Pisgah Church was located in Orange County, Va., south of Clark's Mountain and about six miles southwest of Carter's post near Morton's Ford on the Rapidan River (Gilmer, "Map of Orange County," 1864, Jeremy Francis Gilmer Collection, VHS).

respondence. Tell me your plans when you write. It is now safe for you to return to Pampatike & I advise you to do so as soon as possible so that you may join me, D.V., when we go into winter quarters.[28] My heart turns tenderly to you & our sweet little children every day that passes & never more so than when a battle is imminent. May God ever bless you & if it is his will may we soon be reunited in the inestimable blessings of peace. He has been merciful & gracious to us thus far in preserving William & myself through every danger. To him let us ascribe the praise.

Yesterday, a large box of English bibles & tracts reached me for the Battalion, sent from the Central Pres. Office & bought I presume with the money subscribed by several friends. The men now have bibles enough, I think. I am still desirous of securing a good & zealous chaplain. Do you know one? I promise you to write as soon as I can should the battle come off now.

Once more God bless you. Love to all wherever you are.

Ever y[ou]r devoted husband.

Can you get me government cloth & have a pair of pants made at Beers & Poindexter. I should like a pair of boots also at Francis Thomas Broad Street.[29] I wear No. six. Shirley can attend to it. If you think best I will order the boots in Charlottesville. Those made there for me I allowed Bob Willis to have as he was nearly barefooted.[30]

Oct. 6th. This letter was not sent today & I open it to say that the excitement of yesterday has blown over. In my opinion however the battle is near at hand. Lee will advance if Meade does not.

Please knit me several pairs of coarse cotton socks & send my woollen lined buckskins. Nothing new. Rodes has been presented with a fine boy by his better half—a junior R. E. Rodes.[31] I have heard nothing from you for an age. What is the reason you do not write, paying me off in my own

28. "D.V." is an abbreviation of *Deo volente*, which means "God willing."

29. Francis Thomas was a Richmond shoemaker whose shop was located at 212 Broad Street (*Richmond City Directory, 1866*, 156).

30. Robert D. Willis (b. 1843), an eighteen-year-old clerk from Orange County, Va., enlisted in the Fredericksburg Artillery on 23 April 1861. From March through October 1863 and from January through June 1864, he was detailed as a courier to Carter; from September 1864 until the end of the war, he served in the same capacity for Colonel Carter Braxton. Willis was described as being five feet, nine inches tall with dark hair and light eyes and having a fair complexion (CSR).

31. On 30 September, Hortense Rodes gave birth to the couple's first child, Robert Emmett Rodes Jr. (Collins, *Robert Rodes*, 316).

coin, but I have promised to improve, & am as penitent as you could wish. Wm is still below with his battery.

Good night my precious wife

—॥॥—

[Fragment of letter likely dated October 16, 1863]

{First page(s) missing}

. . . obliteration of the Bristoe Station battle. Every day we miss Jackson & Longstreet.

I send some pictures to my sweet little children which I hope may please them. They were captured at Warrenton Springs by Bob Willis in a very daring act indulged in by his couriership.[32] After I had driven off the batteries[,] Stuart charged across the ford & up the opposite slope upon the Yankee sharpshooters. Bob accompanied him bent on securing a horse, equipment &c. &c. He could be distinctly seen by us. He singled out a cavalryman & dashed at him with pistol in hand. The Yankee took to his heels. Both flew across the open field at full speed[,] Bob gaining rapidly on the Yankee & firing at him from time to time. Finally his horse lapped the Yankee's horse & Bob told him to surrender or he would blow his brains out. The fellow was good pluck but obliged to halt & yield saying very sulkily that if he had a pistol he would show him whether or not he would surrender. Bob captured six pistols, two saddles[,] two overcoats[,] the horse & Lieutenant. The horse has since died. He has given away most of his captured property. Gave me an excellent pistol & wishes me to take any thing I wanted.

Oct. 17th—Nothing new this morning. It has cleared off brightly. The men are enjoying themselves chasing hares over dead men & horses. Bands are playing cheerfully. Such is the indifference occasioned by war.

The reserve Battalions have gone to the rear as far as Warrenton Junction. The Division Battalions are retained here to cover our withdrawal after the railroad is destroyed. The summer campaign is over. We may be pursued by the Yankee Cavalry but the fighting in Va. is over I think for

32. Here, Carter is most likely describing a cavalry skirmish that took place on 12 October near Warrenton Springs in Fauquier County, Va. This activity was part of a general movement of Lee's army across the Rappahannock River and around the right flank of the Army of the Potomac that culminated in the Battle of Bristoe Station on 14 October. Confederate units involved in the skirmish included the 7th, 11th, and 12th Virginia Cavalry with support from 2nd Corps artillery (*OR* 29[1]:445; Long, *Day by Day*, 420–22).

the summer. It is probable one Corps will be sent to the West, but it will not be Ewell's I think. A Campaign can be carried on in the winter at the West but not in this state.

I suppose you are at home now. Have you heard from Mama[?] Tell me every thing of interest. Give much love to all my friends. I am in need of a pair of boots. Think I will get them in Charlottesville or Staunton. Everything is so enormously high [in price] in Richd.

May God bless you & the sweet little folks
Ever your devoted husband

—⁓—

Camp near Rappahannock Station
October 20th 1863

My precious Wife,

Our army crossed to the south side of the Rappahannock yesterday & today we are quiet except so far as necessary changes are made for good encampments. The line of the Rappahannock will be held I think for a while, how long I do not know, but we will probably winter on the Rapidan, as there is nothing but grass in this country & the railroad can hardly supply us having only a single track. The whole country is turned out, not a fence to be seen for miles & not a cultivated field except now & then in a days march[,] a small patch of corn stalks indicating that a crop had been attempted. Indeed the country is uninhabited by white or black. Culpeper Ct H is the dirtiest[,] dingiest[,] poor place imaginable. This line could be held if considered of importance, because our army is small & it is thought will be diminished by a Division at least which will be sent to Bragg. But I don't think it important that it should be held. The enemy will hardly attempt this route again now that we have torn up the railroad for twenty miles & if he should there is nothing worth saving between here & the Rapidan. On the latter river we would be much closer to our supplies & could use our wagons in hauling forage from the surrounding country. My opinion is that we will winter back there. Probably the Artillery will be sent to Albermarle. I hope we may be sent to some more pleasant & habitable section than this wilderness, for I live in the hope of seeing you from time to time this winter. This constant separation is hard indeed. Your stay with me this summer has tended much to spoil me. I regard the summer campaign as over with exception of Cavalry fighting. Doubtless an active campaign will be carried on in the West. Both sides seem to be recruiting for another struggle. Our advance here on the whole has been a success. We have driven back the enemy to his fortifications & he has fled before us without giving battle for which[,] by the way[,] I was not prepared, having confidently expected the contrary. The enemy at the beginning of the campaign held a large portion of Va. & now they are back on the confines of the state. There are some dark spots on the picture—Jackson's death,[33] the reverse at Gettysburg, & the miserable bungling at Bristoe by which a thousand men were placed hors de combat & five pieces of Artillery lost.[34] The Yankee plan of securing good generals is in the main a good one. When one fails try another. By this means they have Gilmore[35] at Charleston, Meade in Va., Rosecrans in Tennessee & Grant on the Mississippi, not an indifferent man in the lot—whereas we have Lee in Va.[,] a good man & the rest very doubtful if we are to judge by results. John Pegram just from the West thinks but for Longstreets generalship this famous Chickamaugua would have been a defeat. He speaks of the conduct of the battle as abominable on our side, with the above-mentioned exception. I don't know how far his views are entitled to credence as he was pretty generally whipped in most of his cavalry battles but I suppose he reflects the views of those who ought to know.

Nothing new here. We fell back unmolested from Bristoe Station, our Cavalry twelve or fifteen miles on the front. Stuart with a portion of his command has gone on a raid. It is thought he has gone to tapp the B & Ohio R.R. He left last Thursday night.[36] Have heard nothing of him since. He conducted himself very handsomely on this expedition, in our fight at Warrenton Springs & at Auburn. At the latter place he got between

33. Lieutenant General Thomas J. Jackson died on 10 May 1863 from pneumonia following the loss of his left arm at the Battle of Chancellorsville (Warner, *Generals in Gray*, 152).

34. Carter is referring to the 14 October Battle of Bristoe Station, in which Lieutenant General A. P. Hill attempted to cut off withdrawing Union troops by sending two of his brigades to attack the Union column near Bristoe Station on the Orange and Alexandria Railroad. Poor reconnaissance failed to disclose that the Union force consisted of most of two corps. The Confederates lost around 1,900 men in the disastrous attack; the Federals suffered around 550 casualties (Boatner, *Dictionary*, 87–88).

35. Major General Quincy Adams Gillmore (1825–88) of Ohio commanded the X Corps and the U.S. Department of the South (Eicher and Eicher, *High Commands*, 255).

36. From 9 to 12 October, Jeb Stuart led a cavalry force of 1,800 men from three brigades on a raid to Chambersburg, Pa. He rode around General McClellan's army, as he had done the previous June, and reached Chambersburg late on the 9th, where the Confederates destroyed a machine shop and many public stores. The next day, Stuart's men, with 500 captured horses, began the ride back to Virginia. On the 12th, the cavalrymen crossed the Potomac River and rejoined Lee's army, having covered 126 miles in four days (Boatner, *Dictionary*, 814).

their lines ~~& spent the night~~ with seven pieces of Artillery & a portion of his command & remained the whole night. He intercepted despatches & in the morning fought his way out. If he had discipline & could keep his command together & in hand he would be a very superior officer. He is certainly brave & fights to the best advantage with the few troops he generally has.

Andrews has written for a place in Richd. He says he is offered the command of the defences around Richd vice Col. Rhett who will be sent to Europe on ordnance business.[37] He will go up a grade, says he will accept if Genl Lee will allow him. A very pleasant berth[,] one I should like except that my sense of duty would harass me to death were I to leave the field.

William Newton's death is indeed a severe loss to our community & to the country. He was a pure & noble gentleman & bid fair to be one of our most prominent men. McClellan, Stuart's A. Genl, told me he was about to be made Lt Col [of] Cavalry & that he was one of their very best officers.[38] Poor Mary Newton. I have felt deep sympathy for her since I heard of his death. A more devoted wife never lived. May God help her to bear her trial. Fitz Lee told me he was shot through the head & lived ten minutes, but he never spoke after his wound. So we go—one by one. Our circle mourns us a few days & then comes endless oblivion. Truly our hope is in immortality of the soul.

I wrote from Bristoe Station. Col Corley promised to send the letter on Sunday morning, so I hope you rec[eive]d it this morning.[39] Yours of the 14th (last Wednesday) reached me last night. I am glad you are at home & have your Aunt's society.

37. Colonel Thomas Smith Rhett (1827–93) of South Carolina, a prewar U.S. Army artillerist and bank clerk in Baltimore, Md., commanded Richmond's artillery defenses in 1862–63. Rhett was ordered abroad on 28 October 1863 to purchase ordnance for the Confederacy (Krick, *Staff Officers*, 253).

38. Major Henry Brainerd McClellan (1840–1904) was an assistant adjutant general on Jeb Stuart's staff (Krick, *Staff Officers*, 206). Captain William Brockenbrough Newton of the 4th Virginia Cavalry was shot in the head while leading a charge against Union cavalry at Raccoon Ford on 11 October 1863. His death prompted Major General Fitz Lee to write in his official report of the fight that Newton was "an officer of extraordinary merit and promise, and his death is deeply felt and mourned." Carter and others thought highly of Newton. Every time he mentioned Newton in his letters, he referred to him as a "noble" fellow. In August 1863 Newton's commanding officer, Colonel Williams C. Wickham, had recommended him for promotion to major based on his "valor and skill" as a cavalryman (CSR; Stiles, *4th Virginia Cavalry*, 37; Johnson, *University Memorial*, 496–514; OR 29[1]:464).

39. Colonel James Lawrence Corley (1829–83) of South Carolina was the chief quartermaster of the Army of Northern Virginia and served on Robert E. Lee's staff (Krick, *Staff Officers*, 103).

I am glad too to hear everything gets on well at Pampatike. You are right to make up my clothes after they are cut out in Richd. All except the uniform coat. I wish a large cape to the overcoat such as can button on. Write to Mary Brown at once about the boots. The pair sent fit me very well, & were good boots.

I sent a Frank Leslie's Illustrated paper to Thomas today. I will try to send one to Miss Jules. Miss Ann Willie Wills is too young isn't she for such things. Love to all. Have you heard anything from Mama lately[?] I think she must be on her way to Pampatike. Get Wm's overcoat. Wms Wickham is at home, was hurt by his horse.

May God bless you my precious.

Ever y[ou]r devoted husband.

Have you sent for Papa's horses? You ought to do so at once. Have the colt (sorrel) brought also. What was done in the Goss case? I hope you left the money at Charlottesville.

You might get the roan horse to help at Pampatike. I think he is not used by Renshaw.

Tom Haines of King Wm was mortally wounded a few days ago.[40] We hear he has since died. You recollect he married Walker Hawes' sister & ran for the County.

I think from present appearances we shall move back to the Rapidan in a few days.

John Edwards returned last night.[41] He is five miles off. Have not yet rec[eive]d the things you spoke of sending by him. Hope to get a letter by him.

—⁂—

40. Thomas Witt Haynes (1827–77), a prewar attorney in King William County, enlisted at West Point, Va., on 10 June 1861 as a first sergeant in Company H of the 9th Virginia Cavalry. On 29 April 1862, he was elected first lieutenant, and two months later, he was promoted to captain (26 June 1862). After suffering a severe wound in the spine near Manassas, Va., on 15 October 1863, Haynes spent the remainder of the war recovering. He finally retired from active service to the invalid corps on 13 March 1865. Haynes was married to the former Mollie Hawes (b. 1835?), sister of Walker Aylett Hawes, who also served in Company H (CSR; 1860 Census, King William County). Undoubtedly, the serious nature of Haynes's wounds led to rumors of his death. His gravestone included the following inscription: "For more than thirteen years he was a helpless paralytic, subject to almost incessant pain caused by a gun shot wound through the spine" (Thomas T. H. Hill, "Record of the Officers of King William County, Virginia," VHS).

41. In July 1863 John Duval Edwards of the King William Artillery had been detailed to the 2nd Corps ordnance train to serve as ordnance sergeant. He remained in this capacity until 28 February 1865 (CSR).

Camp near Brandy
Oct. 31st 1863

Well my precious wife you are taking vengeance on me for all past delinquencies in the letter writing line. Your last letter was the 19th inst. If you are sick & unable to write get someone to do so for you.

I am writing by fire light & at times see the lines indistinctly.

Nothing new with us. Genl Lee is causing to be put down another pontoon bridge for the benefit of the troops across the river & possibly to sally over from time to time. We are fortifying still on the river. Some think the infantry will winter here but I doubt it for many reasons. The Artillery will winter farther back.

Jones has a furlough of twenty days, I suppose to be with his wife during her confinement.[42] He is of course in high glee at his good fortune—a furlough & his first child. It is probable Page will be promoted & assigned to Jones' Battn as Major.[43] Braxton will be assigned to Andrews' Battn I hope. I spoke to Long about it & he promised to do it if possible. Andrews had a mutiny in his camp[,] fifteen men refused to go on guard, & a Company of infantry was ordered down to take charge of the men.

Andrews with all his vaunted resolution is a poor commander I take it. Long tells me that the discipline in his Battn is very bad. I have recommended Wm for Major if another [is] needed. Have you heard anything from Mama?

I suppose you are in Richmond from the fact that you have not written. I am much worried tonight at the loss of my mare. She was turned out & cannot be found tonight. The cavalry are encamped near us & there is danger of losing her entirely. Write soon. Did the children receive the papers sent them?

42. Lieutenant Colonel Hilary P. Jones commanded an artillery battalion in the 2nd Corps of the Army of Northern Virginia (*OR* 29[1]:829).

43. Carter is referring to Captain Richard Channing Moore Page (1841–98) of the Morris Artillery. He enlisted as a private in the 1st Rockbridge Artillery on 14 July 1861 and served with that unit until 21 October, when he was transferred as a sergeant to the Morris Artillery. On 2 May 1862, Page was elected captain of the battery when the unit reorganized. He remained in command of the Morris Artillery until he was promoted to major in March 1864 (to rank from 27 February). For the remainder of the war, he commanded artillery battalions in the Army of Northern Virginia, the Department of North Carolina and Southern Virginia, and the Department of Western Virginia and East Tennessee. After the war, Page earned a medical degree in 1868 at the University of Virginia and practiced medicine in New York City. He also wrote a history of his battery and a Page family genealogy (CSR; *OR* 36[1]:1088, 40[2]:710; Krick, *Lee's Colonels*, 297).

Kiss the precious darlings for me. Wm says Renshaw is not with Dr Gettings now.[44]

God bless you
Ever your devoted husband

—᚛᚜—

Camp near Mitchell's Station
Nov. 6th 1863

My precious Wife,

Your last two letters of the 24th & the 31st ult were rec[eive]d a few days since. They were the first letters rec[eive]d since Oct 19th. I had begun to work my self into a high state of indignation but your last loving letter has dispelled all the clouds which hovered about our house & I am again as affectionate as the husband of such a wife should be.

I enclose a letter from Mr Baylor in which he proposes to buy a place near Greenwood Depot at the foot of the Blue Ridge & desires me to be a partner in the purchase.[45] I am much pleased with the prospect of investing the money in what seems to be [a] safe & judicious purchase & if you agree with me I wish you to write at once to Dr Baylor & make all necessary arrangements.

The place belongs to Misses Langhorne & Scott & I am told by Thompson Brown is as safe a part of the world as we can find. It is near Dr Baylor's father-in-law Mr Bowen's farm.[46]

I shall write to Dr Baylor today but the mails are so uncertain that it would be well for you to communicate with him yourself if you like the plan.

I earnestly desire to make some permanent arrangement for you & the children. The life I now lead is precarious to say the least & while I hope to be spared to my family it is idle to deny that I may be cut off at any

44. Dr. Gettings has not been identified.

45. Greenwood Depot, located in Albemarle County, Va., was a stop on the Virginia Central Railroad. It was originally called Greendwood after the home of the town's founder, Isaac Hardin (Hagemann, *Heritage of Virginia*, 109).

46. Dr. Baylor's father-in-law was James Marshall Bowen (c. 1793–1880), who lived at Mirador near Greenwood Depot in Albemarle County, Va. Bowen's daughter Ann (d. 1901) was married to Dr. John Baylor. Mirador, built around 1832, was later the girlhood home of Viscountess Nancy Astor, the first female member of the British Parliament (Virginia Writer's Project, *Jefferson's Albemarle*, 132–33; Baylor Family Bible Records, 1698–1909, VHS; 1860 Census, Albemarle County).

time. Dr Baylor will explain to you the advantage of the purchase better than I can do.

Since my last letter the Artillery of this Corps has moved back of Culpeper Ct House. We are now some four miles from that place & near Cedar Run on the site of the battle of that name.[47] We are some twelve miles from Orange Ct House & six or seven from Rapidan Station. Our movement was made to secure better grasing. The grass is fast losing its strength which is a source of regret with Artillery-men as it is the main dependence with us for long forage.

There is nothing new with us. Our lines are where they have been since our withdrawal from Bristow Station. No skirmishing since that of Johnson's Division ten days since. Reese's wound turns out to be more serious than was first supposed. The fragment of shell although nearly spent was large & heavy[,] cutting through overcoat & cape & all his clothing & inflicting a severe bruise which will slough off. He has gone home on surgeon's certificate for thirty days.[48] I regret his absence as his subordinate officers are absolutely worthless. Young Christian[,] the cadet assigned to my Battn[,] is of great assistance in the management of the Company.[49] He is young but full of energy & pluck.

47. Carter is referring to the Battle of Cedar Mountain (or Cedar Run), fought on 9 August 1862.

48. William J. Reese enlisted as second lieutenant in the Jeff Davis Artillery at Montgomery, Ala., on 27 July 1861. The battery's first commander, Captain Joseph T. Montgomery, became so unpopular with his men that by December 1861 he had been court-martialed for poor conduct. When President Davis overruled the court's decision to dismiss Montgomery, several of the officers, including Reese, threatened to resign their commissions. In his letter to the secretary of war dated 8 January 1862, Reese stated that Montgomery was "a person for whom I have no respect either as a gentleman or an officer." Having lost control of the battery, Captain Montgomery, despite Davis's efforts, left the unit in February 1862. Meanwhile, Reese remained with the battery, and in the spring of 1863, he was promoted to captain and given command of the unit. He was severely wounded, as described by Carter, in an engagement at Bealton Station on 26 October 1863. He left the army to recuperate a few days later and did not return until the end of February 1864. Two and a half months later, Captain Reese, along with most of the Jeff Davis Artillery, was captured during the 12 May attack on the Bloody Angle at Battle of Spotsylvania Court House. He remained a prisoner at Fort Delaware until his release on 16 June 1865 (CSR).

49. Second Lieutenant Richard H. Christian (b. 1846) of the Jeff Davis Artillery was in temporary command of the battery while its commander, Captain William J. Reese, was recovering from wounds suffered in an engagement at Bealton Station on 26 October. Christian had enlisted in April 1861 at the age of fifteen in the 12th Virginia Infantry, where he served until he was wounded during the Battle of Crampton's Gap on 14 September 1862. After recovering, he was relieved of duty in the 12th Virginia on 5 October 1863 and assigned to the Jeff Davis Artillery. Carter thought highly of the young lieutenant. In January 1864 he recommended him for promotion, stating: "He has exhibited energy[,] courage & a talent for the command of men & there

We hear that Genl Lee says Meade has been ordered to fight us this fall. There may be a battle before we go into winter quarters but it is not expected in the army. I think Long has gone to Richmond to get things for the Artillery. In your letter of the 27th you state that you have not heard from me since I left Mortons Ford. I have written about twice every week since that time & cannot understand why the letters have miscarried. Probably they will turn up at some future time. I hope you will be able to obtain mules in some way for the work of the farm. Indeed it would pay to buy them if there was any certainty that the Yankees would never visit our country again. You will find sorghum one of the best crops to feed the people on the place[,] the children especially. A few acres will give a large quantity of molasses. A farmer close to us is selling it at $16 per gallon & it is decidedly watery at that. I am sorry to hear of Sister Ann's sickness. I hope she is entirely out of danger now. Give my particular love to her when you write.

I am glad you have such charming company with you. Much love to them. I wish most heartily I could join your party. How do you & your old flame Dr Wilkins get on together[?] It is well Lucia is with her spouse. Your old habits of flirtation have enough strength yet to give her trouble.[50]

Some of the Maryland troops have been sent to Hanover Junction— Stewarts Brig & a battery. Cavalry Stuart reviewed his troops yesterday near Culpeper Ct H in the presence of Genl Lee[,] Gov. Letcher &c. I was not present. Several men were seriously injured as usual & one reported to be killed in the charge which was made at full speed.[51]

Tommy Randolph[,] Col R. H. Lee & Washington Nelson have been captured lately. It is a serious matter now to be taken prisoner. Small Pox is said to kill seventeen daily at Fort Delaware.[52] Ditto at other places I presume & no prospect of exchange during the war. Nothing from Mama. Kiss the dear little ones for their Papa who longs to see them &

---

cannot be a doubt that the good of the service will be promoted by his advancement" (CSR; Laboda, *From Selma to Appomattox*, 173, 183; Carter's recommendation filed in Christian's CSR).

50. Dr. Wilkins and his wife, Lucia, have not been identified.

51. Lieutenant Colonel William Richard Carter (1833–64) of the 3rd Virginia Cavalry commented in his diary that the review was a "[g]rand affair! Stuart appeared in all his glory!" But he also noted that "[s]everal men were very seriously hurt by falling from their horses in the *mock charge*" (Swank, *Sabres, Saddles, and Spurs*, 99).

52. Fort Delaware was a Union prisoner-of-war camp located on Pea Patch Island on the Delaware River just east of Delaware City (Hannings, *Forts of the United States*, 52–53).

their precious Mama every day & hour. God bless you all. State to Dr
Baylor what amount of money you can invest.

> Y[ou]r devoted husband

Direct your letter to Culpeper Ct. H.

—⁓—

> Camp near Morton's Ford
> Nov. 10th 1863

My precious Wife,

Here we are again at the same old encampment & the same lines we
occupied one month ago before our expedition to the front. We were
absent one month exactly, having left on the 8th Oct at dark & reached
here the 8th Nov 11 1/2 P.M.

The recent attack of the enemy on Saturday was a great surprise & a
success on their part.[53] They began to advance Saturday afternoon (7th
Nov) at two points in large force. At Rappahannock bridge (pontoon)
they were driven back for some time but about dark they advanced
rapidly & in large force on the two Brigades across the river at that point
& captured the larger portion of both & one of Jones' Batteries with
them. At Kelly's Ford, Rodes' front, they attacked & forced the crossing
in such quick time that the Division was not prepared to meet them.
They captured one hundred & fifty pickets & killed & wounded some
fifty more. Nelson had one battery in earthworks there under Jeff Page
but the enemy ran out three batteries & drove him off.[54] Our line on that
river was weak[,] the ground on the whole being decidedly in their favor.
The Yankees showed decided boldness in this movement. They improve

53. In this paragraph, Carter is describing the 7 November attacks against Jubal Early's and
Robert Rodes's divisions at Rappahannock Station and Kelly's Ford, respectively. At Rappahannock Station, the Union V and VI corps attackers lost 419 soldiers, while Early's men suffered
1,672 casualties. At Kelly's Ford, the U.S. III Corps lost only forty-two men, while Rodes's troops
lost 359 (Graham and Skoch, *Mine Run*, 101–2).

54. Thomas Jefferson Page Jr. (1839–64) commanded the Southern artillery at Kelly's Ford
during the action on 7 November 1863. He enlisted in the Confederate army as a second lieutenant on 23 May 1861 and by November was serving as an ordnance officer and aide-de-camp to
General John B. Magruder. In March 1862 Page was promoted to captain and took command of
the Magruder (Va.) Light Artillery, a rank he held until he became a major on 8 November 1862.
From that date, he served as a staff officer in the artillery. Following the action at Kelly's Ford,
Page took an extended leave of absence from the army and traveled to Europe, where he died
on 16 June 1864 at Florence, Italy (*OR* 29[1]:420; CSR; Krick, *Staff Officers*, 236).

every day as soldiers in consequence of their better discipline & the distinction in classes recognized & carried out in their army. Indeed their men are all regulars now. Our troops labor under many disadvantages, it is true. Short rations & clothing & temptation on the battlefield to scatter & plunder instead of keeping a closed front to reap the fruits of victory. The Yankees are magnificently equipped & uniformed & have no inducement to straggle except to escape the bullets. Then too our policy with the general officers is unfortunate. The Yankee plan is the best. Occasionally a good man might be thrown aside unnecessarily but the principle would be established that success is the only criterion of generalship. It would be folly to discard an officer for the first disaster unless criminal inattention or negligence or incompetency were shown but a repetition ought to cause his dismissal.

The Artillery of the 2nd Corps at the time of the advance was back of Culpeper Ct H. We were suddenly ordered to the front & started at dark[,] reaching camp beyond Stevensburg before 12 that night. At 2 A.M. we were roused up to march back to a line two or three miles in front of Culpeper Ct H.[55] So you see my darling instead of writing to you that night as you desired in your letter rec[eive]d same day I was marching nearly the whole night. I could not help contrasting that night with that of eight years ago when you became my wife. Well it is useless to regret departed happiness. We must look these hardships in the face with unfaltering firmness & trust in the goodness & mercy of God that he will soon bring them to an end & that he will give us in His own good time a name & a place among the nations of the earth.

On Sunday we formed line of battle in front of Culpeper Ct H some two or three miles, but no enemy approached on our front. They attacked A. P. Hill on the left[,] who drove them back handsomely we hear. Sunday night we fell back, forded the Rapidan (& cold fording it was on the poor fellows) & took up our old lines. Since then all has been quiet. The enemy has Cavalry on our front & I presume infantry in their rear. On the whole the expedition of a month's duration has been a failure. In men lost the two sides will probably cancel[,] but nine pieces of Artillery have been lost & worst than all[,] the army has lost prestige & confidence

55. Carter described his battalion's movements in his report of operations during this period: "On the 7th of November, my battalion was ordered from its encampment near Culpeper Court-House to Stevensburg. During the night it joined Rodes' division, and fell back to the base of Pony Mountain, where on the 8th we formed in line of battle. The night of the 8th, we recrossed the Rapidan and returned to the old camp near Morton's Ford" (*OR* 29[1]:423).

in its leaders. I do not know who is to blame in this matter. No one seems to ascribe it to Genl Lee. Now that Longstreet & Jackson are lost to the Army he has no one to strike for him. He is too amiable a man to exercise the proper discipline with his officers. Jackson in this particular was very stern[,] always punishing all who deserved it. You recollect he once arrested A. P. Hill[,] a Maj Genl. It is time to get rid of men when they fail. We can try new men & if they do not succeed put them aside & try others & so on until we must in the nature of things obtain a tolerable general. It may be for our sins that we are destined to carry on this war & decide by the butchery of men rather than by the genius of leaders[,] but were I the ruler the matter should be put to the test. Whether the Yankees will pursue across the Rapidan no one knows. It was thought best not to fight them at Culpeper Ct. H. unless they came on the day we waited for them, the position being very unfavorable to us.

Wm received a letter from Mama yesterday. She was in Clarke, & seemed to have no plans definitely arranged for the winter. Said nothing of coming to Pampatike. I don't think she wants to come for fear Papa will interfere with your plans, & the place is extremely lonesome & always was so distasteful to her. Mary Strange is dead.[56] I will send the letter if Wm does not wish to keep it. Lucy will join Mr Renshaw & Mama & the rest speak of boarding with Mrs Randolph in Millwood, which I think Papa will hardly agree to.[57] I feel sorry to think of them at Annfield without servants. They ought to move some where. I wrote you from Camp near C[ulpeper] C. H. a few days since a letter enclosing one from Dr Baylor in regard to the purchase of a fine tract of grassland in Albermarle near his Father in law's, in partnership with him. I advise that you write to him at once & accept. I did so but[,] as the army moved the same day[,] do not know whether the letters reached their destination. I think it a fine investment with a safe & judicious man. Please state to him how much you can raise in cash &c. I write in a hurry as the mailman has just come for the letter. Nothing new this morning. I think Meade will await the repairing [of] the railroad before he attempts any advance on this line[,] if then. We can't spare James at this time. He is the only servant in the mess. We expect others in a short time. If I can I will send one of the

56. Mary Strange has not been identified.
57. "Mrs. Randolph" is most likely Lucy Nelson Wellford Randolph (1810–82), the wife of Dr. Robert Carter Randolph of New Market, Clarke County, Va. (1860 Census, Clarke County; McGill, *Beverley Family of Virginia*, 173).

boys down after a while. We got some eatables by sending Bob to Orange Ct H & are doing quite well just now. Last night was very cold, had ice a fourth of an inch thick. Our mails are irregular. I write regularly so as to hit the mail days at Old Church. I enclose Mama's letter & one to the little darlings. If they do not understand it tell me & I will try another style. Are they really much pleased to get the letters, & did they enjoy the pictorials[?] I shall write to Mama & Lucy as soon as possible. I wish you would do so too.

The two Brigades lost belonged to Early's Division.[58] Rodes had to admit that with more Artillery he would have saved his men. When ordered to change position in line of battle the other day he asked Genl Lee to be allowed to take my Battalion with him. The old Genl demurred for a while but finally consented. He was anxious for me to hold the position I had. Genl Lee is always as kind & attentive to me as he can well be. I never see him except on the battle field[,] when I am mounted on the meanest & boniest horses I can find not wishing to take my mare into action. He must think me a seedy looking individual. Our Cavalry pickets are a mile across the Rapidan. God bless you my darling in all your undertakings, & our sweet little children. Is little Ann Willie Wills as good as when we were together[?]

Farewell
Ever your devoted husband

—∽—

Camp near Summerville Ford
Nov. 14th 1863

My precious Wife,

I wrote two days ago enclosing a letter from Mama. I also wrote Culpeper Ct. H a week since enclosing a letter from Dr Baylor in regard to the purchase of land in Albermarle in partnership with us. My opinion is decidedly in favor of the purchase & I wish to communicate with him on the subject. I repeat all this lest the other letters may have miscarried

---

58. The brigades commanded by Generals Robert F. Hoke and Harry T. Hays of Early's division were overwhelmed in the 7 November fight at Rappahannock Station by the Union V and VI Corps. Hoke suffered a total of 928 casualties, while Hays lost 702 men (*OR* 29[1]:627, 629–30; Graham and Skoch, *Mine Run*, 101).

as our mails are irregular. I hope in this the abovementioned letters have been rec[eive]d.

My Battalion is now encamped midway between Summerville Ford & Vidiersville[,] the latter place is on the plank road (thirteen miles from Orange Ct House) between Fredericksburg & Orange Ct. House.[59]

It is convenient to the three fords held by Ewell's Corps—viz. Summerville[,] Raccoon & Morton. But we are again about to be on the wing. My wagons at a distance have been recalled with orders to follow on if the Army has moved. We suppose Meade will cross at Germanna or Ely's & we will attack or they are about to move in the direction of Fredericksburg. I do not expect the latter plan because I see no reason for getting themselves opposite to a strongly fortified line when by crossing at Germanna they can fight us on ground unintrenched.

I had thought it probable that the campaign was virtually closed on this line but the recent fine weather seems to have upset all calculations. Meade may be elated at his recent successes & expect to drive us to the wall. We lost in the aggregate at Rappahannock some two thousand men & four pieces of Artillery by the surprise effected on that line.[60] It is bad indeed but we must wade in this time in real earnest & wipe out the stain. I have nothing new to tell, except that I think Lucy Renshaw was in Charlottesville on the 10th inst. Mrs Brown speaks of having called on her & said that she expected to go to the army as soon as the excitement has passed off. From Mama's letter, it must be Lucy. One of Mr Wickham's servants was discovered under guard at Culpeper Ct. H. Mr W. was written to & it turns out the man ran away in July. I supposed he was captured by our forces somewhere. I am trying at Mr W's request to have him sent to Richmond under guard on the cars. His name is Billy Minor.

I will write whenever I can should we move. Always mention what letters you receive from me. A number must have been lost since we parted from remarks that you let fall in those I rec[eive]d.

59. Carter is referring to the tiny crossroads village of New Verdiersville in Orange County, Va. It was located on the Orange Plank Road about a mile directly south of the equally small Verdiersville (or Old Verdiersville) on the Orange Turnpike. Soldiers in both armies often confused these two locations and called them "My Dearsville" in letters home (Hurst, *Soldiers, Stories, Sites, and Fights*, 41; Gilmer, "Map of Orange County").

60. Carter's estimate of Southern casualties at the Battle of Rappahannock Station (7 November) was a slight exaggeration. General Early's report stated that his losses totaled 1,630 (see note 58 above). The "four pieces of artillery" that were captured belonged to Green's Battery (also known as the Louisiana Guard Artillery), commanded by Lieutenant Robert L. Moore. The battery lost one man killed and forty-one captured out of seventy-eight present, expended 400 rounds of ammunition, and lost forty-five of fifty-four horses (*OR* 29[1]:627, 635).

Kiss the precious little ones & may God bless you forever.

Y[ou]r own devoted husband.

—⚋⚋—

[November 19th or 20th, 1863]

{First section of letter missing}

... Richmond. I hope he may get it as Braxton will thereby obtain promotion & a Battalion. If the plan mentioned above ("entre nous ") is carried out I should like him to command my Battalion. Ewell is so much indisposed that he has gone to Charlottesville it is thought for a long time.[61] The fact is he is regarded as having virtually withdrawn from the command of the 2nd Corps. Early now commands by virtue of seniority in rank. I hope he will do well. My only fear is he is such a hardened old sinner, but apart from this serious objection is a firstrate man.

Send Wm his things by Andrew Davis. When will my overcoat be done[?] I want a very large cape. Genl Rodes has the handsomest overcoat I have seen—a beautiful colour of gray & a very large cape. I am having a pair of boots made in Charlottesville—also expect a pair daily from Staunton. Have you heard anything from the chaplain?

Lucy is with Renshaw somewhere, no one knows exactly where. We hope to see them soon. Wm went yesterday to Mrs Taliaferro's. He found Mittie Carter &c. &c. there. All very kind. His battery is mentioned in the papers (Examiner) as having quickly driven off the enemy's battery at Morton's [Ford] on Sunday.[62] I expect a letter from you tonight. I want to see you mighty badly. I wonder if you do care as much for me as I do for you. Kiss the children for me. Did they like the letter?

God bless you, my darling.
Y[ou]r devoted husband.

Send us butter & molasses if you have any to spare but don't overload the horse with things. Andrew will have things to bring for others.

61. Lieutenant General Richard S. Ewell, suffering the effects of an ulcerated stump caused by the use of a faulty wooden leg, was unable to exercise command. General Lee ordered him to turn the 2nd Corps over to Jubal Early. Ewell left for Charlottesville, Va., on 16 November and did not return to the army until 29 November (Pfanz, *Richard S. Ewell*, 346–47).

62. The newspaper reported that on 15 November, General Rodes halted the Army of the Potomac's attempt to cross the Rapidan River at Morton's Ford by ordering the King William Artillery to "drive off" the enemy, "which it succeeded in doing in very short order" (*Daily Richmond Examiner*, 18 Nov. 1863).

Mr Young wrote me about the loss of two of Jack Braxton's horses[,] Jim Crow & a sorrel colt. I will do what I can to recover them but it is almost hopeless.

—— m——

Camp near Pisgah Church
Dec. 12th 1863

My precious Wife,

Your letter of the 8th inst. was rec[eive]d last night. I have written thrice since the recent operations of our army, which you have probably rec[eive]d ere this. There is nothing new with us. All is quiet on the lines. Genl Rodes informed me yesterday that our scouts report the enemy to be reinforced by three Corps supposed to have been drawn from various portions of the South. He also says that the {en}emy has not retired to the north of the Rappa{han}nock but is still near Brandy & Stevensburg. The newspapers report the enemy to be falling back toward Alexandria & the river to be white with transports which would indicate a change of base towards James River. I trust this is not true. Rodes as usual expects another advance of the enemy before we enter winter quarters. The rain now falling will probably interpose Genl. Mud[,] the most powerful general we have. You will see by the above caption that I have changed my camp nearer to Orange Ct H. I am only six miles distant now, a great convenience in the procuring [of] supplies. One battery was left in re-serve at Morton's Ford, Wm's, for a week. He will be relieved at that time by another from my Battalion. One battery will remain on picket during the winter. It will probably be Capt Fry's, & not Wm's[,] as he stayed on picket last winter.[63] I am near Mrs Taliaferro's, & shall visit them in a few days. We moved yesterday to this place. Wm has been several times to Mrs T's. He seems to like Mittie Carter—says she is rather pretty. Mrs Alfred Carter is there with her family. Her husband is the brother of Mrs Taliaferro. He is the gentleman Uncle Hill & I spent some time with while in the South. He owned a place in Fauquier but is a refugee now. His wife is a daughter of Cousin Charles Randolph of the Grove. Lucy was expected at Orange Ct House yesterday. Renshaw has succeeded in getting a room at Mrs Ball's. I am glad she has come & hope to see

63. Captain Charles William Fry (1842–1922) commanded the Orange (Va.) Artillery of Cart-er's battalion (CSR; *OR* 29[2]:902).

something of her. I wrote to her a few days ago. You must do the same. You say in your lett{er} that you are much disappointed that I said nothing of a visit home at Xmas. Nothing would p{lea}se me more but there is no chance of it at all. An order was issued several weeks ago forb{idd}ing all furloughs to officers until further orders except in most urgent cases. You must come to me my darling as soon as we are sent to the rear for the winter. Thompson Brown & I have determined to get rooms together. Thompson is still acting Chief of Artillery of this Corps, in the absence of Long. The latter is suffering with facial paralysis & is in Petersburg. I hope he will soon recover for many reasons[,] among which is the fact that he is a strong friend of mine. Entre nous, there will be a row when they find I am recommended for the command of three fighting Battalions while Brown & Jones will command only two & they in reserve. Thompson is a warm friend of mine but he is very ambitious & would hardly like to see me advanced ahead of him. So I think[,] but I may do him injustice. This plan has been approved by Genl Pendleton & forwarded.[64] I think it probable it will be modified so as to give us each two Battalions, as Bragg's army will need Artillery since its recent loss & some of the reserve of this army may be sent to it—I mean some of Longstreets Artillery which remained in Virginia when his Corps went West. Two of his Battalions are still at Petersburg. One, Coalter Cabell's, is here.[65] It is desired to send { . . . } with a sinecure command & put his Battalion in Jones' reserve. I doubt if these changes will be made until spring so you must say nothing of them, & even then they may be entirely altered. Crutchfield has come to the army on a visit. He is still quite lame but anxious to get a place & is supposed to be hanging around here now for some such purpose.[66] Don't know what will be done with him. Ewell says he is a coward & it is not likely he will get into this Corps. I hope Long will return soon. He has great weight & is withal a man of fine judgment & sense. I will see Lucy tomorrow or next day & give you any news from her. I have heard nothing of Mama since my last. I hope our currency will

64. On 20 November 1863, General William N. Pendleton, as part of a reorganization of the artillery, proposed that Tom Carter be promoted to colonel and given command of three battalions. At the same time, Lieutenant Colonel Hilary Jones and Colonel Thompson Brown would each command two battalions (OR 29[2]:841).

65. Henry Coalter Cabell's (1820–89) artillery battalion consisted of Manly's North Carolina Battery, the 1st Richmond Howitzers, the Pulaski Battery, and the Troup Battery (OR 29[2]:904).

66. At the Battle of Chancellorsville, Colonel Stapleton Crutchfield had been wounded in the right leg by a shell fragment that shattered a bone below the knee. He did not return to active duty until January 1865 (CSR; Dozier, "Stapleton Crutchfield," 593).

soon be restored to its proper condition. It is rumored in Richd that your Uncle Alex will resign. Is there any truth in it?[67]

Rodes' Division will move back a few miles to get into wood in a short time. So will Johnston's.[68] I therefore think they will soon go into winter quarters. I hardly think there will be another battle unless the weather is unusually good. It is entirely too cold to fight & the weather too uncertain for a movement. If Meade had been superseded I should expect an advance.

Kiss the sweet little folks for their Papa & I am much annoyed about the { . . . } It is such a pity her looks should have been injured.

Genl Lee is now in Richmond. I am sometimes afraid he will be sent to the West. A new man here not appreciating the sufferings of this old state already might give up more of its territory. I do not fancy these falling back generals.

God bless you my dearest wife.
Ever your devoted husband

—⟋⟍—

Camp near Pisgah Church
Dec. 15th 1863

My precious Wife,

My time for writing has again come around & although in some haste I must send off a letter. Yesterday I saw Lucy who is now at Mrs Ball's, Orange Ct H. She looks quite as well, if not better, than when I saw her in Clarke, & is quite cheerful considering all things. At times when any remark causes a recollection of her loss, a look of pain crosses her face which she endeavors to hide.[69] She is very affectionate & sweet. A letter from Mama came to her yesterday dated the 28th & 3rd. They are still at Annfield & go through the ceremony of a pack every day or two for a move to Mrs Randolph's Millwood. The first time they had even started

67. The rumors proved false. James Alexander Seddon remained as secretary of war until he resigned because of poor health on 5 February 1865 (Schlup, "James Alexander Seddon," 577).

68. Carter is referring to the 2nd Corps division commanded by Major General Edward "Old Allegheny" Johnson (1816–73) of Virginia (Warner, *Generals in Gray*, 158–59).

69. Lucy Carter Renshaw, Tom Carter's half sister, suffered the loss of her two daughters in a little more than a month. Annie Page Renshaw (1861–63) died on 14 August, and her oldest child, Louis deLuna Renshaw (1860–63), died on 29 September. Both girls were buried at Old Chapel in Clarke County, Va. (McGill, *Beverley Family of Virginia*, 472–73).

to Millwood but while on the way heard Yankee Cavalry had encamped in Millwood the night before, which report turned out to be true. Papa vowed he would go no farther & returned to Annfield. I doubt if they will come to Pampatike this winter though Mama said she hoped it would be convenient for you to have them. She seems in great perplexity & finds difficulties on every side. Mr John E. Page has proposed to live together on shares at Mrs Randolph's in Millwood, which Papa objects to, & indeed Mama is opposed to it & very properly.[70] Papa & Mr Page would never get on as to their meals. My paternal would like to engage in a scold now & then which privilege would be denied him in view of the company. Lucy is decidedly of the opinion that it is best for the family to remain in Clarke. But for the trouble they have & the health of Evelyn & Mama I should agree with her. Lucy thinks everything would be lost at Annfield & she says groceries are now more abundant there than here. We expected to move with the Artillery of this Corps to Frederick Hall (a depot some twelve miles below Louisa Ct. H.) today or tomorrow but the recent news from the valley may detain us longer. Imboden reports a considerable force at Woodstock of Cavalry[,] Infantry & Artillery[,] say four or five thousand.[71] H. H. Walker's Brigade was sent up suddenly in the cars yesterday to Staunton.[72] Passengers who were on the cars were made to get out at the last moment & soldiers put in. There was some rumor of an advance from Bristow Station. I don't know the meaning of this advance up the valley with Infantry (if it is true) unless a diversion is intended while an advance is made on our front. The papers of yesterday state that Averill[73] is pushing towards Lewisburg with the probable intention of cutting Longstreet's communications & also stated that Meade had been superseded by Grant & a large portion of the western army would be brought with him. We have been rather uneasy lest Genl

70. Judge John E. Page (1796–1881) of Pagebrook, Clarke County, Va., was an uncle of Anne Willing Page Carter, Tom Carter's stepmother (Page, *Page Family in Virginia*, 147–48).

71. Brigadier General John Daniel Imboden (1823–95) of Virginia commanded the Valley District of the Army of Northern Virginia (CSR; Eicher and Eicher, *High Commands*, 313).

72. Brigadier General Henry Harrison Walker's (1832–1912) brigade consisted of the 40th, 47th, and 55th Virginia Infantry regiments and the 22nd Virginia Infantry Battalion. The brigade, from Major General Henry Heth's division in the 3rd Corps, was on detached service in the Shenandoah Valley in December 1863 (Warner, *Generals in Gray*, 318; OR 29[2]:901).

73. Brigadier General William Woods Averell (1832–1900) of New York commanded a cavalry division in the Department of West Virginia. While there, he led his command in operations against Confederate supply and communications lines with east Tennessee (Warner, *Generals in Blue*, 12–13).

Lee should be sent West. This plan would prevent it of course. Walker's Artillery (three Batteries) went to the rear yesterday. They will winter at Cobham. Genl Lee has not yet returned from Richmond. Genl Ewell is in command of the Army. The Artillery Quartermaster is now selecting camps near Frederick Hall for us. Two Battalions will remain in the front. Don't know which two. If decided by lot I may have to remain. I should prefer to go back to the railroad but would be content to stay here, but for the picket duty, which is hard on men & horses. When at Frederick Hall I shall be as near to Pampatike as when at Milford say fifty miles, & twenty five miles from James River, not too far for a visit to Sister Ann. If we move back in a day or two I will inform you. I hope we can get a house. Thompson is much disappointed that the Artillery of this Corps was not sent to Albermarle. Yesterday I made several visits, one to Dr Grimes.[74] Today I shall go to Mrs Taliaferro's. I go seldom but being in the way will get through with it at once. I enjoyed my visits quite much as I always do although no one dislikes more to make the start.

How discouraging to all persons is the present condition of things in our Congress. In such a time of trial & emergency to see our lawmakers frittering away the session in contemptible demagoguerism shows that our wickedness is not yet sufficiently punished & that the cup of bitterness is not yet full. Mama says the gentlemen of the north think Lincoln can not . . . {Remainder of letter missing}

—⧓—

Camp near Frederick Hall Depot
Dec. 19th 1863

My precious Wife,

You see we have come to rear rather sooner than I supposed in my last letter. We reached here yesterday. The place is about twenty three miles from Hanover Junction & twenty seven miles to Gordonsville & about thirty two or [thirty] four miles to Raccoon & Morton's Fords. You can come to see me as soon as you choose. I saw Mrs Brown at Fostersville two days since. She had just stopped a day or two with Thompson at that place. He had come down to examine the country for encampments, &

---

74. Carter, though he misspelled the name, is referring to Dr. Peyton Grymes (1791–1878), whose home, known as Selma, was located east of Orange Court House, Va., on the Orange Turnpike.

finding it likely he would be detained a day or two he sent word to her in R[ichmond]. He has returned to the front & will remain there a few days until the two reserve Battalions join us. Cabell's Battalion will do picket duty. He & Mrs B. consigned to my care a lot of turkeys &c. with a view to the housekeeping arrangement. I think there are many difficulties in the way[,] though if you ladies are willing to undertake to furnish a house & bring on servants[,] I think I can get the house. But my advice to you both is to adopt the Goss plan, that is to board at some nice house. There is a large brick house about a half mile from the Depot owned by a wealthy man by the name of Nat Harris.[75] He formerly kept a boarding school & I think will let Mrs B & yourself have rooms. He promised to let me know on Monday morning. There is but one drawback & that is the measles. One of his children has the disease. Our little infant is the only one of our children I think to have the disease. Poor little thing! In your letter of the 15th rec[eive]d since I commenced this, you talk as quietly about a scar from one to one & half inches in size as if it were a beauty mark. I fear she is ruined in appearance. I have been offered a room for you at Dr Mat Pendleton's near here[,] but he cannot take Mrs Brown.[76] The Dr speaks of a vacant house near here without furniture. I can make further inquiries if you & Mrs B have set your hearts on the housekeeping plans[,] though I am sure you will be more comfortable at Harris'. The house is well furnished & neatly kept—unless the measles may be an insuperable barrier.

I have seen Lucy again since {I} wrote. She is very cheerful & I think happy with her husband who is as kind & attentive as possible. He said he supposed you needed the roan horse. Wm says it is in fine order. I have just bought a large fine horse for $600 which I would gladly exchange for a male & possibly it may be done. If not you can work him. He is too large & bony to stand hard usage but under Mr Duling's care would do much work. He is young & powerful but rather clumsy for riding although I am now using him. I bought him on account of the cheap price.

75. Nathaniel W. Harris (b. 1824?), a farmer who lived near Frederick's Hall in Louisa County, Va., owned $36,900 worth of personal property and real estate valued at $32,800 in 1860. The Harris family consisted of Nathaniel; his wife, Ellen; and their eight children, ranging in age from one to sixteen (1860 Census, Louisa County). Flora, the second oldest of the Harris children, is probably the woman who, in 1865, became engaged to Abner Harris of the 4th Virginia Cavalry (see Carter's letter of 25 January 1865).

76. Carter is referring to Dr. Madison Pendleton (b. 1809?) of Louisa County, Va. He was listed in the 1860 census as a fifty-one-year-old doctor and farmer (1860 Census, Louisa County).

Nat could be sent to Hanover Ct House with a pass to Frederick Hall. He will find me two & a half miles from the Depot. Anyone will tell him. To prevent difficulty write to Overton or Phil Winston at Hanover Ct H[,] who will get him on the cars.[77] Tell him to be sure to get off at the right place. I would send James but he is the only servant of any account in the mess. Charles[,] Maj. Braxton's boy[,] always trifling[,] has sprained his wrist, & James has almost everything to do. I will have the roan horse here.

When I write Monday I will give you more definite information about the place for boarding. These people live on the railroad & have R[ichmon]d prices for every thing. You can come as soon as you choose for I will have some place for you. I will try to buy you mules, but they are very scarce. I am glad Genl Lee will return to our army. Many have feared his transfer to the West. Genl Johnston is assigned to the West.[78] I hope he will do well although I am afraid of him. However he is probably the best that can be done.

Be sure to send word to Biers & Spilman to cut my coat large enough.[79] My last uniform coat was entirely too tight. I wish the cape of the over-coat to take off. I have a fine pair of boots from Staunton.

God bless you & the children. Remember me most kindly to Mrs Ellerson.

Ever your devoted husband.

I don't understand Papa's horses looking badly. You had better let Mr Duling take them in hand. They ought to be [?] at with proper attention.

—◦—

77. Carter may be referring to a Phil Winston who lived in a house called Nutshell, which was located behind the courthouse in Hanover County, Va. Apparently, food prepared in Winston's large kitchen was deemed superior to that of the nearby Hanover Tavern, much to the delight of those who had business at the courthouse (Hanover County Historical Society, *Old Homes of Hanover County*, 94). William Overton Winston (1812–62) of the prosperous Winston family of Hanover County is the only "Overton" that could be identified. His death in March 1862, however, disqualifies him from being the subject of Carter's letter (McGill, *Beverley Family of Virginia*, 985).

78. General Joseph E. Johnston formally assumed command of the Army of Tennessee on 27 December 1863 (*OR* 31[3]:873).

79. Beers & Spilman was a merchant tailor operated by William S. Beers and Peter Spilman and located at 104 Main Street in Richmond (*Richmond City Directory, 1866*). The establishment was formerly known as Beers & Poindexter (see Carter's letter of 4 October 1862).

Camp near Frederick Hall

Dec. 27th 1863

My precious Wife,

Your two letters of the 23rd & 25th enclosing one for Mama have just come to hand. I write at once but have some fear the letter will not reach you on Tuesday—not that it is important but one likes the quick going of a letter to its destination.

Mrs Brown has arrived & has gone to Harris'. At first she was much bent on the housekeeping plan but now she thinks herself fortunate in the boarding arrangement. She speaks of the establishment as a second Goss house which you know expresses my idea of comfort & pleasure. The case of measles turns out to be a man who is kept closely confined to his room & who is nearly well. He expected to leave yesterday & I suppose will be off in a day or two if he has not gone already. The only question now that bothers us is whether it will be convenient for Mr Harris to board us all the winter. Mrs Brown suggests that if we leave others will urge him to take in boarders. We intend to ask him on the subject. Mr James Alfred Jones is now with Thompson B.[,] nominally on a hunting excursion but I have thought it possible he may be settling up the property of old Mr Wilcox. I suppose you will stay a day in R[ichmon]d so I shall tell Mr Harris not to expect you until next Wednesday week, the 6th Jan. I regret that you cannot come sooner but think it entirely right that you should attend to duty first & pleasure afterward. Nothing new with us. The cars yesterday were delayed by the troops which were brought from Staunton to Orange[,] so we hear. William has gone to Orange Ct House to spend his Christmas. Always safe to go to the front & no objection raised. I have finished my stables for the battery horses & the winter quarters of the men are nearly completed. They have worked well & it is incredible what an amount a large number of men can do when they work with a will. We met yesterday at Mr Harris's a Mrs Hyde & Miss Hyde of Alexandria.[80] The former once boarded with Cousin Maria Nicholas—[she] is a refugee. She is aunt of Miss Hetty Cary. She says Miss Hetty & Genl Pegram will not be married this winter. The

80. Carter is referring to Eugenia Cary Fairfax Hyde (1812–80) and her daughter, Margaret "Meta" Herbert Hyde (1847–1912). Eugenia's sister Monimia (d. 1875) married Archibald Cary (b. 1808), whose brother Wilson Miles Cary (1806–77) was the father of Hetty Cary (1860 Census, Fairfax County; Sprouse, "Fairfax County in 1860," book 4, Special Collections, Kate Waller Branch, Alexandria Public Library, Alexandria, Va.; Hardy, *Colonial Families of the Southern States*, 130–32).

young lady is bent on a trousseau from Baltimore & intends to run the blockade, a feat attempted once before by her & carried out through many hardships[,] dangers & awkward predicaments for a lady[,] such as three days & nights divided between a small foot boat & cabin with one man.

I spent my Xmas at Dr Mat Pendleton's or rather took my Xmas dinner there with my whole staff. They are most kind & hospitable people & while not fashionable are agreeable & intelligent. His son Capt. William Pendleton was Adjutant Genl for Wm Taliaferro, & lost his leg at Cedar Mountain.[81] He is very agreeable. He showed his wooden leg made in Charlottesville. It is ingenious but he prefers the crutches & gets about nimbly with them whether on foot or horseback. He is a fine handsome fellow, a graduate of the Institute. I suppose his chance for matrimony is much injured & it ought to be infinitely improved. I never see a wounded man that my sympathetic feelings are not deeply excited. The empty sleeve or pants leg should be the passport to attention & respect, for he who has it like Dante has seen hell & risked his life for his country & for those he loves. The girls won't have much choice if they discard such, for should the war continue there will be few sound men save the exempts. All the persons in this neighborhood in the first circle are remarkably kind & attentive. We are very comfortably fixed in a hewed log house nicely daubed & pointed with lime. It was formerly kept as a store.

There is quite a naive pretty girl at Mr Harris'[—]his daughter. She is small but the gentlemen seem to admire her. I hear there is a handsome Miss Pendleton there now. Have not seen her.

Kiss the children for their precious Papa. Have not heard from the mules yet. The horses are ready. Foam is nearly as rapid a trotter as ever. God bless you.

Y[ou]r devoted husband

81. William Barret Pendleton (1838–1914) attended Hampden-Sydney College and graduated in 1860 from the Virginia Military Institute before enlisting as a first lieutenant in the 23rd Virginia Infantry in April 1861. He earned promotion to captain in April 1862 and served as assistant adjutant general on the staff of Brigadier General William B. Taliaferro. Pendleton lost his left leg at the Battle of Cedar Mountain. From January 1863 until his retirement from duty in August 1864, he served as assistant adjutant general on enrolling duty in Virginia (Krick, *Staff Officers*, 241).

CHAPTER SEVEN

------- ⋙ -------

From the Wilderness to the Valley
17 March–31 December 1864

As the year 1864 began, Lieutenant Colonel Tom Carter set himself to work on the business of running a camp in winter quarters. To those men who lived within a reasonable distance of the Frederick's Hall camp in Louisa County, he granted two-week furloughs on a rotating basis throughout January and February. As for himself, he had official paperwork to finish. On 28 January Carter wrote a report of his battalion's activities during the Bristoe and Mine Run Campaigns. In it, he also took the opportunity to point out deficiencies in Confederate ordnance supplied to his batteries. Carter then submitted the report to his superior, Brigadier General Armistead L. Long. On a personal note, he received news from Richmond that the Carter family holdings in Madison Parish, Louisiana, had been "stripped" by Union troops and that the "negroes all went to the Yankees." Carter, however, did have the chance to recover two of the slaves who had left the plantation. Sixteen-year-old Maria and twelve-year-old Nancy had been recaptured and could belong to Carter again for the price of $500 each. Whether or not he went ahead with the transaction is unknown, but it likely reminded him of the personal cost of the war and increased his anxiety over the safety of his family in King William County.[1]

In March, Brigadier General William N. Pendleton traveled to Dalton, Georgia, to meet with General Joseph E. Johnston, commander of the Army of Tennessee, to help him reorganize and find a new chief for his artillery. Johnston initially wanted Edward Porter Alexander, chief of the 1st Corps artillery, but R. E. Lee was unwilling to part with that brilliant officer. On the eleventh, Pendleton formally requested that Tom Carter be promoted to brigadier general and appointed to the position.

---

1. Macaluso, *Morris, Orange, and King William Artillery*, 56; A. R. Hynes to THC, 14 Jan. 1864, Private Collection.

*Postwar portrait of Tom Carter
in Confederate uniform
(Courtesy of James F. Turrell)*

A week later, Richmond authorities responded by sending Brigadier General Francis A. Shoup to Johnston as his new chief of artillery. Pendleton expressed his disappointment over the decision. "I am sorry they did not promote Tom Carter and send him, as he has been so thoroughly tried and found so efficient." If Carter was disappointed over the affair, he was most likely comforted by the fact that he did not have to leave Virginia and by the news that his promotion to colonel, which Pendleton had recommended the previous November, came through on 14 March. His new rank brought with it slightly more responsibility. In early April, General Long reorganized the 2nd Corps artillery into two divisions and placed Carter in command of the second one, consisting of Major Wilfred Cutshaw's and Major Richard C. M. Page's battalions.[2]

<hr>

2. Joseph E. Johnston to Braxton Bragg, 11 Mar. 1864, in Carter's CSR-Officers; Lee, *Memoirs of William Nelson Pendleton*, 315, 317 (quotation); OR 29[2]:841, 33:1267. The fact that General Shoup was a West Point graduate, something the War Department in Richmond tended to favor, may have played a role in the decision (Wise, *Long Arm of Lee*, 734). Carter's new commission bore a date of rank of 27 February 1864 (James A. Seddon to Jefferson Davis, 4 May 1864, Letters Received by the Confederate Adjutant and Inspector General's Office, NARA).

The campaigning season of 1864 opened on the morning of 4 May when the Army of the Potomac, commanded by Major General George G. Meade but under the general direction of Lieutenant General Ulysses S. Grant, crossed the Rapidan River between General Lee's Army of Northern Virginia, located in Orange County, and the town of Fredericksburg. Early that same morning, Colonel Tom Carter and Page's artillery battalion, then on duty at Raccoon Ford on the Rapidan, received orders to rejoin Lieutenant General Richard S. Ewell's 2nd Corps at Locust Grove. Carter and his division of two battalions arrived there early on 5 May and immediately marched east on the Orange Turnpike toward the heavily forested region known as "the Wilderness." That morning, Ewell's men clashed with soldiers from the V Corps on the turnpike not far from Germanna Ford, where they had crossed the night before. On 5 and 6 May, Ewell's men on the turnpike and A. P. Hill's 3rd Corps and James Longstreet's 1st Corps on the Orange Plank Road, three miles to the south, fought in the Battle of the Wilderness against Federals amid dense undergrowth and scattered fields. Carter commanded the guns on the Confederate army's left flank, north of the turnpike. The few open spaces in the region, however, limited the use of artillery by both sides. After two days of inconclusive bloody fighting, the two armies faced each other in hastily constructed earthworks, still within the Wilderness.[3]

On the evening of 7 May, Grant's army began pulling out of its positions and heading toward Spotsylvania Court House, a crossroads village ten miles to the south. Lee's army, however, led by the 1st Corps, moved quicker along roads farther to the west and won the race to the village. On the ninth, the divisions commanded by Major Generals Robert Rodes and Edward Johnson of Ewell's corps constructed strong works along high ground that projected outward from the main Confederate line just north of Spotsylvania Court House. The salient earned the nickname the "Mule Shoe" because of its peculiar shape. In the apex of the Mule Shoe, Colonel Carter placed Page's entire battalion and two of Cutshaw's batteries, interspersed among the infantry. Carter's other guns remained in reserve near the courthouse. Throughout the day, the batteries sparred with Union artillery.[4]

On 10 May the Confederates continued to strengthen their works in the Mule Shoe. Early that evening, twelve Union regiments under the

3. *OR* 36[1]:1038, 1084.
4. Ibid., 1086; Macaluso, *Morris, Orange, and King William Artillery*, 63.

command of Colonel Emory Upton of the VI Corps attacked the left side of the salient and captured about 1,000 Confederates. None of Page's batteries took part in the action. At sunset on 11 May, General Lee—believing that the Federals were withdrawing their army toward Fredericksburg and wanting to arrange his army in such a way as to make pursuit more effective—ordered General Long to remove the artillery from the Mule Shoe that was "so situated as to be difficult to withdraw at night." What the Southerners had seen earlier that day was not a general withdrawal of the Federal army but instead preparations for an assault on the Mule Shoe planned for early on the twelfth. After midnight, Lee, now aware of the impending Union attack, changed his mind. On what Tom Carter later described as a "dark, murky and dripping" night, Long woke him up around 3:30 A.M. on 12 May and ordered him to return his artillery to its former positions in the Mule Shoe. Most of Page's battalion, including the King William Artillery, commanded by Tom's younger brother, William P. P. Carter, and part of Cutshaw's battalion reached the line just in time to be captured by Federals from Winfield Hancock's II Corps, which was then sweeping through the Southern works. Only one gun from Captain Carter's battery unlimbered and fired before William, and most of his men were captured. In twenty minutes of fighting, Page lost twelve guns, and Cutshaw lost eight taken by the Federals. Four days later, Tom wrote to Susan and assured her that "[n]o blame is attached to the Artillery Officer by anyone for the loss of his twenty pieces of Artillery."[5]

In the aftermath of the devastating losses suffered in the second artillery division, Colonel Carter assumed command of his surviving batteries plus a battalion from the first artillery division. On 18 May Grant ordered a major frontal assault where the Confederates had constructed a new line of works along the base of the Mule Shoe salient. This time, with the help of Carter's twenty-nine guns, which "opened a most murderous fire of canister and spherical case-shot," the attack failed. That result lent support to the belief of some officers, Carter included, that had the artillery not been removed from the Mule Shoe the night before the Union assault on the twelfth, that attack would have failed as well.[6]

5. *OR* 36[1]: 1044, 1086, 1088; Macaluso, *Morris, Orange, and King William Artillery*, 63, 66; Carter, "The Bloody Angle," 240; THC to SRC, 16 May 1864.

6. *OR* 36[1]:1087; Carter, "The Bloody Angle," 239. Carter's new command included a battalion made up of the remnants of R. C. M. Page's former battalion, Wilfred Cutshaw's surviving battery, and another 2nd Corps battalion, formerly under Major Robert Hardaway, who suffered a shoulder wound on the twelfth, now under Cutshaw (*OR* 36[1]:1087).

The next two weeks for Carter and the Army of Northern Virginia were essentially a blur of constant movement and armed clashes from Spotsylvania County to the environs of Richmond. Starting with Grant's withdrawal to the southeast on 21 May, Lee sought to counter his opponent's attempts to move around his right flank and win the race to Richmond. The Confederates reached the south bank of the North Anna River in Hanover County by the afternoon of the twenty-second. There, Lee's men dug in behind a line in the shape of an inverted *V*, with the apex anchored on the river. Ewell's corps, with Carter's battalions located on strong ground behind it, occupied the right leg of the *V*. For three days, the two armies fought on both sides of the river to no discernible conclusion. Early on 27 May, Lee's army headed south on the Telegraph Road to counter another move to the southeast by the Federals. This time, the Union army marched farther into eastern Hanover County toward the Pamunkey River crossing at Hanovertown. A series of small engagements over the next few days on farmland broken by forests and fed by the Pamunkey River and Totopotomoy Creek ultimately brought the armies to Cold Harbor, near the site of the 1862 Battle of Gaines's Mill. There, in lines that stretched for several miles north from the Chickahominy River, the Union and Confederate armies fought the bloody Battle of Cold Harbor from 1 to 3 June. During this period of constant movement and sharp encounters, Tom Carter briefly assumed command of the 2nd Corps artillery when General Long fell ill for two days at the end of May. In many of these engagements, Carter fed battalions and individual batteries into action in support of both cavalry and infantry. The butcher's bill for the almost constant fighting in Colonel Carter's artillery division during the Overland Campaign was twenty-one killed, seventy-one wounded, and 276 missing—a total of 368 men lost. Virtually all of the soldiers declared missing were captured at Spotsylvania on the morning of 12 May.[7]

Carter and his battalions spent the next two and a half months east of Richmond engaged in operations with the Confederate navy against Union vessels on the James River. On several occasions, his guns "efficiently patrolled the [northern] bank of the river against the enemy's gun-boats." On 27 June Carter's artillery and Major General Joseph Kershaw's infantry division clashed with Union troops after they had crossed to the north side of the James. The Federals withdrew after a short fight, the purpose of which was to draw more Confederate troops from Petersburg, where

7. *OR* 36[1]:1046–48, 1052; Long, *Day by Day*, 509.

most of the two armies were just beginning their long siege. On 6 August Tom wrote to Susan about an expedition near Berkeley Plantation in which his guns "fired into the [Union] mail steamer, much to the disturbance of the otium cum dignitate of Yankee officers aboard." Until early September, he and his two battalions remained near Chaffin's Bluff in eastern Henrico County. On the second, General Pendleton sent Carter and his batteries to reinforce General Jubal Early's Army of the Valley, which was then opposing Union general Philip Sheridan's Army of the Shenandoah near Winchester. Carter was to replace General Long, who was ill and thus unfit to command Early's artillery. Carter arrived at Winchester on 9 September and reported for duty the next day.[8]

On 15 September Sheridan, aware that Early's army had sent an infantry division and an artillery battalion to Lee's army at Petersburg, decided to pounce on the weakened Confederate force near Winchester. Early on the morning of the nineteenth, Union cavalry began marching west from Berryville in Clarke County toward Winchester. After slowly passing through the two-mile-long Berryville Canyon, through which the turnpike to Winchester ran, the Union force struck the right and center of Early's line at around 11:40 A.M. For the next several hours, the Confederates held their ground and mounted successful counterattacks that almost broke the Federal line. Carter's battalions lent their heavy ordnance to the action. In the midst of this fighting, his close friend, Robert Rodes, was killed. Though the Confederates appeared to be heading toward another victory, Sheridan's decision to commit his reserves—two divisions of cavalry and an infantry corps—to an assault against Early's left flank northeast of Winchester changed the course of the battle. The attack took place at 4:00 P.M. and completely overwhelmed the Confederates on that part of the field. With no other choice, Early ordered a withdrawal through

8. *Official Records of the Union and Confederate Navies in the War of the Rebellion,* 10:352–53, 705, 732, 745–46; *OR* 40[1]:759, 42[1]:859; THC to SRC, 6 Aug. and 13 Sept. 1864. Jubal Early had been promoted to lieutenant general on 31 May 1864 and placed in command of the 2nd Corps following General Ewell's removal from field duty on 29 May. On 13 June, General Lee ordered Early to take most of the 2nd Corps to the Shenandoah Valley to intercept the Union forces under David Hunter that were then threatening Lynchburg (Warner, *Generals in Gray,* 79; Long, "General Early's Valley Campaign," 112). Though Carter's exact whereabouts during this period of time are not easy to determine, it is a certainty that he was not the "Colonel Carter" that Mary Chesnut mentions in her diary entry for 6 August 1864. While that soldier, whom she described as "a bluff Englishman," was dining at her home in Columbia, S.C., Tom Carter was in his camp at Chaffin's Farm, east of Richmond, writing a letter to Susan. The distinguished historian C. Vann Woodward, in his edition of her diary, mistakenly identified the officer as "probably Col. Thomas Henry Carter" (Woodward, *Mary Chesnut's Civil War,* 633).

the town and toward the south (up the Shenandoah Valley). The southern artillery held back Federal pursuers as long as possible. According to Carter, the "guns retired from point to point, halting, unlimbering, and firing, while efforts were made by general officers to rally the infantry." Near the close of the fighting, a shell fragment struck Colonel Carter in the back, forcing him to turn over command of the artillery to Lieutenant Colonel William Nelson, one of his battalion commanders.[9]

Four days after the Battle of Third Winchester, Tom Carter's brother Shirley got the news about his injury and wrote to him: "I have just heard that you were wounded; do let me know if it is a dangerous one. . . . I wrote to Sue this evening; she will of course be perfectly wretched until she hears from you." Fortunately for Carter, the wound proved to be more painful than serious. In the meantime, the wound did keep the colonel out of the army's next battle, which took place on 22 September at Fisher's Hill, south of Strasburg. There, Sheridan won another victory by once again attacking the Confederate left flank with overwhelming force.[10]

The routed Army of the Valley marched to Brown's Gap in the Blue Ridge Mountains, some sixty miles south. Sheridan's men followed Early's army as far as Harrisonburg, where they arrived on 25 September. For the next several weeks, the Union army moved through the upper valley and destroyed anything of value to the Confederacy, including crops, livestock, barns, and mills. Known as "the Burning," this action prevented the Shenandoah Valley from supplying Lee's army ever again. By 10 October Sheridan's Army of the Shenandoah had defeated Southern cavalry at the Battle of Tom's Brook and marched to a point just south of Middletown, where its three corps encamped on high ground north of Cedar Creek.[11]

Fueled by a desire to seek revenge on the Federal treatment of the valley and reinforced by Major General Joseph Kershaw's infantry division and Major Wilfred Cutshaw's artillery battalion, Jubal Early decided to march north and attack Sheridan. By the seventeenth, his army was back at Fisher's Hill, a few miles south of Middletown. The next day, after Confederate reconnaissance revealed that Sheridan's left was unprotected, Early summoned his division commanders and Colonel Carter, now back in service, to a meeting at which they planned a surprise assault on

9. Frye, "Shenandoah Valley Campaign of Sheridan," 1418; *RDD*, 24 Sept. 1864; Carter quotation in Wise, *Long Arm of Lee*, 887.

10. Charles Shirley Carter to THC, 23 Sept. 1864, THCP, 1861–96, VHS; Frye, "Shenandoah Valley Campaign of Sheridan," 1418.

11. Frye, "Shenandoah Valley Campaign of Sheridan," 1418–19.

Sheridan's exposed left flank. The Battle of Cedar Creek began at around 4:30 A.M. on 19 October. Three infantry divisions under Major General John B. Gordon crossed the creek and swept through the unsuspecting Union camps east of the Valley Turnpike. The Confederates drove the Union VIII and XIX Corps north toward Middletown. The Southern artillery rumbled up the turnpike behind Major General Gabriel Wharton's division as it joined Gordon's men. Carter's guns added weight to the overwhelming attack against Federal troops in the fields west of the pike around Belle Grove Plantation. By 10:00 A.M., Sheridan's army had been pushed beyond Middletown to a point about three miles north of its original camps. There, it formed a defensive line and regrouped. "We now held the turnpike," Carter explained to Susan, "our line of battle running across it beyond Middletown." The Confederate attack then ceased for several hours—enough time, according to Percy Hawes, Carter's courier, for Hawes to ride to Middletown and get lunch for both Carter and Gordon.[12]

At 3:30 P.M. the recomposed Union army unleashed its cavalry on Early's left flank, which "broke at once & could not be rallied." The subsequent chaos forced the Confederates to fall back toward Cedar Creek. Carter's gunners occupied high ground just north of Middletown and did their best to slow the Union advance, which had become a general one following the collapse of the Confederate left. It was dusk by the time Colonel Carter had moved his artillery, which included Federal guns that had been captured earlier in the day, across Cedar Creek. In the "dim twilight," pursuing Union cavalry "literally enveloped" the retreating artillerists on the Valley Turnpike. Only the chaos of the moment and the growing darkness prevented Carter and his staff from being captured. Early's weary and demoralized men continued south to the relative safety of their former positions at Fisher's Hill.[13]

A few days later, Jubal Early publically criticized his army's conduct in the battle in a strongly worded address. He blamed the collapse of the Confederate line in the afternoon on "thinned" ranks resulting from his soldiers displaying "a disgraceful propensity for plunder." Carter's men were "incensed" that Early included them in his censure. Carter subsequently spoke with the commanding general about the matter. Early rectified the situation by putting out another order, this time praising the

12. Carmichael, "Cedar Creek, Virginia," 271; THC to SRC, 21 Oct. 1864; Hawes, "Battle of Cedar Creek," 169. Carter had recovered enough from his wound to return to duty on 25 September (Wise, *Long Arm of Lee*, 889).

13. THC to SRC, 21 Oct. 1864; Hawes, "Battle of Cedar Creek," 169.

actions of the artillery. In his official report of the battle, Early stated that the "artillery throughout, from first to last . . . behaved nobly, both officers and men. . . . Colonel Carter and all his battalion commanders richly deserve promotion. They not only fought their guns gallantly and efficiently, but they made the most strenuous efforts to rally the infantry."[14]

The Battle of Cedar Creek ended the fighting in the Shenandoah valley. Early's force was no longer an effective field army. For the rest of October, Carter's artillery remained near New Market. By December, it was in winter quarters at Fishersville, halfway between Staunton and Waynesboro. There, Tom Carter watched as troops boarded cars on the nearby tracks of the Virginia Central Railroad and headed east toward Lee's army at Petersburg.[15]

—⚒—

Camp near Frederick's Hall
March 17th 1864

My precious Wife,

This letter may not find you at Pampatike but I send it there at a venture. In my last I told you I had secured a room, such as it is, at Mr Bibb's.[16] Mrs Brown will occupy the one without a fire place, which is small but comfortable having a carpet & bureau. The large room has no carpet but a fire place[,] two beds & a bureau. Mrs Brown thinks the bureau a great comfort. The people are evidently very plain. I took supper there night before last. It was quite good to a soldier.

The dining room is a basement room with cement floor; a loom stands in it & the cooking was done at the hearth, so that the cakes, made of shorts & very nice, came in piping hot. Mrs Brown is pining for want of your presence. I somewhat expect you the last of this week though you may not be sufficiently recovered. Your note of Wednesday the 9th was rec[eive]d, no other letter since we parted has come to hand, but one may arrive today. I am truly sorry you have been sick & hope to cure you

14. Jubal A. Early, "Soldiers of the Army of the Valley . . . ," 22 Oct. 1864, Imprints Collection, Eleanor S. Brockenbrough Library, Museum of the Confederacy, Richmond; THC to John W. Daniel, 19 Nov. 1894, John Warwick Daniel Papers, 1849–1910, David M. Rubenstein Rare Book and Manuscript Library, Duke University; OR 43[1]:563.

15. THC to SRC, 15 Dec. 1864.

16. Carter is likely referring to the home of forty-five-year-old Robert T. Bibb, who lived with his wife, Bettie, two miles southwest of Fredericks Hall, Va. (1860 Census, Louisa County; Chisholm and Lillie, Old Home Places of Louisa County, 63).

by my love & attention when you join me. It was kind [of] Cousin Nora to visit you. She is a fine & noble woman. What have you decided on in regard to the children? How I shall miss them. Mrs Brown tells me Mrs Long & Mrs Dance[17] will leave Dr Pendleton's in a few days & she has thought of trying to get accommodations there, but I imagine they are like most persons around us[,] pretty well eaten out of house & home.

Mr Brown my chaplain has proved to be a most able & useful preacher & is doing much good in the Battalion.[18] The chapel which holds about two hundred is nearly filled every night. We have been fortunate in securing a man of such talents & usefulness. Mr Taylor, Braxton's brother & law, & his wife are staying a few days at the Miss Gailands. Mr Reed is preaching at the 1st Va. Artillery & Mr Peterkin is expected soon.[19] We hope to have some of the best preachers from Rich[mon]d to preach to the Battalions. All of us have chapels. Braxton is about completing his.

You know Brown is to be Chaplain for our two Battalions as Mr Seddon refused to allow one to each Battn. Half a loaf is better than no loaf. It is probable Wm & Deas[20] will go down on Sunday to be confirmed by Bishop Johns in Richd.[21] They can go on forty eight hours pass.

I am sorry I was unable to obtain France a commission. He is acknowledged to be the most efficient adjutant in the Arty of this Corps & he is

---

17. Margaret C. Dance (b. 1823?) was the wife of Captain Willis Jefferson Dance (1821–87), a prewar attorney from Powhatan County, Va., who commanded the Powhatan Artillery in J. Thompson Brown's battalion (1860 Census, Powhatan County; *OR* 45:1235).

18. The Reverend Abram Burwell Brown (1821–85), a native of Amherst County, Va., attended Washington College and the University of Virginia before becoming a Baptist minister. Known as a "powerful preacher" whose sermons were "clear, forceful, logical and convincing," Brown served as the chaplain for Carter's battalion in 1863–64. After the war, the Reverend Brown preached at a number of churches in Halifax and Pittsylvania Counties, Va. ("List of Virginia Chaplains," 314; Hackley, *Faces on the Wall*, 11).

19. Carter is likely referring to the Reverend Charles H. Read of the United Presbyterian Church, which was located at the corner of Franklin and 8th Streets in Richmond (*Stranger's Guide and Official Directory for the City of Richmond*, 26). The Reverend Joshua Peterkin (1814–92) was the rector of St. James Episcopal Church in Richmond. Like many of his colleagues, Peterkin visited the camps of the Army of Northern Virginia to preach throughout the war. He was also present during General Jeb Stuart's final hours following his mortal wounding at the Battle of Yellow Tavern (Strider, *Life and Work of George William Peterkin*, 18, 45–46; Jones, *Christ in Camp*, 103).

20. William Allen Deas (1838–1920) enlisted in the Regular Confederate army in May 1861 and was appointed second lieutenant. On 4 October 1862, after Deas had recovered from wounds suffered at the Battle of Antietam, Brigadier General William Nelson Pendleton assigned him to the Orange Artillery as senior first lieutenant (CSR).

21. Bishop John Johns (1796–1876) was the fourth bishop of the Protestant Episcopal Church in Virginia (Morton, "John Johns," 75–76).

mortified I think at his position. He regrets no doubt that he ever left his state.[22]

Mr Rutherfoord wrote to me enclosing ~~me~~ a statement of the stocks he had drawn interest on & placed in the Bank of Va in care of Mr Taylor[,] subject to your order or mine. Neither Mr Wortham nor Mr Bruce knew anything of the Va state stock or the West Ten. & Va RR bonds.

Probably you know I left them in Mr Rose's vault[,] Farmer's Bank[,] all in a yellow envelope[,] subject to your order. You have probably drawn interest on them frequently since. Some of them are Coupons.

Mr Ellerson has telegraphed me to know if I would buy Clover seed at $248 per bushel & timothy at $80 per bushel. I have answered that I would not until I had seen you, so as to learn if there is any ready money on hand. When was Wortham's bill settled—was it the 1st [of] January? If so do we owe him anything[?] Did he sell stock to pay for the mules & horses or did he advance the money[?]

I am a little doubtful about buying the seed on account of the last news from Washington in regard to the Spring campaign, which it is thought will be directed chiefly against Va by advice of Grant. If so the peninsula may be used for one army & in that event farming operations at Pampatike will be uncertain.

Kisses to my precious children. God bless you forever.

Y[ou]r devoted husband.

Bring my map of Va

—꩜—

Spotsylvania Ct House
May 16th 1864

This letter my precious Wife, will not reach you until Friday. I therefore telegraphed to Wortham to inform you that I am safe thus far. Wm I am sorry to say was captured with his battery & most of his men. No blame is attached to the Artillery Officer by anyone for the loss of his twenty pieces of Artillery.[23] Most of them were not in position when the Infantry broke & ran out of their breastworks. The Artillery had been

22. Spencer France was a native of Baltimore, Md.
23. Carter's figure of "twenty guns lost" came from R. C. M. Page's battalion, which lost twelve, and Wilfred Cutshaw's battalion, which lost eight, during the fight at the Bloody Angle (*OR* 36[1]:1044).

relieved by order of Genl Lee the night before under the impression that the enemy were moving to our right. Just before day a dispatch was sent for the Artillery to be sent up immediately as the enemy were massing for attack on a salient in our line, which salient was in shape of a horse shoe, say 400 yards across the heels & 3/4 of a mile around the toe. I had protested against this line all the day before to Genl Ewell & Genl Lee thought it extremely objectionable[,] but Rodes & Johnson[,] having made their breastworks[,] insisted they could hold it. So miserable was the shape that when Dole's line was broken on Tuesday I had to get outside the breastwork to meet the attack[,] placing my back to the enemy at that point in order that I might confront him where he had broken the line on Dole's front.[24]

When Wm unlimbered two of his pieces the enemy was only fifty yards from the breastworks. He fired one shot which is said to have staggered the line & was loading the other gun himself when the Yankees gained the works & surrounded him. It was just day & a dense fog obscured everything. The old battery went down as it has fought always—game to the last. Thank God Wm was not hurt. I have heard from him by two prisoners of his Battery who escaped & he is well. Genl Johnson along with most of his Division was captured.[25] The Infantry behaved like curs—ran out of their works without firing a gun. It was Jones' Brigade.[26] He was killed at Locust Grove. All twenty guns were from my Div, & such was the nature of the line that they were captured without being able to fire in their defence[,] even those that were in position. Twenty more have been assigned me but I would give the whole for

24. Around 6:00 P.M. on Tuesday, 10 May, a Union force consisting of twelve regiments under the command of Colonel Emory Upton (1839–81) attacked in column formation the western side of the Confederate salient, known as the Mule Shoe, near Spotsylvania Court House, Va. The assault struck the section of the Southern line held by Brigadier General George Doles's brigade. Upton's attack initially succeeded in breaching the Confederate defenses, but nearby 2nd Corps reinforcements soon arrived and forced the Federals to withdraw. Doles's brigade lost at least 600 men in the attack (Rhea, *Battles for Spotsylvania Court House*, 161–77).

25. Major General Edward Johnson was captured by Union soldiers in the fighting at the Bloody Angle on 12 May 1864. He was later exchanged and commanded a division in the Army of Tennessee. At the Battle of Nashville, Johnson was again captured and subsequently imprisoned at Old Capitol Prison in Washington, D.C. (Rhea, *Battles for Spotsylvania Court House*, 238; Warner, *Generals in Gray*, 159).

26. Brigadier General John Marshall Jones's (1820–64) brigade consisted of the 21st, 25th, 42nd, 44th, 48th, and 50th Virginia Infantry regiments. Colonel William Addison Witcher (1820–87) of the 21st Virginia Infantry commanded the brigade on 12 May because General Jones had been killed (5 May) on the first day of the Battle of the Wilderness (*OR* 36[1]:1023; Warner, *Generals in Gray*, 164–65; Krick, *Lee's Colonels*, 409).

my old Battn on condition that I should have entire control of it, & be subject to no orders as I used to be with Rodes. The enemy were driven back but not far enough to recover the guns.

Grant still holds on without fighting since Thursday. We can't tell what he will do. He has been repulsed on every occasion but the capture of these pieces & several thousand prisoners in this miserable cul-de-sac will have its effect upon the troops & doubtless has prolonged the battle. Their loss has been about 50,000 all told.[27] I hope everything goes well around Richmond. The Yankee papers claim great victories even before the capture of the Artillery which of course is all nonsense. Grant could have marched to Spots Ct H without firing a gun. Our horses are suffering for forage, but we can hold on as long as Grant. There is no intention of going back. I hope we will assume the offensive & drive him in a day or two. Gordon is a Maj Genl.[28] Daniels killed.[29] Davy Watson killed. Hardaway slightly wounded.[30] God has protected me wonderfully thus far. Deas is thought to be killed, also Coleman & Capt Carrington.[31] Wash was killed.[32] Robt Randolph of 4th Cavalry killed.[33]

27. Carter's estimate of total Union losses from the beginning of the campaign through the fight at the Bloody Angle is inflated. According to the official tabulation, Grant's army suffered 29,410 casualties; a modern historian has concluded that the total was more than 33,000 when losses in Ambrose Burnside's independent IX Corps are included in the total (OR 36[1]:195; Rhea, *Battles for Spotsylvania Court House*, 319).

28. John Brown Gordon was commissioned a major general on 14 May 1864 (Eicher and Eicher, *High Commands*, 260).

29. Brigadier General Junius Daniel (1828–64) of North Carolina commanded a brigade in Rodes's division. He was mortally wounded during the 12 May fight at the Mule Shoe salient and died the next day (CSR-Officers; Warner, *Generals in Gray*, 66–67).

30. Major David Watson, second in command of Lieutenant Colonel Robert Hardaway's artillery battalion, was mortally wounded during Colonel Emory Upton's attack on the Confederate lines on 10 May 1864. Hardaway suffered minor wounds in the same attack (OR 36[1]:1044). Watson had enlisted on 3 July 1861 as a second lieutenant in the Albemarle Artillery. He remained with that unit until 1 May 1862, at which point he was elected captain of Company K of the 1st Virginia Artillery Regiment (also known as the 2nd Richmond Howitzers). Watson commanded the battery until 27 February 1864, when he was promoted to major and became Hardaway's second in command. He died from his wounds on 14 May 1864 (CSR).

31. Carter was mistaken about Deas, Coleman, and Carrington. First Lieutenant William Allen Deas of the Orange Artillery was wounded in the leg during the fight on 12 May but escaped capture by lying still among the dead (Macaluso, *Morris, Orange, and King William Artillery*, 65; CSR). Charles Lloyd Coleman, a second lieutenant in the Morris Artillery, and James McDowell Carrington (1839–1911), the six-foot-one captain of the Charlottesville Artillery, were both captured during the attack (CSR; 1860 Census, Albemarle County).

32. "Wash," also mentioned in Carter's letter of 2 April 1863, has not been identified.

33. Colonel Robert Randolph (1835–64) of the 4th Virginia Cavalry was killed on 12 May at Meadow Bridge during the Battle of Yellow Tavern, Va. (CSR).

Keep up your spirits. With God's help we will whip Grant by & by. I want to get out of these works. Kiss the children a hundred times. My tent mate tells me I called Juliet's name frequently last night in my sleep. I think of you always my darling with inexhaustible tenderness. God forever bless you.

—⁂—

Taylorsville
May 24th 1864

My precious Wife,

I have endeavored to communicate with you from time to time. I fear many dispatches have failed to reach you. I have rec[eive]d your letters up to Sunday the 15th, none since. I telegraphed & wrote you that Wm had been captured unhurt. The guns from my Division were unable to defend themselves not being in position but most of them marching to the works. Had they been in position they would easily have driven back the enemy as was done the day before at the same point. Genl Lee ordered them away under the impression that the enemy was moving to the right. He takes the whole blame on himself saying it was one of his blunders. The Yankees deserve no more for their capture than that of so many wagons. Johnson's men behaved badly & broke before the guns could be unlimbered. I was not present but back with Genl Long. It is sad that the old organization should be broken up but if we can crush Grant it won't matter. The 1st Va Battalion has been assigned to my command along with the debris of my old Division which gives me the same number of guns as before. I fear the Yankees have been around you already & have damaged you probably. Still I shall hope to the last that you may escape. Grant's base now is Port Royal & Tappahannock but I fear his Cavalry & flankers will annoy you greatly. I shall direct this to Richmond. I am suffering with Dysentery & intensely at times with Hemorrhoids brought on by it. I ride in the Ambulance until we get to the battlefield & they take my horse. The first disease is almost well. The latter still gives me pain in riding. I have not been so active as usual but have always been with my command in action.

Grant is on our front at the Junction & has crossed a considerable force already. I think the bulk will cross lower down, about Hanover Ct H[,] but as yet there are no signs of this movement. Another battle will be fought this evening or tomorrow. I should like to know where you are & how you are. I fear Pampatike will "go up" this time. We have fresh troops here—Breckenridge's & Pickett's.[34] Genl Lee talks of fighting another defensive battle. We will never do anything with Grant until we attack him. His Army was enormously large when he started. It is about 50,000 less now. He slipped around our flank at Bowling Green without notice on the part of our cavalry, otherwise the line of the Mattapony would have been taken. Dr Baylor has moved everything except his wife who remained. One servant ran off. We will whip Mr Grant in a week more. Keep a brave heart.

God bless you & the little ones

—⁑—

Camp near Chaffin's Farm
Aug. 6th 1864

My precious Wife

Your letter by Hilliard was rec[eive]d two days ago.[35] I have tried in vain to learn beforehand when our wagons would start. Now that you have a regular mail communication I will write regularly. You know however my darling, how entirely you are loved by me & how constantly you occupy my thoughts even when I do not write. The French say it is one party who loves & the other who permits to be loved. I am the first. There! It won't do for us old married folks to be making love afresh.

I have just returned from a lively expedition down to Wilcox's & Berkeley after transports & gunboats.[36] None were sunk but many were bored through. We fired into the mail steamer, much to the disturbance of the otium cum dignitate of Yankee officers aboard.[37] Also fired into a steamer loaded with troops & into Sheridan's Cavalry Camp on the other side of the river.

34. The divisions of John C. Breckinridge and George E. Pickett reinforced Lee's army from the valley and the Bermuda Hundred line, respectively (*OR* 51[2]:943, 36[3]:799).

35. Private Richard Hilliard (b. 1824), a carpenter, enlisted in the King William Artillery on 1 June 1861 at Bond's Store. He was discharged on 10 August 1862 for being over the age of thirty-five but reenlisted in the battery on 1 March 1863. Hilliard was five feet, ten inches tall with a fair complexion, dark hair, and blue eyes (CSR).

36. Berkeley, built in 1726 by Benjamin Harrison IV, was located on the north side of the James River in Charles City County, Va. In the summer of 1862, the Army of the Potomac occupied the plantation following the Seven Days Battles (Loth, *Virginia Landmarks Registry*, 94). In mid-June 1864, the Union army crossed the river three miles east of the plantation at Wilcox's Landing on its movement toward Petersburg, Va. On 3 and 4 August, Carter took part in an expedition to fire upon Federal transports and other vessels on the river. His gunners also lobbed shells into the camps of Union cavalry on the south side of the James (*OR* 42[2]:49–50).

37. *Otium cum dignitate* is literally translated as "leisure with dignity."

Nothing new with us except what the papers give & a dispatch from Hood stating that Sherman's communications are cut & he must fight or starve. I trust so. It is stated here that the enemy attacked a part of our line near Petersburg & was repulsed yesterday evening. You have doubtless seen all about the mine sprung a week ago today & the result. Grant lost between 5[000] & 6000 & we 1200 only.[38]

I have just seen Andrew Davis who passed Pampatike today. He tells me you wrote yesterday by mail. I hope to get the letter tomorrow. In regard to the grinding of the 300 bushels of wheat[,] the only difficulty is the want of team. You have it to haul to mill & then to Richd with less team than is sufficient to put in a crop for next year, but possibly you might do it next winter. The objection to the latter plan is that it is dangerous to keep it on hand. However if you like to try it do so. I am anxious to procure team as I proposed on the plan of grazing condemned horses. Could I go into Richd doubtless it might be arranged. It would be better to buy low priced team even with the certainty of losing it than not to put in a crop this fall. Andrew Davis tells me Alex Dudley has been lent four good mules by the government. The government gets our crops at schedule prices & as the farm is a large & remarkably productive one & has manual labor, I think it to their interest to make some arrangement by which its cultivation can be continued[,] such as the loan of condemned horses. If I can get off to see you when had I better do so[?] You will leave soon now I presume. Mrs Jno Seddon's house having been burnt I suppose she will go to Staunton Hill.[39] Will this prevent you from

38. Carter is referring to the Battle of the Crater, fought near Petersburg, Va., on 30 July 1864. His estimate of Union losses in the battle was slightly exaggerated; the official total was 3,798. The Confederates suffered casualties of around 1,500 men (Wert, "Crater," 190).

39. This is a reference to the destruction of Snowden, the Stafford County, Va., home of Mary Alexander Little Seddon (1826–1910). On 2 August 1864, Major General Benjamin Butler ordered a small Federal expedition to destroy Snowden in retaliation for the burning by Confederates of the Maryland home of U.S. postmaster general Montgomery Blair, which itself had been in retaliation for Union general David Hunter's raid on Lexington, Va. Apparently, Butler may have confused John Seddon, the late husband of Mary Seddon, with his older brother, James A. Seddon, the Confederate secretary of war. Charles Kingsley of the 3rd Pennsylvania Artillery described in a letter home that before destroying the house, the Federals gave John Seddon's widow and her young children an hour to collect their most precious belongings and vacate the property. The *Richmond Daily Dispatch* later commented: "It is, indeed, time for Confederates to treasure up somewhat of the spirit of revenge, and this is one case eminently worthy of retaliation" (Moncure, "The Destruction of Snowden," 1–2; Charles Kingsley to Frank E. Kingsley, 6 Aug. 1864, VHS; "Retaliation," *RDD*, 12 Aug. 1861). Staunton Hill in Charlotte County, Va., was the home of Mary Seddon's sister-in-law Sarah Alexander Seddon Bruce and her husband, Charles Bruce.

getting there[?] You have seen the account of the burning of Chambersburg by McCausland.[40] I trust this retaliation will do some good from the tone of the Washington Chronicle which condemns it strongly & hopes both sides will see in the light of the burning houses of Chambersburg the heinousness of such crimes. It mentions Darien[,] Ga.[,] Alexandria, Louisiana &c. &c. [and] states that the distance from them, [and] the languid feeling in regard to any injury inflicted on us has prevented a proper appreciation of the enormity of the outrage &c. &c. I have just rec[eive]d a letter from Uncle Jno E. Page in regard to Wm his son. I have advised him to enter the Rockbridge Battery. By the way[,] I forgot to tell you how the guns were lost. The left of the infantry supporting it was turned in consequence of the failure of the Cavalry to connect & they fell back without offering resistance. The guns were turned towards the enemy & checked the advance for a time. The infantry however continued to fall back without fighting & the guns had to be abandoned. It was six o'clock in the morning & I was not present[,] not expecting any engagement except with gunboats. That morning Hancock's whole Corps passed over & the force was too strong. The brigadier in command ought to have withdrawn his force or fought long enough to allow the guns to be withdrawn. I wish I had been present but I heard nothing of it until the attack was made & it is impossible for me to be present with every battery of my command. Nothing was lost but the guns, & they were old & the company had recently applied to exchange them for other guns. I have already given them four other ~~new~~ guns which they like better. The infantry lost nothing. A large portion of Sheridan's Cavalry has been sent off on transports supposed to have gone to the Rappahannock to land & attack Early's rear. I fired into his camp on the southside from Berkeley day before yesterday. The Whitworth gun sent two balls into their midst much to their consternation.

I think Grant can do nothing. He is at a deadlock but will hold on until after the election, if possible & I see no way of dislodging him. He may stay until peace. I feel some uneasiness about Atlanta but have much hope too. Hood will certainly fight, & if his recent dispatch is true the condition of things is good.

40. On 30 July 1864, Confederate cavalry under Brigadier General John McCausland (1836–1927) rode into Chambersburg, Pa., and demanded $500,000 in currency or $100,000 in gold as reparations for the Union army's treatment of the Shenandoah Valley. When town leaders could not raise the money, the Confederates set fire to the town and rode off to McConnellsburg (Long, *Day by Day*, 548; Warner, *Generals in Gray*, 197–98).

I have your jars[,] tin bucket &c. & will send them to you. We will be glad to have some butter & vegetables. We are living on very nice beef sent by Early from Yankeedoodledom. I am becoming anxious enough to see you. I am very impatient at times at being so near & yet see so little of you. I enclose you Mama's letter, also one from poor Mary Brown.[41] My heart feels most deeply for her. George Hobson too has been killed.[42] Two out of three of us who were so pleasantly associated last winter are gone, & yet God has spared me who have been in so many more dangers than either of the two taken away.

Keep the bay horse as long as you want. I have three now, Bob Willis having left his horse with me on account of an injury. He has recovered & can be used.

I have just received a dispatch which may require me to go to Culpepper. He writes to know if I can spare a Battalion. I answered that I could. It is to go with Genl. Anderson on some expedition.[43] Say nothing about this. I do not know that I will go. I hate to think of going without seeing you again. If I do have to go I should like to get to Clarke. A soldier's life is a singular one, is it not? I wish I could spend such a happy time with you as at Goss' last year. Indeed I have seen nothing of you this summer.

God bless you my own darling. Kiss the precious children for [their] own dear Papa.

Ever your devoted husband.

Renshaw has lost his place as Q. M. All of that date or batch the Senate refused to confirm. I don't know on what ground. He speaks of staying with me until he decides on what to do. I have asked him to come.

41. Carter is probably referring to Mary Martha Southall Brown, the widow of Colonel John Thompson Brown, who was killed at the Battle of the Wilderness (Krick, *Lee's Colonels*, 68; Johnson, *University Memorial*, 560).

42. George William Hobson (1832–64) of Cumberland County, Va., enlisted as a private in the 2nd Company of Richmond Howitzers at Richmond on 21 April 1861. In October 1861 he transferred out of the unit and into the Amherst Artillery as a newly elected second lieutenant. Promotion to first lieutenant followed on 15 May 1862. Hobson was wounded in the hand on 3 June 1864 at the Battle of Cold Harbor. On 9 July 1864, he was mortally wounded and captured at the Battle of Monocacy. Hobson died on 15 July in a U.S. hospital at Frederick, Md. (CSR).

43. Richard Heron Anderson (1821–79) of South Carolina commanded the 1st Corps in James Longstreet's absence, following that general's wounding at the Battle of the Wilderness. Anderson held the temporary rank of lieutenant general (Eicher and Eicher, *High Commands*, 105). In mid-August 1864, Anderson, with Joseph Kershaw's infantry and Fitz Lee's cavalry divisions, moved from Gordonsville into the Shenandoah Valley to reinforce Early and threaten the Union force at Strasburg. The artillery mentioned by Carter was Cutshaw's battalion, which accompanied Anderson's force on the expedition (OR 42[1]:873, 43[1]:996).

Be sure to write William. I have succeeded in getting the blue pants from the government[,] also a good pair of gaiter sleeves which you can have to walk in if you wish. Mrs Pendleton fixed my coat nicely with the Alpaca & the stars. If I go to the upper country will write tomorrow by mail.

—␣␣—

Camp near Winchester
Sept. 13th [18]64

My precious Wife

I reached here safely on Friday 9th & reported for duty on Saturday. It was unsafe to visit the Millwood neighborhood, our pickets extending no farther than the Opequon. Persons come through to Winchester & in this way I have heard from the family at Annfield. Yesterday I saw John Page. He had seen Papa the day before at Pagebrook. He was well but Mama [was] quite indisposed & had sent for a physician. John knew nothing of the nature of the disease but did not consider her indisposition serious. Evelyn is better. The Yankees have not injured them as much as might have been expected. Papa has one horse left (the best) & the stock has not been driven off. It was feared the house would be used as a signal station. Some officer asked to go to the top. He did so but nothing has come of it thus far. Peter Mayo is still in Winchester. The girls went to the Hall but he was advised to remain in our lines. The Yankees are strongly intrenched at Berryville & send out cavalry scouting parties once or twice weekly to Millwood[,] White Post & nearby to Newtown. Our cavalry with the exception of Fitz Lee's, is much demoralized by the Moorefield disaster & the superiority in numbers of the Yankee cavalry. The latter is said to fight splendidly & having horses without stint can break down our cavalry which is completely cowed. Fitz Lee's Division is swung back to Newtown & Anderson's Div is just in front of Winchester towards Millwood & Annfield.[44] Our whole right wing ought to be thrown forward & to rest on the Shenandoah at Berry's ferry or Snicker's Ferry. As the line now stands the Yankee Cavalry[,] 8 thousand strong[,] can run around by Front Royal & strike the Staunton turnpike at any point in our rear & capture our trains. There are too many leaders

44. Major General Fitzhugh Lee's division consisted of two cavalry brigades, commanded by Brigadier General Williams C. Wickham and Colonel William H. F. Payne, and seven batteries of horse artillery under Major James Breathed (Wert, *From Winchester to Cedar Creek*, 316–17).

here—Early & Anderson in Infantry[;] Fitz Lee & Lomax[45] in Cavalry[;] Cutshaw[,][46] myself & King[47] in Artillery. Anderson's command is entirely distinct from Early's. King is nominally in this Artillery command but Breckinridge is punctilious as to his Corps & Genl Early would not sustain Genl Long. Early & Long do not agree at all. His position is said to have been most disagreeable. This is entre nous. Braxton says Long is a perfect failure. His disease renders him extremely irritable & Early snubbed him in every way.

I have been warmly rec[eive]d by my old friends[,] Cutshaws Battalion very enthusiastic in its cheers & remarks when I rode up. There is skirmishing frequently. Powell has not yet arrived. Came by home. Wagon[,] servants[,] horses arrived safely on Saturday. Artillery horses here very thin. I am in great haste. Have you heard of the call upon Mr Duling to ~~attend a meeting~~ report at some church for duty[?] Mr Seddon to whom Dr Ellerson referred the matter staved it off for the time. Look into the matter. Do you want more mules or horses[?] I can buy cheaply here. Much love to Aunt Cornelia & Cousin Nanny. I will write again in a day or two.

God bless you & our precious little ones.

Y[ou]r devoted husband

—⁊⁊⁊—

45. Major General Lunsford Lindsay Lomax (1835–1913) of Virginia commanded the cavalry of the 2nd Corps (Warner, *Generals in Gray*, 190–91).

46. Wilfred Emory Cutshaw (1838–1907), an 1858 graduate of the Virginia Military Institute and a teacher in Loudoun County, Va., was appointed first lieutenant in the Provisional Army of Virginia on 4 May 1861 and in the Regular Army of the Confederate States on 31 October 1861. From 1 March to 21 April 1862, Cutshaw served as Major General Thomas J. Jackson's acting chief of artillery. He was severely wounded and captured on 25 May 1862 near Winchester, Va., and was not paroled until August 1862. Deemed unfit to return to active duty, Cutshaw served as assistant commandant of cadets and assistant instructor of tactics at VMI until he was arrested in the lower Shenandoah Valley by Federals on 17 April 1863. He was imprisoned at Fort McHenry, Md., and at Fort Monroe, Va., before his exchange on 5 May 1863. Cutshaw returned to duty in September 1863 as inspector general of the 2nd Corps artillery. He was promoted to major on 14 March 1864 (to rank from 27 February) and given command of an artillery battalion. Cutshaw lost a leg on 6 April 1865 at the Battle of Sailor's Creek (CSR; Krick, *Lee's Colonels*, 108; Virginia Military Institute Archives Online, www.vmi.edu/archives/home).

47. Lieutenant Colonel John Floyd King (1842–1915) commanded an artillery battalion in the Army of the Valley in September 1864. In anticipation of the outbreak of war, King enlisted as a lieutenant in the 1st Georgia Regulars on 28 March 1861. In May 1862 he was elected a major in the Confederate army. In the fall of 1863, King became a lieutenant colonel and commanded the 13th Virginia Artillery Battalion. After the war, he returned to his native Georgia and served four terms in the U.S. House of Representatives (CSR; Krick, *Lee's Colonels*, 225; *Biographical Directory of the United States Congress*, http://bioguide.congress.gov/scripts/biodisplay.pl?index=K000206).

Camp near Newmarket
Oct. 10th 1864

My precious Wife,

I fear there is but little prospect that you will receive my letter now that the local troops are in the trenches around Richmond but I will continue to write regularly with the hope that some may turn up safely. Your last letter was of the 25th ult. Doubtless you have written repeatedly but the letters are not forthcoming for the reason above mentioned. Yesterday the Cavalry fought some twenty-five miles down the Valley beyond Woodstock. Our Cavalry, notwithstanding the accession of Rosser's celebrated Brigade commanded by himself, was most outrageously whipped & chased twenty miles back to the neighborhood of this place, losing ten pieces of Horse Artillery, a number of wagons &c.[48] Rosser commands his own Brigade & Fitz Lee's Division[,] three brigades in all. Lomax nominally commands all the Cavalry of this Army but in the fracas yesterday he commanded the right wing & Rosser the left wing[,] the former on the valley turnpike, the latter on the back or Mountain Road. Lomax's command consists of Imboden's, McCausland's, Bradley Johnson's & Jackson's Brigades, some ten or twelve thousand on the rolls but about two thousand present for duty.[49] In the engagement yesterday he took in about six or seven hundred men—who broke & ran back twenty miles. The Yankees literally ran down the Horse Artillery we hear & picked it up while scudding along behind our flying cavalry who could not be induced to stand long enough to enable the Artillery to escape at a gallop. Rosser did better having good troops but was badly whipped. It is said the Yankee Cavalry has been made so formidable by transferring men from the Infantry for special gallantry to the Cavalry. This Valley Cavalry is made up of Western Va men whose homes are in the possession of the enemy. They leave their commands at pleasure & it is impossible to

48. Carter is describing the cavalry Battle of Tom's Brook. Fought on 9 October between Union divisions under Brigadier Generals Wesley Merritt and George A. Custer and Confederate divisions commanded by Brigadier Generals Lunsford L. Lomax and Thomas L. Rosser, the Federals overwhelmed the Southerners and forced them to retreat up the valley from Tom's Brook to Woodstock. In the fight, the Confederates lost around 350 men and eleven cannons, while Union casualties amounted to fewer than sixty men (Salmon, *Battlefield Guide*, 335–36).

49. Carter is referring to Brigadier Generals John Daniel Imboden (1823–95) of Virginia, John McCausland (1836–1927) of Missouri, and Bradley Tyler Johnson (1829–1903) of Maryland and Colonel William Lowther Jackson (1825–90) of Virginia, each of whom commanded a brigade in Lundsford Lindsay Lomax's cavalry command (*OR* 43[1]:566; Warner, *Generals in Gray*, 147, 153–54, 156–57, 190–91, 197–98).

recover them unless they choose to return. The consequence is that there can be no discipline with them.[50] Vaughan commanding a Cav Brigade from East Tennessee was sent to South Western Va a short time since to follow his Brigade which had preceded him in squads of stragglers.[51] He took with him only sixty men—the rest having taken themselves off. The only course to pursue with these men is to put them in Infantry & give their horses to better men. If this were done I really believe good Cavalry might be made. I hope it will be done. Sheridan's Infantry is supposed to be at Fisher's Hill near Strasburg. It may be further back but since the disaster to our Cavalry it is impossible to learn anything except through scouts. We are about to go forward to ascertain their whereabouts, so I judge from the orders today to cook two days rations & be ready to move at sunrise tomorrow. I fear there will be difficulty in subsisting the army down the valley. It is sad to see the destruction of barns & mills & forage in this country. The Yankees are determined we shall not campaign in the lower valley this fall. Indeed it will be difficult to do so next summer[,] the advance of the enemy having put a stop to seeding & all farming operations. They have taken off many horses[,] a hundred from this immediate neighborhood, animals needed badly by our Country. I have just seen a letter from Mama to Mr Lee her brother-in-law. She is extremely anxious about me, had heard of my wound & feared it was much more serious than reported. I wrote a week ago & Wms Wickham had written the day before. I hope therefore she has heard from one source or the other of my safety. Nothing could be more affectionate than her expressions in relation to me. They are in low spirits in Clarke. The enemy are rebuilding the Manassas Gap road to Strausburg as if they intended to keep an army at that place. I have just heard from Wm[.] He is at Morris Island & well. Heard through Lieut Hawes who is also there. Direct your letters to Wm [as] "prisoner of war[,] Morris Island[,] S.C.[,] Charleston by flag of truce" & without U.S. stamp. Write to him often.

50. Toward the end of October, Major General John C. Breckinridge (1821–75), commander of the Confederate Department of East Tennessee and Western Virginia, wrote to Major General Lundsford L. Lomax about the problem of Confederate deserters and stragglers from Lomax's command. He assured Lomax that he was doing all he could to find and return men to Lomax's command in the Shenandoah Valley, including using troops to search the countryside (OR 43[2]:906).

51. Brigadier General James Crawford Vaughn (1824–75) of Tennessee commanded a cavalry brigade in Major General John C. Breckinridge's division of the 2nd Corps. At the beginning of October, Vaughn was sent to join the Confederate Department of East Tennessee and Western Virginia (Warner, Generals in Gray, 316–17; Eicher and Eicher, High Commands, 544; OR 43[2]:892).

We are nearly reinstated in Artillery except of course the Horse Artillery with which I have nothing to do save to help them if I can. The Cavalry deserves no Artillery. Mrs Gordon has returned to Staunton to remain absent. Gordon has done right in this matter. Mr Lee thinks our folks can do well enough in Clarke. Some wheat was left.

Kiss the precious little folks. Tell me about them Mother. I suppose you are wending your way homeward. I hope you can get the old island in grain this fall. If I can help you in any way let me know. My mare is worse & worse—fear she will die. Hope to get a horse in a few days. Shirley wrote me an affectionate note when he heard of my wound. Love to him. I shall direct this to Dr Ellerson as probably the best way of getting it to you. I think of you always darling & with inexpressible affection.

May God ever bless you.

Y[ou]r devoted husband

Send my flannels by first opportunity & a couple of towels.

—◆—

Camp near New Market
Oct. 21st 1864

My precious Wife,

Here we are again after a long, tedious battle at Cedar Creek & Middletown on the 19th. The first part of the day we carried the heights on Cedar Creek by a flank movement in brilliant style & with trifling loss carried Middletown & the whole battle field[,] sweeping everything before us like chaff before the wind. The attack was made a little before daybreak by Rosser on the left just to engage their attention on that flank. Gordon in command of four Divisions moved during the night to the right & just at daybreak fell upon their left flank. Attack suits our soldiers & suits Gordon above all men I have known, & nothing seemed to stand before their impetuosity. I moved all the Artillery on the turnpike & as soon as Gordon reached the turnpike, crossed Cedar Creek & joined him, having previously engaged the enemy's fire so as to relieve ~~Gordon~~ him in his attack on the right. The Army having reached the turnpike made a right wheel & again carried all before it. At 8 A.M. we had won the battlefield, seventeen pieces of Artillery, their tents, a number of wagons & ambulances & 1400 or 1500 prisoners, [and] with a loss of say 400 men, had disorganized the 8th & 19th Corps & had before us the 6th Corps only & a small force of Cavalry[,] the main force of the latter arm being on our left in front of Rosser.[52] We now held the turn-pike[,] our line of battle running across it beyond Middletown. At this period the fatal error which lost us Gettysburg was again repeated—we *halted.* Early crossed the Creek with my command & after this success was too well pleased to complete the victory & ensure his own safety by demolishing the rest of the Infantry. He was unwisely afraid to advance when really the safety of his army consisted in it. It is true a good many men had straggled to plunder the Yankee camps but the enemy was badly broken & demoralized & their lines yielded before a slight pressure whenever made. The stragglers too were soon driven into ranks & all supposed we would advance. It was not done, however. Early was disposed to rest on his laurels & we remained idle until about 4 P.M. by which time the enemy had recovered from their surprise. They in turn attacked our left, more I think as an experiment than with any hope of success. Unfortunately Gordon's Division held the left, without connection with our Cavalry, that body of troops being too few to reach this point. This Division stands an attack badly since the Fisher's Hill & Winchester engagements. Kershaw's Div[,] absent from these unlucky places[,] would have been much more staunch. Gordon's Division broke at once & could not be rallied. Kershaw's Div stood like a rock[,] every attack against its front[,] until the enemy having broken Gordon on its left enveloped its flank, & they fell back. I succeeded in running five Napoleons on a crest just behind Kershaw & opened upon the enemy[,] advancing & cheering like hungry devils. They were checked until a thin line of Kershaw's men could be rallied to meet them. We held them one hour & a quarter when the ammunition of these Napoleons being exhausted & the infantry lines thinned out they again advanced & we retired.

The Artillery as usual had to do all the fighting in the retreat as our infantry are utterly worthless when once broken. I fought them retiring & got every piece of Artillery & all the captured artillery across the Cedar Creek which was our supposed harbour of rest. We were marching complacently along the turnpike with all our plunder congratulating ourselves on the escape when just before dark the Yankee Cavalry struck us on the right flank at a charge. Although thousands of Infantry marched on each side of the train in a disorganized state none could be

52. The VI and XIX Corps were commanded by Major Generals Horatio G. Wright and William H. Emory, respectively. Carter misidentified the VIII Corps as being the third component of the Army of the Valley. The Army of West Virginia, commanded by Brigadier General George Crook, was the force serving with the two corps.

induced to offer resistance to the enemy. One hundred men could have saved the train. We had thousands but the wonderful difference between an organized body of men & a mob was never more-clearly illustrated. I was at the rear of the Artillery keeping everything well up. The first charge, they came on my right to within fifty yards & fired their pistols[,] wheeled & retired. It was now nearly dark. They sounded the bugle for another charge[,] came up at full speed & captured a few of the rear pieces. They would ride along the column killing the horses & occasionally the driver by way of varying the amusement. Most of the latter however at the last moment slipped from their horses & escaped through the darkness. I kept just ahead of them guided by their cheering & the sounds of the pistol shots. Sixteen pieces only escaped of thirty nine carried in & the seventeen captured [from the enemy]. They escaped by reaching Fishers Hill before the Yankees reached so far up the train. The ambulances & ordnance wagons about Strausburg were captured with the wounded &c. Had the Yankees pressed on that night with this Cavalry they could have captured the whole army save those escaping to the mountains. Fortunately Fishers Hill frightened them. When we reached it there was not an organization of any kind except in the few pieces of escaped artillery. Not three men could be found to stand together with

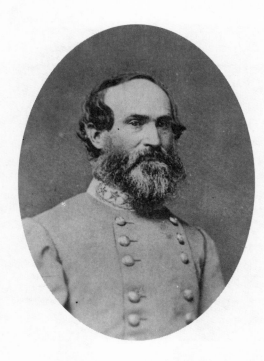

Jubal A. Early
(Library of Congress)

that shoulder to shoulder confidence which makes an army. In the morning these men were lions, in the evening lambs. Such facts are incredible to one who has not witnessed them but they are unfortunately too true.

Ramseur was mortally wounded & captured in the Ambulance.[53] Rob Randolph was killed (brother of Wm Randolph).[54] The loss in killed & wounded & prisoners is small[,] not over 1,000, that of the enemy two or three times larger.[55] But for the miserable termination which compelled our retreat the affair would have been one of the most brilliant of the

53. Major General Stephen Dodson Ramseur was shot through both lungs and fell into Union hands on 19 October during the Battle of Cedar Creek. He was taken to a nearby house, called Belle Grove, where he died the next morning (Warner, *Generals in Gray*, 252).

54. Robert Carter Randolph Jr. (1840–64) was the son of Dr. Robert Carter Randolph of New Market, Clarke County, Va. Young Randolph, who listed his occupation as farmer, enlisted as a second lieutenant in the 2nd Virginia Infantry on 18 April 1861 at Millwood, Va. On 9 September 1861 he was promoted to the rank of first lieutenant. Randolph continued to serve with the regiment until his death on 19 October 1864 at the Battle of Cedar Creek. See Carter's letter dated 9 November 1861 for mention of his brothers Archie and William (CSR; McGill, *Beverley Family of Virginia*, 173).

55. Carter underestimated the opposing armies' total losses at the Battle of Cedar Creek. A modern study of the 1864 Shenandoah Valley Campaign estimates the following casualty figures for the battle: Confederate army—2,910 total, consisting of 320 killed, 1,540 wounded, and 1,050 missing; Union army—5,665 total, including 644 killed, 3,430 wounded, and 1,591 missing (Wert, *From Winchester to Cedar Creek*, 246).

war considering the disparity in numbers. It was suggested[,] planned & carried out by Gordon after the Jackson style. He really has military genius. Whether he has general capacity enough is doubtful & his administrative ability is certainly not of a high order. He lacks discipline, but he is a giant on the field, not only by his personal courage but by that sort of instinct which teaches a leader to do the right thing at the right time & in the right manner. As soon as Early took immediate command after crossing the Cedar Creek the whole affair languished & subsided into a lackadaisical failure. Early is a staunch man with courage & fortitude in disaster & has sustained himself well in retreat, but on the field he is a blank, sees nothing with the eye of genius, is slow & do-nothing in policy & always trying to play a safe game which is generally an unsafe one. He has sense enough but no system & no discipline. We are anxious to remodel the army organization, to abolish the elective system for officers & to inaugurate a discipline which will make the men obey on the battlefield & elsewhere. Unless we do we are lost. The Yankee discipline is immeasurably superior to ours. Think of their men turning on us after such a disaster & surprise & forcing us back. As to their Cavalry it is fast becoming equal to that of Europe. I saw them charge Infantry & break it repeatedly, while ours has dwindled down to a mere handful by straggling & they run at the sound of their horses hooves. Our Company officers & many field officers are utterly worthless exercising no authority whatever at any time & running as fast as the fastest in battle. Had we a system which could at once reduce these men to ranks something might be done. We are too democratic to have a good army. Our legislators are not patriots but demagogues. Green Peyton hopes to have two or three officers shot for misbehavior before the enemy.[56] I hope so. It is useless to

56. Major Moses Green Peyton (1828–97) was the assistant adjutant general on the staff of Major General Stephen D. Ramseur at the time of the Battle of Cedar Creek. Peyton, a graduate of the University of Virginia, was a civil engineer who worked in Richmond for the Norfolk & Western Railroad before the war under future Confederate general William Mahone. Green Peyton enlisted as a first lieutenant in the Albemarle Artillery at Charlottesville, Va., on 3 July 1861. In August 1862 Peyton became captain and assistant adjutant general to Brigadier General Robert E. Rodes. He served with Rodes, first as captain and then as major, until the general's death at the Battle of Third Winchester. Service on Ramseur's staff followed until his death at Cedar Creek a month later. Until the surrender at Appomattox, Peyton functioned as assistant adjutant general to Bryan Grimes, who had inherited Ramseur's division and who, in February 1865, became the last man in Lee's army promoted to major general. In 1868 Peyton was elected proctor and superintendent of grounds and buildings at the University of Virginia, a position he held until his death in 1897. His successor was Tom Carter (CSR; Krick, *Staff Officers*, 242; Richey, *Memorial History of the John Bowie Strange Camp*, 50–51).

tell you that the Artillery behaved splendidly. The whole army admits it & wonders at it. I supposed it is due to better discipline. It is deplorably helpless however. I applied today for muskets for some of my cannoneers to establish a corps of sharpshooters for the protection of the Artillery. This Infantry cannot be depended on when attacked since the recent defeats. The cannoneers were cool & easily controlled even when charged in flank on the march by Cavalry. I got your note today by Willy Mann. I hope you are getting on well at Pampatike. We will do nothing here for sometime unless ordered to Richd or unless the enemy's Cavalry come down & take a till at us alone.

I have a big disgust on me, as old Ewell would say.

Kiss the sweet little ones for me.

May God ever bless you darling.

Ever your devoted husband

—⋙—

Camp near New Market

Oct. 26th [18]64

My precious Wife,

I wrote on the 22nd inst giving an account of the battle of the 19th & telling you of my safety. I have nothing new to relate. Yours by Jno Edwards was duly received. Unfortunately some servant stole one pair of the flannel drawers at Dr Defainette's [in] Spotsylvania County.[57] I was too glad to get off so well to complain at all. Jno Edwards is much annoyed about it. The same servant stole both flannel shirts belonging to young Turner. Edwards wished to punish him but his master objected on the grounds that he would run off & stated that he could keep nothing of his own. The flannel shirts came safely to hand & are splendid. I shall enjoy them the more because they were made entirely by your own dear hands. Also the socks & one pair of flannel drawers, toothbrush & book. Had you not better make another pair of drawers as soon as possible? My summer drawers are ripping in many places. I can make out with the old ones until you can complete another pair. Were I to wear the new pair without change to same thickness of flannel it might give cold. The socks are soft & nice. You recollect my objection to the socks last winter was the hardness of the thread. These are much softer.

57. Possibly Joseph S. Defarnette (b. 1826?), who was listed as a thirty-four-year-old farmer in Spotsylvania County in 1860 (1860 Census, Spotsylvania County).

Col. Venable, Genl Lee's staff, is here on an official visit[,] the object of which is doubtless to ascertain the tone of the army & the cause of our disasters.[58] It is attributable to three causes[:] 1st want of an adequate force of Cavalry[;] 2nd want of discipline[;] 3rd want of a good general. I understand there is no intention to relieve Genl Early. He has many good qualities of a soldier but is no Genl. On the battle field he is without particular aim or plan & the fighting under his control is languid, in small detachments & without vigor. Gordon's management of the 19th is going to Early's credit. Although doubtful of Gordon's general capacity I would willingly try him in preference to Early. He certainly has military talent & that sort of intuition which teaches him to go straight to success. Early I am told is now claiming the plan as his own. He deserves credit for carrying it out or rather for allowing it to be carried out thereby assuming the responsibility of its failure. This shows good nerve on his part but nothing more. Poor Ramseur is dead. I recollect at the meeting of the Division Commanders & myself at Genl Early's Hd Qrs the evening before the battle to plan the attack, fix the hour, set watches together &c. he said "if we whip these people I must have a furlough to go home to see my baby." You know he was married to Nelly Richmond a year or so ago.[59] He was one of the bravest of the brave. He thought himself mortally wounded, sent his watch & messages to his wife. The ambulance containing him was captured the night of the battle. Sheridan makes a great glorification over the victory, claims everything to himself. His success is far more due to our shortcomings than to his generalship. Nothing could show more conclusively the propriety of our continuing the advance than his description of the condition of things on his arrival.

Well it is no use to reprove—it is all right. I am afraid I shall have trouble to keep my couriers. Detailed men of every description are required to go before an Examining Board of Surgeons to be returned to the ranks & their places to be filled by disabled men. I trust I shall not lose Powel

58. Lieutenant Colonel Charles Scott Venable (1827–1900) was the assistant adjutant general on the staff of General Robert E. Lee. He was a native of Prince Edward County, Va., and a graduate of Hampden-Sydney College, where he later taught. Early in the war, Venable served with the Hampton Legion Infantry and the 2nd South Carolina Infantry. In May 1862 he began his career as a staff officer as a major and assistant adjutant general to Brigadier General Martin L. Smith. In June he joined the field headquarters of the newly formed Army of Northern Virginia. Venable, who became a lieutenant colonel on 25 February 1864, remained with Robert E. Lee for the remainder of the war. After the war, he taught math at the University of Virginia (Krick, *Staff Officers*, 292–93).

59. Ellen "Nellie" Richmond married Stephen Dodson Ramseur on 28 October 1863 at Woodside, the Milton, N.C., home of the Richmond family (Gallagher, *Ramseur*, 84).

& Percy.[60] We are gradually increasing the Artillery again, possibly for Genl. Early to turn it over to Sheridan. He intends I understand to make special notice in general orders of the splendid behavior of the Artillery in all his reverses. He is late enough about it considering the contrast in the conduct of the Artillery & Infantry & Cavalry. Gentlemen through the lines tell us that the Yankees admit that the Artillery at Winchester was splendidly served. It is great injustice to these men & they feel & speak of it that the Cmdg Genl should not notice their good conduct. I shall ask Genl Early to attend to it.

Venable speaks in the most cheering manner of things at Richmond. Thinks we can hold it. Hopes a good deal from Hood's maneuvers.[61]

I am glad to hear you are doing so well at Pampatike. Was any clover seed raised? I am sorry to hear the sorgum is a failure. It may turn out better than you suppose. The oxen ought to be fed with some grain if worked regularly. If they enter the winter thin they will die next spring.

They have worked faithfully to put in the old island in wheat. What does the Doctor think of Winny & Collins?[62] I hope they have no serious disease. Love to Martha & Nannie if they are with you.

60. Robert Powel Page (1846–1930) served on Carter's staff and was a cousin of his stepmother, Anne Willing Page Carter. Page was a student at Episcopal High School in Alexandria, Va., when the war began in 1861. At the age of seventeen, he enlisted as a private in the 1st Rockbridge Artillery on 1 May 1864. The next day, Colonel Carter detailed him to serve as a courier on his staff. Page remained with him until both men were paroled at Appomattox. After the war, Powel Page returned to his native Clarke County, Va., where he purchased Saratoga, the former home of Revolutionary War general Daniel Morgan, and took up farming. His older sister Lucy married Carter's brother William in 1867 (History of Virginia, 5:185–86; CSR; McGill, Beverley Family of Virginia, 471, 527).

Captain William Alexander Percy (1834–88) had been an assistant adjutant general on the staff of Carter's artillery battalion since June 1864. Percy, a graduate of Princeton and the University of Virginia and a prewar planter and lawyer from Greenville, Miss., had begun the war out west as assistant adjutant and inspector general on the staff of Brigadier General John S. Bowen. Percy was captured at Vicksburg when that city fell in July 1863. Three months later, on 8 October 1863, he came east and served as assistant adjutant general to Brigadier General Armistead Lindsay Long, chief of artillery for the 2nd Corps of the Army of Northern Virginia. Appointment to Tom Carter's battalion staff followed in June 1864; he remained there until he returned to Long's staff in November 1864. At the end of the year, Percy went back to the western theater, where he served as a lieutenant colonel in the 24th Mississippi Cavalry Battalion. After the war, he served in the Mississippi state legislature (CSR; Krick, Staff Officers, 241).

61. General John B. Hood's Army of Tennessee was marching through Alabama on its way toward Tennessee in an effort to cut Union general William T. Sherman's lines of communications and threaten central Tennessee. Sherman reacted to Hood's maneuvers by sending Major General George H. Thomas to command Union forces in Tennessee. Thomas's army eventually met and decisively defeated Hood's Confederates at the Battles of Franklin (30 November) and Nashville (15–16 December) (Boatner, Dictionary, 305–9).

62. It is unclear whether Carter is referring to family slaves or to a pair of horses at Pampatike.

The Cavalry here is being put into severe training. Lomax has thirty officers under arrest. Rosser has a large number also. Several of his Colonels[,] Welby Carter of Fauquier among the number[,] are to be tried for cowardice.[63] Some of them will be shot. Col. Forsythe [of the] 3rd Ala[.,] the same whose pretty wife you saw at Orange Ct H at the review[,] is on trial for cowardice.[64] Rosser's course has had already a good effect, as seen in the recent engagements. Lomax was attacked yesterday by the cavalry & repulsed them. Kiss the sweetest little ones.

God forever bless you. Shall I continue to direct [letters] to Dr Ellerson[?]

Ever y[ou]r devoted husband

—⟋⟍—

Camp near Newmarket
Oct. 31st [18]64

My precious Wife

Your letter of the early part of last week was rec[eive]d yesterday evening with much pleasure, also the verses which accompanied it for which I am much obliged. I have nothing of interest to relate but write on an average two letters weekly that you may not be uneasy about me & with the hope that the receipt of my letters give you something of the pleasure that yours impart to me. I have written twice since the battle of the 19th & directed the letters to care of Dr Ellerson. Shall I continue to direct them there or does this arrangement delay them? My last told you about the flannels by Jno Edwards, that one p[ai]r of drawers had been stolen by a servant & requested you to make another pair as soon you could conveniently. We are recruiting here quite rapidly considering all things & a very much more rigid discipline is enforced[,] the effect of which will be beneficial. Whether the morale will be sufficiently good to enable us to fight successfully another battle this fall is doubtful. I am inclined to the opinion that Early will try one more engagement if possible. He is smarting under the newspaper articles at this time. His

63. Colonel Richard Welby Carter (1837–88) commanded the 1st Virginia Cavalry at the Battle of Tom's Brook, and for his disgraceful actions during the fight, he was later cashiered for cowardice (CSR; Krick, *Lee's Colonels*, 82–83).

64. Colonel Charles M. Forsyth (d. 1872) of the 3rd Alabama Infantry was court-martialed for cowardice on 24 October and found guilty. His sentence, however, was remitted by President Davis in November because of Forsythe's previous reputation as a gallant officer. He remained in command of the 3rd Alabama (CSR; Krick, *Lee's Colonels*, 143).

civil & political life renders him particularly sensitive to these strictures. I have known no man in the army so morbidly sensitive on this subject as himself. His jealousy & hatred of Gordon is openly displayed, a most unfortunate circumstance, for could they work in harmony a great victory might be won. I believe Early to be a patriot but a selfish man who is desirous of monopolizing all the glory. He has sense enough for any command but lacks generalship, just the quality in which Gordon excels. I have some doubt as to Gordon's general capacity, it seems not at all above mediocrity but on the field he has the instincts of a general. Early[,] having followed a profession of reflection rather than action[,] is slow on the field & at a loss what to do. The halt at Middletown was the cause of the disaster—every man in the army believes it now. Had we pushed on between 9 A.M. & 10, my letters would be now dated on the Potomac. On our front (the right) with portions of three Divisions intact & twenty five or thirty cannon we could have advanced without a halt, for Cavalry only confronted us. Our advance would have necessarily occasioned the falling back of the enemy on our left or my Artillery would have smashed them by an enfilading fire. Early seemed in favor of pushing on but one or two of his Div commanders opposed it. I believe all thought an advance desirable but each wished someone else to make it. Time wore on & it was not made & the enemy made a feeble attack on our left where Gordon's Div held the line & away they ran before the enemy even closed with them. Well I got seven Napoleons to bear on this column & gallant Ramseur & Major Goggin induced a thin line of their men to rally on the Artillery to hold the position.[65] I ordered up six more Napoleons & had the order been promptly obeyed the line could have been held until dark. As it was we held them one hour & a quarter until the last round was fired. The infantry will not even make an effort without the Artillery. The fresh guns reached the spot soon after the others retired & opened a heavy fire but the infantry refused to stand longer & their [the enemy's] lines through the woods [were] so close that the guns were withdrawn. Still we apprehended no disaster. It was only after crossing Cedar Creek & when approaching Strausburg on the march that a handful of Cavalry stampeded the whole infantry & captured the

65. Major James Monroe Goggin (1820–89), an assistant adjutant general on the staff of Joseph Kershaw, commanded the brigade in Kershaw's division formerly led by Brigadier General James Conner (1829–83) of South Carolina, who had suffered a severe leg wound in a skirmish at Cedar Creek on 13 October (CSR; Warner, *Generals in Gray*, 59–60). The brigade consisted of the 2nd, 3rd, 7th, 8th, 15th, and 20th South Carolina Infantry regiments and the 3rd South Carolina Infantry Battalion (*OR* 43[1]:566).

trains. I do not know what will be done as to a new commander. I think Early will remain. He will probably endeavour to fight partial engagements & not risk a general action. The Old Man is kind to me & I feel sorry for him. Could he but harmonize with Gordon he might do well. The present state of feeling greatly impairs Gordon's usefulness. He has great confidence in Gordon's ability but is worried at the reputation he has won, & they are at daggers draw now.

I agree with you about the corn. It had better be gathered at once, or you will suffer before another crop comes in. The oats will do well if sowed in February.

I can't say what will be done in the Valley. We cannot winter where we are. Forage is scarce already & has to be hauled a long distance. We might possibly winter near Staunton but Sheridan cannot winter far from Martinsburg or Harpers Ferry & at such a distance neither Army would accomplish much, & [we] would most likely be ordered to Richd in any emergency. Still we may winter here (in the Valley) or on the Central near Gordonsville. I begin to feel as if we might see each other soon. Our Cavalry will find it difficult to winter here since the destruction of the grain by the enemy. It is improving in its discipline. Many officers have been charged with cowardice & are being courtmartialed, Welby Carter[,] Col. of 1st Regt Cavalry[,] among the number. I wish he had some other name & title at this time. Eugene Blackford is also charged with cowardice & many others.[66] Don't forget to write to Wm at Charleston. I see by the papers there is some chance of an exchange between Foster & Hardee.[67] The suitability of Hardee or Dick Taylor for this command is discussed in the army.[68] The papers state that Dick Taylor has taken S. D. Lee's Corps in Hood's Army.[69]

66. Major Eugene Blackford (1839–1908) of the 5th Alabama Infantry was cashiered by a court-martial for "misbehavior before the enemy at Cedar Creek." On 11 February 1865, President Davis reinstated him after Davis had received numerous petitions testifying to Blackford's qualities as a man and a soldier (CSR; Krick, *Lee's Colonels*, 52–53).

67. Major General John Gray Foster (1823–74) of New Hampshire commanded the U.S. Department of the South in October 1864. Lieutenant General William Joseph Hardee (1815–73) of Georgia commanded the Confederate Department of South Carolina, Georgia, and Florida in October 1864 (Eicher and Eicher, *High Commands*, 241, 279).

68. Lieutenant General Richard Taylor (1826–79), son of President Zachary Taylor, commanded the Confederate Department of Alabama and Mississippi (Warner, *Generals in Gray*, 299–300).

69. Stephen Dill Lee (1833–1908) was the youngest lieutenant general in the Confederate army. He commanded a corps in the Army of Tennessee from June 1864 until that army surrendered to Sherman's forces in North Carolina in late April 1865. Obviously, the story Carter cited from the newspaper proved to be a false rumor (Warner, *Generals in Gray*, 183–84).

I hope Ann Willie Wills is better in every respect & Mother she can't be a "torn down little piece." She is too sweet for such epithets. And how are my other two darlings[,] my little man & sweet daughter. I long to see you all & squeeze you tight—to use a homely phrase. May God forever bless you.

                                                    Y[ou]r own devoted husband.

Early has invited Peyton to become his A. A. Genl. Peyton gave a doubtful answer, & there the matter rests. You have seen Early's address to his troops. Knowing he had no allusion to the Artillery I informed him that his address was too general in its denumeration. He at once addressed me an official letter to be read to the command which is highly complimentary to it.[70] As his address was published I asked & obtained his permission to publish the letter & sent it today to the Examiner. The spirit of troops can never be maintained unless justice is done them, praise & punishment when deserved. Their sense of justice is as acute as that of educated classes, & some of them are men of education & even talents. I am much grateful to find that my efforts to do my duty have been appreciated by Genl Early, as shown by his remarks to your Uncle Alex.

—⁓—

                                                    Newmarket
                                                    Hd Qrs, Arty V.D.
                                                    Nov. 15th [18]64

My precious Wife,

I received your letter of the 9th inst written at Richd. I am devoutly thankful to God for his crowning mercy to me in sparing your life. At times I feel this war & the separation from you to be almost intolerable, but to lose you in whom my earthly happiness is so bound up would be misery insupportable. I trust myself & our darling children will be spared such a trial.

70. Early's address to his army, which was critical of its conduct at Cedar Creek, was published in the *Richmond Enquirer* on 27 October. Two days later, the general wrote to Carter, stating: "I wish you to Express to the officers and men of the Artillery my high appreciation of their good conduct and gallantry at Winchester, Fisher's Hill and on the 19th instant near Middletown." Furthermore, he assured Carter that the "strictures contained in my address of the 22nd are not applicable to your command" (Jubal A. Early to THC, 29 Oct. 1864, Jubal A. Early Collection, Eleanor S. Brockenbrough Library, Museum of the Confederacy, Richmond).

How did you contract the disease[?] You will not go home until all danger is past of imparting the disease to the children. Your throat has always been peculiarly susceptible to inflammation[,] less so however since your marriage than before & I had hoped you would be troubled no more by this disease. Why are you wearing Aurc? Simply because it is time I imagine. I inferred from your letter that you were out of danger. I cannot realize that your life has been in peril. What should I do without you my darling wife. How could I live. The castles I build & the bright spots in [the] future are all associated indissolubly with you. God grant us a happy reunion in peaceful days when our land shall be no more blighted by the scourge of war. And the sweet little ones, mother, what would they do without you & your protecting care. Dear little innocent things, I could never console them or take care of them in your absence. You must therefore take care of yourself. No doubt the attack was owing to your ride to Richd to get me a piece of flannel. You will kill yourself to keep me in clothes. I am doing very well. My last winter flannels are still good enough to wear & will last some time yet. I shall not use the new shirts until the weather becomes colder as they are very thick & warm.

We have just returned from another train down the valley. On Thursday the 10th [of November] 1864 we moved towards the enemy. Our Cavalry engaged the enemy at Middletown & Newtown[,] our infantry & artillery were not engaged. McCausland (Lomax's Cavalry) lost two pieces of horse Arty & was badly whipped. Rosser was driven back but rec[eive]d reinforcements & in the end got the advantage of the enemy. We found the enemy encamped at the Opequon near Kernstown some five miles this side of Winchester, & strongly entrenched. We remained in their front part of Friday & all day Saturday. On the last mentioned day the Cavalry engagement took place. At one time Saturday appearances seemed to indicate an attack on their part but fortunately for us they did not do so. Our men in all probability would have given way. There was certainly a most uneasy feeling all down the line. Early went down to ascertain if the 6th Corps had left[,] which fact had been reported to Genl Lee. The report of a good scout would have obtained the desired information as well as the march of eighty miles (to & fro) of the whole army not to say anything of the hazard of the movement in the present condition of the Army. "All's well that ends well" however. While near Newtown we captured the books of Chief Med Director of Sheridan's Cavalry on the 3rd Sept. Torbert had 11,218 men present in the

Cavalry.[71] At that time Fitz Lee had about 4,000 & a majority of them badly armed. Their cavalry is armed too with repeating rifles (seven & sixteen shooters) pistols & sabres & horses ad libitum. I believe we have expected too much of our Cavalry & have censured them too severely. On the 15th Oct. they had 7,250 Cavalry, showing a diminution of some 4,000. We are now nearly on an equality in Cavalry, & if the men can get arms may be at them.

Sheridan's army is represented as a very large one by all the inhabitants along the turnpike. The citizens of Middletown say they boast but little of the victory of the 19th ult., that their loss in killed was at least five to our one. They believe in Sheridan. Considering his great numerical superiority he has not availed himself of his victories. Had he done so this army would have been annihilated. I send you a long & most affectionate letter from dear Mama. She sent one at the same time to Wm which I forwarded by mail to Charleston. She sent me two shirt & two prs of socks by Col. Morton Marye who is now in Richd.[72] I wish you would find out if they arrived safely & get them. Capt Marye could tell you probably if you are unacquainted with Morton. I have put on my last winter flannel shirts. They are very good still. You will hardly be in Richd when this letter arrives.

I fear from Mama's letter that there is little hope of Eva's recovery.[73] What is the matter with her have you any idea? I have none. Lucy wrote

71. Brigadier General Alfred Thomas Archimedes Torbert (1833–80) of Delaware commanded the cavalry of the U.S. Middle Military Division in the Shenandoah Valley. His cavalry routed the Confederates at the Battle of Tom's Brook on 9 October 1864 (Warner, *Generals in Blue*, 508–9).

72. Morton Marye (1831–1910), a twenty-nine-year-old merchant in Alexandria, Va., enlisted as captain of Company A of the 17th Virginia Infantry on 17 April 1861. When the unit reorganized in April 1862, he was elected lieutenant colonel. On 28 June 1862, Marye was captured during the Seven Days Battles and sent to Fort Warren in Boston, Mass. Two months later, on 27 August, he was exchanged for Second Lieutenant George T. Rowler of the 64th New York Infantry and returned to the 17th Virginia in time to lead his regiment in the Battle of Second Bull Run. During the fighting on 30 August, Marye suffered a bullet wound to his left knee joint and had the leg amputated above the knee. While convalescing, he was promoted to colonel on 1 November 1862. Colonel Marye never fully recovered and finally retired from active service on 8 July 1864. He remained in Richmond for the rest of the war and served on various examination and inspection boards. Captain Edward "Ned" Marye of the Fredericksburg Artillery was Morton's younger brother. They grew up at Brompton, the Fredericksburg, Va., home of the Marye family, which was located on the high ground that James Longstreet's men defended during the Battle of Fredericksburg. Morton Marye stood five feet, nine and a half inches tall and had dark hair, hazel eyes, and a florid complexion (CSR; *OR*, Series 2, 4:443).

73. Rosa Evelyn Carter, Tom Carter's half sister, died in Philadelphia from her unidentified illness on 8 April 1865 (McGill, *Beverley Family of Virginia*, 471).

a postscript to Wm's letter on Nov. 1st in which she said Mama & Evelyn would start the next day to Baltimore with Alfred Byrd. Is it not sad to think of the change in Mama's appearance & spirits & yet withal she is so sweet & affectionate & such a true Christian. Renshaw wrote Wm Nelson that he had not yet been reinstated nor had he heard from his application but expected to do so soon. Genl Long is now in Staunton with his family. He has taken two rooms there & draws his rations. He finds he can live more cheaply in that way. I have not heard whether his wife has yet presented him with an heir. He will hardly return to this command until the close of the campaign. Says he is anxious to return but his physicians tell him it would be hazardous to do so. His voice has not yet returned & he has placed himself under the treatment of some new physician in Staunton. It is thought to be connected with paralysis. His throat is externally swollen. When he returns I hardly know what I shall do. Cutshaw is here & Hardaway at Richmond. Genl Alexander commands on the North side of the James & Hardaway now reports directly to him. In many respects the command of a Division is awkward at times. I suppose something will turn up however. I am willing to serve in any way that I can be useful. I see by the papers that Willie Pegram has been given temporary rank of Brigadier & put in command of Archer's Brigade.[74] If he intends to remain in the Army as I understand he does he is right to take the change. For my ~~Command~~ own part I would not change for the additional rank. I was sorry to hear that France was not doing so well at one time last week—only a fever of two or three days. I did not understand that he was in danger. He wrote me that he was most kindly treated by the ladies of Charlottesville[,] furnished with eatables[,] flowers[,] books &c. &c. [and] in a most comfortable hospital. Fez Page is here trying to get through to Clarke, have not seen him yet.[75] Scouts report the Harper's Ferry & Winchester R-road complete to Charlestown & to be built to Winchester which indicates a permanent lodgment of the Yankees at Winchester or thereabouts. I presume this Artillery will encamp for the winter at Staunton or near Charlottesville, unless the campaign takes a new turn by order of Genl Grant. When [you] send my things send me

---

74. The *Richmond Daily Whig* reported the rumor that Lieutenant Colonel William R. J. Pegram was about to be promoted to brigadier general and given the infantry brigade formerly commanded by James J. Archer, who had died in Richmond on 24 October 1864. General Lee, however, believed that Pegram was too young and did not approve his promotion (*Richmond Daily Whig*, 5 Nov. 1864; Warner, *Generals in Gray*, 11; Carmichael, *Lee's Young Artillerist*, 150–51).

75. Fez Page has not been identified.

the helmet or hood made for me by Lucy Lindley. It is possible that one Division of this Army may go to Rich[mon]d. We regard the campaign as closed here unless some Cavalry raids are made which may require us to return to the march. Wm Page is very ill with typhoid fever. He went to Nanny Meriwether's house before he was seriously sick.[76] Have not heard from him for a few days. How is Thomas Smith?[77] I was sorry to see by the papers that Col Robins was again wounded.[78] Col Haskall will lose an eye but will not be disfigured.[79]

Kiss the dear little ones & may God bless you & keep you, for Christ's sake.

Y[ou]r devoted husband.

—⟁—

Camp near Newmarket
Nov. 21st [18]64

My precious Wife

Your letter of the 16th inst was rec[eive]d a few hours since & I am rejoiced to find you are again well & that the dearest little ones had done well in your absence. Would that I could participate in the delights of their company. We are quietly encamped here with little prospect of further movement this fall. { . . . } are looking forward to winter quarters. We will probably winter on the railroad between Waynesboro & Staunton or across the mountain in Albermarle. I am inclined to think

76. Carter is probably referring to Anne Willing Page Meriwether (1835–75), who lived at the Meadow in Clarke County, Va. She was a first cousin of his stepmother, Anne Willing Page Carter (Page, *Page Family in Virginia*, 148).

77. Thomas Smith has not been identified.

78. William Todd Robins (1835–1906) began the war in July 1861 as acting sergeant major in the 9th Virginia Cavalry. On 30 October 1862, he was appointed captain and assistant adjutant general on the staff of Brigadier General W. H. F. Lee. Robins subsequently served as lieutenant colonel of the 40th Virginia Cavalry before and after it merged with the 42nd Virginia Cavalry in the summer of 1863. He became colonel of the 24th Virginia Cavalry on 14 June 1864. The previous February, he had suffered an injury to his side after being struck by a falling tree. Following his promotion to colonel, he was wounded in the left arm on 14 August and in the right foot on 26 October 1864. Robins surrendered with the army at Appomattox Court House. After the war, he practiced law in his native Gloucester County, Va. (CSR; Krick, *Lee's Colonels*, 326).

79. Colonel Alexander Cheves Haskell (1839–1910) commanded the 7th South Carolina Cavalry. He was wounded in action on the Darbytown Road east of Richmond on 27 October 1864. Earlier in the war, Haskell had served as aide-de-camp and assistant adjutant general on the staffs of Brigadier Generals Maxcy Gregg and Samuel McGowan and been wounded in the Battles of Fredericksburg, Chancellorsville, and Cold Harbor. He surrendered with his regiment at Appomattox Court House on 9 April 1865 (CSR; Krick, *Lee's Colonel's*, 185–86).

the former place will be selected. We are now in the midst of a rainy season of some five days without intermission which will render the roads very bad. Corn is becoming distant & is hauled some sixty miles (120 round trip) & our horses will suffer unless we move soon which I think we will do in a week or two. I wrote you a letter a week ago just after the return of this army from Newtown, enclosing a long letter from Mama. I have heard since by a man from Millwood that Mama & Eva had started to Baltimore. I am not sure that he { . . . } the fact positively, he may have inferred { . . . } the report to that effect. I hope they have gone.[80] It will be a comfort to think that everything has been done for Evelyn should her case terminate fatally. The disease has lasted nearly a year & I fear the worst without knowing the character of it. Lucy has remained with Papa. Mama hoped to hear from Wm while in Baltimore. I forwarded her letter to him at Morris Island. I see by the papers that prisoners are now allowed to receive supplies from friends, the supplies to be under care of officers paroled for the purpose. It is stated that a large quantity of cotton is to be sent from Mobile to New York the proceeds of which will go to the purchase of blankets[,] clothes &c. for our prisoners in Yankee hands. It is also stated that a subscription of $90,000 was raised in London for same purpose, & Slidell's daughter has also started a subscription to the same end. So that Wm will not suffer.

If he is made comfortable where he is it may be as well that he is not exchanged. Here, he would be {in} danger always. There he is comparatively {safe}. I hope it is not unpatriotic to wish that some of those we love may be safe from harm.

Fez Page went to Clarke on Wednesday last; he goes to try his chance with Mary Francis, whom he hopes to induce to marry him without delay in the few days he has to stay in that neighborhood. They are not engaged but were conditionally engaged some years ago which understanding was broken off. I think he will fail in the speedy marriage but may succeed in bringing on an engagement. She is said to be a fine woman. He is not certain as to his future movements & would like to

80. Carter's mother and sister had reached Baltimore by 27 November. Their journey to that city drew the attention of no less a person than the Union commander in the Shenandoah Valley. On the 27th, Major General Philip Sheridan wrote to Major General Lew Wallace, informing him that "Mrs. Thomas Carter and daughter" along with seven other "intensely secession ladies" had reached Baltimore from the vicinity of Millwood, Va. Sheridan ordered Wallace to "detain them in [Baltimore] until they get authority from me for their return." According to the commanding general, "I am satisfied that they are unsafe people and should be watched closely" (*OR* 43[2]:682).

remain in Va. Wm Page has been at the point of death, if he is not now
dead, at Nanny Meriwether's in it { . . . }. She had but little hope in a
letter of the 15th { . . . } will recover for his Father's sake as well as his
own, for he is the idol of the old man's heart. We are quite uneasy here
about Hood's Army & the Western campaign. Capt Percy[,] Long's A. A.
Genl[,] has just returned from the South & speaks of his army as about
25,000 muskets & the morale not good.[81] The army & the people of the
whole South are clamorous for the reinstatement of Johnston. He says
Hood's loss around Atlanta was some 20,000 men[,] two & a half times as
much as Johnston loss from Dalton to Atlanta on his retreat. Sherman[82]
is said to have remarked to a Genl Govan of Arkansas—captured & afterwards exchanged—that the removal of Johnston was equal to a victory
to him[,] that he had regarded him as an able man in the old service but
had no conception of his real talents until this campaign.[83] If Hood cannot beat a part of Sherman's army now confronting him at the Tennessee
river, he stands no chance of contending successfully with the whole.
Sherman's destination is still unknown whether to Charleston[,] Savannah or Mobile via Selma & Macon. I hope this rain is falling in torrents
where his army now lies & that he may be mud bound until his army
is lost. The enlistment of negro troops is much discussed by members
of Congress.[84] I think some fifty thousand should be mustered in immediately & their freedom given the day they are mustered. Many would
desert if they could with safety—so would the whites. Strict discipline
would prevent this evil to any serious extent. If we do not enlist them
the Yankees will. They may take all between 18 & 45 except Martin &
James, for my part. The males under 18 & over 45 with the women would
produce enough for the country. I fear Congress will not be equal to the
occasion. They will repeat the old cry that the Yankees can't get men

81. Official returns for the Army of Tennessee, dated 6 November 1864, state that Hood's army
had 30,599 effective soldiers present for duty and an aggregate total of 44,832 (*OR* 39[3]:893).

82. Major General William Tecumseh Sherman (1820–91) commanded all the Union armies
in the western theater. By the date of Carter's letter, Sherman was in the early phase of his
March to the Sea (Eicher and Eicher, *High Commands*, 484–85).

83. Brigadier General Daniel Chevilette Govan (1829–1911) of North Carolina commanded a
brigade in Patrick Cleburne's division of the Army of Tennessee. Govan was captured on 1 September 1864 at the Battle of Jonesboro and held prisoner for three weeks. On 20 September he
was exchanged, at General William T. Sherman's request, for Union general George Stoneman
(Eicher and Eicher, *High Commands*, 260–61; *OR*, Series 2, 7:792, 851).

84. Earlier in November, Confederate congressmen had debated the issue of enlisting black
soldiers and determined that the military situation did not warrant such action (*Journal of the
Congress of the Confederate States*, 7:247).

& delude themselves with an underestimate of their numbers as { . . . } have done this campaign from beginning to end. Next spring Grant[,] She{rida}n & Sherman will start with the overwhelming numbers of the early { . . . } of this campaign. Let us { . . . } now for this condition of things. Detailed men & will not fill the ranks s{uf}ficiently. Negroes as teamsters[,] pioneers &c. ought to be brought into service at once.

Genl Long is boarding {at} Staunton. His wife is about {to be} confined. He talks of returning to {his} command in two or three weeks & is said to be somewhat better as to his voice. Did you learn anything of the two shirts & two pairs [of] socks sent to me by Mama through Col. Morton Marye[?] I wrote to ask you to find out & let me know. I am now wearing my last winter flannel shirts & drawers; they are in good condition & will last several months if not the whole winter with some repair. I am sorry to hear of Armistead's behavior—he is crazy. What grief he has brought upon his family. Did you hear who ran off with Mrs Fanny Dudley daughter of Mr Brookes[?] It is reported with us that she ran off with a married man leaving her infant with her grandmother. Did Armistead carry money with him? He will find it difficult to make a livelihood in the North. Will Clay Dallam get a situation as a Military Ct. [?] Those appointments are political & I imagine Maryland stands a poor chance. How are the carriage horses[?] In good order I hope.

Kiss the precious little ones for their own dear Papa & take many many many for yourself. May God bless you now & forever.

Y[ou]r devoted husband.

Nov. 22nd—
The enemy cavalry is reported advancing. A reconnaissance probably. Do not know that any infantry is with them. A little snow fell last night.

—⚍—

Camp near Newmarket
Nov. 28th [18]64

My precious Wife,
Your letter of the 23rd inst was rec[eive]d yesterday. You make no mention of the receipt of letters from me. I presume therefore that they have reached you regularly. Some ten days since I enclosed you a letter from Mama. I think she is now in Baltimore. L[uc]y Page is expected from Clarke daily & I shall know positively whether [Mama] & Evelyn

went at the time designated. We are still quiet here. The cavalry I mentioned in my last came within five miles of Newmarket where we met it with infantry[,] Artillery & one Brigade of cavalry & drove it back. Our cavalry lost some fifty in killed & wounded. The enemy lost more as they caught the fire of our Artillery & of the infantry skirmishers. It was only a reconnaissance to learn if we had gone to Richmond. No infantry accompanied the cavalry force. Rosser has gone on a secret expedition to Cumberland[,] Md. where he will subsidize the town for a half million dollars in greenbacks, which failing to pay it will be burned. He goes however chiefly to procure cattle for our commissariat which is at this time too low to be comfortable, so much so that we are likely to move back soon nearer our railroad communications. We are not likely to secure any great quantity of supplies by this step however for we are pretty closely confined to the valley by Genl Lee. As soon as the winter sets in & the enemy goes into winter quarters we will do so too—say three weeks hence—unless the campaign in the South & the movements at Richmond should necessitate further movements on our part.

Hood's campaign thus far is the most lame & impotent conclusion of the year. It would seem now plain enough that Johnston should not have been removed. Capt Percy[,] Long's A.A.G.[,] says his popularity in the South is equal to Lee's here. Sherman it seems is on an expedition to Savannah. He will do us much damage by destruction of railroads, supplies &c. It is improbable that any force can be collected sufficient to injure his army seriously. I { . . . } too the ironclads are collecting in James River either as a feint to prevent troops from being sent to Hardee or for a real attack which is not improbable. Congress seems to be idling away its time as usual. Hope it will do something before it adjourns. Gold has gone up to 45 from 28! Hood's Army unable to whip the minor portion of Sherman's. The President gets the credit of the recent movement of Hood. Strategy does not seem to be his fort[e].

I am sorry to tell you that Wm Page died on Monday the 21st inst at Dr Merriwether's. His case which was simple in the beginning when he left here became complicated with pneumonia. His poor father's heart will be wrung by grief. He idolized him, I understand. I am glad I took him in my mess & tent & sent him to his sister's when attacked by the disease. He was quiet & reserved with me the little while he stayed but seemed happy & attended well to his duties. Today I sent Powel with his horse to Dr Merriwether who thought it best it should be sent there.

I wrote to Nannie by Powel & must write to his father today. I am sorry to hear of the death of the black horse. Poor Cuffee will be careless & lazy so long as he lives. I wish you could get more team. Can't say, however, that the crops will justify it this year. You are the best judge of that, for I really know nothing of the finances now. If you desire it I will purchase you two horses when we go into winter quarters. I do not now know where I can obtain a furlough. Not before Xmas I am sure. Genl Long is much improved he writes but says nothing of his return. His wife has lately presented him with a fine boy. They are living in Staunton. Wm Nelson expects to go to housekeeping in Newmarket soon. Mary is expected from Clarke in a short time.

If possible I wish you would purchase a piece of grey cloth to re-inforce my grey pants. They are quite good yet with that exception. When you come, they can be turned & reinforced & will be nearly as good as new. It is not necessary to get a piece exactly of the same colour. You recollect the manner you fixed a pair for me at Mr Goss' house.

I am now wearing the new pair of drawers you sent me; they fit unusually well. Hope they won't shrink. I alternate with a pair of the old winter drawers[,] still quite good with a little darning & which will probably last all winter with some repairing. You had as well make me another pair however to replace the pair lost by Jno Edwards.

Have you heard anything from Morton Marye about the two pairs [of] socks & the two shirts Mama sent me? I hope they will not be lost. I hate to lose things. I will write to Wm soon. Do write constantly to him. Has Shirley any affair on hand[?] I hear the Preston girls have returned. Has Ann finished cutting her teeth? I must write the children a little note[,] dear little things.

> God bless you my darling wife.
> Y[ou]r devoted husband.

One of the servants here has the itch. It is Southall's servant. Quite a fair prospect of its spreading. Archie Randolph has just recovered from an attack. Fitz Lee will be up the middle or last of this week. France writes he will be able to sit up soon & hopes to get a furlough as soon as he gets on crutches. He had rec[eive]d a letter from his wife of the 25th ult. She had heard nothing of his wound.

—⁂—

My precious Wife,

We have at last marched back to the Va Central for the winter. The ground is covered with snow & has been since the 9th, last Friday, & the animals are suffering much for forage. Now that we are back there is still difficulty in subsisting the horses but I trust they will get more forage after a while. Today a number of trains have passed to Staunton to carry down Rodes old Division & we are not certain that all the infantry may not go, & in that event the Artillery would go also.[86] Gordon & Pegram you know have already gone. I think Wharton's Division will be left & no other except Cavalry.[87] If so the Artillery will remain on account of the better facilities for forage. Gordon's & Pegram's Divisions were put far down on the right below Petersburg, a mean country for wood[,] people &c.[88] We are therefore not anxious to go. We regret that our quarters are not east of the Blue Ridge. Dr Straith, Stanard, (the same we saw so much of at the Alleghany Springs) & myself have been trying to get room together.[89] Straith married in Charlestown just before the disasters, stayed three days with his bride & has not seen her since. She is to run the blockade. He is a fine intelligent man. Stanard & his wife you know. The people here have been unmolested by the Yankees except in a Cavalry raid, & many of them have large ~~considerable~~ means but a stingier meaner set you have never seen. We have today succeeded in

---

85. THC to SRC, 15 Dec. 1864, Private Collection.

86. On 13 December General Early ordered Brigadier General Bryan Grimes (1828–80), who took command of Robert Rodes's division after the Battle of Cedar Creek, to march the division to Staunton, Va., board the trains, and take the Virginia Central Railroad to Richmond (*OR* 43[2]:938).

87. Brigadier General Gabriel Colvin Wharton (1824–1906) of Virginia commanded a division in the Confederate 2nd Corps (*OR* 43[2]:928; Warner, *Generals in Gray*, 331).

88. On 9 December 1864, the divisions of John B. Gordon and John Pegram left Early's Valley Army to reinforce Lee's lines around Petersburg, Va. By 17 December both divisions were encamped near Hatcher's Run southwest of that city (*OR* 42[3]:889, 1025; McDonald, *Make Me a Map*, 247).

89. Dr. John Alexander Straith (1835–72) was the chief surgeon of the 2nd Corps artillery. He was an 1854 graduate of the medical school at the University of Virginia. On 25 August 1864, Straith married Jane Charlotte Alexander (1835–85) in Charlestown, W.Va. In December 1864 he was a member of a board that examined medical officers in General Early's command. Earlier in the war, Straith had served as an assistant surgeon with the 2nd Virginia Infantry and as surgeon with the Stonewall Brigade (Hayden, *Virginia Genealogies*, 181; Link, *Marriages of Jefferson County, Virginia*, 551; CSR). Stanard has not been identified.

getting three rooms in one house in this place. Fishersville has a half dozen indifferent houses in it; the one ~~we~~ at which we secured rooms is the best looking in the place. I did not see the rooms but Stanard says they are large & neatly kept. The owners would sell their souls for money, like the rest around here, but yet . . . {remainder of letter missing}

—∿—

[Fragment written from Fishersville
during the week of Dec. 19th, 1864]

{First section of letter missing}

. . . I told him it might be an evil, although I did not believe it[,] but among the crying evils of our army to single it out as the chief was ridiculous. I quoted some pretty good authority on him in the persons of Jackson, Rodes, Gordon[,] Rooney Lee & all who had wives except Genl Lee. His wife is a cripple & of course cannot come. Genl Early discourses at length on the importance of self denial & good example on the part of officers & in the very act indulges in every creature comfort that his heart can desire that is obtainable. He stays in houses & never in a tent. He cares nothing for home having no family. Says no soldier should have ties, which is true enough provided the war could be carried on by single men. While staying in a large brick house by a good fire on this last trip, when the cold was intense in an open tent pitched in the snow & without a chimney, the old thing told me of Charles XII [of] Sweden sleeping on the snow in his cloak, & eating rations which soldiers complained of.[90] You have doubtless heard how he lives at home; he lives openly with a white woman of the lower class & has raised four or five children by her. These children he has sent to school with his nephews, whereupon his brother in law took his children away: "He compounds for sins he is inclined to/ By damning those he has no mind to." The old thing & I get on very well. I tell him I shall marry him off to a widow with whom he is now staying.

In regard to your coming[,] Straith[,] Stanard & I have ~~employed~~ engaged rooms for you ladies at the house of one Schmenker, a Dutch skinflint, who asks thirty cents a day for ~~the~~ each room in specie, or its

90. Charles XII of Sweden (1682–1718), who reigned beginning in 1697, was known for his dashing personality and military genius. His habit of enduring hardships with his soldiers won him their praise and devotion.

equivalent in Confed currency. He furnishes bedding & linen & does the washing of same[—]nothing else. If you rake up a little specie three months will cost you only twenty seven dollars but in Confed currency some thirteen or fourteen hundred as gold is now fifty for one & likely to rise as our reverses are worse & worst. We propose to put up a large hospital tent with a chimney & plank floor to take our meals in. It will be put by the house. The room is large & has several beds in it. I wish I could have secured another room for the children. It would have been far more pleasant. We can get some plates & dishes from the hotel at Staunton[,] the proprietor of which is an old friend of Straith's but you will have to bring some few things[—]not many. Schmenker promises to help us out. As to the eatables I shudder to think of them but Stanard is a good caterer & you can get some of the substantials from home by sending down occasionally. Mrs Stanard will not come until you do. I suppose you will come week after next[,] first week of January. You understand that . . .

{missing page of letter}

. . . Savannah will be taken & then Augusta. Congress waits to feel public sentiment. The army is in favor of the enlistment of negroes—a great change has taken place in this respect. The Yankees have used them successfully & so can we if their freedom is given them when conscribed—or enlisted. The negroes in the Yankee Army are not there *now* from choice but by compulsion, although they may have volunteered originally. If they can be held there by proper discipline & by the death penalty they can be held here. White soldiers would desert in larger numbers but for fear of detection & death. As to the remnant of the slaves to be turned loose after the war no great number will be left. The few remaining might be kept in the standing army—a large one will be required. It is the choice between our use of them & the Yankees. {There} may be another choice as I sincerely believe[—]the use of them or ultimate subjugation.

God bless you always.
Y[ou]r devoted husband.

I was delighted to get the letters from the children[,] precious little things. We are preparing to have a little eggnog tonight in which I will drink your health.

—⁂—

My precious Wife,

As James will probably arrive tonight by the cars I write that my letter may be ready for Martin in the morning. I hope James will bring me good tidings of you all. I fear you will be uncomfortable on your trip up here & after your arrival. I have never yet crossed a people so set on making money as these, & so little disposed to put themselves to inconvenience to accommodate soldiers who are sacrificing everything to save their property & their rights. Southall says while at home for three days at Xmas he heard the remark a dozen times that the people at home care nothing for the army except so far as it is a means to an end, and it seems to be true. Farmers cheerfully give up their sons & brothers to go to death & when it is reached they seem to bear it with marvelous fortitude, as the fate of war, but only suggest the necessity of taking a cuffee or two or some other property & what a storm is aroused. They would sooner risk the butchery & destruction of the small army of whites now in the field with the hope that something might arise to save the nigger property than let negroes be used in the army.

After agreeing to give $9 a month in specie or its equivalent in Confederate money (which is between $450 & $500) for a room with the plainest furniture, without fuel or lights furnished in a miserable little village of eight or ten indifferent houses, we have to haggle about every trifle in addition. Old Mrs Skinflint agreed to furnish a bed this evening in our room for Celia, but it was impossible to get one for Susan or Betsy. I am inclined to think you had better leave ~~the~~ Thomas & Juliet at H. Hill until you come up & stay three or four days; you could then see what is best to be done. The old scamp refused us a room to mess in & since has given up his dining room to Major Rogers,[91] Dr McGuire[92]

91. Major John Dalrymple Rogers (1830–89) was acting chief quartermaster for the 2nd Corps. He was a farmer from Middleburg, Va., before beginning his Confederate service as quartermaster for the following generals: Nathan G. Evans (4 October 1861), Daniel Harvey Hill (February 1862), and Robert E. Rodes (19 May 1863) (CSR; Krick, *Staff Officers*, 257).

92. Dr. Hunter Holmes McGuire (1835–1900) was the medical director of the 2nd Corps. He began the war as medical director at Harpers Ferry, Va., in May 1861. Later that summer, McGuire became the surgeon of the 33rd Virginia Infantry. On 4 May 1863, he was temporarily relieved of his duties as 2nd Corps medical director and assigned to oversee Stonewall Jackson's recovery from wounds he suffered at the Battle of Chancellorsville. McGuire tended to Jackson until the general's death from pneumonia on 10 May 1863. McGuire remained with the army until the surrender at Appomattox. According to a letter in his compiled service records, he dropped the use of his middle name sometime in 1861 (CSR).

& Dr Morrison;[93] also a kitchen that Stanard tried to secure was refused & afterwards granted to the same. We are about to pitch a tent (a large one)[,] floor it & put a chimney to it. We shall also have to cook in a tent I suppose. There is a rag carpet on our room & everything is exceedingly neat. One bed has been taken out leaving two in the room. Mrs Stanard will come I suppose on Wednesday. If either should arrive before the other it will not matter. We are allowed to use the drawing room to sit in but not as a dining room. Mrs Smencher . . . {remainder of letter missing}

93. Doctor Samuel Brown Morrison (1828–1901) was the medical inspector of the Army of the Valley (as of 10 October 1864). Earlier in the war, he had served as surgeon of the 58th Virginia Infantry (9 October 1861) and as chief surgeon of Jubal Early's division (by Spring 1863) (CSR).

CHAPTER EIGHT

———〰〰———

War's End

1 January – 7 March 1865

Colonel Carter began the year 1865 at Fishersville still in command of the artillery of Lieutenant General Jubal Early's Army of the Valley because Brigadier General Long had not yet returned from sick leave. Carter spent most of January trying to secure a thirty-day furlough for himself. He also was doing his best to keep his former battalions together in the face of requests that they be returned to Richmond and converted into heavy artillery. In frustration, Carter considered asking for a transfer to another arm of the service, but in the end, he chose to remain where he was. To Susan he proclaimed: "I would rather be a Lieutenant in the Artillery than a Colonel of Infantry."[1]

On 31 January, Carter received his long-hoped-for furlough from the War Department. As he later explained, "It was the parting favor of Ja[me]s A. Seddon . . . as he left office & was succeeded by [John C.] Breckinridge." Two days later, Carter boarded a train at the nearby depot and made his way to Richmond. With him rode the men and ordnance of Carter Braxton's and Wilfred Cutshaw's battalions.[2]

———〰〰———

January 1st 1865

My precious Wife,

Since writing the enclosed letter I received a letter from Genl Long in which he states that he will go to Richd tomorrow & on his return in a few days will resume his duties. I therefore send Martin down to tell you not to come as I will apply for a furlough of twenty days as soon as

---

1. *OR* 46[2]:1083; THC to SRC, 28 Jan. 1865.
2. Special Orders No. 25, 31 Jan. 1865, in *Special Orders of the Adjutant and Inspector General's Office*, 85; THC to Robert Powel Page, 11 Jan. 1897, THCP, 1850–1915, VHS; *OR* 46[1]:513.

Long takes command. I presume he will take command about tomorrow week & I will apply at once for leave, if Genl Early refuses it[,] which I do not expect[,] you can then come on. It is best I should get my furlough now so as to save you a trip. Otherwise you would make two probably. This management will not interfere with Stanard & Straith. I will send them James to cook. I am sorry you have kept James. It will subject me to inconvenience to be without either himself or Martin. You kept Martin last summer over his time; it is always best not to interfere with my arrangements because I make them knowing many circumstances which you cannot know. I am not certain whether you will come to H[ickory] Hill or to Richd. I will send Martin by Hanover Ct House so as to hear of you there & telegraph to Richd in case you come that way. I fear you will have started & have had the discomfort of the carriage journey in either event, but I only heard today from Genl Long that he would come so soon. Send James up as soon as you get this.

I imagine there will be no difficulty in getting my leave of absence next week. When Genl Long assumes command my duties will be merely nominal, a stepping stone between his office & the two Battns (if I get another with Cutshaw's) which is not necessary & which has not existed in the Army except in the 2nd Corps & A.V. D. by order of Genl Long.

If there is a difficulty then you will come at once.

Heard a good sermon today from Mr Lacy.[3] I am glad to hear Genl Lee favours the enlistment of negroes. Shirley writes me today that you got the little books for the children.

I will write you when to send for me. I will go to Richd.

God bless you. Kiss the dear little ones.
Y[ou]r devoted husband

---

3. The Reverend Beverley Tucker Lacy (1819–1900) was a Presbyterian minister who served as chaplain at large for the 2nd Corps. He had been a particular favorite of General Jackson. Campbell Brown, General Ewell's assistant adjutant and inspector general, wrote after the war that Lacy "was very fond of eating & jokes—some not very clerical." Brown also remembered that although Lacy could deliver "an eloquent sermon, [he] did not advance the cause of religion much at our Hd. Qrs. while he staid there" (Pitts, *Chaplains in Gray*, 147; Jones, *Campbell Brown's Civil War*, 53).

Camp at Fishersville
Jan. 3rd 1865

My precious Wife,

James reached here last night in safety as to himself & the things you sent me but had his carpet bag stolen at the depot of this place after his arrival. It seems he waited some {tim}e there with the hope that someone would go down, but not expecting him, I sent no one; he then asked two cavalrymen standing by the fire to watch his boxes & carpet bag until he could come to my Hd Qrs some four hundred yds distant; on his return the cavalrymen had decamped with his carpet bag. He brought up the small box, fearing they might make away with that. The others were too large to be carried.

Powel & Corbin Wellford, accompanied by James, immediately started in pursuit, & inspected a cavalry camp near here, but without success.[4] James lost two prs of pants of his own, & one pair of Martin's; also Martin's shoes (new); the pants were all old, possibly quite good though. The shoes you will have to make good to Martin by giving him another pair. James also lost some other things—two prs of drawers, & some little things of value to him, I suppose, by the way he spoke of them. I had supposed from his destitution that you had kept him to come with you & therefore sent Martin down in haste to halt you before you had undergone the journey to the cars. Genl Early is still absent & all furloughs to officers have come back "disapproved for the present" & a circular stating that applications for leaves of absence by officers have become too frequent.

The tendency is therefore still towards a refusal of such indulgence. Still I think it probable my application will be granted, as there is but little need of my presence here after Genl Long's arrival. I presume he will resume command the early part of next week.

I see Early is floating about Richd, invited to a seat in Congress during his stay. H{e is} doubtless endeavoring to set his triggers so as to save his military carcass. I think however he need give himself no uneasiness; there is no intention to relieve him, so far as I can learn. He would render

---

4. Richard Corbin Wellford (1842–87) enlisted in the 2nd Company of Richmond Howitzers as a private on 26 June 1861. A year later, he transferred to the Morris (Va.) Artillery as a sergeant. Wellford was wounded at the Battle of Chancellorsville on 2 May 1863 and was captured on 29 February 1864 at Frederick's Hall, Va., during Dahlgren's Raid on Richmond. Two months later, he was exchanged and returned to duty. On 31 October 1864, Wellford was detailed to Carter's staff. Sergeant Wellford was paroled at Winchester, Va., on 4 May 1865 (CSR).

better service to his army by giving his attention to its wants. I believe he does this to a certain extent; himself first, the army afterwards, also country & everything else. His selfishness is his besetting sin, everything must bend to that.

The horses here are literally starving; they go without corn as long as ten days occasionally[,] living meantime on hay & straw in small quantity; once or twice they have been two or three days without anything. I drew up a statement of the case at Early's request which he took down to Genl Lee. It is to be hoped something will be done. Nelson's wagons returned last night after an absence of a fortnight with enough sheaf oats to feed his Arty horses once. The railroad does not haul a pound of hay or corn. Genl Lee's Army we hear is well fed—the horses receiving 8 or 9 lbs corn each daily, besides long forage. There is an impression that this valley is inexhaustible; it is a rich country & one of wonderful resources, but these people would see every horse in this army starved before they would deny themselves a toothpick or take government price for anything they can avoid. The impressment laws are such that they are not of practical use. They are as mean & stingy as the people of the lower valley are patriotic & liberal. One idea alone pervades {the} mass of them viz money making & that too {in} a time like this. When the Yankees visit this country I shall regret it for only so far as it affects injuriously our cause. A visit will do them good; it will develop their sense of duty; it will sweep away in a twinkling their ill gotten gains.

We are trying to make arrangements to feed the horses by establishing depots on the railroad to which the wagons will haul & deposit instead of returning over mountains & rivers & hundreds of miles to camp with the handful of feed left by the teams hauling. Several weeks ago I applied for two cars for this purpose. Nothing of course has been heard from it as a paper meanders through the official channels, pigeon holes &c.[,] until such time as their lordships choose to give it their august attention. Meantime horses starve & die. It is to be hoped Early's visit may accomplish something as by his admission he went for the purpose of getting forage. I have a large supply of corn in Giles & Monroe [Counties] after which a large detail has been sent. It will last a couple of months with good management. Some assistance must be furnished or the men must be allowed to take the horses, one to each man, to his home to take care of, leaving a Battn here which could be foraged with all the wagons.

The ground is covered with snow & has been for three weeks with the exception of a few days.

An effort is being made in Staunton to give this army a dinner. By last accounts they had $1000 which would about feed a dozen men at a feast. However they have revived the project & posted flam{boyant} handbills announcing that on Saturday next the dinner will certainly be forthcoming. I can't speak for Staunton but if dependent on Fishersville & vicinity for much of their feast, next Saturday will see us pulling through the same old things—beef & biscuit. I have had your barrels & firkin locked up; they will keep doubtless a month or so. James says they are all packed in straw. Do you think they will keep? Your box was very acceptable. We dived into it last night & were much edified. We are all longing for the good old country of Louisa, where kindness & hospitality to the soldier were the unexceptional rule. There is no chance of inducing Smencher to reduce his charge. He knows our predicament too well. Your diamonds will have to melt I fear or you must give me up this winter after the furlough. Indeed I am a little uneasy lest the postponement in taking the room may occasion the loss of it. I would like to take the old fellow in one battle that he might hear shells & minies about his ears; it would open his heart. The hospital tent has been put up for your dining saloon; the chimney will soon be built. Unless I get a furlough I shall have to take a tent soon anyway, as Genl. Long will have the house I now occupy. Nothing new from the Yankees.

Love to Mrs Laura & Andy. Kiss my sweet little folks. God bless you always.

Y[ou]r devoted husband.

{Mrs} Stanard comes too. Don't know as to Mrs Straith.

—ɯ—

Fishersville
Jan. 20th 1865

My precious Wife,

I have not written for some time past because I had hoped to be with you by the time a letter could reach you. I still hope to join you soon but enclose a letter from the A.A.G. which tells all I know. The "final arrangements" therein referred to are probably in allusion to sending the guns to some safe place for the winter, a proposal submitted by me to Genl Early two weeks ago. Now that most of the horses have been sent back it is proper the guns should be removed to Lynchburg[,] Richd or some other comparatively safe place. But I can not understand the necessity of keeping me here for so simple an operation. The guns are at the depot, the harness boxed up, a guard with them to put them on the cars, & I can be of no use. We retained six pieces of Artillery with horses. I have recommended that four of these be ~~sent~~ dis-horsed as have been the others on account of scarcity of forage. No answer has come to this suggestion & Genl Early may have referred the matter to Genl Lee as he did about sending the guns to Lynchburg. Possibly his letter refers to this matter. The cannoneers remaining behind will be armed with muskets temporarily until the return of the guns. Genl Long has reported for duty & has his Hd Qrs in Staunton. He has taken command generally of all the Artillery in this Army including the horse Arty (that which is attached to Cavalry) & the Battalion under King which has gone for the winter to Giles Co near Dublin Depot on the E. Ten & Va R.R.

He has put me in command of the Arty of the 2nd Corps under him; this is composed of Nelson's[,] Braxton's & Cutshaw's Battns. He has been very kind & attentive to me [and] was anxious I should move my Hd Qrs to Staunton which would have been much more agreeable to you & to me. Genl Early made some objection which I should not have regarded had I not thought that it was too far from my command—seven miles. Southall[,] Straith & Stanard are all gone there & are nicely fixed—the two last with their wives. They get rooms & board (save fuel & lights, both of which they can get without cost from the government though I am not certain about lights) for $250 per month each, $500 for the couple of man & wife. While Old Skinflint here with gold at seventy as I hear it is, would have rec[eive]d some $630 per month for a couple, simply for the use of one room.

I have pretty much determined to bring you to this house here. I am solitary & alone, except Powel; he & the adjutant . . . {remainder of letter missing}

—⚬—

Fishersville
January 25th 1865

My precious Wife,

I wrote you a long letter on Friday last enclosing one from Mama & one from Genl Early's A.A. Genl. In the last was stated that Genl Early would approve my application for leave as soon as the final arrangements for the Artillery were made. What he means by this expression

I am at a loss to know. I suppose it is a sufficient pretext to keep me from furlough, a species of indulgence which he abhors, having no occasion to go home himself. It unfortunately keeps me in such a predicament that I cannot advise you what to do. Were you to start to me the leave might come down the day of your arrival & you would have the double trip to perform. When he will hear from Genl Lee in regard to the final arrangements alluded to I have no idea.

Today I read a telegram from Dr Ellerson stating you were in Richd. It was dated the 20th inst & has been five days on the way. There is no office (telegraph) here & this accounts for the delay. I shall send this to Richd as you may still be there. My letter referred to above probably reached Old Church on Tuesday (yesterday). If you have gone home you will understand the cause of my delay—if still in Richd this will explain. Early is perfectly arbitrary & it is useless to try to do anything with him unless one is willing to flatter & fawn which I am not at all disposed to do. So that there is nothing to be done but to have patience.

I suppose I may calculate on getting off sometime in the next fortnight. I regret we shall lose so much of the winter apart from each other but so much for having muleish people to deal with. There is nothing new here. Miss Flora Harris is to be married on the 1st prox. to Abner Harris.[5] Osborne has been invited to be one of the groomsmen; he expects to attend in that capacity. Tom Taliaferro speaks of a letter he mailed in Richd from you to me. It has not been rec[eive]d; possibly it was directed to Staunton & may turn up at some future day.

I have seen Lieut Rodes Massie lately paroled & sent home; he was one of Wm's messmates, he says they were very comfortable at Fort Delaware but suffered greatly at Morris Island, not so much at Fort Pulaski.[6]

5. Abner Harris enlisted at Powhatan Court House, Va., as a private in the 4th Virginia Cavalry on 9 April 1862. In November 1862 he was detailed to the brigade commissary, followed by duty in the division commissary in 1864–65. Harris was paroled as a captain in Richmond on 20 April 1865 (CSR). Flora Harris, Abner's intended bride, was probably Flora A. Harris (b. 1846?) of Louisa County, Va. (1860 Census, Louisa County; see Carter's letter of 19 December 1863).

6. D. Rodes Massie enlisted as a corporal in the Charlottesville Artillery on 20 March 1862. He was promoted to second lieutenant on 25 June 1863. On 12 May 1864, Massie was captured in the fighting at the Bloody Angle near Spotsylvania Court House and sent to Fort Delaware, where he was confined with Carter's brother William. He was paroled at Charleston, S.C., on 15 December 1864 and returned to duty with Cutshaw's artillery battalion (CSR). Both Massie and William Carter were part of the group of Confederate soldiers who, after the war, became known as the "Immortal Six Hundred" because of the privations they suffered as prisoners of war in Charleston.

At Morris Island they were nearly starved, for six weeks they were not free from the sensation of hunger. The Yankees said their treatment was in retaliation for that on their own officers. They began by giving the prisoners one cracker a day—12 of which make a pound—& this cracker was filled with worms & weevil. Our rations are a pound & two ounces of flour daily & some men eat it. The Yankees soon found that all would die at this rate & increased the rations to two & three & I believe to four crackers. He says they thought & talked about little else than eating, & that they had no blankets except my old black poncho blanket which you gave me when we entered the service; they laid on the sand & covered with this. While at Delaware Fort[,] Mrs France sent Wm fifteen fine hams & four or five barrels of vegetables & they lived well. He says Wm is as quiet as ever but that crowsfeet are gathering around his eyes. I wish he could be exchanged as he is kept in discomfort.

Rec[eive]d a letter from Mr Jno E. Page thanking me for my letter of condolence & kindness to Wm his son.[7] He thinks Eva will not recover from what he hears. I have seen Mary Frances & Mrs Bev Randolph. Nothing very new from Clarke. Since little Jno Page & Mr Jno E. Page have procured guards they have not been molested. The Yankee guards are entire protections they say, which shows a very much better discipline than in our army.

I called on Mrs & Miss Straith[;] the former is not pretty but I expect a fine woman. The latter is pretty but small.

I took tea with Mrs Long. She is much interested in housekeeping. I think she will visit you next summer, or rather spring. Stanard & his wife are nicely fixed in a parlor.

Mrs Dabney Carr Harrison is staying with Lucy Page at Saratoga in Clarke. They undertook a trip to Winchester without a passport. The pickets allowed them to pass. Sheridan was so enraged that he had the carriage cut down & the horses killed & then sent them home in an ambulance.

Kiss the dearest little folks. May God bless you always.

7. William Byrd Page (1848–64) died in March 1864 at Kinloch, Albemarle County, Va. (Page, *Page Family in Virginia*, 148).

Fisherville
Jan. 28th 1865

My precious Wife,

I wrote you a letter yesterday morning & directed it to Richd care of Dr Jno Ellerson. Your telegrams of the 20th & 21st reached me on the 25th & 26th in consequence of the hailstorm which had broken down the wires. I rec[eive]d your letter of the 26th an hour or two since.

In my letter of yesterday I hoped you were still in Richmond & that you could run up & stay with me until the return of my application for leave of absence. Now that you have gone home you must use your own judgment in the matter. If you have to bring any of the children, the trip is not worth the trouble & risk of cold &c. & the drive to the cars[,] for I do not imagine my application can be detained much longer. I can get you a comfortable room & James can cook for us. Genl Early has again sent me word that he will approve my application as soon as the final arrangements about the Artillery have been made. I have at last discovered the meaning of the "final arrangements." Genl Pendleton has written a letter containing an official endorsement of Genl Lee to the effect that there is no prospect of horsing all of the Battns of Artillery of this Army in the spring & that the guns & horses of the other four Battalions should be turned into two Battns & the other two to be sent to Richmond to man the heavy guns from Drewry's Bluff to Howlett's. This will leave but two Battns with this Army. I presume I should have to go with the two that take the heavy guns. Of course we are all opposed to the smash up. Heavy Artillery is the stepping stone to Infantry. The men are drilled with muskets & made to use them on the lines occasionally & if the heavy guns are ever abandoned or captured the men go regularly into Infantry. The heavy Arty is used to gild the pill. Long & Early are carrying on a correspondence with Genls Lee & Pendleton. The result is not yet known. If Genl Lee adheres to the plan it will probably be executed next week, & if he abandons it I can get off on leave[,] so it seems to me I cannot be delayed much longer. It seems a pity that such splendid light Artillery as our old Battns should be transferred to another arm of the service, but every thing is done to increase the Infantry which is the main arm of the service. With Genl Pendleton those around him get the crumbs of comfort & as we are distant & have been smartly crippled by the last campaign we are to be the sacrifice. I suggested that only three Battns should be fitted up & the remaining Battn (that from South West

Va which is not so well drilled in Artillery) should be made into a Corps of Sharpshooters for the Artillery. Having an interest in the Arty they could be relied on to defend it in time of defeat which is more than can be said for the infantry. Dont know what will be done. The 2nd Corps & Wharton's Division will be quite a respectable army & will need Artillery in the Spring. Probably if more Arty is needed for this force than the two Battns to be left with it[,] enough will be taken from some of the other corps for the purpose. If we are put into Heavy Arty I think I shall make a break for something else, possibly Cavalry or the Artillery attached to it. I would rather be a Lieutenant in Artillery than a Colonel of Infantry.

Having been identified with light Arty so long I prefer it. I know more about it & can render more service in this branch, but if the change is to be made to another arm, & I can effect it[,] I am inclined to think I shall try Cavalry. Of course I shall have to start afresh with my studies & I don't know when I should get a command unless my old Division (Page & Cutshaw, when the prisoners are exchanged, if they ever are) could be mounted. However there are many, & perhaps insuperable difficulties in the way of this plan which may float me into the heavy business. I look upon the horse objection as a real difficulty only to some extent. We can get them in this country, but there is probably an excess of light Arty as compared with the infantry[,] although I don't think it is the case in this army, for this reason, it is desired to convert it into Infantry. We having been considerably damaged & being farthest from the ear of the old Chief of Arty are the sufferers. I am inclined to think it will take as many horses to fit up any Artillery at Richd to act with the 2nd Corps next spring (and it will require more than the two Battns left with it) as it will to fit up three Battns, the other serving as sharpshooters. However I shall calmly abide any arrangements that may be made. I am too old a soldier not to know that we have no rights, except to die[,] for the indulgence of which privilege we are allowed many favorable opportunities.

I don't wish you to say anything about this until I write again; the matter is not yet settled & we are anxious to keep it from the officers & men, who will be much mortified at & opposed to the plan. Moreover it may not take place. They are so elated at the praise they have rec[eive]d for their splendid conduct this fall that it will be a sad blow to their hopes of a refit this spring. If it is necessary or best I think it should be done whatever the objection.

Now you must do exactly what you think best about coming. I have given you all the data known to me. If you are compelled to bring Ann

I think you had better not come. The weather is intensely cold & I am always uneasy about moving children in the winter. If you can come alone, bringing little Betsy[,] you might undertake it, even in this case you had best be guided by the condition of the roads & weather. While in Richd the trip would have been nothing as you [would] get here by sundown, & I am only four or five hundred yds from Fisherville Depot. The correspondence between Genls Lee[,] Pendleton[,] Early & Long ought to come to a close next week or sooner. This letter will reach you Tuesday. Should I get off I will endeavor to save you the trip & meet you in Richd should you determine to come. The various trips to Richd must be hard on your horses. I regret particularly that I did not receive your telegrams when they were sent.

It is not necessary for me to tell you how much I want to see you & how much this continued postponement has annoyed me. Of course if I had had the least idea of any such delay I should have sent for you long ago but every day I expected the return of the papers. It is the worst possible state of things. A decision one way or the other would have been preferable.

May God bless you always. Love to Mrs Laura & Andy if with you.

Y[ou]r devoted husband

—⟋⟍—

Richmond
March 7th 1865

My precious Wife,

We arrived safely last night at dusk after a tedious journey. The roads are almost impassable. I have never seen them as bad. A carriage could not pass over them at all without first rate horses. We stopped one hour at Ingleside. All were as kind as possible. On the way we were cheered by the report from a soldier, who seemed to know me, that William had returned. On our arrival however it proved untrue. Shirley says Col Ould told him the officers at Hilton Head will be exchanged at once.[8] The order has been issued but he was ignorant of the point of exchange.

8. Judge Robert Ould (1820–82) of Georgetown, D.C., was a prewar lawyer, judge, and district attorney in Washington, D.C. He moved to Richmond following Virginia's secession and was appointed assistant secretary of war. In July 1862 Ould became the commissioner for the exchange of prisoners. After the war, he defended Jefferson Davis against charges of treason and conspiracy to mistreat prisoners of war; served a term in the state senate; represented Richmond in the Virginia House of Delegates; and was president of the Richmond, Fredericksburg, and Potomac Railroad Company (Hall, *Portraits*, 185–86).

It is said that Hampton has whipped Kilpatrick & that he excited great enthusiasm in South Carolina.[9] It is rumored here that I am to be promoted & sent to Hardee's Corps. I don't know how true it is—will learn this evening from Genl Pendleton. I will learn at 3 P.M. & spend the night there. I should not be surprised if it proves as well for me to go to N. Carolina. Our 2nd Corps Artillery is smashed up & Long has come to Drewry's Bluff & it is said will command the line. Genl Early's whole command has been scattered or captured by the Cavalry that moved up the valley. The force was estimated at 6000 Yankees—all cavalry. Early attempted to make a stand near Waynesboro with Wharton's two Brigades numbering about five hundred, Nelson's Battn of six guns & one hundred Cavalry under Rosser.[10] After a fight of some three hours our force was utterly routed & scattered. Early & some of his staff escaped. Long & Southall & some others of the Arty escaped. The Arty was captured. The other guns had been sent to Lynchburg. The Yankees surrounded the force taking possession of the fords on Little River in their rear & it was difficult to escape. The cavalry (Yankee) came on to Charlottesville[,] burnt the bridges over the Rivanna & have gone off[,] either back or towards Lynchburg. Genl Early does not know which. He is near Charlottesville with some of his staff. Long was here yesterday but went to Petersburg in the evening train. He has ordered Nelson, who escaped, to gather up what men he can find & report to him at Drewry's Bluff. My two Battns report to different persons on the line, one to Jones & the other to Cabell. They have muskets already, although serving the heavy guns, & are doing picket duty, along with the infantry. Osborne tells me there was considerable talk of promoting me over Walker & keeping me

9. Carter is referring to fighting between opposing cavalry forces in North Carolina commanded by Confederate general Wade Hampton and Union general Hugh Judson Kilpatrick. Following the capture and near total destruction of Columbia, S.C., in mid-February, William T. Sherman's army continued its march through the Carolinas. Hampton's cavalry engaged the advancing forces in a series of small delaying actions. Three days after Carter wrote this letter, Hampton's command fought Kilpatrick's force in the Battle of Monroe's Crossroads—the last all-cavalry battle of the war.

10. Carter is describing the Battle of Waynesboro, fought on 1 March 1865 between the remnants of Lieutenant General Jubal A. Early's army and Union cavalry under Brigadier General George A. Custer (1839–76). Carter's estimate of Confederate numbers is understated. Early had around 1,600 men, all of whom were captured after Custer's force attacked simultaneously the Southern front and left flank. Early and a few others, including Brigadier General Gabriel C. Wharton (1824–1906), escaped. This battle brought an end to the 1864 Shenandoah Valley Campaign (Salmon, *Battlefield Guide*, 373–74).

here but he thinks [Walker] got his brigadiership yesterday. I am glad he got it. My promotion over him would have given rise to much healburning & I really care nothing about it. I am sorry if I shall have to leave Virginia but there is a good prospect of the armies operating near each other if not together in the coming campaign. I hear Johnston's army is at Raleigh[,] so if I should have to go it will [not be] far.[11] However this is all speculation. I know nothing positively. If this army moves much of the Arty will be destroyed & my best chance to remain in Light Artillery would be to go off somewhere. The Southern Army is moveable & must always have light Arty. I do not know who is Chief [of] Arty in that Army—probably Elzey.[12] I will write you fully as soon as I know anything.

Powel is here. He left Staunton the evening before the Yankees came into the place. While at Greenwood the Yankees fired into the train & killed Bev Randolph, Junior by his side. Genl Lee is in the city & has just sent for me. Fitz Lee's Cavalry is moving & he may want me to do something. Mrs Ellerson sends six yards of osnaburg for my drawers. May God ever bless you. Our horses (mine) are almost dying for something to eat.

Kiss the dearest children

—⚋—

Tom Carter returned to the army after a month's rest to find the artillery in the middle of yet another reorganization. After Early's army suffered its final defeat at Waynesboro on 2 March, General Long had returned to Richmond and assumed command of the Confederate artillery on the Bermuda Hundred line between the capital city and Petersburg. Under the new organization, Colonel Carter retained command of the 2nd Corps artillery, which once again included the battalions of Nelson, Braxton, and Cutshaw. Generals Pendleton and Long had convinced R. E. Lee to permit Carter to refit and redesignate his former battalions as field artillery. Until around the twentieth of March, Carter set up his headquarters at Chaffin's Bluff, east of Richmond. At that time, General Lee ordered

11. General Joseph E. Johnston, in command of the Army of Tennessee since 25 February 1865, assumed command of all Confederate forces in North Carolina on 6 March. His army, then near Fayetteville, N.C., was attempting to block Union general William T. Sherman's advance toward Goldsboro and Raleigh (OR 47[2]:1274, 1334).

12. Major General Arnold Elzey (1816–71) of Maryland was acting chief of artillery for the Army of Tennessee (Warner, Generals in Gray, 82–83).

Carter to Lynchburg to reorganize the remnants of Jubal Early's artillery. The colonel was back in Richmond by the end of the month.[13]

On the morning of 2 April, Carter was at St. Paul's Church near the capitol. During the service, President Davis, also in the congregation, received a message from General Lee stating that earlier that morning, a massive Union assault had broken through the thin Confederate line southwest of Petersburg and that the army could no longer defend Richmond. Carter and other officers present soon left to make their preparations to evacuate the city. Later that night, the colonel and one of his staff members crossed Mayo's Bridge and rode south to join the rest of Lee's army. As they made their way through Chesterfield County, the darkness was lit only by the explosions of Confederate gunboats in the James River near Drewry's Bluff.[14]

The next six days saw constant movement punctuated by sharp engagements as the Army of Northern Virginia marched along roads that headed west away from Grant's pursuing Federals. On the fifth, Carter and his reunited artillery camped at Amelia Court House. The next day, when Lee lost nearly a third of his force (around 8,000 men) at the battle of Sailor's Creek, Carter's guns helped prevent the capture of the rest of the army. After two more days of hard marching with no time for meaningful rest or meals, Carter's battalions reached a point on the road to Lynchburg about two miles east of the village of Appomattox Court House. That night, the eighth of April, Carter received orders to assemble three artillery battalions in preparation for an attack the next morning. Lee intended to use Carter's guns along with John B. Gordon's infantry and Fitzhugh Lee's cavalry to brush aside what he thought was Union cavalry, which would then allow the Confederates to escape farther west to Lynchburg. Gordon's line advanced to about a half mile west of Appomattox Court House. Around 7:00 A.M. on 9 April, the Confederate attack began and seemed to succeed at first. The Lynchburg Stage Road had been cleared. But the arrival of Union infantry soon ended the hopes of escaping to the west. By 10:00 A.M., the fighting was over and the Confederates had retreated east

13. *OR* 46[3]:1316–17, 1329. Precisely when Carter went to Lynchburg is unknown. On 18 March he wrote to Colonel William Nelson and informed him that he "may go to Lynchburg in a day or two" (THC to William Nelson, 18 Mar. 1865, THCP, 1865–1909, VHS). In a postwar letter to his former courier, Robert Powel Page, Carter remembered that he traveled to Lynchburg a "week or two before the fall of Petersburg" (THC to Robert Powel Page, 11 Jan. 1897, THCP, 1850–1915, VHS).

14. THC to Robert Powel Page, 11 Jan. 1897; Hawes, "Last Days of the Army of Northern Virginia," 342.

of the village. After a cease-fire had been declared, word spread that Lee was going to surrender the army. The general met with Grant later in the afternoon at the home of Wilmer McLean and accepted the Union commander's terms of surrender.[15]

The war in Virginia was over. On a parole document dated 9 April 1865, the colonel signed his name as "T. H. Carter Col comdg Arty Battns Long's Arty Corps." Below his signature were those of fifty-eight fellow artillery officers who all agreed not to "serve in the armies of the Confederate States, or in any military capacity whatever, against the United States of America." Carter remained at Appomattox Court House for the next two days, securing rations for his men and horses and overseeing the final disposition of his guns. Early on the twelfth, he "broke camp for the last time about sunrise" and rode off toward home and an uncertain future.[16]

15. Hawes, "Last Days of the Army of Northern Virginia," 342–43; Robert Powel Page, "Appomattox Recollections," THCP, 1861–96, VHS; Long, *Day by Day*, 670–71. Major General John Brown Gordon commanded half of Lee's reorganized army on the retreat from Petersburg (Warner, *Generals in Gray*, 111).

16. Appomattox Parole, 9 Apr. 1865, THCP, 1865–1909, VHS; Page, "Appomattox Recollections."

CHAPTER NINE

Life after the War

Tom Carter's journey home from Appomattox Court House took several days, as it did for the majority of Lee's army. In many cases, weeks passed before those soldiers from states farther south reached their final destination. Colonel Carter and his traveling companion, a Mr. Drane, reached Goochland County by the evening of 14 April. There, they passed by Sabot Hill, the home of Susan Carter's uncle, former Confederate secretary of war James Alexander Seddon. His daughter Elvira recorded in her diary that Carter and Drane "stopped for a short time and took supper" and that both men were "sad" with the "memory of the surrender" still "fresh" in their minds. Elvira sympathized with the former soldiers: "If the women feel as I do, bitter and resentful, what must the men experience?"[1]

A day or two later, Carter arrived at his home in King William County, where he found his wife and three young children waiting for him. He also found a farm that had experienced the hard hand of war. To support the Confederacy, Susan Carter had sold fodder and hay to the quartermaster's office when it sent agents to the farm in 1862 and 1863. As to the harsher side of the war, the Carters' son, Thomas, later recalled that Union soldiers visited the farm four times and "swept the place clean." The tally included "forty-two horses and mules . . . cattle, hogs and sheep," and "of the negroes[,] only the old men, women and children, amounting to some ninety in number, remained." Tom Carter returned to find "two old broken down mules" and "nothing but desolation."[2]

Not all visitors to Pampatike were unwelcome, however. Two months after the surrender at Appomattox, Robert E. Lee rode down the farm's

1. "The Diary of Elvira Bruce Seddon, Part III," 10.
2. Receipts for the purchase of provisions on 28 Feb. 1862, 20 Nov. 1863, and 7 Dec. 1863 in Susan Carter's file, Confederate Papers Relating to Citizens or Business Firms, 1861–65, RG109, NARA; TNC to IBC, 14 Jan. 1915.

long, cedar-lined driveway to visit his cousin. The general had grown "weary of [Richmond]" and "of the crowds of persons of all sorts and conditions striving to see him." An excursion into the countryside to visit friends and family seemed the best solution. Lee spent a few days at Pampatike playing with the children and talking with Carter. They spoke little about the war. Perhaps the painful memories were too fresh in their minds. One subject that did come up, however, was the difficult transition that southern farmers now faced. Lee looked around and noticed the relatively large number of former slaves who remained at Pampatike. His advice to his younger cousin was to "get rid of the negroes left on the farm" and let the federal government provide for them. Lee suggested that Carter hire white laborers in the future. That, according to the general, would provide a more stable workforce. After his brief visit, Robert E. Lee left to spend time with others nearby before returning to Richmond to face his uncertain future.[3]

Many others shared Carter's immediate situation. From owners of large plantations down to those who had only a few slaves, all faced a difficult and dramatic transformation. As much as every southerner had benefited in some way from the existence of the institution of slavery, those who directly depended on the labor of the enslaved faced a new world in 1865.

When Carter returned to Pampatike, he found a large farm that needed the labor of many, but now he would either have to pay for that work or make some other arrangement that would satisfy the new system of postwar labor relations. At Pampatike, Carter struggled to compensate his farmworkers. The system he adopted involved providing housing, food, and medical treatment for his workers throughout the year and, once the income from the sale of crops was received, paying each of them at the end of the year. One man, Robert Smith, challenged Carter and reported him to the local field office of the Freedmen's Bureau. He claimed that Carter owed him for four months' work. On 14 May 1866, Carter appeared before the bureau at King William Court House to defend his actions. Smith had a wife, four children under the age of eleven, a small garden, and four hogs. Sometime before the end of 1865, Robert Smith left the farm and took his hogs with him. Now he wanted the wages that Carter had not paid him at the end of the year. The bureau court heard the case and ruled that because Carter continued to feed and care for Smith's wife and chil-

3. Lee, *Recollections and Letters*, 166–68.

dren though they did not work for him, Smith was "not entitled to anything more than he has received." The case was promptly dismissed.[4]

Despite the advice that Lee had given him the year before and his brush with the Freedmen's Bureau, Carter retained mostly black labor at Pampatike. When his wife's uncle, William Patterson Smith, wrote to Tom about the prospects of finding African Americans to work for him for long periods of time on his Gloucester County farm, Carter responded with his own advice and, in the process, revealed some of the benefits and problems associated with hiring black workers. On the positive side, Carter suggested that Smith find married men to work for him because they tended to be "tied to the soil by their families." If he could afford to hire a large number of African Americans, that would be best because, as Carter believed, they are "gregarious & a crowd offers attractions to them." On the negative side, Carter pointed out that the proximity of Richmond to his own county tended to offer greater opportunities for blacks looking for work. The same might hold true for Smith because of the oyster industry that flourished in Gloucester County. Also, white small farmers in King William, seeking extra income, had a tendency to rent land to African American farmers, thus reducing the pool of available laborers. In frustration, Carter noted that white labor had not yet "found its way" to the county and that "all our capital, all our skill & all our energies are taxed for the benefit of the negro[,] whose wages absorb within a fraction of everything made on the farm."[5]

Financial strains remained a constant for Carter during the years immediately following the war. To earn a living, he continued to farm Pampatike throughout the late 1860s and into the 1870s. Every fall, he recorded in his farm account book the annual yields in wheat: 451 bushels in 1867, 494.5 in 1868, 389 in 1869, 390 in 1870, and 147 in 1871. The sale of lumber from the forests on the estate supplemented Carter's farming income, but most of that went toward paying the burdensome $1,000 annual rent that he owed his father for the farm. Those former slaves who remained at Pampatike helped to keep the farm in operation, but their lives had changed forever. Freedom meant the ability to come and go at will. On one particular day in October 1867, Carter recorded in his account book the rea-

---

4. *Robert Smith v. T. H. Carter*, 14 May 1866, Letters sent, vol. 1: Feb.–Aug. 1866 and Dec. 1868, 161, Records of the Field Offices for the State of Virginia, Bureau of Refugees, Freedmen, and Abandoned Lands, 1865–72.

5. THC to William Patterson Smith, 14 Nov. 1866, THCP, 1850–1915, VHS.

son for the absence of his farmworkers. "Election day," he noted, "negroes gone to the Ct. House to vote."[6]

In 1868 Carter made an important decision, one that would affect his life and that of his wife for the next twenty years. He needed a source of income to supplement the meager sum generated by farming, and his ten-year-old son, Thomas, needed to attend school. To kill two birds with one stone, Carter established a school at Pampatike. His son would learn the basics the same way his father had as a boy in Clarke County.[7]

Sixteen boys from the neighborhood, which included Richmond twenty-five miles away, each paid an annual tuition of $250 to attend the Pampatike Male Academy from 1 October to 30 June. According to a former student, the boys studied under a University of Virginia graduate who taught them everything from "reading, writing, spelling, and history, to arithmetic, algebra, Latin, and Greek." There was no separate building for the academy, so the students lived and studied in the main house, which a former student later described as a "jumble of frame structures, built at different periods, and without pretence to architectural design or beauty."[8]

Although it was Tom Carter's name that appeared in newspaper advertisements promoting the school, it was his wife, Susan, who actually ran the academy. Henry A. Wise, who attended Pampatike in the 1880s, "fell under the influence of [Susan Carter], who stamped upon every boy . . . the impress of her singular refinement and high character." Another former student remembered her as "a person of remarkable force of will and executive capacity." One former pupil described "Colonel Carter," as Tom was still known, as being of "medium height, and rather slender build, [with] clear-cut military features [that] were lit by an eye with an expression which could pass from that of the eagle to that of the gazelle, as occasion demanded." He exuded a "quiet dignity" and the "simplicity of a country gentleman" who was "accustomed to command." Both Tom and

6. Thomas Henry Carter Account Book, 1859–88, VHS. The annual totals in wheat were derived from the following dated entries in the account book: 14 Nov. 1867, 2 Oct. 1868, 8 Nov. 1869, 18 Nov. 1870, and 14 Oct. 1871. Carter's reference to blacks voting at the courthouse appears in his entry for 22 October 1867.

7. The 1868 date for the establishment of the school is based on a newspaper advertisement in the fall of 1880 that declared the upcoming session to be the twelfth (*Richmond Dispatch*, 14 Sept. 1880). Carter's daughters, Juliet and Anne Willing, attended a school in Richmond (TNC to IBC, 14 Jan. 1915).

8. *Richmond Dispatch*, 14 Sept. 1880, 8 Oct. 1880, 30 July 1881, 20 Aug. 1882, and 23 Sept. 1883; *Richmond Dispatch*, 21 Sept. 1884 and 27 Aug. 1885; Henry Alexander Wise, memoir, 1874–88, Wise Family Papers, 1840–67, VHS; Wise, *Diomed*, 180.

Pampatike, King William County, Virginia (Virginia Historical Society)

Susan Carter expected the students to behave with the "highest moral, religious, and social standards." Accordingly, on Sundays, the boys accompanied the Carters to worship at nearby Acquinton Church.[9]

Life at the school, however, was not all work for the boys. Shooting was the most popular leisure activity. According to one former pupil, at the time he was there, all sixteen boys at Pampatike had shotguns. Tom Carter himself, however, reportedly had "no particular predilection for shooting." Perhaps he had done enough during the war to last a lifetime. On one hunting expedition in February 1873, a tragedy occurred that had a lasting effect on the Carter family. A pupil named Spencer Leslie France, the son of Carter's wartime adjutant, and two other boys treed a raccoon. When they cut down the tree with the raccoon in it, a branch from another tree snapped off and struck young France in the head. He died before the doctor could arrive. Spencer's mother visited the farm a few months later, around the time that Susan Carter gave birth to her last child, and asked her to name the baby after her son. Tom and Susan's fourth child and second son was christened Spencer Leslie Carter.[10]

9. Wise, *Col. John Wise of England*, 219; Wise, *Diomed*, 181; Bruce, *Recollections*, 45.
10. Bruce, *Recollections*, 46–48; TNC to IBC, 14 Jan. 1915. Spencer Leslie Carter was born on 10 May 1873 (McGill, *Beverley Family of Virginia*, 471).

Tom Carter in the 1870s
(Virginia Historical Society)

Throughout the years that followed the Civil War, Tom Carter shared in the experience of being a former Confederate. His personal journey of remembrance began not too long after he returned home. In December 1866 a letter arrived from Jubal Early, his former commander in the Shenandoah Valley, who was then living in Canada. In the letter, Early notified Carter that his *Memoir of the Last Year of the War* had just been published. The book included accounts of the Battles of Third Winchester, Fisher's Hill, and Cedar Creek, three of Carter's most important engagements during the war. Early hoped that Carter would be satisfied with his portrayal of Confederate artillery. In closing, Early let loose the anger toward his former enemies that would shape most of his postwar life. "Do you think if the Gates of Hell were spread wide open that it would belch forth such another set of infernal scoundrels as the Yankees?"[11]

Beginning in the 1880s, Carter corresponded with other former Confederates as they sought to pass on their memories or challenge others' accounts of the war. Samuel J. C. Moore, a former Confederate staff officer, wrote to Carter asking for details about the artillery at Cedar Creek. The

11. Jubal A. Early to THC, 13 Dec. 1866, Lee Family Papers, 1732–1892, VHS.

response to Moore brought to its author a flood of emotion, particularly when Carter defended Jubal Early's leadership on that October day in 1864. "Pardon this infliction," Carter wrote, "but when an old Confed[erate] gets on war memories, and feels anew the old heart throbs, he is apt to be prolix." In 1898 Dr. F. A. Dearborn sent Carter a letter containing a series of questions relating to the artillery at the Battles of Spotsylvania Court House and Cedar Creek, once again forcing Carter to confront his memories. His most active correspondence concerning his wartime experiences, however, took place over a ten-year period beginning in 1894. In letters to U.S. senator and former Confederate staff officer John Warwick Daniel, Carter related details about the Battles of Third Winchester and Cedar Creek and offered a passionate defense of the role and conduct of the artillery of the Army of Northern Virginia. In his notes about the battle of Cedar Creek, Carter, though concerned that he not appear too critical, stated that "[John B.] Gordon in defence is not Gordon in attack." As for the artillery, Carter asserted that he "never saw so much as a single gun detachment fail to do everything asked of it, and to do it with unfaltering zeal and courage, regardless of surrounding conditions." In the romantic tone of much of the postwar writings, he wrote: "Looking back through the vista of many years, in fancy I see them again, through rifts of smoke and dust, reeking with sweat, begrimed with powder, without murmuring, dead and dying comrades around, standing defiantly and dauntlessly to their guns—for themselves, the half starved and in tatters, asking nothing but orders, hoping nothing but victory, and fearing nothing but defeat."[12]

As a former Confederate officer, Carter actively participated in public gatherings, reunions, and memorial dedications. On 3 November 1870, less than a month after the death of Robert E. Lee, a group of veterans led by Jubal Early met at the First Presbyterian Church in Richmond to organize the Lee Monument Association, whose stated purpose was to raise public and private funds to erect a monument to the general in the former capitol of the Confederacy. Tom Carter was present that day, and his colleagues elected him to serve on the executive committee of the new association. Two months later, the Virginia legislature officially incorporated the Lee Monument Association in legislation that included

12. THC to Samuel J. C. Moore, 15 Oct. 1889, Samuel Johnston Cramer Moore Papers, 1861–1904, VHS; F. A. Dearborn to THC, 15 May 1898, THCP, 1898, VHS; Bland, "John Warwick Daniel," 682–83; THC to John Warwick Daniel, 19 Nov. 1894 and 28 Nov. 1894, both in John Warwick Daniel Papers, 1849–1910, David M. Rubenstein Rare Book and Manuscript Library, Duke University.

Carter's name as a member of the executive committee. He also joined the Virginia Division of the Association of the Army of Northern Virginia when it formed in November 1871. A year later, at the group's second annual meeting, Carter was elected to its governing board. The association's annual meetings took place in the hall of the House of Delegates in the Virginia State Capitol followed by a banquet in a nearby hotel, where former Confederates would address the membership on war-related topics. Except for brief service as vice president of the association in 1880, Carter remained on the executive committee throughout the 1870s and 1880s. On 29 May 1890, Carter and many of his aging comrades rode in the parade as marshals during the lavish celebration surrounding the unveiling of the Robert E. Lee statue on Richmond's Monument Avenue. Almost exactly three years later, he attended the dedication of the Soldiers' and Sailors' Monument on Richmond's Libby Hill, and a few days later, on 31 May 1893, Carter marched in Jefferson Davis's funeral procession to Hollywood Cemetery.[13]

Unlike many former Confederates, Carter did not publish a memoir of his wartime experiences. He was not a regular contributor to the *Southern Historical Society Papers*. His only writings to appear in that publication included an article on the events surrounding the capture of Confederate artillery during the major Union attack on the Mule Shoe near Spotsylvania Court House on the morning of 12 May 1864 and a letter, written by Carter in 1899, to a Mrs. Turner in which he offered his assessment of former Confederate general Richard S. Ewell. The Spotsylvania article was a reprint of a long editorial letter published in the *Richmond Times* in 1893, and the letter to Mrs. Turner appeared in the *Southern Historical Society Papers* six years after Carter's death. The only other printed piece that bore any relation to Tom Carter was a 1919 recollection published in *Confederate Veteran* magazine. Written by his former courier Percy Hawes, the article, reportedly submitted at Carter's request, detailed the Confederate retreat from Petersburg to Appomattox.[14]

13. Jones, *Army of Northern Virginia Memorial Volume*, 37, 48; *Acts and Joint Resolutions Passed by the General Assembly, 1870–71*, 47; Foster, *Ghosts of the Confederacy*, 53; "Editorial Paragraphs," 160, 252; "Annual Reunion of the Virginia Division," 283–84; "Annual Reunion of the Virginia Division, A.N.Va. Association," 385; "Annual Reunion of the Association of the Army of Northern Virginia," 85; *RDD*, 28 Oct. 1880; "Unveiling of the Statue of General Robert E. Lee," 266; "Unveiling of the Soldiers' and Sailors' Monument," 336; *New York Times*, 1 June 1893.

14. Carter, "The Bloody Angle," 239–42; *Richmond Times*, 12 Feb. 1893; Hawes, "Last Days of the Army of Northern Virginia," 341–44.

Tom Carter's presence among his fellow Confederate veterans and his role as the operator of Pampatike Academy led to the start of a new career in the mid-1870s for the King William County farmer. The war had all but destroyed the railroad industry in Virginia. Miles of track had been the target of both the Union and Confederate armies as they marched across the state for four years, laying waste to whatever might be useful to their opponent. In the early postwar period, railroad companies in the commonwealth began to rebuild and expand. By 1877 the industry was in need of some method of control and standardization. To provide this, the General Assembly established the office of railroad commissioner for the state of Virginia, whose duty it would be to supervise rates, safety issues, and legal compliance. On 31 March 1877, the assembly created the two-year position, and Robert Ryland, a former officer in the King William Artillery and current delegate representing the county in the General Assembly, knew the right man for the job. Two days later, he nominated Carter, and the House of Delegates voted 119 to 1 to appoint him as the first railroad commissioner. On 5 April Tom Carter swore an oath before the Richmond Circuit Court that he would faithfully perform his duties and that he was not a stockholder or an owner or employee of any railroad in the state.[15]

Carter settled in almost immediately at his new job. For a salary of $3,000 a year and with the help of a clerk, he was expected to arbitrate a wide range of issues and occasionally inspect the conditions of the railroads. Numerous letters landed on Carter's desk, complaining about everything from excessive freight charges by the York River and Chesapeake Rail Road to "frequent and destructive fires" caused by locomotives on the Virginia Midland and Great Southern Rail Road and the killing of a cow by a train on the Chesapeake and Ohio Railway. In each case, Carter did his best to mediate between the parties to resolve the issue. For four years, he served the commonwealth in this capacity, during which time, to ease the strain of traveling by horse between Richmond and King William County, he rented a room in the city at a boarding house at 543 East Franklin Street.[16]

15. *Acts and Joint Resolutions Passed by the General Assembly, 1876–77*, 254–55; *Journal of the House of Delegates, 1877–78*, 447–48; Leonard, *General Assembly of Virginia*, 526; Virginia Railroad Commissioner's Oaths of Office, 1877–89, Library of Virginia, Richmond. The one vote cast against Carter went to Bradley T. Johnson (1829–1903), former Confederate general and current Virginia state senator (*Journal of the House of Delegates, 1877–8*, 448; Warner, *Generals in Gray*, 157).

16. *Acts and Joint Resolutions Passed by the General Assembly, 1876–77*, 257; *First Annual Report of the Railroad Commissioner*, 15–16; *Third Annual Report of the Railroad Commissioner*, 43; 1880 Census, Richmond.

Carter's tenure as commissioner of railroads ended abruptly at the end of 1879 when he and his fellow Democrats were swept from power following the fall General Assembly elections. The Readjuster Party, led by former Confederate general William Mahone, took control of both houses of the legislature in the fall elections. On 12 December 1879, Carter stood for reelection against Asa Rogers Jr., the Readjuster candidate. Democratic senator John W. Daniel, who nominated Carter, delivered a two-hour-long speech in which he took the opportunity not only to support Carter but also to attack the Readjusters. In the end, the assembly voted 65 to 53 to replace Carter with Rogers. A few days later, a local Democratic newspaper reported the following: "The people of King William [County] will regret to learn that Col. Carter . . . has not been re-elected to the position he has filled with so much ability and credit alike to himself and to the state." The reason for his defeat was obvious to the reporter. Carter would have continued to render valuable service "had it not been" for "the fact that he was a Democrat," which "doomed him . . . as a victim of the relentless partisanry of Mahone." Carter continued to serve as commissioner until the following March, when he resigned to become a member of the board of arbitration of the Southern Railway and Steamship Association.[17]

Tom Carter took up his new duties as arbitrator in May 1880 and remained with that organization for the next sixteen years. Initially, he continued to live at Pampatike, but because the Southern Railway and Steamship Association oversaw all railroads south of the Ohio and Potomac Rivers and east of the Mississippi River, Carter's involvement in resolving disputes between railroad companies, primarily relating to rate control and charges of unfair competition, forced him to travel fairly regularly. While he had been commissioner of the railroads in Virginia, he had gone to the annual national convention of railroad commissioners in Columbus, Ohio. Now, he attended regular meetings in New York City; Washington, D.C.; and Atlanta. According to his son, these were "very happy times" for Carter.[18]

From 1888 to 1892, Carter served as the commissioner of the association, a job that required him and Susan to relocate to Atlanta, the home

17. Wallenstein, *Cradle of America*, 234; *Journal of the Senate, 1879*, 50; unidentified newspaper clipping, [Dec. 1879], Juliet Carter Scrapbook, 6, THCP, 1850–1915, VHS; *Shenandoah Herald*, 17 Dec. 1879; *RDD*, 30 Mar. 1880; "Elections and Official Changes," 417.
18. "Elections and Official Changes," 417; Hudson, "Southern Railway and Steamship Association," 72; *First Annual Report of the Board of Railroad Commissioners*, 73–74; *Second Annual Report of the Railroad Commissioner of the State of South Carolina*, 259, 265; *New York Times*, 17 June 1893, 25 Aug. 1894; TNC to IBC, 14 Jan. 1915.

of the organization since its establishment in 1875. They remained in that city until the association abolished the office of commissioner in 1892. Shortly thereafter, the couple moved to Washington, D.C., where for the next few years, Carter again served on the association's board of arbitration. By 1897 the board had been dissolved, and he continued to work on occasional cases for the association. The cases, however, were "few and far between," and the work was not steady enough to "keep the union between 'the buckle and the tongue.'" Having reached the end of his railroad career, Carter wrote to his King William County neighbor and friend William Roane Aylett to ask him to help him find "some employment." As Carter explained in his letter, he needed a more reliable source of income, and since the death of his father in 1883—and the subsequent division of the farm among Tom and his siblings—"[f]arming on my share of Pampatike is not sufficiently profitable either."[19]

The specific job that Tom Carter mentioned to Aylett was the post of proctor at the University of Virginia. The current proctor, Moses Green Peyton, was planning to resign for health reasons in the early spring of 1897, and he let Carter know of his plans. Carter was well acquainted with Peyton, who had served as Robert Rodes's adjutant general during the war and thus had worked closely with Carter. In his letter to Aylett, Carter, though himself an alumnus of the university's medical school, was anxious to get all the help he could in succeeding Peyton. He did not have to wait long. On 19 April, a little more than a month after Carter wrote to Aylett, Green Peyton died. Before that happened, however, the board of visitors of the university met on 2 April and elected Tom Carter to replace the ailing Peyton. Also at that meeting, the board resolved to combine the positions of proctor and superintendent of grounds and buildings. Carter's new career, which promised an annual salary of $2,000, would begin on 15 September 1897. With Peyton's death occurring only two weeks after the board meeting, however, Carter assumed the office of proctor almost immediately. He and Susan moved into their new home in Pavilion III on the West Lawn of the university, and on 1 May Carter took charge of the proctor's office.[20]

19. TNC to IBC, 14 Jan. 1915; *Alexandria Gazette*, 2 Oct. 1888; "Notes of the Week," 705; THC to William Roane Aylett, 8 Mar. 1897, THCP, 1850–1915, VHS.

20. THC to William Roane Aylett, 8 Mar. 1897; Krick, *Staff Officers*, 242; Minutes of the Board of Visitors of the University of Virginia, 2 Apr. 1897, Papers of the Proctors of the University of Virginia, 1809–1905, RG-5/3/1.111, UVA; *Richmond Dispatch*, 27 Apr. 1897; *Annual Reports of Officers, Boards, and Institutions of the Commonwealth of Virginia for the Year Ending September 30, 1897*, 184.

In his capacity as proctor and superintendent of grounds and buildings, Carter dealt with a variety of responsibilities and issues. Overseeing the physical campus of the university proved a daunting task that kept him busy. In addition to his regular duties, he supervised the replacement of aging gas pipes, authorized major repairs to the boiler, and supervised the carving of new capitals for the columns of the Rotunda, which was undergoing reconstruction following its near destruction by fire in October 1895. He also managed various university investments and accounted for payments to the school. In the last sentence of a December 1897 letter to the rector, Carter proudly announced that "of 465 students matriculated to date, in which checks large and small have been accepted[,] not one check has failed to be paid on demand." One major issue that drew Carter's attention during his tenure involved the governance of the university. The subject of much debate during the 1890s was whether or not the school should create the office of president. At the time, most of the faculty were against the idea, while the board of visitors and the alumni favored the plan. Carter saw no need for a president as long as the board remained a strong one. Plus, the decision, according to him, was not up to the school to decide: "A President would either be a figurehead, or the whole fabric of the charter, or laws, as they now stand, and were intended to stand by the Founder, would have to be altered, and this could only be done by the Legislature." In the end, the board of visitors chose to elect a president and in 1902 offered the job to Woodrow Wilson, then president of Princeton, who turned it down. Two years later, Edwin A. Alderman of Tulane University accepted and became the first president of the University of Virginia.[21]

While Tom Carter was worrying about gas pipes and tuition checks, raising funds for the repairs to the Rotunda, and arguing over the merits of hiring a president, he and his wife were becoming popular among the students at the university. Like they did when they ran Pampatike Acad-

21. THC to the Rector and Board of Visitors of the University of Virginia, 7 Dec. 1897, Papers of the Rector and Board of Visitors of the University of Virginia, 1854–1903, UVA; *Richmond Dispatch*, 25 June and 18 Sept. 1902; Dabney, *Mr. Jefferson's University*, 40, 42; THC to Jack Williams, 16 July 1897, Thomas Henry Carter Correspondence, 1897–1903, UVA. Another issue that Carter faced concerned a proposed plan in the Virginia General Assembly to combine the medical school at the University of Virginia with the Medical School of Virginia in Richmond. The one in Richmond would teach the practice of medicine, while the school at the University of Virginia would teach the theory of medicine. Carter opposed the plan, calling it "absolutely ruinous to our medical school." The plan did not pass (THC to Armistead Churchill Gordon, 21 Nov. 1903, Armistead C. Gordon Correspondence, 1900–1907, UVA).

Tom (seated, fourth from left) and Susan Carter posing with students, who called themselves "Colonel Carter's Colts," at the University of Virginia in the late 1890s (Courtesy of Eda Carter Williams Martin)

emy, the couple opened their home to some of the young boys. Those students who ate meals with them on a regular basis adopted the name "Colonel Carter's Colts." Susan Carter treated her "dear boys" almost as members of the family, dealing out equal measures of encouragement and praise to suit the occasion. That arrangement, however, came to tragic end when Susan died on 9 November 1902 at the age of sixty-nine after "an illness of several months." Two days later, she was buried at Hollywood Cemetery in Richmond. Almost immediately, friends and family members sent condolence letters to comfort the grieving husband. Two days after Susan's death, George Washington Custis Lee assured Carter that his "heart has been, and is with [him] in all [his] affliction." Tom's cousin, the writer Thomas Nelson Page, expressed his "unspeakable sympathy" and "affection" in a letter in which he went on to praise Susan as the "handsomest and most gracious matron [he] ever knew." In February 1903, Page published a three-and-a-half-page tribute to her in the *University of Virginia Magazine*. Two weeks after his wife's death, Tom Carter assured two friends that in the midst of his grief he found comfort "in knowing that she is absolutely free from pain, sorrow, crying & death."[22]

After Susan's death, Carter continued to live and work at the University of Virginia until 1905, when a stroke that paralyzed the left side of his body forced him to retire. Unable to cope on his own, he went to live with his daughter Juliet and son-in-law Robert E. Lee Jr. at Romancoke in King William County. There, on 2 June 1908, eleven days short of his seventy-seventh birthday, Carter died, leaving an estate valued at $81,000. The next day, his body was taken to 205 West Franklin Street in Richmond, the home of his oldest son, Thomas Nelson Carter. That day, many of the city's residents turned out to watch a parade honoring the centennial of Jefferson Davis's birth. The chief marshal, former Confederate artillerist J. Thompson Brown, ordered the various military units in the parade to march in funeral time as they passed the Carter house. A newspaper correspondent recorded that "[s]everal of the bands played funeral marches, the infantry passing with guns presented, while the Howitzers passed the house uncovered, their buglers sounding the funeral dirge." On 4 June,

22. Martin, *Remarkable Women of Pampatike*, 37–38; *Richmond Dispatch*, 11 Nov. 1902; George Washington Custis Lee to THC, 11 Nov. 1902, and Thomas Nelson Page to THC, 18 Nov. 1902, both in THCP, 1902, VHS; Page, "Mrs. Susan Roy Carter," 274–77; THC to Norma and Hope, 24 Nov. 1902, THCP, 1850–1915, VHS.

following a well-attended funeral service at All Saints Episcopal Church, Thomas Henry Carter was buried next to his wife on a hilltop near President's Circle in Hollywood Cemetery.[23]

23. Martin, *Remarkable Women of Pampatike*, 39; "Daily Court Record," *Richmond Times-Dispatch*, 9 June 1908; "Death Claims Colonel Carter," *Richmond Times-Dispatch*, 3 June 1908; "Honor to Colonel Carter," *Richmond Times-Dispatch*, 4 June 1908. Between 1887 and 1904, all of Susan and Tom Carter's children married—Thomas Nelson Carter to Agnes Atkinson Mayo in 1887, Anne Willing Carter to Henry Rozier Dulany in 1888, Juliet Carter to Robert E. Lee Jr. in 1894, and Spencer Leslie Carter to Roberta Atkinson in 1904 (McGill, *Beverley Family of Virginia*, 220, 349, 472). The house at 205 West Franklin Street was built in 1895 by Peter H. Mayo for his daughter, Agnes, and her husband, Thomas Nelson Carter. It still stands and is currently owned by the Junior League of Richmond (Mayo-Carter House File, VHS). When it came time for Anne Willing Carter to get married in 1888, her parents worried that Pampatike was too remote for the wedding. To solve the problem, Anne's cousin, Fitzhugh Lee, then governor of Virginia, offered to host the ceremony at the governor's mansion in Richmond. The thrilled family graciously accepted. One of the guests of honor was Celia Grymes, the former Carter family slave who raised Tom's children. For her, the high point of the day was when Governor Lee personally escorted her to the dining room after the ceremony. According to Anne, Celia "never lost her poise in the slightest degree" ("Mammy Celia," in Dulany, *Some Recollections*). Celia Grymes died in 1907 at the age of 101 and was the subject of an article on the front page of the *Richmond Times-Dispatch* ("Mammy Celia Dead," *Richmond Times-Dispatch*, 19 Dec. 1907). In September 1929 those members of the Carter family who had been buried in the graveyard at Pampatike were relocated to the family plot at Hollywood Cemetery. They included Tom Carter's mother, Juliet Muse Gaines Carter; two of his and Susan's infant children, William Roy and James Carter; his brother, Julian M. Carter; his aunt, Cornelia Gaines Meaux; and Dr. Randolph Turner (*Hollywood Cemetery*, http://www.webcemeteries.com/Hollywood [accessed 30 Sept. 2013]).

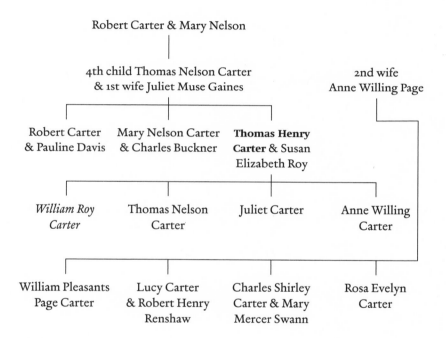

This abbreviated chart shows the Carter family descended from Tom's grandfather, Robert Carter. It also includes only those children of Tom and Susan Carter who were born before 1865 and thus mentioned in his letters. After the war, the couple had two more sons: James, who died as an infant, and Spencer Leslie.

Italic type = died as an infant

BIBLIOGRAPHY

MANUSCRIPT COLLECTIONS

Alexandria, Va.
   Special Collections, Kate Waller Barrett Branch, Alexandria Public Library
      Edith Moore Sprouse, "Fairfax County in 1860: A Collective Biography"
Berryville, Va.
   Clarke County Historical Association
      Annfield Title Abstract, 1900
      Carter Family Genealogical Files
Charlottesville, Va.
   Albert and Shirley Small Special Collections Library, University of Virginia
      Thomas Henry Carter Correspondence, 1897–1903
      Armistead C. Gordon Correspondence, 1900–1907
      Papers of the Proctors of the University of Virginia, 1809–1905
      Papers of the Rector and Board of Visitors of the University of Virginia,
         1854–1903
Durham, N.C.
   David M. Rubenstein Rare Book and Manuscript Library, Duke University
      John Warwick Daniel Papers, 1849–1910
Lexington, Va.
   Archives, Preston Library, Virginia Military Institute
      Thomas Henry Carter Alumni File
      Class Standings
      1848 Regulations
N.p.
   Private Collection
      Thomas Henry Carter to Susan Roy Carter, 22 June 1861
      Thomas Henry Carter to Susan Roy Carter, 18 August 1862
      Thomas Henry Carter to Susan Roy Carter, 15 December 1864
      A. R. Hynes to Thomas Henry Carter, 14 January 1864
Raleigh, N.C.
   North Carolina Division of Archives and History
      Daniel Harvey Hill Papers

Richmond, Va.
 Eleanor S. Brockenbrough Library, Museum of the Confederacy
  Jubal A. Early, "Soldiers of the Army of the Valley . . . ," 22 October 1864
  Jubal A. Early Collection
 Library of Virginia
  Mathews County Marriage Records, 1854–1935
  Records of the Field Offices for the State of Virginia, Bureau of Refugees,
   Freedmen, and Abandoned Lands, 1865–72 (microfilm)
  Virginia Railroad Commissioner's Oaths of Office, 1877–89
 Virginia Historical Society
  Baylor Family Bible Records, 1698–1909
  Braxton Family Bible Records, 1789–1941
  Brockenbrough Family Bible Records, 1778–1887
  Bruce Family Papers, 1665–1926
  Bruce Family Papers, 1715–1906
  Carter Family Bible Records, 179[?]–1811
  Robert Carter to His Children, 12 October 1803
  Thomas Henry Carter Account Book, 1859–88
  Thomas Henry Carter Papers, 1850–1915
  Thomas Henry Carter Papers, 1861–96
  Thomas Henry Carter Papers, 1898
  Thomas Henry Carter Papers, 1902
  Jeremy Francis Gilmer Collection
  Thomas T. H. Hill, "Record of the Officers of King William County,
   Virginia"
  J. Ambler Johnston Papers, 1784–1902
  Thomas Catesby Jones, "War Reminiscences"
  Charles Kingsley to Frank E. Kingsley, 6 August 1864
  Lee Family Papers, 1732–1892
  Mayo-Carter House File
  Minor Family Papers, 1810–1932
  Samuel Johnston Cramer Moore Papers, 1861–1904
  Randolph Family Bible Records, 1825–1901
  Alice Cabell Horsley Siegel Papers, 1898–1963[?]
  Virginia State Convention of 1861, "An Ordinance to Reorganize the
   Militia," Confederate Imprint #2261
  Ella More Bassett Washington to Winfield Scott Hancock, 25 July 1865
  Wise Family Papers, 1840–67
Washington, D.C.
 National Archives and Records Administration
  Compiled Service Records of Confederate General and Staff Officers and
   Nonregimental Enlisted Men. RG109. M331.
  Compiled Service Records of Confederate Soldiers Who Served in
   Organizations from the State of Virginia. RG109. M324.
  Confederate Papers Relating to Citizens or Business Firms. RG109. M346.

Letters Received by the Confederate Adjutant and Inspector General's
Office, 1861–65. RG109. M474.
Letters Sent by the Confederate Secretary of War, 1861–65. RG109. M522.
U.S. Census of 1830. Population Schedules. Microfilm M19.
U.S. Census of 1850. Population Schedules. Microfilm M432.
U.S. Census of 1850. Slave Schedules. Microfilm M432.
U.S. Census of 1860. Population Schedules. Microfilm M653.
U.S. Census of 1860. Slave Schedules. Microfilm M653.
U.S. Census of 1880. Population Schedules. Microfilm T9.

NEWSPAPERS

Alexandria Gazette   *Richmond Daily Whig*   *Shenandoah Herald*
Daily Richmond Examiner   *Richmond Dispatch*   *Staunton Spectator*
Harper's Weekly   *Richmond Enquirer*   *Winchester Evening Star*
New York Times   *Richmond Times*
Richmond Daily Dispatch   *Richmond Times-Dispatch*

PUBLISHED PRIMARY SOURCES

Acts and Joint Resolutions Passed by the General Assembly of the State of Virginia, at the Session of 1870–'71. Richmond, Va.: Superintendent of Public Printing, 1871.
Acts and Joint Resolutions Passed by the General Assembly of the State of Virginia during the Session of 1876–77. Richmond, Va.: Superintendent of Public Printing, 1877.
Annual Reports of Officers, Boards, and Institutions of the Commonwealth of Virginia for the Year Ending September 30, 1897. Richmond, Va.: Superintendent of Public Printing, 1897.
"Annual Reunion of the Association of the Army of Northern Virginia." *Southern Historical Society Papers* 17 (1889): 85–112.
"Annual Reunion of the Virginia Division, A.N.V." *Southern Historical Society Papers* 6 (1878): 283–89.
"Annual Reunion of the Virginia Division A.N.Va. Association—Address of Col. Archer Anderson on the Campaign and Battle of Chickamauga." *Southern Historical Society Papers* 9 (1881): 385–418.
Carter, Thomas Henry. "The Bloody Angle." *Southern Historical Society Papers* 21 (1893): 239–42.
Catalogue of the Trustees, Officers, and Students of the University of Pennsylvania, Session 1851–52. Philadelphia: L. R. Bailey, 1852.
Catalogue of the University of Virginia, Session of 1850–'51. Richmond, Va.: H. K. Ellyson, 1851.
The City Intelligencer; or, Stranger's Guide. Richmond, Va.: Macfarlane & Fergusson, 1862.
"The Diary of Elvira Bruce Seddon, Part III." *Goochland Historical Society Magazine* 23 (1991): 9–18.
Dulany, Anne Willing Carter, *Some Recollections*. Washington, D.C., 1936.

"Editorial Paragraphs." *Southern Historical Society Papers* 2 (1876): 159–60, 252–56.

"Elections and Official Changes." *Railway World* 6 (1880): 416–17.

"Experiments with Bone Manure." *Farmers' Register* 9 (1841): 23–28.

First Annual Report of the Board of Railroad Commissioners for the Year Ending June 30, 1878. Des Moines, Iowa: R. P. Clarkson, 1878.

First Annual Report of the Railroad Commissioner of the State of Virginia. Richmond, Va.: Superintendent of Public Printing, 1877.

Hawes, George Percy. "The Battle of Cedar Creek." *Confederate Veteran* 31 (1923): 169–70.

———. "Last Days of the Army of Northern Virginia." *Confederate Veteran* 27 (1919): 341–44.

Hawthorne, J. B. "Sermon before the Reunion." *Confederate Veteran* 5 (1897): 411–12.

Hewitt, Janet B., Noah Andre Trudeau, and Bryce A. Suderow, eds. *Supplement to the Official Records of the Union and Confederate Armies.* 100 vols. Wilmington, N.C.: Broadfoot Publishing Company, 1994–2001.

Hoge, William J. *Sketch of Dabney Carr Harrison: Minister of the Gospel and Captain in the Army of the Confederate States of America.* Richmond, Va.: Presbyterian Committee of Publication of the Confederate States, 1863.

"The Honor Roll of the University of Virginia." *Southern Historical Society Papers* 33 (1905): 43–56.

Hotchkiss, Jedediah. *Map Me a Map of the Valley: The Civil War Journal of Stonewall Jackson's Topographer.* Edited by Archie P. McDonald. Dallas: Southern Methodist University Press, 1973.

Jones, Terry L., ed., *Campbell Brown's Civil War: With Ewell and the Army of Northern Virginia.* Baton Rouge: Louisiana State University Press, 2001.

Journal of the Congress of the Confederate States of America. 7 vols. Washington, D.C.: Government Printing Office, 1904–5.

Journal of the House of Delegates of the State of Virginia for the Session of 1877–8. Richmond, Va.: Superintendent of Public Printing, 1877.

Journal of the Senate of the Commonwealth of Virginia: Begun and Held at the Capitol in the City of Richmond, on Monday, the Second Day of December, in the Year One Thousand Eight Hundred and Sixty-One—Being the Eighty-Fifth Year of the Commonwealth. Richmond, Va.: James E. Goode, Senate Printer, 1862.

Journal of the Senate of the Commonwealth of Virginia: Begun and Held at the Capitol in the City of Richmond on Wednesday, December 3, 1879, Being the One Hundred and Fourth Year of the Commonwealth. Richmond, Va.: Superintendent of Public Printing, 1879.

Journal of the Sixty-Sixth Annual Convention of the Protestant Episcopal Church in Virginia, Held in St. Paul's Church, Richmond, on the 16th and 17th of May, 1861. Richmond, Va.: C. H. Wynne, 1861.

Lee, Robert E., Jr. *Recollections and Letters of General Robert E. Lee.* Garden City, N.Y.: Garden City Publishing, 1924.

Lee, Susan P. *Memoirs of William Nelson Pendleton, D. D.* Philadelphia: J. B. Lippincott Company, 1893.

"List of Virginia Chaplains, Army of Northern Virginia." *Southern Historical Society Papers* 34 (1906): 313–15.

Long, Armistead Lindsay. "General Early's Valley Campaign." *Southern Historical Society Papers* 3 (1877): 112–22.

Martin, Joseph. *A New and Comprehensive Gazetteer of Virginia, and the District of Columbia* ... Charlottesville, Va.: Joseph Martin, 1836.

Moore, Frank, ed. *The Rebellion Record: A Diary of American Events, with Documents, Narratives, Illustrative Incidents, Poetry, etc.* 11 vols. New York: D. Van Nostrand, 1866–69.

"Notes of the Week." *Railway World* 18 (1892): 704–6.

The Official Atlas of the Civil War. New York: Thomas Yoseloff, 1958.

The Richmond City Directory, 1866: Containing a Business Directory of All the Persons Engaged in Business, Classified according to the Business. Richmond, Va.: E. P. Townsend, 1866.

Ruffin, Edmund. *The Diary of Edmund Ruffin.* Edited by William Kauffman Scarborough. 3 vols. Baton Rouge: Louisiana State University Press, 1972–89.

Runge, William H., ed. *Four Years in the Confederate Artillery: The Diary of Private Henry Robinson Berkeley.* Chapel Hill: University of North Carolina Press, 1961. Published for the Virginia Historical Society.

Sears, Stephen W., ed. *The Civil War Papers of George B. McClellan: Selected Correspondence, 1860–1865.* New York: Ticknor & Fields, 1989.

Second Annual Directory for the City of Richmond, Va.: To Which Is Added a Business Directory for 1860. Compiled by W. Eugene Ferslew. Richmond, Va.: W. Eugene Ferslew, 1860?

Second Annual Report of the Railroad Commissioner of the State of South Carolina. Columbia, S.C.: James Woodrow, 1880.

A Sketch of the University of Virginia together with a Catalogue of Professors and Instructors, the Graduates in Law and Medicine, and the Masters and Bachelors of Arts since the Foundation of the Institution. Washington, D.C.: Henry Polkinhorn, 1859.

Sneden, Robert Knox. *Eye of the Storm: A Civil War Odyssey.* Edited by Charles F. Bryan Jr. and Nelson D. Lankford. New York: The Free Press, 2000.

Sorrel, G. Moxley. *Recollections of a Confederate Staff Officer.* New York: Neal Publishing, 1905.

Special Orders of the Adjutant and Inspector General's Office, Confederate States, 1861–1865. 5 vols. Washington, D.C.: Government Printing Office, 1885–87.

The Statutes at Large of the Provisional Government of the Confederate States of America: From the Institution of the Government, February 8, 1861, to Its Termination, February 18, 1862 ... Edited by James M. Matthews. Richmond, Va.: R. M. Smith, 1864.

The Stranger's Guide and Official Directory for the City of Richmond. Richmond, Va.: Geo. P. Evans & Co., 1863.

Third Annual Report of the Railroad Commissioner of the State of Virginia. Richmond, Va.: J. W. Randolph & English, 1879.

U.S. Naval War Records Office. Official Records of the Union and Confederate

Navies in the War of the Rebellion. 30 vols. Washington, D.C.: Government
Printing Office, 1894–1922.

U.S. War Department. *The War of the Rebellion: A Compilation of the Official Records of the Union and Confederate Armies*. 128 vols. Washington, D.C.: Government Printing Office, 1880–1901.

"Unveiling of the Soldiers' and Sailors' Monument." *Southern Historical Society Papers* 22 (1894): 336–80.

"The Unveiling of the Statue of General Robert E. Lee, at Richmond, Va., on May 29th, 1890." *Southern Historical Society Papers* 17 (1889): 262–306.

"The Widow's Moan." *Confederate Veteran* 4 (1896): 40.

Woodward, C. Vann, ed. *Mary Chesnut's Civil War*. New Haven: Yale University Press, 1981.

SECONDARY SOURCES

Ailsworth, Timothy S., and others, comps. *Charlotte County, Rich Indeed: A History from Prehistoric Times through the Civil War*. Charlotte Court House, Va.: Charlotte County Board of Supervisors, 1979.

Andrews, J. Cutler. *The South Reports the Civil War*. Princeton: Princeton University Press, 1970.

Atkinson, Dorothy Francis. *King William County in the Civil War: Along Mangohick Byways*. Lynchburg, Va.: H. E. Howard, 1990.

Bearss, Edwin C. "David Rumph Jones." In *The Confederate General*, vol. 3, edited by William C. Davis, 200–201. Harrisburg, Pa.: National Historical Society, 1991.

Berkeley, Edmund, Jr. "Robert Carter." In *Dictionary of Virginia Biography*, vol. 3, edited by Sara B. Bearss and others, 84–86. Richmond: Library of Virginia, 2006.

Biographical Directory of the United States Congress, 1774–1989. Washington, D.C.: Government Printing Office, 1989.

Blanton, Wyndham B. *Medicine in Virginia in the Nineteenth Century*. Richmond, Va.: Garrett & Massie, 1933.

Boatner, Mark Mayo, III. *The Civil War Dictionary*. Revised ed. New York: David McKay Company, 1988.

Brown, Kent Masterson. *Retreat from Gettysburg: Lee, Logistics, and the Gettysburg Campaign*. Chapel Hill: University of North Carolina Press, 2005.

Brown, Stuart E., Jr. *Burwell: Kith and Kin of the Immigrant, Lewis Burwell (1621–1653): And Burwell Virginia Tidewater Plantation Mansions*. Berryville, Va.: Virginia Book Company, 1994.

Brown, Stuart E., Jr., Lorraine F. Myers, and Eileen M. Chappel. *Biographical and Genealogical Record of Persons Buried at Old Chapel*. Vol. 2 of *Annals of Clarke County, Virginia*, edited by Stuart E. Brown Jr. Berryville, Va.: Virginia Book Company, 1983.

Bruce, John Goodall, comp. *The Bruce Family: Descending from George Bruce, 1650–1715*. Parsons, Va.: McClain Printing Company, 1977.

Bruce, William Cabell. *Recollections*. Baltimore: King Bros., 1936.

Bullard, CeCe. *Goochland, Yesterday and Today: A Pictorial History*. Virginia Beach, Va.: Donning Company, 1994.

Carmichael, Peter S. "Cedar Creek, Virginia." In *Encyclopedia of the Confederacy*, vol. 1, edited by Richard N. Current, 271–72. New York: Simon & Schuster, 1993.

———. *Lee's Young Artillerist: William R. J. Pegram*. Charlottesville: University Press of Virginia, 1995.

Carter, William R. *Sabres, Saddles, and Spurs*. Edited by Walbrook D. Swank. Shippensburg, Pa.: Burd Street Press, 1998.

Chisholm, Claudia Anderson, and Ellen Gray Lillie. *Old Home Places of Louisa County*. Louisa, Va.: Louisa County Historical Society, 1979.

Clarke, Peyton Neale. *Old King William Homes and Families: An Account of Some of the Old Homesteads and Families of King William County, Virginia, from Its Earliest Settlement*. Louisville, Ky.: J. P. Morton and Company, 1897.

"Col. Thomas H. Carter, C.S.A." *Proceedings of the Clarke County Historical Association* 3 (1943): 40–42.

Collins, Darrell L. *Major General Robert E. Rodes of the Army of Northern Virginia: A Biography*. New York: Savas Beatie, 2008.

Colvin, Steven A. *On Deep Water*. Verona, Va.: McClure Print Company, 1983.

Cooper, William J., Jr. *Jefferson Davis, American*. New York: Random House, 2000.

Couper, William. *One Hundred Years at V.M.I.* 4 vols. Richmond, Va.: Garrett and Massie, 1939.

Crute, Joseph H. *Units of the Confederate States Army*. Midlothian, Va.: Derwent Books, 1987.

Dabney, Virginius. *Mr. Jefferson's University: A History*. Charlottesville: University Press of Virginia, 1981.

Davis, Richard B. "John Syng Dorsey Cullen." In *Dictionary of Virginia Biography*, vol. 3, edited by Sara B. Bearss and others, 595–96. Richmond: Library of Virginia, 2006.

Davis, Virginia Lee Hutcheson. "Mangohick Church, c. 1730, King William County." *Tidewater Virginia Families: A Magazine of History and Genealogy* 10 (2002): 207–8.

Denson, C. B. "William Henry Chase Whiting, Major-General C.S. Army." *Southern Historical Society Papers* 26 (1898): 129–81.

Dorman, John Frederick, comp. *Claiborne of Virginia: Descendants of Colonel William Claiborne, the First Eight Generations*. Baltimore: Gateway Press, 1995.

Dozier, Graham T. "Stapleton Crutchfield." In *Dictionary of Virginia Biography*, vol. 3, edited by Sara B. Bearss and others, 593–94. Richmond: Library of Virginia, 2006.

Driver, Robert J. *1st Virginia Cavalry*. Lynchburg, Va.: H. E. Howard, 1991.

Eckert, Ralph Lowell. *John Brown Gordon: Soldier, Southerner, American*. Baton Rouge: Louisiana State University Press, 1989.

Edmunds, John B., Jr. "Francis Wilkinson Pickens." In *American National Biography*, vol. 17, edited by John A. Garraty and Mark C. Carnes, 470–72. New York: Oxford University Press, 1999.

Eicher, John H., and David J. Eicher. *Civil War High Commands*. Stanford, Calif.: Stanford University Press, 2001.

Evans, Emory G. "John Carter." In *Dictionary of Virginia Biography*, vol. 3, edited by Sara B. Bearss and others, 73–75. Richmond: Library of Virginia, 2006.

Fall, Ralph Emmett. *People, Postoffices, and Communities in Caroline County, Virginia, 1727–1969*. Roswell, Ga.: W. H. Wolfe Associates, 1989.

Fleet, Benjamin Robert. *Green Mount; a Virginia Plantation Family during the Civil War: Being the Journal of Benjamin Robert Fleet and Letters of His Family*. Edited by Betsy Fleet and John D. P. Fuller. Lexington: University of Kentucky Press, 1962.

Foster, Gaines M. *Ghosts of the Confederacy: Defeat, the Lost Cause, and the Emergence of the New South*. New York: Oxford University Press, 1987.

Freeman, Douglas Southall. *Lee's Lieutenants: A Study in Command*. 3 vols. New York: Charles Scribner's Sons, 1942–44.

———. *R. E. Lee: A Biography*. 4 vols. New York: Charles Scribner's Sons, 1934–35.

Frye, Dennis E. "Shenandoah Valley Campaign of Sheridan." In *Encyclopedia of the Confederacy*, vol. 3, edited by Richard N. Current, 1417–19. New York: Simon & Schuster, 1993.

Gallagher, Gary W. "Robert E. Lee." In *Encyclopedia of the American Civil War: A Political, Social, and Military History*, edited by David S. Heidler and Jeanne T. Heidler, 1152–63. New York: W. W. Norton & Company, 2000.

———. *Stephen Dodson Ramseur: Lee's Gallant General*. Chapel Hill: University of North Carolina Press, 1985.

Gordon, Armistead Churchill, Jr. "Muscoe Russell Hunter Garnett." In *Dictionary of American Biography*, vol. 7, edited by Dumas Malone, 158. New York: Charles Scribner's Sons, 1946.

Gottfried, Bradley M. *The Artillery of Gettysburg*. Nashville, Tenn.: Cumberland House Publishing, 2008.

Graham, Martin F., and George F. Skoch. *Mine Run: A Campaign of Lost Opportunities, October 21, 1863–May 1, 1864*. Lynchburg, Va.: H. E. Howard, 1987.

Green, Bryan Clark, Calder Loth, and William M. S. Rasmussen. *Lost Virginia: Vanished Architecture of the Old Dominion*. Charlottesville, Va.: Howell Press, 2001.

Hackley, Woodford B. *Faces on the Wall: Brief Sketches of the Men and Women Whose Portraits and Busts Were on the Campus of the University of Richmond in 1955 . . .* Richmond: Virginia Baptist Historical Society, 1972.

Hagemann, James. *The Heritage of Virginia: The Story of Place Names in the Old Dominion*. Norfolk, Va.: Donning, 1986.

Hall, Virginius Cornick, Jr., comp. *Portraits in the Collection of the Virginia Historical Society*. Charlottesville: University Press of Virginia, 1981. Published for the Virginia Historical Society.

Hamilton, Daniel W. "Confederate Sequestration Act." *Civil War History* 52 (2006): 373–408.

Hannings, Bud. *Forts of the United States: An Historical Dictionary, 16th through 19th Centuries*. Jefferson, N.C.: McFarland & Company, 2006.

Hardy, Stella Pickett. *Colonial Families of the Southern States of America: A History and Genealogy of Colonial Families Who Settled in the Colonies prior to the Revolution*. New York: Tobias A. Wright, 1911.

Harrison, Noel G. *Fredericksburg Civil War Sites, April 1861–November 1862*. 2 vols. Lynchburg, Va.: H. E. Howard, 1995.

Hassler, William Woods. *Colonel John Pelham: Lee's Boy Artillerist*. Chapel Hill: University of North Carolina Press, 1960.

Hayden, Horace Edwin. *Virginia Genealogies: A Genealogy of the Glassell Family of Scotland and Virginia; also of the Families of Ball, Brown, Bryan, Conway, Daniel, Ewell, Holladay, Lewis, Littlepage, Moncure, Peyton, Robinson, Scott, Taylor, Wallace, and Others of Virginia and Maryland*. Wilkes-Barre, Pa.: E. B. Young, 1891.

Heinemann, Ronald L., John G. Kolp, Anthony S. Parent Jr., and William G. Shade. *Old Dominion, New Commonwealth: A History of Virginia, 1607–2007*. Charlottesville: University of Virginia Press, 2007.

Hennessy, John J. *Return to Bull Run: The Campaign and Battle of Second Manassas*. New York: Simon & Schuster, 1992.

Hewitt, Lawrence L. "William Henry Chase Whiting." In *The Confederate General*, vol. 6, edited by William C. Davis, 132–33. Harrisburg, Pa.: National Historical Society, 1991.

"Historical and Genealogical Notes and Queries." *Virginia Magazine of History and Biography* 8 (1901): 322–35.

History of Virginia. 6 vols. Chicago: American Historical Society, 1924.

Horner, Frederick. *The History of the Blair, Banister, and Braxton Families before and after the Revolution with a Brief Sketch of Their Descendants*. Philadelphia: J. B. Lippincott, 1898.

Howe, Daniel Walker. *What Hath God Wrought: The Transformation of America, 1815–1848*. New York: Oxford University Press, 2007.

Hudson, Henry. "Southern Railway and Steamship Association." *Quarterly Journal of Economics* 5 (1890): 70–94.

Hughes, Charles Randolph. *Old Chapel: Clarke County, Virginia*. Berryville, Va.: Blue Ridge Press, 1906.

Hurst, Patricia J. *Soldiers, Stories, Sites, and Fights, Orange County, Virginia, 1861–1865, and the Aftermath*. Rapidan, Va.: P. J. Hurst, 1998.

Johnson, John Lipscomb. *The University Memorial: Biographical Sketches of Alumni of the University of Virginia Who Fell in the Confederate War*. Baltimore: Turnbull Brothers, 1871.

Jones, J. William. *Christ in Camp; or, Religion in Lee's Army*. Richmond, Va.: B. F. Johnson & Co., 1887.

———, comp. *Army of Northern Virginia Memorial Volume*. Richmond, Va.: J. W. Randolph & English, 1880.

Jones, Terry L. *Lee's Tigers: The Louisiana Infantry in the Army of Northern Virginia*. Baton Rouge: Louisiana State University Press, 1987.

Kilbride, Daniel. "Southern Medical Students in Philadelphia, 1800–1861: Science and Sociability in the Republic of Medicine." *Journal of Southern History* 4 (1999): 697–732.

Krick, Robert E. L. *Staff Officers in Gray: A Biographical Register of the Staff Officers of the Army of Northern Virginia*. Chapel Hill: University of North Carolina Press, 2003.

Krick, Robert K. *Civil War Weather in Virginia*. Tuscaloosa: University of Alabama Press, 2007.

———. *Fredericksburg Artillery*. Lynchburg, Va.: H. E. Howard, 1986.

———. *Lee's Colonels: A Biographical Register of the Field Officers of the Army of Northern Virginia*. 5th ed. Wilmington, N.C.: Broadfoot Publishing Company, 2009.

———. "'We Have Never Suffered a Greater Loss Save in the Great Jackson': Was Robert E. Rodes the Army's Best Division Commander?" In *The Smoothbore Volley That Doomed the Confederacy: The Death of Stonewall Jackson and Other Chapters on the Army of Northern Virginia*, 117–43. Baton Rouge: Louisiana State University Press, 2002.

Laboda, Lawrence R. *From Selma to Appomattox: The History of the Jeff Davis Artillery*. New York: Oxford University Press, 1994.

Lancaster, Robert A. *Historic Virginia Homes and Churches*. Philadelphia: J. B. Lippincott Company, 1915.

Lane, Martin S. "Carter Moore Braxton." In *Dictionary of Virginia Biography*, vol. 2, edited by Sara B. Bearss and others, 201–2. Richmond: Library of Virginia, 2001.

Lattimore, Ralston B. *Fort Pulaski National Monument*. Washington, D.C.: National Park Service, 1954.

Lee, Edmund Jennings. *Lee of Virginia, 1642–1892: Biographical and Genealogical Sketches of the Descendants of Colonel Richard Lee*. Philadelphia: Franklin Printing Company, 1895.

Leonard, Cynthia Miller, comp. *The General Assembly of Virginia, July 30, 1619–January 11, 1978: A Bicentennial Register of Members*. Richmond: Virginia State Library, 1978.

Link, J. Lester, comp. *Marriages of Jefferson County, West Virginia, 1801–1890*. Westminster, Md.: Heritage Books, 2007.

Long, E. B. *The Civil War Day by Day: An Almanac, 1861–1865*. Garden City, N.Y.: Doubleday & Company, 1971.

Loth, Calder, ed. *Virginia Landmarks Register*. 4th ed. Charlottesville: University Press of Virginia, 1999. Published for the Virginia Department of Historic Resources.

Louse, Mark A. "West Virginia." In *Encyclopedia of the American Civil War: A Political, Social, and Military History*, edited by David S. Heidler and Jeanne T. Heidler, 2090–92. New York: W. W. Norton & Company, 2000.

Lund, Jennifer. "Conscription." In *Encyclopedia of the Confederacy*, vol. 1, edited by Richard N. Current, 396–99. New York: Simon & Schuster, 1993.

Macaluso, Gregory J. *Morris, Orange, and King William Artillery*. Lynchburg, Va.: H. E. Howard, 1991.

MacDonald, Rose M. E. *Clarke County, a Daughter of Frederick: A History of Early Families and Homes*. Berryville, Va.: Blue Ridge Press, 1943.

Magill, John. *The Beverley Family of Virginia: Descendants of Major Robert Beverley (1641–1687) and Allied Families*. Columbia, S.C.: R. L. Bryan Company, 1956.

Martin, Eda Carter Williams. *The Remarkable Women of Pampatike: Stories in Black and White*. Williamsburg, Va.: Eda Carter Williams Martin, 2006.

Maxwell, W. J., comp. *General Alumni Catalogue of the University of Pennsylvania*. [Philadelphia]: General Alumni Association of the University of Pennsylvania, 1922.

McMurry, Richard M. *Virginia Military Institute Alumni in the Civil War: In Bello Praesidium*. Lynchburg, Va.: H. E. Howard, 1999.

Melton, Maurice. "Charleston, S.C., Du Pont's attack on." In *Historical Times Illustrated Encyclopedia of the Civil War*, edited by Patricia L. Faust, 131. New York: Harper & Row, 1986.

Moncure, T. M., Jr. "The Destruction of Snowden." *Newsletter of Historic Stafford County* 11 (January 1991): 1–2.

Moore, Robert H., II. *Miscellaneous Disbanded Virginia Light Artillery*. Lynchburg, Va.: H. E. Howard, 1997.

Morris, Thomas R. *Virginia's Lieutenant Governors: The Office and the Person*. Charlottesville: Governmental and Administrative Research Division, University of Virginia, 1970.

Morton, Richard L. "John Johns." In *Dictionary of American Biography*, vol. 10, edited by Dumas Malone, 75–76. New York: Charles Scribner's Sons, 1946.

Murfin, James V. *The Gleam of Bayonets: The Battle of Antietam and Robert E. Lee's Maryland Campaign, September 1862*. 1965; reprint, Baton Rouge: Louisiana State University Press, 1982.

Musick, Michael P. *6th Virginia Cavalry*. Lynchburg, Va.: H. E. Howard, 1990.

Nevins, Allan. *The War for the Union*. 4 vols. New York: Charles Scribner's Sons, 1959–1971.

Nitzsche, George E. *University of Pennsylvania: Its History, Traditions, Buildings, and Memorials*. Philadelphia: International Printing Company, 1918.

Norfleet, Fillmore. *Saint-Mémin in Virginia: Portraits and Biographies*. Richmond, Va.: Dietz Press, 1942.

Norford, William L. *Marriages of Albemarle County and Charlottesville, Virginia, 1781–1929*. Charlottesville, Va., 1956.

Norris, Walter Biscoe, Jr., ed. *Westmoreland County, Virginia, 1653–1983*. Montross, Va.: Westmoreland County Board of Supervisors, 1983.

Old Homes of Hanover County. Hanover, Va.: Hanover County Historical Society, 1983.

Page, Richard Channing Moore. *Genealogy of the Page Family in Virginia: Also a Condensed Account of the Nelson, Walker, Pendleton, and Randolph Families*. 2nd ed. New York: Press of the Publishers' Printing Company, 1893.

Page, Thomas Nelson. "Mrs. Susan Roy Carter." *University of Virginia Magazine* 46 (1903): 274–77.

Parks, Joseph Howard. *General Edmund Kirby Smith, C.S.A.* Baton Rouge: Louisiana State University Press, 1954.

Parrish, T. Michael, and Robert M. Willingham Jr. *Confederate Imprints:*

A Bibliography of Southern Publications from Secession to Surrender. Austin, Tex.:
    Jenkins Publishing; Katonah, N.Y.: G. A. Foster, 1987.

Pecquet du Bellet, Louise. *Some Prominent Virginia Families.* Lynchburg, Va.: J. P.
    Bell Company, 1907.

Pfanz, Donald C. *Richard S. Ewell: A Soldier's Life.* Chapel Hill: University of North
    Carolina Press, 1998.

Pitts, Charles Frank. *Chaplains in Gray: The Confederate Chaplains' Story.* Nashville,
    Tenn.: Broadman Press, 1957.

Pratt, Dorothy, and Richard Pratt. *A Guide to Early American Homes: South.* New
    York: McGraw-Hill, 1956.

Pryor, Elizabeth Brown. *Reading the Man: A Portrait of Robert E. Lee through His
    Private Letters.* New York: Viking Press, 2007.

Quitt, Martin H. "John Carter." In *Dictionary of Virginia Biography*, vol. 3, edited
    by Sara B. Bearss and others, 72–73. Richmond: Library of Virginia, 2006.

Rable, George C. *Fredericksburg! Fredericksburg!* Chapel Hill: University of North
    Carolina Press, 2002.

Rasmussen, William M. S. *The Portent: John Brown's Raid in American Memory.*
    Richmond: Virginia Historical Society, 2009.

Register of Former Cadets: Memorial Edition. Lexington, Va.: Virginia Military
    Institute, 1957.

Rhea, Gordon C. *Battles for Spotsylvania Court House and the Road to Yellow Tavern,
    May 7–12, 1864.* Baton Rouge: Louisiana State University Press, 1997.

Richey, Homer, ed. *Memorial History of the John Bowie Strange Camp, United
    Confederate Veterans, Including Some Account of Others Who Served in the
    Confederate Armies from Albemarle County . . .* Charlottesville, Va.: Press of the
    Michie Company, 1920.

Robertson, James I., Jr. *Stonewall Jackson: The Man, the Soldier, the Legend.* New
    York: Macmillan Publishing, 1997.

Sale, Marian Marsh. "Disaster at the Spotswood." *Virginia Cavalcade* 12 (Autumn
    1962): 13–19.

Salmon, John S. *The Official Virginia Civil War Battlefield Guide.* Mechanicsburg,
    Pa.: Stackpole Books, 2001.

Schlup, Leonard. "James Alexander Seddon." In *American National Biography*,
    vol. 19, edited by John A. Garraty and Mark C. Carnes, 575–77. New York:
    Oxford University Press, 1999.

Sears, Stephen W. *Landscape Turned Red: The Battle of Antietam.* New York:
    Ticknor & Fields, 1983.

Sommers, Richard J. "William MacRae." In *The Confederate General*, vol. 4, edited
    by William C. Davis, 136–37. Harrisburg, Pa.: National Historical Society, 1991.

Stiles, Kenneth. *4th Virginia Cavalry.* Lynchburg, Va.: H. E. Howard, 1985.

Strider, Robert Edward Lee. *The Life and Work of George William Peterkin.*
    Philadelphia: G. W. Jacobs & Co., 1929.

Taylor, George Braxton. *Virginia Baptist Ministers, 6th Series, 1914–1934.*
    Lynchburg, Va.: J. P. Bell Company, 1935.

Tillson, Albert H., Jr. "Charles Carter." In *Dictionary of Virginia Biography*, vol. 3, edited by Sara B. Bearss and others, 57–59. Richmond: Library of Virginia, 2006.

Tyler, Lyon Gardiner, ed. *Encyclopedia of Virginia Biography*. 5 vols. New York: Lewis Historical Publishing Company, 1915.

———, ed. *Men of Mark in Virginia, Ideals of American Life: A Collection of Biographies of the Leading Men in the State*. 5 vols. Washington, D.C.: Men of Mark Publishing Company, 1906–9.

Virginia Writer's Project. *Jefferson's Albemarle: A Guide to Albemarle County and the City of Charlottesville, Virginia*. Charlottesville, Va.: Jarman's Incorporated, 1941.

Wallace, Lee A., Jr. *1st Virginia Infantry*. Lynchburg, Va.: H. E. Howard, 1984.

———. *A Guide to Virginia Military Organizations, 1861–1865*. Revised 2nd ed. Lynchburg, Va.: H. E. Howard, 1986.

———. *Richmond Howitzers*. Lynchburg, Va.: H. E. Howard, 1993.

———. *3rd Virginia Infantry*. Lynchburg, Va.: H. E. Howard, 1986.

Wallenstein, Peter. *Cradle of America: Four Centuries of Virginia History*. Lawrence: University Press of Kansas, 2007.

Warner, Ezra J. *Generals in Blue: Lives of the Union Commanders*. Baton Rouge: Louisiana State University Press, 1964.

———. *Generals in Gray: Lives of the Confederate Commanders*. Baton Rouge: Louisiana State University Press, 1959.

Welsh, Jack D. *Medical Histories of Confederate Generals*. Kent, Ohio: Kent State University Press, 1995.

Wert, Jeffry D. "Beverley Holcombe Robinson." In *The Confederate General*, vol. 5, edited by William C. Davis, 96–99. Harrisburg, Pa.: National Historical Society, 1991.

———. *Cavalryman of the Lost Cause: A Biography of J. E. B. Stuart*. New York: Simon & Schuster, 2008.

———. "The Confederate Belle." *Civil War Times Illustrated*, August 1976, 20–27.

———. "Crater, Battle of the (Petersburg, Va.)" In *Historical Times Illustrated Encyclopedia of the Civil War*, edited by Patricia L. Faust, 190. New York: Harper & Row, 1986.

———. *From Winchester to Cedar Creek: The Shenandoah Valley Campaign of 1864*. Carlisle, Pa.: South Mountain Press, 1987.

———. *General James Longstreet: The Confederacy's Most Controversial Soldier— A Biography*. New York: Simon & Schuster, 1993.

Whitley, William Bland. "John Warwick Daniel." In *Dictionary of Virginia Biography*, vol. 3, edited by Sara B. Bearss and others, 681–85. Richmond: Library of Virginia, 2006.

Williams, Helen Dearborn Tyler, and Bernice Roy Johnson, comps. *Roy Genealogy*. Richmond, Va., 1943.

Wingfield, Edward Maria, comp. *A History of Caroline County, Virginia: From Its Formation in 1727 to 1924*. Richmond, Va.: Trevvet Christian, 1924.

Wise, Jennings Cropper. *Col. John Wise of England and Virginia (1617–1695): His Ancestors and Descendants*. Richmond, Va.: Bell Books and Stationary Company, 1918.

———. *The Long Arm of Lee; or, The History of the Artillery of the Army of Northern Virginia.* 2 vols. Lynchburg, Va.: J. P. Bell, 1915.

———. *The Military History of the Virginia Military Institute from 1839 to 1865.* Lynchburg, Va.: J. P. Bell Company, 1915.

Wise, John Sergeant. *Diomed: The Life, Travels, and Observations of a Dog.* Boston: Lamson, Wolffe, and Company, 1897.

Woods, Edgar. *Albemarle County in Virginia; Giving Some Account of What It Was by Nature, of What It Was Made by Man, and of Some of the Men Who Made It.* Charlottesville, Va.: The Michie Company, 1901.

Wright, Raleigh Lewis. *Artists in Virginia before 1900: An Annotated Checklist.* Charlottesville: University Press of Virginia, 1983.

ONLINE RESOURCES

Antietam National Battlefield (http://www.nps.gov/anti/)

Biographical Dictionary of the U.S. Congress (http://bioguide.congress.gov/)

Centers for Disease Control and Prevention (http://www.cdc.gov/)

Clemson University (http://www.clemson.edu/)

The Confederate War Department (http://www.csawardept.com/history/Cabinet/)

Hollywood Cemetery (http://www.webcemeteries.com/Hollywood)

Virginia Military Institute Archives Online (www.vmi.edu/archives/home)

INDEX

Bracketed text signifies probable identifications.

Bruce, Sarah Alexander Seddon ("Aunt
  Sally"), 19, 27, 76, 93, 101, 107, 135,
  139n, 248n
Buckner, Dr., 134
Buckner, Simon Bolivar, 105n
Buell, Don Carlos, 111–12
Bull Run, First Battle of, 25, 54, 105;
  Confederate failure to advance fol-
  lowing, 3, 28, 34–35
Bull Run, Second Battle of, 128, 136
"Burning, The" 239
Burnside, Ambrose Everett, 86, 88, 129,
  143n; and Army of the Potomac com-
  mand, 155, 157, 159, 175n
Burwell, George, 39
Burwell, Isabella Dixon, 39
Burwell, Nathaniel, 42
Burwell, Susy, 15
Butler, Benjamin, 248n
Byrd, Alfred, 269
Byrd, Francis Otway, 38n

Cabell, Henry Coalter, 225, 229
Cabell, Mary Walker "Polly" Carter, 106
Calhoun, John C., 29
Cape Hatteras, 50
Carlisle, Pa., 197
Carraway, Mr. [George], 185, 187
Carrington, 124
Carrington, James McDowell, 245
Carroll, Lu, 29
Carter, Agnes Atkinson Mayo
  (daughter-in-law), 311n
Carter, Alfred Ball, 112
Carter, Anne Willing (daughter), 164,
  189, 192, 206–7, 213, 221, 266, 290–91;
  birth of, 171n; wedding of, 311n
Carter, Anne Willing Page (step-
  mother), 38, 44, 63n, 99, 112, 149, 220,
  227, 251, 269; in Baltimore, 271, 273–
  74; burial plot, 311n; Carter's letter to,
  152–53; marriage, 10
Carter, Ann Hill (great-aunt), 8a
Carter, Charles, 106
Carter, Charles (great-grandfather),
  8, 114
Carter, Charles Shirley (half brother),
  15, 22, 133, 282; on half brother's

wound, 239, 255; and marriage, 148,
  189, 191
Carter, Hill (uncle), 112
Carter, James (son), 311n
Carter, John (great-great-grandfather), 8
Carter, John (great-great-great-great-
  grandfather), 7
Carter, John Hill, 106
Carter, Julian M. (brother), 10n, 112,
  311n; in artillery company, 30, 38, 92,
  99, 107, 119; death of, 128, 133
Carter, Juliet (daughter), 31, 68, 87, 246,
  310; birth of, 20; health of, 91, 93;
  marriage, 311n
Carter, Juliet Muse Gaines (mother), 7,
  9, 10, 311n
Carter, Lucy (half sister). See Renshaw,
  Lucy Carter
Carter, Lucy Randolph Page (sister-in-
  law). See Page, Lucy Randolph
Carter, Mary (great-aunt), 24n
Carter, Mary Nelson (sister), 10n
Carter, Mittie, 223–24
Carter, Mrs. Alfred, 224
Carter, Pauline Davis (sister-in-law),
  38, 87
Carter, Richard Welby, 263
Carter, Robert (brother), 10n, 34, 87, 89,
  178–79
Carter, Robert (grandfather), 8–9, 13,
  58n
Carter, Roberta Atkinson (daughter-in-
  law), 311n
Carter, Robert "King" (great-great-
  great-grandfather), 7–8, 178n
Carter, Rosa Evelyn (half sister), 15, 133,
  191, 227, 251; fatal illness of, 268, 271,
  288
Carter, Sarah Ludlow (great-great-
  great-great-grandmother), 7
Carter, Spencer Leslie (son), 301, 311n
Carter, Susan Roy (wife): biographical
  information, 18; daguerreotype of,
  76–77, 80, 82; death of, 5, 310; gives
  birth, 19–20, 164, 301; husband's
  relationship with, 3–4; husband's
  visit with, 250, 293; illnesses of, 154,
  265–66; management of farm by, 297;

marriage, 17; moves to Richmond, Atlanta, and Washington, D.C., by, 306–7; and Pampatike school, 300–301; visits to husband by, 103–4, 113–14, 208, 210, 277–79, 289–91; visits to Richmond by, 115, 214

Carter, Thomas Henry

—biography: birth, 7, 10; children's births, 18–20, 164, 301; death and funeral, 310–11; as doctor, 14–16; enlistment in Confederate army, 21; growing up at Pampatike, 10; marriage, 17; at medical school, 13–14; middle name, 2, 7n; and Pampatike school, 300–301; as plantation manager, 4, 16–17, 19–20; primary schooling, 10–11; as railroad commissioner, 305–6; as University of Virginia proctor and superintendent, 307–10; at Virginia Military Institute, 11–13; work for Southern Railway and Steamship Association, 306–7

—camp life: clothing, 44–45, 57, 107, 143, 168, 172, 208, 213, 251, 260, 267, 273, 275, 283; efforts to obtain furloughs, 84–85, 87, 89, 93, 97, 103, 122, 133, 170, 178, 225, 286–87, 289, 307–8; food, 29–30, 76, 125, 183, 188, 192, 221, 250; furlough granted, 281, 293; mess of, 30, 44, 147, 166, 168, 172–73, 274; slaves as servants, 4, 23, 33, 35, 44, 48, 59, 130, 149, 175, 185, 188, 220, 272, 279, 281–83, 289; weather, 47, 49–50, 97, 100, 168, 175, 187, 222, 226; wife's visits, 250, 293

—health: battle wounds, 129, 239, 254; illness concerns, 22–23, 51, 59, 64, 116, 123, 246. *See also* Disease

— personality and tastes: appearance, 22; personality, 2–3; religion, 100; sense of discipline, 4

—promotions and commands: to brigadier general (recommended), 233–34; to colonel, 234; as D. H. Hill's chief of artillery, 129, 153; of 1st Virginia Battalion, 246; invitation to North Carolina command, 1, 4, 127n, 164, 180–82, 184; of King William Artillery, 2,

21–22, 79, 86, 123; to lieutenant colonel, 163–64, 189–90, 192; to major, 130, 154n, 160; news concerning, 97, 101, 225, 292; of 2nd Corps artillery, 234, 237, 286, 292–93

Carter, Thomas Nelson (father), 7, 31, 52, 63–64, 112, 133, 227, 271; asks Thomas to manage Pampatike, 16; biographical information, 9–10; horses of, 38, 183; Louisiana land purchase by, 19, 147n

Carter, Thomas Nelson (son), 59, 125–26, 297, 300, 310; birth of, 19; illness of, 122–24

Carter, Welby, 263, 265

Carter, William, 9

Carter, William Pleasants Page (half brother), 19, 54, 68, 70, 82, 113, 139, 147n, 168, 179, 188, 220, 231; as battery commander, 153, 174n, 202n, 207, 209; in battles, 162, 236; and Lucy Page engagement, 142, 183, 189, 191; in officer elections, 123, 125; poetry by, 98; as prisoner of war, 243–44, 246, 254, 271, 287; Thomas Henry Carter and, 57, 112, 172–73, 214

Carter, William Richard, 217n

Carter, William Roy (son), 18, 311n

Cary, Hetty, 189, 231

Cedar Creek, Battle of, 216, 239–41, 255–60, 302–3; criticism of Confederate conduct at, 3–4, 256, 258–59, 261, 264

Centreville, Va., 64–65, 102, 194

Chaffin's Bluff, 238, 293

Chambersburg, Pa., 165, 211–12, 249

Chancellorsville, Battle of, 2, 164–65

Charles (slave), 23

Charleston, S.C., 182, 187–88

Charles Town, Va., 145, 155

Charles XII (Sweden), 277

Charlottesville, Va., 88, 133, 201, 205, 222–23, 269; Union army in, 292

Chenault, Mr., 77, 80, 99

Chericoke, 95

Chesterfield Depot, 181

Chickahominy River, 121, 125, 237

Chickamauga, Battle of, 203, 211

Chilton, Robert Hall, 181, 188
Christian, Richard H., 216–17
Claiborne, Mrs. [Mary Anna McGuire Claiborne], 23
Clarke, Martha, 23
Clarke's Mountain, 201, 204
Clemson, Anna Maria Calhoun, 29
Clothing, 44–45, 57, 107, 143, 168, 172, 208, 213, 251, 260, 267, 273, 275, 283
Cobham, Va., 228
Cocke, Edward J., 30
Cocke, Mrs., 150
Cocke, Philip St. George, 84
Coffman, 186
Cold Harbor, Battle of, 237
Coleman, Charles Lloyd, 190, 245
Coleman, Lewis Minor, 184
Coles Rutherfoord, Helen, 176
Colquit, Alfred Holt, 156
Colston, Raleigh E., 12
Confederacy: Carter apprehensions about, 83, 87, 98, 175; and Confederate army leadership, 61n, 90–91, 114; currency, stocks, and bonds of, 113, 137, 172, 185, 187, 192, 195–96, 225–26, 243, 278–79; demagoguery in, 69, 228, 259; draft and militia system in, 4, 79–81, 83, 85, 120n, 121, 139, 284; popular attitudes in, 85, 105, 272, 279, 284; and secession, 20; Sequestration Act of, 84; and utilization of black troops, 272–73, 278–79, 282; war fever in, 20–21
Confederate army: Carter's criticisms of leadership in, 3–4, 28, 34–35, 53–54, 73, 185, 244, 253, 256, 258–59, 261, 264, 274; casualties, 40, 41n, 42, 54n, 117, 124, 127, 129, 141, 162, 165, 198, 199n, 218, 222n, 237, 248, 258n, 274; cavalry of, 102, 167, 253–54, 263, 265, 267–68, 274, 290; court-martials in, 92, 100, 145n, 146–47, 151, 175n, 216n, 263, 265; Davis and, 61n, 90–91, 114; and defense of forts, 125; deserters and stragglers from, 130, 137, 139, 142, 253–54, 278; and discipline, 112, 220, 254, 259, 263, 265; election of officers in, 86, 112–13, 121, 123, 125, 180, 259;

flanking movements by, 131, 146–47, 255; furloughs in, 81, 92, 99, 102–3, 225, 283; hiring of substitutes in, 131, 179; morale of, 94, 116, 254; northern invasions by, 128, 139, 165–66, 195–97; and pillaging, 112, 139, 165–66, 195–96, 249; recruitment to, 21, 97, 102, 211, 263; reenlistments, 83, 87, 92, 95, 97, 99, 103, 123; reinforcements, 85–86, 206, 246–47; reorganizations of, 60–61, 91, 94–98, 100–101, 163, 165, 170–71, 182, 225; troop strength, 35, 53, 58, 137, 145–46, 207, 267–68; twelve-month volunteer enlistment period in, 79, 83, 85, 87, 94, 97–98, 112; veteran reunions of, 303–4; Virginia positioning of, 40–41, 58, 85–86, 107, 111, 119–21, 127, 129–30, 170, 197–99, 240. See also Battles and skirmishes
Confederate Veteran, 304
Conner, James, 264n
Conrad, Henry Tucker, 54
Conrad, Holmes Addison, 54
Conscription, 4, 85, 119–21, 139, 284
Cooke, John Esten, 55n
Cooper, Samuel, 3, 28
Corcoran, Dennis, 76n
Corley, James Lawrence, 212
Cornday, Dr., 23
Court-martials, 100, 145n, 175n, 216n, 263, 265; of Courtney, 146, 147, 151; Davis and, 216n, 263n, 265n; of Montgomery, 92, 216n
Courtney, Alfred Ranson, 146–47, 151
Crater, Battle of the, 248n
Crenshaw & Co., 70
Crittenden, George Bibb, 98
Cropper, Thomas T., 130n
Croreton, V., 206
Croxton, William Virginius, 72
Crump, Charles Alfred, 124
Crutchfield, Stapleton, 163–64, 180, 182, 190, 225
Cullen, John Syng Dorsey, 26, 58
Culpeper Court House, 210, 216, 219
Cumberland, Md., 274
Cumberland Gap, 150

in Shenandoah Valley, 58, 109, 111, 119n, 129, 155; "Stonewall" nickname of, 40; wife of, 158
Jackson, William Lowther, 253
James (slave), 33, 35, 48, 59, 130, 149, 185, 188, 220, 272, 279, 282–83, 289
James River, 85, 121, 130, 224, 237–38
Johns, John, 242
Johnson, Bradley Tyler, 253
Johnson, Colonel, 146
Johnson, Edward "Old Allegheny," 226, 235, 244, 246
Johnston, Albert Sidney, 98, 109, 111; Carter's assessment of, 109, 112
Johnston, Joseph Eggleston, 36, 56, 66, 73, 92, 108–9, 125, 272; and Carter, 26, 101; Carter's assessment of, 28, 53, 109; and Davis, 90, 114; in North Carolina, 293; on recruitment, 102; in Tennessee, 105, 230, 233–34; Virginia forces commanded by, 60–61, 119
Jones, David Rumph, 29, 142–43
Jones, Hilary Pollard, 153–55, 214
Jones, James Alfred, 231
Jones, John Marshall, 244
Jones, Sarah Rebecca Taylor, 29
Jordan, Thomas, 66; Carter's assessment of, 3, 93

Kearny, Philip, 175
Kelley, Benjamin Franklin, 58
Kelly's Ford, Battle of, 198, 218, 221
Kemper, Delaware, 65
Kernstown, Battle of, 111n
Kershaw, Joseph, 237, 239, 256
Key, Philip Barton, 66
Kilpatrick, Hugh Judson, 292
King, Festus, 48n, 180n, 202
King, Georgia P., 89n
King, James Hill, 48–49, 71
King, John Floyd, 252
King, Rosena, 50
King, Rufus, 121n
Kingsley, Charles, 248n
King William Artillery: in battle, 127, 128–30, 140–41, 147, 160–62, 223n; Beauregard review of, 65–66; Carter's leadership of, 2, 21–22, 79, 86, 123; de-

serters from, 130; disease in, 68, 71, 98, 101, 133; election of officers in, 86, 123, 125, 180; encampments of, 25, 43, 57, 74, 77–78, 85, 115–16, 127–29, 148–49; foraging expeditions of, 31–32, 150; fortifications of, 46, 119; furloughs in, 81, 92, 94, 97, 99; Hill praise for, 127, 149; incidents and disputes in, 180, 202; marches and movements by, 85, 114, 129, 131n, 134, 155, 158–59; morale in, 116; organization of, 21–22; practice firing by, 60; reenlistments to, 83, 92, 95, 97, 99, 103; reinforcements to, 127, 129–30, 144; reorganizations of, 30n, 86, 123, 129; in Richmond, 114, 127–28, 130n; Rodes and, 25, 138; training and drilling of, 25, 98; troop strength of, 135, 148, 152; unit attachments of, 25, 28, 129, 152–53; William Pleasants Page Carter and, 153, 174n, 202n, 207, 209

Lacy, Beverley Tucker, 282
Lacy, James, 178
Lane, James Henry, 201n
Lawton, Alexander Robert, 161
Leach, Charles Hunton, 82
Leake, Walter Daniel, 144, 174
Lee, Agnes, 188
Lee, Evelyn Byrd Page, 42n
Lee, Fitzhugh, 251–52, 275, 293, 311n; in battles, 71, 157, 253, 294; on William Newton death, 212
Lee, George Washington Custis, 36n, 310
Lee, James Kendall, 41
Lee, John Mason, 75
Lee, Juliet Carter. See Carter, Juliet (daughter)
Lee, Mary Anna Randolph Custis (R. E. Lee's wife), 11n, 36n, 49n, 63n, 128, 133n
Lee, Mary Custis (R. E. Lee's daughter), 36–37n, 38, 75
Lee, Richard Henry, 42, 115, 217
Lee, Robert E., 23, 28, 134, 159, 163, 181, 214, 233, 247, 274; at Antietam, 142; Carter's assessment of, 3, 75, 110, 211,

Mayo, Peter Helms, 39, 251
McCall, George Archibald, 121n
McCausland, John, 249, 253, 267
McClellan, George Brinton, 46, 55, 58, 66, 74, 101, 120, 139; avoidance of attack by, 53, 84, 153; Carter's assessment of, 53, 97, 131, 155; estimate of Confederate strength by, 145–46n; movements by, 52, 134; relieved of command, 155, 175
McClellan, Henry Brainerd, 212
McCormick, Cyrus, 10
McDowell, Irvin, 121
McGowan, Samuel, 201n
McGuire, Hunter Holmes, 279
McKinney, Dr., 88
McLaw, Lafayette, 134, 140, 153, 200n
McLean, Wilmer, 295
Meade, George Gordon, 199, 211; anticipated advances by, 200, 205, 217, 220, 222, 226; and command of Army of the Potomac, 197, 227, 235
Measles, 89, 229, 231
Meaux, Cornelia Gaines, 134, 150, 191, 194, 252, 311n
Meriwether, Anne Willing Page "Nanny," 270, 272
Merrimack, USS, 121
Merritt, Wesley, 253n
Merriwether, Dr., 274
Mexican War, 12
Middletown, Va., 240, 267–68
Milford (guard), 182–83
Milford Depot, 163–64
Millwood, Va., 220, 225–26, 251
Milroy, Robert Huston, 165, 183
Mine Run, 199, 233
Minor, Billy, 222
Mississippi River expedition, 61–62, 69, 124, 188
Mitchell's Ford, 45
Monocacy River, 136, 138
Monroe's Crossroads, Battle of, 292n
Montgomery, Joseph T., 92, 216n
Montville, 135
Moore, Ann Butler, 8
Moore, James Donald, 89

Moore, Patrick Theodore, 27n
Moore, Samuel J. C., 302–3
Moorefield, Battle of, 251
Morale, Confederate, 85, 94, 105, 116, 254, 272
Morgan, Major [John Tyler], 32
Morrill Tariff, 62
Morris Artillery, 184n, 197, 198, 214n
Morris Island prisoner of war camp, 135n, 254, 271, 287–88
Morrison, Samuel Brown, 279–80
Morton's Ford, 199, 224, 228; Battle of, 199, 222, 249
Mule Shoe, 235–36, 244
Murfin, James, 146n

Nancy (slave), 233
Nat (slave), 33
Naval forces and warfare, 79, 188n; blockade, 88, 182; ironclads, 121, 175–76; James River battle, 237–38; Mississippi River expedition, 61–62, 69, 124, 188; Port Royal, 50, 52
Nelson, Benjamin Cary, 68
Nelson, Dr. [Mann Page], 141
Nelson, Hugh Mortimer, 42–43
Nelson, Mary, 8–9
Nelson, Thomas, 8–9
Nelson, Washington, 217
Nelson, William, 52, 118, 239, 269, 275, 293
New Kent County, Ky., 49n
Newman, William B., 30, 123
Newmarket, Battle of, 274
New Orleans, La., 93, 124
Newton, Mary, 68, 212
Newton, Mr. [Willoughby], 24
Newton, William Brockenbrough, 24n, 65, 84, 102–3, 119; Carter's assessments of, 42, 107, 212; Carter's relationship to, 29, 42, 99; death of, 212
Newtown, Va., 267–68
New Verdiersville, Va., 222
New York Tribune, 171
Nicholas, Lizzie [Elizabeth Byrd], 134
Nora, Cousin. *See* Macon, Nora Crena Brexton

North Carolina: Carter offered command in, 1, 4, 127n, 164, 180–82, 184; Confederate command in, 131, 163–64, 167–68; Union army campaign in, 85, 131, 171

Oakley, 38
O'Brien, Michael, 76n
Old Church, Va., 77
Orange Court House, Va., 113, 222, 231
Osborne, Nathaniel Montgomery, Jr., 179, 206, 287, 292–93
Ould, Robert, 291
Overland Campaign, 2, 235–37, 245–46, 249
Overton [William Overton Winston], 230
Owen, William M., 1–2

Pae, Mr., 81
Page, Ann Randolph, 11n
Page, Archie, 42, 54, 72
Page, Evelyn Byrd Nelson, 10
Page, Fez, 269, 271
Page, Jack, 118
Page, John E., 227, 249, 251, 288
Page, John Randolph, 116–17
Page, Lucy Randolph, 142, 183, 189, 191, 288
Page, Mary Frances, 55, 106
Page, Richard Channing Moore, 214, 234
Page, Robert Powel, 261–62, 274, 283, 293
Page, Thomas Jefferson, Jr., 218
Page, Thomas Nelson, 310
Page, William Byrd, 10, 38, 84, 93, 270, 272, 274, 288
Palham, Mr., 44
Palmer, William P., 172
Pampatike plantation, 8–10, 228–29; black farmworkers at, 298–300; Carter as farm manager at, 16–17, 19–20; Carter's letters referring to, 33, 43–44, 49, 55–57, 63, 67, 71–72, 99, 104–7, 124, 148, 154–55, 159–60, 200, 206, 217, 243, 248, 265, 275; Carter's youth at, 10; financial strains after war, 299; Robert E. Lee's visit to,

297–98; school established at, 300–301; slaves at, 4, 16, 19, 33, 43–44, 64, 99, 113, 118–19, 159; Union occupation of, 118, 125, 194, 251, 297
Pamunkey River, 8, 9, 33, 49n, 77n, 154, 237
Patterson, Robert, 24
Patton, John, 76
Pay, 33, 48
Payne, William, 29
Payne, William H. F., 251n
Peace sentiment, 88, 157, 171, 196
Pegram, John, 189, 211, 231, 276
Pegram, William Ransom Johnson, 162, 269
Pelham, John, 182
Pemberton, Lewis Howard, 141
Pendleton, Alexander Swift "Sandie," 193
Pendleton, Madison, 229, 232
Pendleton, Mrs., 251
Pendleton, William Barret, 232
Pendleton, William Nelson, 54, 85, 119, 143, 156, 207, 289; artillery reorganization by, 163, 225, 233; and Carter, 182, 225, 233–34, 238, 293
Pennsylvania Hospital, 14–15
Pensacola, Fla., 69
Percy, William Alexander, 261–62, 272, 274
Perrin, Abner Monroe, 202n
Perryville, Battle of, 150
Peterkin, Joshua, 242
Petersburg, Va., 130, 159, 225; Lee's army at, 184, 238, 241, 276; Union attacks on, 237–38, 248, 294
Peyton, Moses Green, 259, 266, 307
Peyton, Mrs., 205
Philadelphia, Pa., 13–15
Phillips, Nannie O. Meaux, 134, 252
Pickens, Francis Wilkinson, 159
Pickett, George Edward, 155, 181, 184, 194, 247
Pisgah Church, 207
Planter, 123
Pneumonia, 98, 122, 274
Poague, William T., 1–2
Pohick Church, 31

Pope, John, 128, 134n
Porter, Fitz John, 155, 175
Port Royal, S.C., 50, 52, 129
Powel. *See* Page, Robert Powel
Powell, Dr., 55
Prisoners of war, 217, 254, 271; exchanges of, 217, 265, 291; treatment and conditions of, 135n, 217, 271, 287–88
Pryor, Roger Atkinson, 119, 121

Railroads: Carter as commissioner of, 305–6; pilfering on, 68–69
Rains, Gabriel J., 147
Raleigh, N.C., 293
Ramseur, Stephen Dodson, 156, 204, 258–59, 261, 264
Randolph, Archibald Cary, 52, 275
Randolph, Bev, 293
Randolph, Charles, 224
Randolph, Charles Carter, 29n
Randolph, George Wythe, 160
Randolph, Nelson Randolph, 15, 220, 226
Randolph, Robert, 29, 245
Randolph, Robert Carter, 15n, 39, 72, 159
Randolph, Robert Carter, Jr., 258
Randolph, Tommy, 217
Randolph, William Wellford, 52, 54, 57, 133, 148
Rapidan River, 111, 137, 213, 219; Confederate defenses on, 165, 198–99, 210, 213, 235; Union efforts to cross, 164, 198, 223, 235
Rappahannock River, 8, 163; Confederate army and, 85, 111, 198, 210; skirmish on, 193, 218, 222; Union army and, 114, 175, 183, 193
Rappahannock Station, Battle of, 198, 218–19, 221n, 222
Ravensworth, Va., 36
Readjuster Party, 306
Recruitment, 21, 97, 102, 211, 263
Redoubt no. 5, 117
Reed, Mr. [Charles H. Read], 242
Reese, William J., 216
Religion, 100, 186
Renshaw, Annie Page, 186

Renshaw, Lucy Carter (half sister), 63n, 121, 133, 227, 268–69; daughters' deaths, 226; visits of, 142, 220, 222–26, 229
Renshaw, Robert Henry Aloysius, 39, 52, 76, 98, 112, 121, 133–34, 191, 201, 215, 224, 250, 269
Rhett, Thomas Smith, 212
Richard's Ford, 166
Richmond, Ellen "Nellie," 261
Richmond, Va., 89, 127–28, 130, 133, 159, 299; Carter's wife in, 115, 214; Confederate abandonment of, 294; defense of, 114, 212, 237, 253, 293; free blacks from, 48; Spotswood House in, 108
Richmond College, 25
Richmond Daily Dispatch, 21, 25, 95, 248n, 269n
Richmond Examiner, 56
Richmond Times, 304
Richmond Whig, 56
Ripley, Roswell Sabine, 132, 152, 156
Roanoke Island, Battle of, 107
Robertson, Beverly Holcombe, 40, 43, 102
Robins, Mr., 124
Robins, William Todd, 270
Robinson, Lucien Dabney, 135–36, 180
Robinson, Thomas, 123
Rock Castle, 27
Rockville, Md., 138
Rodes, Hortense, 78, 135, 194, 206, 208
Rodes, Robert Emmett, 74, 108, 116, 205–8, 223–24; association with Carter, 12, 30–31n, 55–56, 82, 130, 150, 164, 180; in battles, 140, 164, 197–98, 218, 221, 223n, 235, 244; becomes division commander, 163, 167; Carter's assessment of, 3, 45–46, 167; death of, 238; and furlough for Carter, 102, 122; and King William Artillery, 25, 87, 123, 138; promotion of, 46, 151, 155–56
Rogers, Asa, Jr., 306
Rogers, John Dalrymple, 279
Romney, Va., 22–23, 52, 58, 89
"Rory O'Moore," 203–4
Rosecrans, William Starke, 50, 176, 204, 211